Africa-China Relations

"The scholarly literature on Africa-China relations continues to expand with remarkable works on the changing trends of Africa's engagement with China. Lloyd Adu Amoah's new book not only extends earlier works on Africa-China relations on topics such as diplomatic engagement, trade, economic, and technology issues, but the new volume offers new insights and novel ideas into our understanding of China's rise, geopolitical influence, and increasing footprints in Africa. The systematic integration of theoretical ideas with relevant supporting examples elevates the volume to a different new level. The book is also comprehensive with persuasive arguments which add great value to the growing field of Africa-China relations. I highly recommend this book to everyone."

—Dr. Felix Kumah-Abiwu, Associate Professor and Director, *Center for African Studies, Kent State University, Ohio-USA*

"China-Africa relations is an under-examined yet crucial issue. It is under-examined because China's comprehensive and energetic interventions in Africa have in recent times expanded greatly and analysis and understanding have lagged behind. It is a crucial issue because of the scale, capacity and effects of China's multiple engagements with many African countries. Lloyd Amoah is to be congratulated on assembling a fine group of contributors with knowledge and understanding of current China-Africa relations, while the editor himself provides enlightening and thought-provoking contributions to the volume. The result is a must-read book for anyone with an interest in one of the most important recent developments affecting Africa: China's comprehensive regional involvement."

—Professor Emeritus Jeffrey Haynes, *London Metropolitan University, UK.*

"This edited volume is an important book that comes to us at the right time. Avoiding the polemics currently fashionable in political discussions around Africa-China relations on all sides, it offers a collection of scholarly and well-rounded assessments that in their entirety present a fascinating variety of cases and different angles of a continuingly complex story. This book will be much welcomed by specialists, students of the subject and general readers alike."

—Prof. Dr. Ralph Weber, Professor for European Global Studies, *Institute for European Global Studies, University of Basel*

"*Africa–China Relations: Partnership, Peonage or Pawnage*? is a captivating, groundbreaking and unapologetically African-centered interrogation of one of the most consequential geopolitical relationships of the 21st century. Through the pertinent questions it raises, the book succeeds in cutting through ideological noise, and challenges us to think again. A well written book, it masterfully foregrounds African agency while confronting uncomfortable truths about dependency and strategic vulnerability by weaving history, political economy, and diplomacy into a cohesive narrative. *Africa–China Relations: Partnership, Peonage or Pawnage*? is undoubtedly an important contribution to the burgeoning literature on sovereignty, development studies, Africa-China relations, African studies, international political economy, and South–South cooperation in a changing global order."

—Dr. C. Amo-Agyemang, *Department of Political Science, University of Ghana, Accra, Ghana*. Distinguished Visiting Professor of Africa's International Relations, *Schwarzman College, Tsinghua University, China*

"This volume brings together distinguished and emerging thinkers who critically examine Africa's relationship with China. It offers a timely and incisive account of Africa–China relations at a moment when African scholarship is redefining its place in global knowledge production while reassessing the continent's own strengths and vulnerabilities. The contributors approach the grand promises of China and other external powers with measured skepticism, moving within and beyond conventional paradigms of (neo)colonialism/imperialism and debt-trap diplomacy. They persuasively as well reposition the debate within the shifting dynamics of infrastructure and global interdependence that will shape the decades ahead."

—Tom Hoogervost, Senior Researcher, *Royal Netherlands Institute of Southeast Asian and Caribbean Studies (KITLV)*, and Adjunct Professor at the *Universitas Negeri Malang*.

"Lloyd Amoah has put together an excellent volume on China-Africa relations, along with contributions from several eminent scholars. They offer meticulously researched essays that explore African agency and South–South cooperation, both in theory and in practice, while engaging with topical debates in the field of China-Africa studies. This compendium will serve as a seminal text for students and scholars of Politics, International Relations, African Studies, and East Asian Studies."

—Dr. Renu Modi (Retired), Professor and Former Director, *Centre for African Studies, University of Mumbai, Mumbai*

Lloyd G. Adu Amoah
Editor

Africa-China Relations

Partnership, Peonage or Pawnage?

palgrave
macmillan

Editor
Lloyd G. Adu Amoah
Department of Political Science
University of Ghana
Accra, Ghana

ISBN 978-981-95-4369-4 ISBN 978-981-95-4370-0 (eBook)
https://doi.org/10.1007/978-981-95-4370-0

Cover illustration: boonchai wedmakawand/ getty images

This Palgrave Macmillan imprint is published by the registered company Springer Nature Singapore Pte Ltd.
The registered company address is: 152 Beach Road, #21-01/04 Gateway East, Singapore 189721, Singapore

To the Pioneers of Africa–Asia Studies in Africa from Africa
Emmanuel Hevi, Chinweizu, Ali A. Mazrui, Alaba Ogunsanwo, Kweku Ampiah, Ernest Aryeetey, Adams Bodomo

Special mention:
Teoboldo Filesi *and* Tareq Y. Ismael, *for their seminal contributions in the then very nascent field, when it was not fashionable and indeed was very testing to produce scholarly work on Africa–Asia Studies.*

Preface and Acknowledgements

The year 2025 has proved quite momentous for the following reasons. It marks the 70th anniversary of the Bandung Conference. It is also a remarkable year because it designates the first 25 years of the twenty-first century. Within this quarter of a century, China has become the largest economy in the world after the US, and the Chinese Communist Party (CCP) commemorated its centennial since its founding in the then French Concession of Shanghai on July 1921 in an all-girls' boarding middle school. Within these 25 years, the relations between African nations and China have deepened and come to encompass an astonishingly unprecedented and diverse range of areas, as this volume shows. But vexing questions have come to plague these relations. At the heart of disquisitions trying to make sense of these relations is whether China is a force for good for Africa's development or one cast in the mould of predatory imperialist powers. This book makes its contribution to these questions, taking advantage of the flow of time and the more coherent organization of data from China (to be sure, it is still a big challenge laying hands on easily available credible data from China and even African states with which it deals) and elsewhere. This contribution is no doubt informed and aided by the momentous events that have rocked the international political economy in the last 25 years, such as the COVID-19 pandemic, the rise of artificial intelligence, the derisking and decoupling of major corporations and firms from China as Xi Jinping consolidated his power, the emergence of BRICS, the deepening of the climate crisis and the responses to them.

As an undergraduate and graduate student in Ghana and right through my doctoral studies in China, I have long grappled with attaining some clarity on the questions referred to. In this work, this burden has been made lighter with empirical, conceptual and theoretical insights from nineteen emergent and established researchers and scholars from four continents, who have weighed in with such perspicacity on the subject matter. It is my hope that the positions canvassed in this work will prove useful for better understanding and framing Africa–China relations and spur the necessary feedback and critique to inspire even more research on the subject matter. I will be remiss if I do not acknowledge the work of reviewers (especially double-blind reviews of draft chapters) for all the texts (from the abstract selection to the draft chapter stages), which helped to sharpen and clarify the largely novel and groundbreaking arguments made in this volume.

Last but not least, I must thank profusely Jacob Dryer at Palgrave Macmillan, who saw the value of the project when I first pitched it.

Accra, Ghana
September 7, 2025

Lloyd. G. Adu Amoah

Contents

Notes on Contributors

Lloyd G. Adu Amoah, Ph.D is an Associate Professor in the Department of Political Science, University of Ghana, Legon, and is the founding and first director of the Centre for Asian Studies (CAS) at the same university. He was also the former acting director of the Centre for European Studies at the University of Ghana. His research focuses on administrative theory, political theory, strategy in government, Africa–Asia relations, technopolitics and ICT policy in the Global South and the political economy of space, spatiality and architecture in the Global South. He is the author of ten books (two sole-authored, four edited and four co-edited).

Amabilly Bonacina is currently a Ph.D. candidate and lecturer at the University of Montreal. As part of her thesis, she is studying South-South cooperation and science diplomacy in Brazil and South Africa from a comparative perspective. In 2023, she was selected to participate in the pilot training on science diplomacy, FORMHYDS, a science diplomacy training program in French, intended for early-career professionals working in the field of science and international relations. Between August and October 2024, Amabilly was a visiting doctoral student in the Department of Political Science at the University of Pretoria (South Africa).

Alexander Demissie holds an MA in China Studies and International Relations from the University of Cologne, Germany, and Sichuan University, Chengdu, PRC. He is the Founding Director of ChinaAfricaAdvisory, an Africa and China-focused advisory firm that assists governments, international organisations, and businesses. With two decades of experience in Africa–China relations, his interests include

Special Economic Zones and their potential for sustainable industrialisation in African countries, the use of technology to leapfrog development within a country-specific context in Africa, as well as strategy development for African businesses engaging with Chinese stakeholders. He is a visiting lecturer and a Ph.D. candidate at the University of Bonn, Germany. He is a regular media contributor on matters pertaining to Africa–China relations.

Kwaku Obeng Effah is a PhD student in the Department of Government and International Affairs at Lingnan University. His research is situated within the Department's *China in the World* research stream of international politics. His doctoral thesis examines the mechanisms of Peaceful Order Change, exploring how China seeks to assert its power and influence in shaping the international system through non-military pathways of transformation. Beyond his doctoral research, he engages with scholarship on Africa–China political and economic relations, as well as the broader field of International Political Economy.

Costanza Franceschini is a postdoctoral researcher and Lecturer in Cultural Anthropology at the Institute of Cultural Anthropology and Development Sociology, Faculty of Social and Behavioural Sciences, Leiden University, the Netherlands. Her research focuses on the ethnographic study of Africa-China and Ghana-China relations, with a particular focus on Sino-African infrastructural entanglements, the localization strategies of Chinese firms, everyday Afro-Chinese encounters, labour relations, linguistic formations, and brokerage practices.

Elisa Gambino is Lecturer in Globalisation, Trade, and Development at the Global Development Institute of the University of Manchester, UK, and an Adjunct Researcher at the Centre for Asian Studies of the University of Ghana. Her research explores the intersection of China's outward economic engagement and African countries' development trajectories. She studies the internationalisation of Chinese capital in the trade, manufacturing, and infrastructure sectors in Africa, placing particular emphasis on the role of embeddedness in fostering the spatial expansion of Chinese companies. Her most recent project, titled "African hubs, Chinese trade, and global circulation", explores the internationalisation of Chinese private capital and its impacts on West African regional integration and industrialisation. Previously, she has worked on the market expansion of Chinese state-owned enterprises in Kenya's infrastructure sector as part of the

European Research Council (ERC)-funded project "African governance and space: transport corridors, border towns and port cities in transition".

Emmanuel Graham is a Business Intelligence Consultant, Natural Resource Governance Consultant, and a PhD Candidate (ABD) at York University, Department of Politics, in Toronto, Ontario, Canada. His dissertation examines resource nationalism in Africa through a Neo-Gramscian analysis of Ghana's petroleum industrialization, exploring the interplay of global capital, state policy, and local community contestations in shaping oil governance and development outcomes. In terms of research interests, Graham's focus is on the political economy of the extractive sector, energy politics, and climate change in Ghana and West Africa. He is also interested in the social and political thought of Kwame Nkrumah, Karl Marx, and Antonio Gramsci. His research has been on the role of civil society in escaping the resource curse in Ghana, oil exploration and production in sub-Saharan Africa, and energy policy. He is also interested in electoral politics, political vigilantism, and democratic consolidation in Ghana and West Africa. He has some publications in international peer-reviewed journals such as Extractive Industry and Society, Africa Review, Insight on Africa, and Journal of African Elections. He can be reached at graham19@yorku.ca or kofigraham@gmail.com

Katja Kalkschmied received her PhD in Economics from the University of Graz (Austria). She is currently employed as a postdoctoral fellow at the Department of International Economics at the Vienna School of International Studies (Austria) after holding a similar position at Ruhr University Bochum (Germany). Her research contributes to understanding how institutions shape economic development by looking at the economic, political, and ecological conditions under which they evolve and how they feed back into this environment. A central strand of her work investigates China's role as a development financier and how it challenges the Western-led global order, with particular attention to infrastructure development in the Global South and Europe's periphery. Her broader interests span development and growth, institutional economics, international political economy, development finance, and trade, bridging economics and political science. Her work is published in peer-reviewed journals, book chapters, and edited volumes.

Adam Laroussi is a postdoctoral researcher at the National School of Public Administration of Canada, director of the "Ideas" division of the

French think tank "Raisonnances Humanistes," and director of the Africa department at the Institute for Applied Geopolitical Studies (IEGA). Adam LAROUSSI holds a Ph.D. in Political Science from the University of Montreal and is a member of the Groupe d'études et de recherche sur l'international et le Québec (GERIQ), the Groupe interuniversitaire d'études et de recherches sur les sociétés africaines (GIERSA), and the Pôle de Recherche sur l'Afrique et le Monde Émergent (PRAME).

Fathia Lawal holds an Advanced Master's degree in International Studies from the Vienna School of International Studies (Austria), where she specialized in International Relations, International Law, and Economics. Her research examines dependency dynamics in Ghana's renewable energy transition, focusing on how multilateral development banks and Chinese development financing align with the country's development priorities. She earned her BA in Political Science with Information Studies from the University of Ghana. She is developing *Sustainability Mosaic,* a nonprofit initiative bridging sustainability and climate research with actionable project implementation. Her academic and professional interests span international political economy, development finance, and sustainability and climate policy, with particular emphasis on Africa's green transition, circular economy, and sustainable food systems.

Abdou Rahim Lema holds a Ph.D. in Political Science from the Université de Montréal and a Master's degree in China Studies from Peking University. He is a former Vanier Scholar and Yenching Scholar. His areas of specialisation include international relations, comparative politics, and South–South cooperation. In addition to a co-authored book and book chapters, his academic work has been published in peer-reviewed journals such as *African Studies Quarterly*, *Cogent Social Sciences*, the *International Journal of Conflict & Reconciliation*, etc. Several of his sole-authored manuscripts are currently under review in *Development Policy Review*, *Global Social Challenges Journal*, and the *Canadian Journal of African Studies.* In addition to his scholarly publications, Lema has contributed to public scholarship through platforms including *Africa at LSE*, *The Diplomat*, *Foreign Policy*, *Africa is a Country*, the *Munk School of Global Affairs*, etc.

Yen-Chi Lu is a research fellow and Ph.D. student at the Center for Advanced Security, Strategic, and Integration Studies at the University of Bonn. He co-led the research project "Surveying Strategic Digital Politics" with Prof. Maximilian Mayer at the University of Bonn in 2021. His research focuses on China's Digital Silk Road, digital autonomy and dependence, and the impact of China's rise and digital technologies on the global political economy.

Maximilian Mayer is Junior Professor of International Relations and Global Politics of Technology at the Center for Advanced Security, Strategic, and Integration Studies (CASSIS), University of Bonn. His research interests include the global politics of science and technology; China's foreign and energy policy; global energy and climate politics; and theories of International Relations. He is co-editor of *The Global Politics of Science and Technology* (2014, two volumes), *Art and Sovereignty in Global Politics* (2016), editor of *Rethinking the Silk-Road: China's Belt and Road Initiative and Emerging Eurasian Relations* (2018), co-editor of the Routledge *Handbook on Global China* (2024), and led the research group on "Infrastructures of China's Modernity and Their Global Constitutive Effects", funded by the Ministry of Culture and Science of the State of North Rhine-Westphalia.

Paola Minoia is an Associate Professor of Geography at the University of Turin, Italy, and an Adjunct Professor of Global Development Studies at the University of Helsinki, Finland. Her academic work combines critical geographical analysis with a focus on political ecology and an ethical commitment to engaging with movements and scholars dedicated to advancing social transformation grounded in epistemic and territorial justice. As the principal investigator in numerous research projects, she has critically examined international cooperation policies and interventions—particularly on water, food, and Indigenous peoples' rights—and explored possibilities for decolonial alternatives, drawing on fieldwork conducted in several countries across Africa, Latin America, and Europe.

Lou Mo is a Chinese Canadian artist and curator. She lives and works in France. She graduated from Ecole des hautes études en sciences sociales in Paris with a degree in Asian Studies. Her research is focused on modern and contemporary Afro-Asian connections and Third World artists' creative practices. She is also interested in issues of diaspora, identity, and perception in relation to post-colonial history and the centre-periphery model. She was invited curator of the 14th Dakar Biennial in Senegal, where she presented 'Havana, Forging the Souths' exhibition at the Musée Théodore Monod—IFAN. Recently, she curated 'Hot Flux: Modern and

Contemporary Photography in Taiwan and Africa' at Tainan Art Museum. As a member of the School of Mutants collective, her works have been exhibited in venues such as the 12th Taipei Biennial, Centre Pompidou Metz, the 12th Berlin Biennial, the 4th autostrada biennale and Glasgow International.

Asaah Sumaila Mohammed is a scholar affiliated with CK Tedam University of Technology and Applied Sciences in Ghana, where he has been contributing to the field of environmental science and sustainable development since 2019. His research primarily focuses on the intersection of community livelihoods, environmental management, and resource extraction, particularly within the Ghanaian context.

Mohammed's recent publications reflect a commitment to addressing pressing local issues through rigorous analysis and community engagement. Notable works include studies on solid waste disposal site selection using analytical hierarchy processes, gender-disaggregated analyses of sustainable agricultural practices, and the challenges faced by coastal communities in accessing livelihoods. His research has been published in reputable journals such as *Heliyon* and the *African Journal of Science, Technology, Innovation and Development*, showcasing his dedication to advancing knowledge in his field. In addition to his academic pursuits, Mohammed has received sponsorship from esteemed institutions, including the National Institutes of Health and Jimma University, which underscores his contributions to research and development in Ghana in particular and globally more generally.

Thierry Pairault a socioeconomist and sinologist, is an Emeritus Research Director at France's National Centre of Scientific Research (CNRS) and at the EHESS Research Centre on Modern and Contemporary China (CECMC), where he co-organises and runs a seminar on Chinese Presences in Africa.

Mariasole Pepa is a Research Fellow at the Department of Historical and Geographic Sciences and the Ancient World at the University of Padua and an affiliated researcher at CEDEJ-Khartoum. Her work lies at the intersection of critical geographies and decolonial approaches to development, with a particular focus on water and land. She is interested in transformative research methodologies/practices and disobedient pedagogies. She also serves as Vice-President of the Italian Association for African-Chinese Studies (AISAC).

Hagan Sibiri, PhD is a senior research fellow at the Africa-China Centre for Policy and Advisory (ACCPA) and a member of the Ghana Institute of International Affairs (GhIIA).

He holds a PhD in International Politics from the prestigious Fudan University in Shanghai, a Master of Law from the University of International Business and Economics, and a Bachelor of Arts from the University for Development Studies (Ghana). In addition, he holds a PhD Masterclass certificate in Economics of International Business from the University of Reading's Henley Business School (England, UK), an Executive Education certificate in Governments in Times of Crisis from the Mohammed Bin Rashid School of Government (Dubai, UAE), and a certificate in Advanced Training Programme for Young Diplomatic Talents from Fudan University (Shanghai, PRC).His research is in the area of international relations with a focus on African-Sino relations and South-South cooperation. His work has appeared in top international peer-reviewed journals such as *East Asian Community Review*, *Insight on Africa*, *Africa Spectrum*, *African Studies Quarterly*, *Harvard Africa Policy Journal*, *Kennedy School Review*, *Journal of Entrepreneurship in Emerging Economies*, *China Quarterly of International Strategic Studies*, *Health Policy and Technology*, *Ethics, Medicine and Public Health*, among others.Aside from academics, he has years of corporate and IT experience. He worked for Microsoft Global Support as a senior technical support engineer for Microsoft 365 cloud services. He is also a former student leader, serving as the chapter president of the National Union of Ghana Students and vice president of the Fudan University African Students Association.

List of Figures

China–Africa Agricultural Cooperation and the Promises of Modernization

Mediterranean Africa, China and the European Union

The Ecological Implications of Africa–China Partnership in the Extractive Sectors of Africa: Lessons from Artisanal and Small-Scale Mining in Ghana

List of Tables

China in Africa: A Sub-imperialist Power?

Chinese Finance for African Infrastructure: Credit Enhancements as Means for Doing Business or Politics?

Trading Natural Resources for Infrastructure: A Sustainable Approach to Financing Africa's Infrastructure Gap?

Mediterranean Africa, China and the European Union

The Ecological Implications of Africa–China Partnership in the Extractive Sectors of Africa: Lessons from Artisanal and Small-Scale Mining in Ghana

Introduction: Africa-China Ties: Lifting the Veil Through Three Themes

Lloyd G. Adu Amoah

Don't hate China – but don't trust her either. Trust ourselves – have faith in Africa.
—Hevi (1963, p. 136)

Introduction

I begin this introduction with the very important work of Emmanuel Hevi on Africa-China relations, which seem to have fallen into oblivion in an era in which China has become globally ascendant. Hevi was a Ghanaian student who was sent by the Government of Ghana through the Ghana Trades Union Congress (GTUC) to study medicine in China. Arriving on 27th November, 1960, Hevi left in April 1962 without completing his five-year medical studies (at the Peking Medical College).On leaving China, Hevi wrote his now well-known book *An African Student in China* (1963) and then followed it up with his second book, *The Dragon's embrace: the Chinese Communists and Africa* (1967). In the first book,

L. G. Adu Amoah (✉)
Department of Political Science, University of Ghana, Accra, Ghana

Centre for Asian Studies (CAS), University of Ghana, Accra, Ghana
e-mail: alloydgeorgeadu@ug.edu.gh

L. G. Adu Amoah (ed.), *Africa-China Relations*,
https://doi.org/10.1007/978-981-95-4370-0_1

Hevi recounts his rather sombre experiences of China as a student marked especially[1] by anti-black racism insisting, "The Chinese have so long posed as defenders of the African and the persecuted races that it must really come as a shock to many people to hear that racial discrimination is practised in China. Chinese racial discrimination is not of the kind that springs spontaneously from the people. It is a deliberate attempt by the Communist Party to assert and to make the African accept once and for all the idea of the superiority of Yellow over Black" (1963, pp. 135–136). In the second book, Hevi is concerned about China's imperialist tendencies and warns Africa not be seduced by its claims of genuine interest in the continent's welfare and offers some caution: "Since the imperialism of these new nations can affect us as profoundly as, and sometimes even more profoundly than, the same vice in the traditional imperialists, it will pay us to study, with all the care we can give to the subject, the political mentality and attitude of these new and unfamiliar imperialist nations" (1967, p. 2). This position is further reinforced in Hevi's reflections on Zhou Enlai's 12-nation tour of Africa from 14th December, 1963 to 4th February, 1964. These reflections are fleshed out in eight points of which a couple are worth reproducing here:

> 1. *To win friends and allies in the bid to end China's political isolation.* China has no real friend in the Western world and, since the eruption of the Sino-Soviet ideological dispute, most communist countries—with the notable exception of Albania—have aligned themselves with the Soviet Union. Peking will find it easier to win friends in the relatively uncommitted new countries than in either the East or the West.
>
> 3. *China is making a bid for the leadership of 'we coloured peoples'* (Chou's [referring to Zhou Enlai: author's comment] phrase). Having worsted India and dethroned it as the leading Asian power, China, seeking to isolate the Soviet Union with the argument that the Russians are non-Asians, aims to dominate all future Afro-Asian gatherings. At the time of Chou's tour of Africa, a 'second Bandung' was envisaged by Peking as a forum for condemning both the Western 'imperialists' and the Soviet Union which, by Chinese definition, now belongs to the despicable imperialist species. Thus, China presents herself to us as a coloured, underdeveloped, anti-imperialist and anti-colonialist country—and therefore 'one of us'. At the same time, we in the underdeveloped world are supposed to realise and accept that, though a member of our 'poor-man's club', China is ahead of us in all respects, including economic development, population and military power. So, clearly, China must lead us—so the Chinese communists say.

> 4. *To present China as the sole champion of the Third World, and Russia as a betrayer of the cause of the oppressed peoples.* Confronted by grim nuclear reality, the Soviet Union is now more cautious and sophisticated in furthering communism and her own national interests... Of immediate importance to China is the winning of Africa's moral support in the Sino-Soviet dispute. Since most of Africa has shown the desire to steer clear of this cold war in the communist camp, Peking's aim here can only be achieved by a roundabout method, one which will manoeuvre China into a position of leadership in the developing world. This achieved, African support—Peking calculates—will follow automatically.
>
> 7. *To seek new trade partners outside the Soviet orbit.* Sino-Soviet trade having been affected by the breach between the two countries, China must go farther afield for markets and raw materials. Africa is a fertile field for both. (Hevi, 1967, pp. 142–143)

It is clear that in the heat of the Cold War era, Hevi, drawing on his firsthand experience of China, was trying to understand the very nature of Africa-China relations by lifting the veil of official tropes and drilling down to the facts for his interpretation. This need then and now is necessitated by what Adie (1964) describes as the difficulty of making sense of China policy if one fails to allow for "the traditionally Sinocentric cast of Chinese thought, or for the disparity between talk and reality in a word, the sense of theatre—which is still found in the present Chinese rulers' attitude to the outside world" (43). Adie (1964) points in addition to China's interest in Africa's natural resources, its anti-Black racism as well as its manipulation of Africa in order to bolster its international standing. Ogunsanwo (1974) weighed in as well (in one of the most trenchant, seminal, and early book length reflections and in a crucial time frame, 1958–1971) on this puzzle claiming that generally Africa-China interactions have been shaped and conditioned by China's diplomatic initiatives which reality generated necessary questions:

> *On the whole Chinese policy in Africa has resulted from the diplomatic initiative of the People's Republic of China, rather than of the African States themselves. This immediately suggests questions requiring examination.* Why is China interested in Africa? Has there been a coherent policy towards Africa in the period under consideration or is it simply a policy of fomenting revolutions every and especially in places where revolution is detrimental to the interests of imperialism? *Is there a genuine desire for the independence and welfare of the African people or is there a grand strategy aimed at bringing the*

> *whole continent under the aegis of China*? Again, is the Chinese record in Africa merely a chain of failures resulting from their lack of understanding, their lack of communication with, and misperception of, the situation in Africa and the way the leaders of the new states choose to conceive their national interests? (1; italics added)

Paring down the questions these selected early classic reflections on Africa-China relations grappled with, three themes emerge that frame the analysis in this book: partnership, pawnage and peonage. This volume contends that these themes have proved quite enduring in the literature on the subject matter shaped as they constantly are by new realities in the international system as well as national contexts in both Africa and China and therefore require a fresh critical appraisal. I lay down in a broad outline in the next section these international and national contexts in order to define the framework through which the volume engages its three themes.

Africa and China and the Flux of Political Economy

The year 2025 marks the seventieth anniversary of the Afro-Asian Conference held in Bandung, Indonesia in 1955. The 29 countries from Africa and Asia in attendance at Bandung sought to essentially use the international platform it provided to "confront colonialism and the divisive nature of the Cold War" (Ampiah & Naidu, 2008, p. 6). The conference was a watershed in Chinese diplomacy because it afforded China the opportunity to cast itself not just as a champion of Afro-Asia solidarity and interests (Ismael, 1971) but also catalysed the opening of new economic relations with especially African countries. These new economic opportunities and the political capital they offered were important for China given that it had laboured under embargoes and controls from the West led by the US on the outbreak of the Korean War in 1950. Indeed these embargoes meant that between 1950 and 1955 China had become economically dependent on the Soviet Union for military hardware, many types of machinery and a whole range of other capital goods. In sense, Bandung proved a boon because by the time of the Sino-Soviet split in the 1960s, China had entered into diplomatic, trade, economic and cultural relations with many African and Global South countries allowing it to present itself as a trustworthy friend as against the imperialist Soviet Union and the United States. These developments among others definitely laid the groundwork for the sorely needed rapprochement between China and the United States in 1971(Litwak, 1984).

The 1970s proved tough for Africa politically and economically. Following on heels of the 1960s in which newly independent African states were led largely by visionary leaders who were determined that their nations will undergo rapid socio-economic transformation, the 1970s were marked by among other crises the misrule of the army, political instability, debt crises and economic stagnation and decline. The 1970s, thus marked egregiously by crises, came to be described in the academic literature and popular discourse as Africa's lost decade (Adjei et al., 2014; Stimson,[2] 2025). The 1970s turned out to be a decisive decade for Africa and China in the ways it shaped their development trajectory in the first two decades of the 21st century. For China, the decade long (1966–1976) (in)famous Cultural Revolution ended with the death of Mao in 1976 paving the way for the return to power of Deng Xiaoping and the adoption of a raft of policies which set China on the road to capitalist transformation (Li & Kotz, 2021). The political, economic and social crises Africa experienced in the 1970s led nations across the continent to solicit for and adopt the World Bank (WB)/International Monetary Fund (IMF) Structural Adjustment Programmes (SAP)/Economic Recovery Programmes (ERP), which were anchored in political and economic conditionalities under a collection of ideas known as the Washington Consensus:

> The international recession of the early 1980s left many less developed countries in a precarious position as their exports collapsed, private capital flows were sharply reduced and interest rates rose. Major aid donors, in particular the World Bank, responded with fundamental changes in aid policy – the introduction of 'structural adjustment lending'. Under this new policy, financial flows to developing countries were made conditional on changes in policy, generally of a type that reduced the level of government intervention in the economy. (Mosley et al., 1991, p. 1)

These changes in policy were made by African countries in exchange for especially financial support as well as technical aid. The WB/IMF led development process however constricted the policy space of African countries without any far-reaching economic and social dividends and before long these countries were casting about at the turn of the twenty-first century for other sources of funding and support. At this critical juncture, China having undergone its transformation into a neoliberal capitalist state under the aegis of America (Hung, 2018; Hui, 2017) was battling its overaccumulation crisis (Hung, 2022) and saw Africa as a critical spatial and political fix for this problem. It is within this adumbrated account of the shifts and gyrations of the political economy of Africa and China at the national and international scales that China has become the leading creditor to Africa rivalling only the WB. The ties between the two have expanded and deepened to cover politics, trade, culture, architecture, technology, infrastructure, migration, education among others on a scale that is unprecedented in modern history. It is within this framework, further complicated by significant regional, sub-regional, continental and global events— such as the return of coups[3] in West Africa in which great power rivalry is playing out, the COVID-19 crisis, the Russo-Ukraine War, the European Union's Global Gateway Project, Xi Jinping's tightening grip on power (and the attendant delinking and derisking response by major global firms and corporations from China), Trump's rise to power in 2017 and 2025 (and with it the stringent measures to contain and degrade China's technological capabilities and rise), the Palestine-Israeli war and the 100th anniversary of the Communist Party of China—that this volume takes a fresh critical look at Africa-China interactions wound around the three themes already mentioned. What this volume does is to extend and complicate earlier book-length treatments of Africa-China relations (such as those by Ampiah & Naidu, 2008; Brautigam, 2011; Oqubay & Lin, 2019) by taking into account new realities and tackling otherwise taboo questions such as imperialism and moving beyond the arguably tired and irksome economistic foci to address other pertinent developments such as a rereading of architecture and infrastructure and China's increasing digital footprints in Africa. At this juncture it will be useful to offer some working understandings of partnership, pawnage and peonage as deployed in this work.

Partnership as understood and critiqued in this work points fundamentally to diplomatic relations without which African states cannot build trade, economic and other ties (that embody and express the partnership) with the China party-state (or state-party as Thornton [2021] suggests). It is instructive that as at March 2025, China had established diplomatic ties with 53 out of the 54 African states (Etswatini being the only exception). Given the obvious power asymmetry between African countries and China, the often-claimed partnership needs to be subjected to continuous scrutiny. Digging deeper beyond the official tropes of partnership constantly enunciated, the literature also gestures at Africa as already indicated as a pawn and in peonage in its relations with China. The *Oxford Advanced Learner's Dictionary* (Gimson & Cowie, 1989) describes a pawn as "person or group whose actions are controlled by others" (908). *Cambridge Dictionary* (online) gives the meaning of pawn as "a person or organization that does not have any real power but is used by others to achieve something". Drawing on these two lexical meanings, pawnage in this work refers to a group of people without real power (as opposed to without any power) used by others to achieve their own ends. Peonage essentially refers to being in debt and having to make restitution on the debtor's terms and the power and control this confers on the creditor. The debt question especially has come to mark Africa-China relations leading to debt trap diplomacy charges against China and the real danger of African nations becoming China's debt peons and geostrategy pawns. The next section shows how the chapters in this volume engage the three themes of partnership, pawnage and peonage as fleshed out.

Arguments of the Book

This book contains 14 chapters including this introductory chapter. In Chap. 2, Amoah takes on China's conduct in Africa, which has been variously characterized or worse mischaracterized as imperial, neo-imperial, colonial and neocolonial (these terms are usually used interchangeably). In his view theoretically and empirically, these descriptions struggle to accurately capture China's Africa forays. He provides an intervention (given the benefit of the now longer time span of China's presence in Africa and with it available data and information which are still spotty to be sure) in Chap. 2 by engaging critically with the literature on these claims and then drawing on dependency theory generally and Ruy Marini's sub-imperialism framework in particular, to argue and demonstrate that China's activities in Africa may more accurately depict that of a sub-imperialist state. Chapters 3 and 4 take on the much storied and vexed question of China's purported debt trap diplomacy in its interactions with African nations. Effah and Amoah in Chap. 3 wade into the China debt trap diplomacy debate and introduce the debt peonage framework as a more plausible and empirically realistic way of unpacking the question of debt in Africa-China interactions. In Chap. 4, Kalkschmied and Lawal insist that the claim of debt trap diplomacy cannot be reasonably sustained unless it can be proven that Chinese state and non-actors have intentions to ensconce their African counterparts in debt from the outset. Anchoring their analysis on no recorded case of debt-equity swaps in Africa-China relations thus far, they rather point to the prevalence of debt and equity financing as the two sides undertake projects. This argument is fleshed out using the empirical cases of the Sonangol Project in Angola, Kenya's Standard Guage Railway Project and the Ethiopia-Djibouti Gas Pipeline Project. In Chap. 4, Kalkschmied and Lawal, while debunking the idea of debt diplomacy acknowledge the present and future dangers of Chinese debt power—and therefore present and future peonage and pawnage—over African nations. Chapters 5, 6, 7, 8, and 9 reflect on Africa-China relations through an expansive and variegated infrastructure lens. Lou tackles in Chap. 5 cultural infrastructure in Africa-China relations through Senegal's ill-fated University of African Future (UFA) and the controversial Museum of Black Civilizations (MCN). Taiwan (UFA) and China (MCN) were involved in the financing and construction of both buildings. Lou shows how contending diplomatic interests, Pan-African ideals and the interests of the Senegal people intermingle and collide over decades in what otherwise seems the straightforward construction of buildings. In Chap. 6, Franceschini underlines the ways in which partnerships involving African nations and China require a nuanced understanding in what she describes as heterogeneous partnership. Franceschini establishes her position through the interrogation of the construction of marine and fishing facilities along Ghana's coast that involved collaboration and contestation between Ghanaian officials at many levels and European actors. In Chap. 7, Gambino wades into the Africa-China infrastructure debate by showing how the construction of transport infrastructure in particular involving Chinese loans and contractors has increasing ties with domestic African politics through political legitimacy or contestation. Gambino argues that this is an area worthy of further exploration and research. Sibiri in Chap. 8 makes the case that China's interest in Resource for Infrastructure (RFI) financing model provides a viable alternative for financially hardpressed African nations so long as these nations show evidence of the required state capacity to handle this. Mayer, Yen-Chin and Demisse in Chap. 9 focus on Africa-China interactions with respect to digital infrastructure. This is a critical area of both current and futuristic import given the way artificial intelligence in particular and digitalization more generally are shaping contemporary life and society. In three key areas with respect to the Chinese role (mostly through state actors and state-linked entities, including companies like Huawei and ZTE;

state-firm coordination as Mayer Yen-Chin and Demisse describe them) in constructing digital infrastructure—namely physical infrastructure (backbone and broadband), cloud infrastructure and platforms—in Africa, Mayer, Yen-Chin and Demisse show the unassailed technological dominance of China. Ethiopia is used to empirically demonstrate this—and presented as emblematic of the African digitalization reality—through unpacking its technology stack configurations (at the hardware level where it matters most) tied to Huawei and ZTE. Africa-China cooperation in the agriculture sector is the central theme of Chap. 10. Through a discourse analysis of FOCAC documents spanning the years 2000–2024, Mariasole and Minoa conclude that Africa-China cooperation in agriculture as expressed in technology modernization and green development are at the core about China's (with the tacit support of Africa's elites and governments) investments, market penetration and the reproduction of the failed green revolution of the last century. In Chap. 11, Pairault focuses on North African states in what he describes as the Mediterranean Five (namely Morocco, Egypt, Tunisia, Algeria and Libya) and analyses their ties with China through their engagements with the European Union. For Pairault, the comparative lens allows for a more insightful understanding of China's engagement with North Africa, which is woefully understudied. Pairault's ultimate claim in Chap. 12 is that North Africa is valuable for China only in instrumental terms as a bridgehead to establish a foothold in the prized EU market. In Chaps. 12 and 13, the ecological dimension of Africa-China relations enter into the discussions for this volume. Graham and Mohammed in Chap. 12 paint a very grim picture of the ecological catastrophe in Ghana as Chinese nationals partner Ghanaians in Artisanal and Small Scale Mining (ASM) known popularly as *galamsey*. Chapter 12 unpacks the sheer scale of environmental, social and economic degradation as Chinese technology and technology from China obliterates traditional modes of ASM in Ghana. In Chap. 13, Lema, Bonachina and Laroussi argue that China has become a formidable partner as Africa turns to greener sources of power generation. China's partnership in this regard according to the trio is because of its accumulation of massive generation and technological capacities in the wind and solar energy sectors. Drawing on the ideational, regulatory, supervisory and other processes that were marshalled for the construction of Garissa and Sakaï solar power plants in Kenya and Central Africa Republic respectively, Chap. 13 insists on African agency through co-construction with Chinese entities. Lema *et al* recognize though the power asymmetries between Africa and China and therefore describe the partnership between the two sides as asymmetrical partnership. Chapter 14 concludes by drawing together the various insights of the chapters and suggesting in particular the need for research to begin to focus more explicitly on the structure of globalized capitalism of the international political economy, how this shapes Africa's agency especially at the level of the actions of its states and China's role in deepening or dismantling this structure. Such an explicit research focus should help provide further, better and less idealized particulars on Africa-China relations going forward.

Abbreviations

ERP	Economic Recovery Programme
GTUC	Ghana Trades Union Congress
IMF	International Monetary Fund
SAP	Structural Adjustment Programme

Notes

1. He was not also enthused at all by what he considered Marxist and Maoist indoctrination that was imposed on foreign students like himself in that era.
2. Simson (2025) poignantly recalls the good life in the 1960s in Africa in sharp contrast to the turmoil of the 1970s and 1980s:

   > Many older, middle-class Africans will recall a 'before' and 'after'. The 'before' of the 1960s and 70s, when a secondary school teacher or mid-ranking bureaucrat in Accra or Dakar could comfortably support a family in the city and perhaps purchase a car or an apartment with the help of a subsidized mortgage scheme. And an 'after' the crisis years of the 1980s and 1990s, when the way to make ends meet was through a patchwork of income streams – an unpredictable salary, perhaps a small business or farm, and the occasional remittance from a brother or sister overseas.(1)

3. This has led to the dismembering and weakening of the Economic Community of West African States (ECOWAS) with Burkina Faso, Niger and Mali leaving the sub-regional body and forming their own organization, the Alliance of Sahel States (AES) which is meant to be a mutual defense, development and security organization aimed at responding to security challenges in the Sahel.

References

Adie, W. A. C. (1964). Chinese policy towards Africa. In S. Hamrell & C. G. Widstrand (Eds.), *The Soviet Bloc, China and Africa* (pp. 43–63). Pall Mall.

Adjei, P. O.-S., Kyie, P. O., & Afriyie, K. (2014). Global economic crisis and socio-economic vulnerability: Historical experience and lessons from the "Lost Decade" for Africa in the 1980s. *Ghana Studies, 17*, 39–61.

Ampiah, K., & Naidu, S. (2008). *Crouching tiger, hidden dragon? Africa and China*. University of KwaZulu-Natal Press.

Brautigam, D. (2011). *The dragon's gift: The real story of China in Africa*. Oxford University Press.

Gimson, A. C., & Cowie, A. P. (1989). *Oxford advanced learner's dictionary* (4th ed.). Oxford University Press.

Hevi, E. J. (1963). *An African student in Peking*. Frederick A. Praeger, Inc.

Hevi, E. J. (1967). *The Dragon's embrace: The Chinese communists and Africa*. Pall Mall Press.

Hui, E. (2017). Putting the Chinese State in its place: A March from passive revolution to hegemony. *Journal of Contemporary Asia, 47*(1), 66–92.

Hung, H. (2018). Rising China, Asia and the global south. *Review of Contemporary Economics, 22*(1), 1–26.

Hung, H. (2022). *Clash of empires: From "Chimerica" to the "New Cold War"*. Cambridge University Press.

Ismael, T. Y. (1971). The People's Republic of China and Africa. *Journal of Modern African Studies, 9*(4), 507–529.

Li, Z., & Kotz, D. M. (2021). Is China imperialist? Economy, state, and insertion in the global system. *Review of Radical Political Economics, 53*(4), 600–610.

Litwak, R. S. (1984). *Détente and the Nixon Doctrine: American foreign policy and the pursuit of stability, 1969–1976*. Cambridge University Press.

Mosley, P., Harrigan, J., & Toye, J. (1991). *Aid and power: The World Bank and policy-based lending*. Routledge.

Ogunsanwo, A. (1974). *China's policy in Africa, 1958–1971*. Cambridge University Press.

Oqubay, A., & Lin, J. Y. (2019). *China–Africa and an economic transformation*. Oxford University Press.

Simson, R. (2025). Africa's lost decades, 1974–1994. In E. Frankema, E. Hillbom, U. Kufakurinani, & F. M. z. Selhausen (Eds.), *The history of African development: An online textbook for a new generation of African students and teachers. African Economic History Network E-Book*. https://www.aehnetwork.org/textbook/africas-lost-decades-1974-1994/

Thornton, P. M. (2021). Party all the time: The CCP in comparative and historical perspective. *The China Quarterly, 248*, 1–15.

China in Africa: A Sub-imperialist Power?

Lloyd G. Adu Amoah

If capitalism is restored in a big socialist country, it will inevitably become a superpower ... If one day China should change her colour and turn into a superpower, if she too should play the tyrant in the world, and everywhere subject others to her bullying, aggression and exploitation, the people of the world should identify her as social-imperialism, expose it, oppose it and work together with the Chinese people to overthrow it.
—*Deng Xiaoping* (1974)

Introduction

On Wednesday, April 10, 1974, Deng Xiaoping, then Executive Premier of the People's Republic of China (PRC; hereafter China) delivered a speech before the United Nations (UN). Deng was the first Chinese leader to speak at the UN after 1949 when China was proclaimed as a new republic at the Tiananmen Square by Chairman Mao. It is important to consider the peculiar regional and global political economy circumstances which

L. G. Adu Amoah (✉)
Department of Political Science, University of Ghana, Accra, Ghana

Centre for Asian Studies (CAS), University of Ghana, Accra, Ghana
e-mail: alloydgeorgeadu@ug.edu.gh

L. G. Adu Amoah (ed.), *Africa-China Relations*,
https://doi.org/10.1007/978-981-95-4370-0_2

provided the context for this speech. By 1974, the Sino-Soviet split had clearly become unbridgeable, and China was fancying itself, during the Cold War, as the leader of the Third World within the Maoist Theory of the Three Worlds (People's Daily [n.d.]). Mao (People's Daily, n.d.) described the Three Worlds as follows: the "First World" was made up of the rich and nuclear-armed Union of Soviet Socialist Republics (USSR) and United States (US); the "Second World" referred to Japan, Europe, Australia, and Canada; the "Third World" covered the undeveloped countries of Africa, Latin America, and Asia.

Deng's speech came exactly 48 days after Mao had expounded on his conception of the Three Worlds and he attempted following Chinese Communist Party (CCP) practise to elaborate and reinforce the idea before a global audience. By the 1970s, many colonized and semi-colonized territories across the world were transforming or had transformed into newly independent nations. Indeed, Mao's interlocutor when he theorized on the Three Worlds idea was Kenneth Kuanda, who led the East African country of Zambia to independence a decade earlier in 1964. The era of independence did not however obliterate entirely the vestiges of an imperialist world as Nkrumah (2004) was at pains to point out: "neo-colonialism is also the worst from of imperialism. For those who practise it, it means power without responsibility and for those who suffer from it, it means exploitation without redress" (xi). Deng (1974) railed against imperialism in his speech and mentioned the word (in the English version of the speech) and its cognates 31 times. It is important to stress that Deng (1974)[1] clearly drawing on Marxist political economy in the works of Luxemburg, Hilferding, Bukharin and Lenin (Brewer, 1980) understood imperialism as fundamentally the product of the workings of the capitalist mode of production even as he insisted (in veiled reference to the USSR) that a superpower socialist country can be imperialist by practising "socialism in words and imperialism in deeds" (6). By a superpower, Deng (1974) meant this: "……an imperialist country which everywhere subjects other countries to its aggression, interference, control, subversion or plunder and strives for world hegemony" (9). To the extent that the China of his times was socialist, was a big country and could convert to capitalism, Deng warned that it could become an imperialist state by wearing "the hat of social imperialism" (社会帝国主义的帽子).

It has been 51 years (at the time of writing) since Deng issued his caution on China as a potential imperialist state. China has undergone phenomenal changes in the last 50 years including its transformation into a capitalist economy and its historically unprecedented influence and presence in Africa. Hitherto, distant and rather tentative in its engagement with Africa beyond the ideological and rhetorical, the Chinese party-state, institutions, businesses and citizens have established a close, tangible presence in Africa that is as unprecedented as it is confounding in the history of Africa-China relations. Across Africa, the Chinese now live cheek and jowl in African countries. They are hawking on the streets; building roads, railways, residences, digital relays and digging for minerals; influencing politics, business, education and virtually all facets of African society including the linguistic regarding which a whole generation of Africans is being exposed to Mandarin as a language of choice and power. All this has arguably been made possible especially by China's globally consequential economic rise and the need to sustain it.

Given the obvious power asymmetry between Africa and China, the latter's conduct on the continent has been variously characterized or worse mischaracterized as imperial, colonial and neocolonial (these terms are usually used interchangeably). Theoretically and empirically, these descriptions struggle to accurately capture Africa's China forays. I provide an intervention (given the benefit of the now longer time span of China's presence in Africa, available data and informatiom) in this chapter by engaging critically with the literature on these claims and then drawing on dependency theory generally and Ruy Marini's sub-imperialism framework in particular, to argue and demonstrate that China's conduct and actions in Africa may more accurately depict a variant of sub-imperialism. The next section provides an overview of imperialism with an emphasis on its classical Marxist renderings as well as the most germane contemporary debates on the subject. This is followed by sections that examine whether or not China can be considered imperialist on a global scale and sub-imperialist in Africa. A conclusion rounds up.

Imperialism: An Overview of the Career of a Concept

Imperialism is a decidedly very modern concept and practice with an interesting career in the reflections of both Marxist and liberal thinkers. Arrighi (2006) reiterates this modern provenance: "The concept of 'imperialism' was introduced at the beginning of the twentieth century to deal theoretically and practically with an unexpected development of the capitalist world economy" (284). Given that imperialism is not as 'hot' a topic as it was in the nineteenth and twentieth centuries many scholars of our times (except those still engaged in work on it) will be surprised that imperialism was given its most elaborate analysis and conceptualization by the liberal scholar Hobson (1902 [2016]). Initially ignored, it is ironic that it was Marxist thinkers who placed it at the centre of their analysis of the global political economy in the first two decades of the twentieth century and thereby popularized it. In popularizing the idea, these Marxist thinkers while differing in their perspectives and the nature of its causal links to capitalism agreed that imperialism was the product of a maturing capitalism (triggering a search for outlets) in the core Western capitalist countries such as Britain and France and with it interstate territorial rivalry (leading to war) as capitalism spread to non-capitalist parts of the world.

Hilferding's (2006) addition to the menu of capitals represented a crucial moment in the conceptualization of imperialism. Observing capitalism in Germany and Austria, Hilferding pointed to three key interrelated tendencies in capitalism's heartlands viz. the increasing concentration and centralization of capital, the spread of monopolistic practices and the dominance of finance capital[2](the integration of financial capital with industrial capital) over industrial capital. For Hilferding, the rise of finance capital as a novel form of capital and its export was central to understanding the rise of imperialism. Indeed, it is important to stress that Hilferding's idea of finance capital was an important conceptual novelty that laid the basis for theorizing the idea of imperialism. I follow Brewer (1980) and Callinicos (2009) in giving Bukharin (1929 [1966]) the credit he deserves for his analysis and extension of the theory of imperialism given that his work antedated Lenin's (1950) more famous pamphlet on the subject. Bukharin essentially "elaborated on and systematised Hilferding's analysis making the link between capitalism and imperialism explicit." (Noonan, 2017, p. 2). Hilferding's understanding of imperialism was directed at the concentration and centralization of capital in which financial capital came to dominate industrial capital by the former becoming far less removed from the latter historically. Bukharin's (1929 [1966]) rationalisation of imperialism on the other hand focused on "the *internationalisation* and *nationalisation* of capital, the growth of international interdependence, of the world economy, and its division into national blocs" (Brewer, 1980, p. 103). Bukharin (1929 [1966]) points to the emergence of monopoly capitalism as the driving force of this nationalisation and internationalisation of capital:

> The destruction, from top to bottom, of old, conservative, economic forms that was begun with the initial stages of capitalism, has triumphed all along the line. At the same time, however, this "organic" elimination of weak competitors inside the framework of "national economies" (the ruin of artisanship, the disappearance of intermediary forms, the growth of large-scale production, etc.) is now being superseded by the "critical" period of a sharpening struggle among stupendous opponents on the world market. The causes of this phenomenon must be sought first of all in the internal changes that have taken place in the structure of "national capitalisms," causing a revolution in their mutual relations. Those changes appear, first of all, as the formation and the unusually rapid spread of capitalist monopoly organisations: cartels, syndicates, trusts, bank syndicates. We have seen above how strong this process is in the international sphere. It is immeasurably greater within the framework of "national economies." (64)

For Bukharin these two reinforcing tendencies linked to the rapid formation of cartels, syndicates, trusts (monopoly control of the market) behind a wall of tariffs intensified competition on a worldwide scale and made interstate rivalry and therefore war for markets inevitable. Lenin (1950) extended these ideas and in doing so drew attention to other ones such as the drawing of non-capitalist regions into the orbit of capitalist development, the rise of a rentier class (foreshadowing financial capitalism) and the centrality of the control and extraction of raw materials from undeveloped regions of the world. It is important to emphasize here that classical Marxism's rendering of capitalism paid very close attention to interstate rivalry for territories and markets and military coercion.

Changes in the post-World War II world especially the delegitimization of war under the United Nations charter undercut classical Marxist explanations and predictions of the global political economy. The upshot of this was a Marxist response to imperialism that introduced the idea of the "development of underdevelopment" in economic, psychological, moral, political and other spheres to make sense of global capitalism under US hegemony. The works of a diverse ensemble of theorists (including the dependency theorists) such as Nkrumah (2004), Fanon (1967), Frank (1969a, b, 1972, 1978), Baran (1973), Baran and Sweezy (1968), Wallerstein (1974, 1979), Arrighi and Saul (1973), and Marini (1972; I return to this scholar later) exemplify the Marxist derived novel explications of imperialism in the 1960s to the 1990s. To be sure, there have been fresh reflections and debates on imperialism of the late twentieth century and early decades of the twenty-first century in what has come to be labelled as new (neo)-imperialism (Wood, 2003; Harvey, 2003; Hardt & Negri, 2000; Brenner, 2006).

China in Africa: Imperialist or Not?

Overview

Having sketched above the career of the idea and practise of imperialism over the last 100 odd years I now focus in this section on a response to the question whether China's contemporary presence and conduct in Africa can be plausibly characterized as imperialistic. My response is framed simultaneously as a counterpoint to the work of Li and Kotz (2021) and an extension of it.

Given China's rise as a major global political and economic power following in particular policy decisions after the Third Plenum of the Eleventh Central Committee (hereafter 3/11) and its subsequent forays into Africa, scholars have tried to make sense of contemporary Africa-China relations. In this regard China's actions in Africa in a variety of spheres have been variously analysed in the literature as imperial, neo-imperial, colonial and neo-colonial (French, 2014; Alden, 2007; Lumumba-Kasongo, 2011; Alden et al. 2008; Sautman & Yan, 2007, 2008; Li & Kotz, 2021; Jian & Donata, 2014; Dickson, 2024). On the whole though this literature may be categorized into those which insist (Imperialist School)that China is imperial, neo-imperial, colonial and neo-colonial; those that outrightly reject the idea (Rejectionist School); and those that straddle these two views and thus call for a more complex-and therefore less simplistic-and situated reading (the Agnostic School).

French (2014), for example, insists that China is an imperial presence in Africa in the way its conduct recalls

> the patterns of empires past. The most frenzied period of imperial expansion the world has ever seen was not driven by arms alone, but also by an unprecedented expansion of global trade between the mid-eighteenth and early twentieth centuries. The new manufacturing centers of the West were only able to sustain growth of this magnitude by continually opening up new markets and inundating them with their goods. To do so required new infrastructure, and today one easily forgets that ports, railways, roads, and the administrative districts that became the downtowns of capitals around the world were built on an extraordinary scale all over the world by Westerners

in the driven pursuit of their own interests. As manufacturing powers, they needed their goods to circulate, and they needed the raw materials from far-flung places in order to make them. (286–287)

For French (2014, p. 287) the resemblance of contemporary China's imperialism in Africa to that of the past is most exemplified in the increasing numbers of Chinese migrants making the continent their home. Alden (2007, p. 125) exemplifies the Agnostic School: "The central question here is whether China's role in Africa can best be characterized as that of development partner, economic competitor or colonizer. It should be evident by now that these characterizations oversimplify what are complex and overlapping interactions which are themselves nested within the diverse African political and economic landscape." Li and Kotz (2021, p. 600) are truly representative of the Rejectionist School in presenting "evidence that China's role in other parts of the world does not fit the Marxist concept of imperialism. We argue that the nonimperialist character of China's external relations stems from China's particular political economy."

I must add here that while one engages the literature on China's imperialism, new (neo)-imperialism, colonialism and neo-colonialism, one is hard-pressed to encounter analyses that take into full and explicit account the Marxist roots of these claims. Li and Kotz (2021) and Lumumba-Kasongo (2011) are notable exceptions in that they present their arguments by steeping their claims fully in the Marxist tradition of imperialism. I turn to the next section to this kind of analysis by engaging the work of Li and Kotz (2021).

Is China Imperialist?

Is China[3] imperialist? Li and Kotz (2021) adroitly attempt to answer this question by drawing on Lenin (1950). They answer in the negative. This focus on Lenin (1950) essentially situates their work in the classical Marxist school of imperialism, which has been overtaken by both new historical realities and extended. The duo unpack their argument by postulating a strict-and rather tenuous-distinction in the Chinese political economy between a capitalist production base and a non-capitalist ruling class. This tenuous distinction is demonstrated empirically, and more convincingly in terms of the capitalist transformation of China's economy than with the capitalist control or absence of control of state power. In terms of the former, data is provided by the Li and Kotz (2021, pp. 602–605) regarding asset ownership in the industrial sector and the percentage shares of employment in the private and public sector. The data provided regarding asset ownership in the Chinese industrial sector shows that

> …the share of assets in the industrial sector held by our category of public enterprises fell from 68.8 percent in 1998 to 38.8 percent in 2018, while the share of private enterprises rose from 31.2 percent to 61.2 percent over the period. For determining how big the state's role is in guiding the economy, the share of assets is the best measure. It roughly indicates how large state investment will be relative to whole economy. (602)

With respect to China's labour profile, Li and Kotz (2021) argue

> …that the share of employment in public enterprises in the industrial sector fell from 60.5 percent in 1998 to 17.9 percent in 2018, while the share of private enterprises rose from 39.5 percent to 82.1 percent. Since over 80 percent of the industrial labor force works in private enterprises, we conclude that the ownership structure in China corresponds to the definition of a capitalist economic base. (603)

On whether state power in China is controlled by capitalists Li and Kotz (2021) make the following claim

> In China, a capitalist economy was given birth and nurtured by the policies of the CCP, a political party originally with a base of workers and peasants that seized power in a civil war. The CCP continues to control the state in China. In 2001, CCP rules were changed to admit "entrepreneurs," a euphemism for capitalists, to party membership. Some have joined the CCP, *but there is no evidence that capitalists now control the CCP or can dictate state policy*. The CCP has a self-perpetuating leadership group that runs the state (italics added). (605)

With reference to the italicized phrase in the quote above, any evidence to the contrary will clearly challenge the argument made that the Chinese ruling class has no capitalists among its ranks who control the CCP and or dictate policy. In addition to this a legitimate query from a logical point of view is how at all a capitalist economy was constructed by non-capitalists in power in China?

By the 1980s under Deng Xiaoping, China began to put in place the rules, regulations and institutions for running a society and economy underpinned by the capitalist logic of private ownership, profit motive, and market competition. This logic was ultimately consolidated beyond the 1980s because intellectuals and party leaders like Li Yining, Ma Hong, Wu Jinglian, Zhou Xiaochun, Li Jiange, Zhao Ziyang, Hu Yaobang, Deng Xiaoping, Jiang Zemin, Zhu Rongji, Hu Jintao among others made the case for and implemented capitalist policies and programmes or what Wu (2005) described as a "market economy" (81). Of course the economic reforms under Deng Xiaoping generated resistance from Marxist-Leninist Maoists such as Peng Zhen, Li Peng and Chen Yun leading to the compromise enunciated in the Four Basic Principles (socialist road, people's dictatorship, party leadership, and Marxism-Leninism-Mao Thought) adopted in the resolution on culture and ideology at the 6th Plenum of the Twelfth Central Committee on September 28, 1986 (Wang, 2002; for a comprehensive overview of these debates see Wu [2005, 2013]). Just 7 years later in 1993, the Central Committee of the Communist Party of China (CCCPC) adopted the *Decision on Issues Regarding the Establishment of a Socialist Market Economic System* (hereafter *Decision*) encompassing a ten-point road map. Point 3 of *Decision* was explicit on the necessity to "cultivate and develop a market system" (Wu, 2005, p. 83).

I raise the aforementioned points as a prelude to my rejection of the rather obtuse claim of Li and Kotz (2021) that the CCP remained a pristine Marxist-Leninist Maoist political formation ideologically without the presence of not just influential but dominant members who insisted on and formulated capitalist policies for China and by that token influenced and dictated China state policy for capitalist ends. The building of China's sovereign wealth fund together with its formidable financial system which exemplifies the influence of leading capitalist minded cadres of the CCP is ably expounded on by Liu (2023). From a paltry amount of US$167 million in 1978, China's foreign exchange reserves rose to a staggering US$3.2trillion in 2021(Liu, 2023, p.55). Indeed, in 1997 during a CCP Central Financial and Economic Leading Small Group meeting, Jiang Zemin "signaled to the apparatus of the state that financial security was the top priority of the party" (Liu, p. 53). If their (Li & Kotz, 2021) claim is true that no capitalists were part of the ruling party nor had any influence how then did capitalist policies get formulated and implemented?

By the CCP's own admission, the Deng Xiaoping inspired "building socialism with Chinese characteristics (建设有中国特色的社会主义)"

which began in the 1980s saw China at the primary stage of socialism which required that it could not "take the socialist road without going through the stage of fully developed capitalism" (Wang, 2022, p. 60). If "ideology enlists commitments, motivates action, and creates a collective conscience to the extent that actors accept and internalize it in their personality through a process of socialization" (Chai, 2003, p. 164) then within this putative primary stage of socialism requiring capitalism to be built, it can be claimed that capitalism was if not the dominant at least one of key ideologies of the ruling class in China. It can thus be argued (even if one accepts the claims of China's elites about the primary stage of socialism) plausibly that in terms of sequencing on the long march to advanced socialism that capitalism was and is all the rage and therefore actively pursued and deployed by a capitalistic CCP. It bears stating though that it is intriguing that Marx's description of the historical stages of the mode of production expounded in his *A Contribution to the Critique of Political Economy* will be essentially repurposed by China's political elites to justify the embedding of the capitalist logic into the Chinese political economy in the 1980s:

> In the social production which men carry on they enter into definite relations that are indispensable and independent of their will; these relations of production correspond to a definite stage of development of their material powers of production. ... At a certain stage of their development, the material forces of production come in conflict with the existing relations of production, or—what is but a legal expression for the same thing—with the property relations within which they had been at work before... Then comes the period of social revolution... In broad outline we can designate the Asiatic, the ancient, the feudal and the modern bourgeois modes of production as so many epochs in the progress of the economic formation of society. (Finley, 1983, p. 20, see Marx, 1904)

In Marx's periodization of history, capitalism *naturally* emerges (through class struggle) and then via "social revolution" gives way to socialism. In the Chinese case, capitalism is *unnaturally* constructed, nay artificially built it would seem, as a transition period to socialism. In a sense, Marx's historiography and social theory are turned on their heads. All this may make sense given that the kind of political economy China has built is anchored in and profoundly influenced by Mao Zedong Thought with its idiosyncrasies which challenged Marxist Thought (I will return to China and Lenin later).

Lin Biao's effusive praise of Mao Zedong Thought in his preface to the second edition of the *Little Red Book* published in 1966 is telling: "Once Mao Zedong's thought is grasped by the broad masses, it becomes an inexhaustible source of strength and a *spiritual atom bomb of infinite power*" (cited in Cheek, 2002, p. 172; italics added). While Lin's words could be described as bombastic and hagiographic, they reflect in some measure the way in which the CCP came to view Mao's ideological prominence in the party and China. I make this point because on Mao's demise and following a comprehensive review of his life, thought and times, the CCP concluded in 1981 that in spite of all his shortfalls "Mao Zedong Thought[4] is the valuable spiritual asset of our Party. It will be our guide to action for a long time to come" (Cheek, 2002, p. 216). As Mao embarked on the sinification of Marxism he made key contributions of which his ideas on contradictions are germane for my analysis here. Mao's analysis of contradictions departed from both the renderings in traditional Chinese thought and in Marxism (Pye, 1976; Wang, 2002; Chen, 1963; Schurmann, 1968). Pye (1976) argues that

> Indeed, the zigzags of Chinese policies over two decades seem to reflect in large measure Mao's bemusement with the very concept of contradictions. Some scholars have argued quite convincingly that the most striking characteristic of Mao's political thought is his fascination with the notion of contradictions……. in his own philosophical writings Mao has concentrated to a large degree on the question of contradictions. Yet when reviewing Mao's use of the concept of contradictions it does not require any special perceptiveness about personal styles to recognize that Mao's fascination with contradictions has gone beyond that of most Marxists, and that his concept of the dialectic has at times been extraordinarily idiosyncratic, indeed to a point which would make it seem to be non-Marxian. (224)

For Mao contradictions are the very essence of life and political economy and his malleable view of contradictions is such that "little endures for anything can change into its opposite" (Pye, 1976, p. 224) and back again in an unending cycle. In this sense and given the enduring hold of Mao Zedong Thought on the CCP and its policy formation, it can be plausibly argued that the CCP can be Marxist and then capitalist and then Marxist again depending on the circumstances. If this current phase of the CCP (in terms of both the kind of economy that has been built and the very nature of the CCP itself) is to be considered capitalist as I insist then the bifurcation that Li and Kotz (2021) offer crumbles. In this vein, I reframe their argument regarding China and imperialism thus: a capitalist China is not imperialist in Africa or elsewhere. Following Li and Kotz (2021), I agree that while China has been on a global search for natural resources, surplus value and markets it has not used violence and war in pursuing this. The germane question for me though is whether regarding Africa what China is if not imperialist? In the next section I argue that China in Africa may well be considered a sub-imperialist power.

China in Africa: A Sub-Imperialist Power?

The Return of Sub-imperialism

In the last 15 odd years, Marini's (1972) perceptive sub-imperialism analytical framework seems to be enjoying a resurgence for understanding the era of US led imperialism in the wake of the rise of new powers such as China, Brazil, India, Turkey and South Africa among others. Moyo and Yeros (2011) and Bond (2013a, b, 2020) are arguably among the first scholars to point out the analytical value of sub-imperialism for critically assessing Africa-BRICS relations in general and in particular South Africa's African engagements:

> Since the era of Lenin's (as I insist Bukharin holds the honours) imperialism, the system has evolved into a far more complex network responsible for managing global capital's commodification of everything under the sun, in part by displacing its crisis tendencies via more extreme uneven and combined development. We need conceptual tools — especially sub-imperialism, although the term is very alienating for Third World nationalists — to attack each of these processes. (Fuentes, 2024 in interview with Patrick Bond; parenthesis added)

The works in which sub-imperialism is employed as an analytical framework initially tended to focus on geopolitical and economic entities such as the BRICS (Bond & Garcia, 2015; Satgar, 2020) but in recent times the analytical gaze has shifted to the sub-imperialist tendencies of specific countries such as Turkey (Uysal, 2021; Amoah, 2024). The literature focusing on specific states and their sub-imperialism in the Global South has been rather hesitant and indeed coy on clearly identifying China's conduct in Africa as sub-imperialist (Katz, 2022; Luce, 2015; Moyo & Yeros, 2015) even though it has gestured at it. Katz (2015) argues for example, regarding China's sub-imperialism that "The restoration of capitalism is extremely advanced, but it has not been completed."[5] (90). On the same theme, Moyo and Yeros (2011) insist that one "cannot foreclose on these questions without further debate and analysis" (18).Over the last 15 years new developments and the availability of data and information make it possible to attempt some foreclosure regarding China in Africa which is the focus of this chapter broadly and to which I turn in the next sub-section specifically.

What Does it Take to Be Sub-imperialist?

For a state to be considered sub-imperialist it must exhibit certain key characteristics (see Table 1); what Luce (2015) describes as "determining elements" (33). These characteristics are drawn from Marini's (1972) classic work and more recent writings (Uysal, 2021; Luce, 2015; Amoah, 2024) on the subject.

I have insisted *contra* Li and Kotz (2021) that China can be considered capitalist (on this point see also Gonzalez-Vicente, 2024) at the level of both its economy and its politics. Indeed, using a Gramscian reading Hui (2017, 2023) makes the claim that China has undergone the shift to a full-blown capitalist political economy by going through three stages viz. passive revolution (under Deng and Jiang); emergent hegemony (under Hu and Wen) and eroding hegemony (under Xi). I have also argued above that China cannot be properly described as an imperialist state even though it is a capitalist state. Can capitalist China be described as sub-imperialist in its pursuit of capital accumulation and surplus value in Africa? One can claim so given that Brazil and Turkey have been so described based on the determining elements already alluded to. China can be said to arguably exhibit these elements. I will follow the determining elements (enumerated in Table 1) in making my case.

Sub-Imperialist China in Africa?

Strong State and Dependent Capitalism

Hui (2017) has convincingly showed that the Chinese state apparatus was reconstructed under Deng Xiaoping and Jiang Zemin (spanning over two decades) to make possible the construction of a capitalist economy under the hegemony of Western particularly American capital (Beckley, 2025,

Table 1 Characteristics of the Sub-imperialist State

Simplified determining elements for a state to be sub-imperialist	
Elements	*Brief description*
Strong state	State apparatus reconstructed to foster by legal, institutional, political and other means the internationalization of capital; to be precise monopoly capital.
Dependent capitalism	Dependence on imperial powers for export markets, capital inflows, advanced technology and managerial expertise; a reflection of late capitalism
Externalist orientation	Foreign policy geared at the pursuit of surplus value and capital accumulation regionally and internationally.
Fractions	Various sections of the national bourgeoisie; also known as the power bloc; their specific characterization is based on their relation to capital.
Antagonistic cooperation	Cooperation with dominant core Western nations in particular the US (the imperial fount) marked in turns by antagonism and non-antagonism.
Limits of the market	"The problem of the market constitutes the axis of the sub-imperialist scheme" (Marini, 1972, p. 15).

refers to China as a protectorate of America). States like the Chinese one under Deng and Jiang which make a turn to the accommodation of the internationalization of capital acquiesce ultimately to the ways in which this "…. deeply affects the politics and institutional forms of these states by including them in a system of interconnections……" (Poulantzas, 1976, p. 73). In this sense the Dengian-Jiangian Chinese party-state was retooled to effectively engineer the contradictions between capital-capital and labour-capital germane to the internationalization process and this by means of coercion given the absence of an existent capitalist class: "the party-state had to navigate the passive revolution with naked power so as to quell social protests and political opposition against the capitalist project" (Hui, 2017, p. 71). China under Deng and Jiang thus entered the dependent capitalist phase marked by the ideas of external orientation (*waixiangxing*, 外向型) and idolizing and fawning over anything from the West (*chongyangmeiwai,* 崇洋媚外). Ultimately, these ideas were aimed at securing China access to foreign markets, capital, advanced technology,[6] and managerial expertise. China's joining of the World Trade Organization (WTO) in December 2001 laid the formal basis for its access to the world market. China thus became the much-touted factory of the world on the back of unorganized and cheap labour and the very privileged entrenchment of multinational corporations (MNCs) in the Chinese market. As a dependent capitalism goes the MNCs made fabulous profits in the Chinese market aided by the new capitalist class inside the Chinese bureaucracy and within the MNCs as well:

> For the MNCs lobbying was a two-way process. They actively lobbied with the Chinese government for greater market concessions, thereby *reaping extraordinary profits* that would have been challenging to attain elsewhere. The Chinese government secured the endorsement and support of these influential economic players, who became advocates for the political interests of the CCP, utilizing their influence to lobby their home-country governments to maintain stable relations with China. (Yue, 2024, p. 114; italics added by author)

Limits of the Market and Externalist Orientation

Unprecedented levels of foreign capital in the form of Foreign Direct Investment (FDI) and credits poured into China in the passive revolution phase as "The market-friendly measures taken by the Party to attract foreign capital were a near-immediate success" (Liu,[7] 2023, p. 49). While in 1979 foreign capital was almost non-existent, by 1985 realized[8] foreign credits and FDI had risen cumulatively to US$21.8 billion and continued to peak reaching US$55 billion in 1996. Committed foreign credits and FDI peaked at US$123.27 billion by 1993. As large amounts of capital flowed into China it began to experience the "limits of the market" (Marini, 1972, p. 15) or the realisation problem. Kenway (1990) describes the realisation problem thus: "At its simplest, the realization problem amounts to this: is there sufficient monetary demand for the commodities which have been produced to be sold, and sold at their value?" (326). Liu (2023) captured this quandary aptly:

> Since the Asian financial crisis, Party leaders had contemplated how to broaden China's participation in global markets and redirect domestic surplus capital into foreign investment to ease speculative investment at home and temper appreciative pressure on the renminbi to maintain the competitiveness of Chinese exports in global markets. (56)

To deal with this quandary, by 1998 China set its sights on Africa and other areas of the developing world to find what Harvey (2003) describes as a spatial fix to offload domestic surplus capital. Jiang Zemin (2016) argued that "regions like Africa, the Middle East, Central Asia, and South

America with large developing countries [have] very big markets and abundant resources; we should take advantage of the opportunity to get in. We should organize a group of SOEs with sufficient capacity to invest there and set up operations" (385).

Since the "going out strategy" (*zou chuqu zhanlue*; 走出去战略) enunciated in the 10th 5 Year Development Plan, China's financial, trade, economic and investment presence in Africa has been historically unprecedented. Over the last 20 odd years, China's FDI (see for example Table 2) has poured into Africa providing therefore the conduit for capital accumulation and surplus value and making the East Asian nation "the single largest source of imports for African countries, supplying manufactured goods and machinery" (International Monetary Fund [IMF], 2023, p. 2). In 2021, China's FDI flows into Africa was about US$3 billion (IMF, 2023, p. 3)

My analysis here is also interested in China's development financing given that this has tended to be strongly correlated with China's current account surplus "which supplied foreign currency that could then be leveraged through sovereign finance" (Ray, 2023, p. 2). Again "the political focus on ODA means that its data is generally more comprehensive than that on other forms of official finance" (Development Initiatives, 2015, p. 34). China issues such development finance commitments[9] through its

Table 2 China FDI in Africa

China FDI Inflows into African Countries in Descending Order (2000–2020)	
Country	*FDI Value in Millions ($)*
South Africa	367
Democratic Republic of Congo	185
Zambia	165
Nigeria	139
Kenya	115
Ethiopia	108
Angola	97.3
Zimbabwe	76.1
Ghana	75
Mauritius	69.5
Tanzania	67.2
Mozambique	61.4

Table constructed by author using data from Iddrisu *et al.* (2023)

"two main development finance institutions (DFIs), the China Development Bank (CDB) and Export-Import Bank of China (CEXIM)" directed at "…governments, inter-governmental bodies, majority state-owned entities and minority state-owned entities with *sovereign guarantees*" (Ray, 2023, p. 2). Clearly, through these sovereign guarantees, China secures the extraction of surplus value from recipient developing states with highly reduced risks of non-payment. At the time of writing some of the most recent authoritative data publicly available (2008–2021)[10] regarding development finance shows that while there has been a drop in total value of China's overall development finance globally, Africa is still one of the three most important destinations worldwide (accounting for US$104.5 billion; 21% of global total), and Angola (US$ 32.9 billion) ranks third in the league of its ten leading borrowers globally.

China's development finance footprint in West Africa is instructive. I point to West Africa because it is the region where China has some of its longest modern diplomatic relations on the continent with Guinea and Ghana. I also use West Africa to highlight the extent and reach of China's development finance on the African continent as a means of extracting surplus value. At the global level, Chinese development finance in the years in question have been channelled into three top sectors: transportation, power (generation and distribution) and extraction/pipelines. These are fundamentally infrastructural in nature. China's development finance in West Africa follows this infrastructural trajectory in large measure but with telecoms (building the telecom infrastructure) making a very strong showing (see Table 3). As Table 3 shows, China's surplus value extraction

Table 3 Top sectors by value for Chinese Development Finance in West Africa, 2008–2021

Sector	*Value*
Transport	US$8.4 billion
Power	US$4.7 billion
Telecom	US$2.6 billion
Water and sewerage	US$1.3 billion
Social sector	US$943 million
Extraction and pipeline	US$953 million
Other construction	US$64 million
Grand total	US$18.95 billion

Source: Compiled by author using data from CODF (Boston University, 2023)

in West Africa is located in virtually all the critical sectors of the region's political economy including the new key strategic one, telecoms. Out of the 16 West African countries, China is financing the telecoms sector in 11 of them (Amoah, 2024).

It is worth mentioning here that China's FDI inflows into Africa as a percentage of China's total stock is still relatively small; it is stood at paltry 4.4 % in 2021. This however masks the reality that China has strategically channelled its FDI inflows into resource rich Africa countries (for example Angola, Nigeria, DRC and Zambia) in primarily construction and mining (IMF, 2023) where the prospects for surplus extraction are bright. China has also emerged as the largest holder of Africa's bilateral official debt: "The share of the region's total external debt-service cost attributable to China's official bilateral loans is 12 percent as of 2019, based on International Debt Statistics data. Moreover, sub-Saharan African countries that are either in debt distress or at high risk of debt distress account for about 40 percent of the total public debt stock to China at the end of 2020" (IMF, 2023, p. 2).

Fractions

The mention of state-owned enterprises (SOEs) by Jiang Zemin above provides a clue about the capitalist fractions built in China since 1978 without which there is no way China could become capitalist and then sub-imperialist. Drawing on Hui (2017, 2023), Ho (2013), China's Ministry of Commerce (MOFCOM) (2023) statistics and Yue (2024), one can construct a contemporary and credible sketch of China's fractions. I follow the categorisations in the literature but add my own category, capitalist-turned-cadre (see Table 4). Fractions (different sections of the bourgeoisie) emerged once capitalism was built in China and came to constitute a power bloc under the leadership, protection and control of the party-state. These capitalist social formations reflect this tight almost inseparable co-constitutive ties between the bureaucracy, party-state and commercial entities (MNCs, Town and Village Enterprises [TVEs] and SOEs) in what has been described as market Leninism (Yue, 2024) and bureaucratic capitalism (Ho, 2013). Surplus value circulates (in a process of appropriation and transmission) in a tensional, simultaneous and contradictory movements from China to the traditional imperial centres (the core) and then from Africa to China and back to the traditional imperial centres. The driving forces of the process are China state finance (embodied in the thriving financial system built by 2000), the businesses (see Table 4 for a sample of the areas of operation) and unorganized and cheap labour.

Table 4 China's fractions

	Nature of China's fractions				
Entities/groups/ individuals	*Foreign capitalists*	*Cadre-turned-capitalist*	*Capitalist-turned-Cadre*	*Family and friends*[a]	*Businesses/SOEs*
Foreign Invested Enterprises (FIEs)[b]	✓				
Rong Yiren		✓			CITIC[c]
Wang Jun				✓	CITIC
Rong Zhijian				✓	CITIC Pacific Ltd
Kong Dan				✓	CITIC
He Pengfei				✓	Polytechnologies Inc[d]
He Ping				✓	Polytechnologies Inc
Deng Pufang				✓	Kanghua
Jiang Mianheng		✓		✓	Shanghai Alliance Investment Ltd
Jiang Mianheng		✓		✓	China Netcom
Li Xiaopeng		✓		✓	Huaneng
Li Xiaolin				✓	China Power
Hu Haifeng		✓		✓	NucTech(Tsinghua Holdings)[e]
Capitalists invited in 2001 to join CPC under Jiang's Three Represents Theory			✓		

Constructed by author drawing on Hui (2017, 2023), Ho (2013), China Ministry of Commerce (MOFCOM) statistics and Yue (2024).

[a] Key here are the children and in-laws of Chinese leaders (Deng Xiaoping, Jiang Zemin, Li Peng, Hu Jintao) who played key roles in China's capitalist transformation lie at the core of these fractions.

[b] According to MOFCOM (2023) data the FIEs from the European Union (EU) increased from 40 in the year 1987 to 2846 in the year 2005; beyond 2005 the numbers have remained above 1000 right up to 2022 (1376).

[c] Initially started out introducing advanced technology and equipment into China. Currently it is engaged in a diverse portfolio of businesses like metals, oil and gas, construction, food and financial services.

[d] Trading group for missiles.

[e] Business focus on start-ups, hi-tech industries, innovation services, finance, creative industries and online education.

Antagonistic Cooperation

With its new-fangled status as an intermediate centre of accumulation within the "hierarchic arrangement of capitalist countries in the form of a pyramid" (Marini, 1972, p. 25; cited in Luce, 2015, p. 30), China's interactions with especially the USA have become antagonistic. This antagonistic interaction is born out of the search for relative autonomy. Luce (2015) puts it well: "in sub-imperialism antagonistic cooperation with centre imperialism expresses a search for relative autonomy in international politics and for control over a part of surplus value, so that the economy not only transmits but also appropriates surplus value" (39). According to the sub-imperialism framework not all sub-imperialist states are able to display antagonistic cooperation. The capacity to do so depends on a concatenation and balance of political, military, historical, economic and other factors conducive to displays of episodes of subordination and tendencies directed at relative autonomy in self-serving even opportunistic ways. The military factor in the form of high military expenditures is important here serving as it does as the "escape valve" to deal with the limits of the market problem by being "the only effective means of wasteful expenditure" (Marini, 1972, p. 22). In effect a sub-imperialist state like China that engages in antagonist cooperation is able to do so in large part because of its military capabilities; this acts as a bulwark against wanton military reprisals from the imperialist centres (which continue to resort to it in direct violation of Chapter 7 of the UN Charter). China's Anti-Access/Area Denial (A2/AD) system (Mastro, 2017) by which it seeks to prevent through advanced precision technology access into the Indo-Pacific waters by America is a case in point. No wonder Schindler et al. (2023) argue that China and the US are engaged in a network-centric non-zero sum Second Cold War for centrality of global proportions in the key areas of infrastructure, digitalization, production and finance involving both interdependence and rivalry. The Chips and Science Act of 2022 captures this antagonistic cooperation. China effectively rode (Chinese students attended Ivy League universities in droves; there existed joint Sino-American research technological and scientific projects; and blue-chip companies like Apple built their R&D operations in China) on the back of American technological breakthroughs to build its own technological capabilities. As China built its technology with American cooperation, China was a dutiful subordinate capitalist state. With for example the emergence of its 5G technology, this has occasioned technological rivalry with the US as China sought to assert its autonomy. This had to be checked with the passage of the Chips and Science Act, which seeks among other things to constrain China's "ability to obtain advanced computing chips, develop and maintain supercomputers, and manufacture advanced semi-conductors" (US Department of Commerce, 2022,p.1).

Conclusion

This chapter has concerned itself with the vexing question of the overarching nature of the political economy of China's presence in Africa within the general scheme of contemporary Africa-China relations. Framed as a critical intervention and contribution (utilising a Marxian political economy lens) directed at descriptions of China's activities and conduct in Africa in the literature as colonial, neo-colonial and (neo)imperialist, the chapter accepts the argument canvassed by Li and Kotz (2021) that China is not imperialist on a global scale nor in Africa. In contradiction though to Li and Kotz (2021), I argue that China can be considered a full-blown capitalist state at the levels of its economy and politics and that its actions in Africa can therefore be described as sub-imperialist in its search for surplus value and capital accumulation on the continent.

The question to pose at this juncture is whether as a sub-imperialist state China's presence in Africa can be characterized as partnership, pawnage or peonage. I will submit that this presence encompasses all three descriptors operating in concert to allow the China party-state to pursue and realize its surplus value and capital accumulation ends. Partnership here must be understood first and foremost as the euphemism for diplomatic relations without which the China party-state cannot build trade, economic and other ties with African states for its sub-imperialist ends. It is clearly instructive that as at March 2025 China had established diplomatic ties with 53 out of the 54 African states (Etswatini being the only exception). It must be stressed though that given the sub-imperialistic nature of the links between China and Africa, the latter is by definition the subordinate partner in the partnership. Woods (2006) has brilliantly shown how in the imperialist orbit, notions of liberal equality (which is entrenched in the dominant multilateralist view of international politics following the English School) are simply a basis for catalysing exploitation effected by a cultivated disjuncture between a political sphere where some putative equality exists and its economic opposite where power and exploitation rule.

Digging deeper beyond the official tropes of partnership enunciated yearly at the Forum on China-Africa Cooperation (FOCAC), I argue that one is confronted with Africa as a pawn and in peonage in its relations with China. The *Oxford Advanced Learner's Dictionary* (Gimson & Cowie, 1989) describes a pawn as "person or group whose actions are controlled by others" (908). Cambridge Dictionary (n.d.) gives the meaning of pawn as "a person or organization that does not have any real power but is used by others to achieve something." Drawing on these two lexical meanings pawnage in this chapter (reiterating the meaning in the introductory chapter in this volume) is understood as a group of people without real power (as opposed to without any power) used by others to achieve their own ends. Sub-imperialist China in Africa can be construed therefore as pawning Africa to access raw materials as well as energy to feed its industries; as a market for its cheap industrial and other products; and projecting itself as leader of the global South in its dream to be a superpower among others. And this precisely because Africa has no real power (technological, military, industrial, scientific etc.) which China itself strove to acquire from the 1950s. Peonage or more to the point debt peonage (see Chap. 3 in this volume for a fuller explication) essentially refers to being in debt and having to make restitution on the debtor's terms. As I have shown above, African countries constitute the group most heavily indebted to China. Indeed 22 low-income (40.1% of the total number of African states) (Vines et al., 2023) African countries are reportedly either already in or at high risk of debt distress providing China enormous leverage and influence over these countries which include geopolitically and geoeconomically important and resource rich ones such as Angola, Zambia, Nigeria and the Democratic Republic of Congo. Again, I have shown above how China flush on its capital account with excess liquidity resorted to lending to other countries to ease appreciative pressure on the renminbi and head off speculative investment and thus protect the Chinese economy overall.

I will reiterate in conclusion that a sub-imperialist account of China's presence in Africa brings to the fore much more forcefully and realistically the exploitative aspects of Africa-China relations than has so far been arguably suggested or attempted especially theoretically in existing research on the subject. The theoretical and empirical value for scholars of the claims of this chapter lie in its general utility for further research. Africa's policy-makers in particular who must engage a China whose geopolitical and geoeconomic impact is bound to be felt for a very long time to come may also find both theoretical and practical value for this chapter's positions.

Abbreviations

A2/AD	Anti-Access/Area Denial
CDB	China Development Bank
CEXIM	China Export and Import Bank
CODF	China's Overseas Development Finance
CCP	Chinese Communist Party
DFI	Development Finance Institutions
DRC	Democratic Republic of the Congo
FDI	Foreign Direct Investment
IMF	International Monetary Fund
MNCs	Multinational Corporations
MOFCOM	Ministry of Commerce
PRC	People's Republic of China
R&D	Research and Development
SOEs	State-owned Enterprises
TVEs	Town and Village Enterprises
UN	United Nations
USD	United States Dollar
USSR	Union of Soviet Socialist Republics

Notes

1. Deng was ideationally greatly influenced by Bukharin (He, 2021) whose work (Bukharin & Preobrazhenski, 1969) on the fundamentals of communism he was exposed to while studying in Moscow.
2. This is the only capital not theorized by Marx.
3. By China in this work, I mean the party-state and logically so given that contemporary international relations still continues to privilege the state(in its Westerncentric construct going back to Hobbes) than any other entity.
4. The CCP it must be noted saw Mao Zedong Thought as the collective ideology of the party embodying the ideas of its leading members with Mao as the fount or lead theoretician:

    Mao Zedong Thought is Marxism-Leninism applied and developed in China; it constitutes a correct theory, a body of correct principles and a summary of the experiences that have been confirmed in the practice of the Chinese revolution, a crystallization of the collective wisdom of the Chinese Communist Party. Many outstanding leaders of our Party made important contributions to the formation and development of

Mao Zedong Thought, and they are synthesized in the scientific works of Comrade Mao Zedong ...(Cheek, 2002, p. 216)

This collegial view of Mao Zedong Thought with Mao as the lead theoretician had not always been the dominant one as Schram (1969) stresses until fairly recently: "'Mao Tse-tung's thought' as used today in Peking refers to a body of ideas which are presumed to have sprung full-blown from Mao's brain sometime around 1920, and to have been handed down ever since as absolutely immutable and universally valid truths" (9). Schram therefore within the context of his times tries to make a distinction between the political thought of Mao Zedong and Mao Zedong Thought which distinction is now superfluous given the recent amendments that acknowledge Mao's own thought and that of others.

5. Capitalism is a necessary condition for sub-imperialism to be sure.
6. See Hannas and Tatlow (2021) for a comprehensive account of how China sought advanced technology from the West.
7. I lean heavily on Liu for the data on Chinese capital.
8. Chinese financial statistics make a distinction between committed and realized capital. The former are essentially pledges like contracts and credit lines while the latter are more concrete in the form of value of actual construction and the amount drawn on credit lines.
9. Commitments according to the China's Overseas Development Finance (CODF) Database (Boston University, 2023) refer to the financial undertakings made by Chinese Development Finance Institutions related to 'tracking the pipeline and network of supported projects.' (Ray, 2023, p. 4).
10. I refer here to the CODF Database (Boston University, 2023) from which I draw heavily for data on China development finance around the globe including Africa.

References

Alden, C. (2007). *China in Africa*. Zed Books.

Amoah, L. G. A. (2024). Diplomacy of architecture and the Ghana National Mosque Complex: Concrete sign of a soft Turkish Imperium? *Third World Quarterly*, *0*(0), 1–24.

Arrighi, G. (2006). Imperialism. In W. Outhwaite (Ed.), *The Blackwell dictionary of modern social thought* (pp. 284–287). Blackwell Publishing.

Arrighi, G., & Saul, J. S. (1973). *Essays on the political economy of Africa*. Monthly Review Press.

Baran, P. (1973). *The political economy of growth*. Penguin.

Baran, P., & Sweezy, P. (1968). *Monopoly capital*. Harmondsworth Penguin.

Bond, P.(2013a). BRICS in Africa: Anti-imperialist, sub-imperialist or in between? a Brics reader for the Durban Summit.

Bond, P. (2013b). Are BRICS sub-imperialists? *Pambazuka News*. Retrieved March 1, 2025, from https://farmlandgrab.org/post/21847-are-brics-sub-imperialists

Bond, P. (2020). Subimperial BRICS: Enter the Bolsonaro-Putin-Modi-Xi-Ramaphosa. In V. Satgar (Ed.), *BRICS and the new American imperialism: Global rivalry and resistance* (pp. 105–139). Wits University Press.

Bond, P., & Garcia, A. (2015). *BRICS: An anti-capitalist critique*. PlutoPress.

Boston University Global Development Policy Center. 2023. *Chinese Loans to Africa Database*. Retrieved January 23, from http://bu.edu/gdp/chinese-loans-to-africa-database.

Brenner, R. (2006). What is, and what is not, imperialism. *Historical Materialism, 14*(4), 79–105.

Brewer, A. (1980). *Marxist theories of imperialism: A critical survey* (1st ed.). Routledge and Kegan Paul Ltd..

Bukharin, N. (1929[1966]). *Imperialism and world economy*. Howard Fertig.

Bukharin, N., & Preobrazhenski, E. (1969). *The ABC of communism*. Penguin Books.

Callinicos, A. (2009). *Imperialism and global political economy*. Polity Press.

Cambridge Dictionary (n.d.). Retrieved March 25, from https://dictionary.cambridge.org/dictionary/english/pawn

Chai, W. (2003). The ideological paradigm shifts of China's world views: From Marxism-Leninism-Maoism to the pragmatism-multilateralism of the Deng-Jiang-Hu Era. *Asian Affairs: An American Review, 30*(3, Fall), 163–175.

Cheek, T. (2002). *Mao Zedong and China's revolutions: A brief history with documents*. Palgrave.

Chen, W.-T. (1963). *A source book in Chinese philosophy*. Princeton University Press.

Deng, X. (1974). *Speech By Chairman of the Delegation of the People's Republic of China, Deng Xiaoping, At the Special Session of the U.N. General Assembly*. Retrieved September 18, from https://www.marxists.org/reference/archive/deng-xiaoping/1974/04/10.htm

Development Initiatives. (2015). *Investments to end poverty*. Development Initiatives.

Dickson, E. M. (2024). Major powers and the new scramble for Africa in the 21st century: Interrogating China-Nigeria engagements. *African Journal of Political Science and International Relations., 18*(4), 146–153.

Fanon, F. (1967). *The wretched of the earth*. Penguin Books.

Finley, M. (1983). Ancient society. In T. Bottomore, L. Harris, V. G. Kiernan, & R. Miliband (Eds.), *A dictionary of Marxist Thought* (pp. 19–22). Blackwell.

Beckley, M. (2025). The Stagnant Order and the End of Rising Powers. Foreign Affairs. Retrieved December 30, 2025 from https://www.foreignaffairs.com/united-states/stagnant-order-michael-beckley#:~:text=THE%20AGE%20OF%20ASCENT,on%20a%20steady%20upward%20trajectory

Frank, A. G. (1969a). *Capitalism and underdevelopment in Latin America*. Revised edition, Modern Reader Paperbacks, New York, and London, first edition published 1967.

Frank, A. G. (1969b). *Latin America: Underdevelopment or revolution*. Monthly Review Press.

Frank, A. G. (1972). *Lumpenbourgeoisie: Lumpendevelopment*. Monthly Review Press.

Frank, A. G. (1978). *Dependent accumulation and underdevelopment*. Macmillan.

French, H. (2014). *China's second continent: How a million migrants are building a New Empire in Africa*. Alfred Knopf.

Fuentes, F. (2024). *US imperial dominance, BRICS sub-imperialism and unequal ecological exchange: An interview with Patrick Bond*. Retrieved January 23, 2025, from https://www.cadtm.org/US-imperial-dominance-BRICS-sub-imperialism-and-unequal-ecological-exchange

Gimson, A. C., & Cowie, A. P. (1989). *Oxford advanced learner's dictionary* (4th ed.). Oxford University Press.

Gonzalez-Vicente, R. (2024). In the name of the nation: Authoritarian practices, capital accumulation, and the radical simplification of development in China's global vision. *Globalizations, 21*(6), 1041–1056.

Hannas, W. C., & Tatlow, D. K. (2021). *China's quest for foreign technology*. Routledge.

Hardt, M., & Negri, A. (2000). *Empire*. Harvard University Press.

Harvey, D. (2003). *The new imperialism*. Verso.

He, L. (2021). Bukharin inspired Deng Xiaoping to Change China. *Translations, 25*, 1–16.

Hobson, J. A. (1902). *Imperialism: A study*. James Pott and Company.

Hobson, J. A. (2016). *Imperialism: A study*. Routledge.

Ho W-C. (2013). The New 'Comprador Class': the re-emergence of bureaucratic capitalists in post-Deng China. *Journal of Contemporary China, 22*(83), 812–827.

Hui, E. (2017). Putting the Chinese State in its place: A march from passive revolution to hegemony. *Journal of Contemporary Asia, 47*(1), 66–92.

Hui, E. (2023). The development of labor policies in China: From passive revolution to eroding hegemony. In C. Scherrer, A. Garcia, & J. Wullweber (Eds.), *Handbook of critical political economy and policy* (pp. 279–292). Edward Elgar Publishing.

Iddrisu, K., Abor, J., Insaidoo, M., & Kannyiri, B. (2023). Does China's flow of FDI and institutional quality matter for poverty? Evidence from Africa. *Journal of Asian and African Studies, 60*(2), 1250–1275.

International Monetary Fund (IMF). (2023). *At a crossroads: Sub-Saharan Africa's economic relations with China. In regional economic outlook: Sub-Saharan Africa—Light on the Horizon?* IMF.

Jian, J., & Donata, F. (2014). Neo-colonialism or De-colonialism: China's economic engagement in Africa and the implications for world order African. *Journal of Political Science and International Relations, 8*(7), 185–201.

Katz, C. (2015). Capitalist mutations in emerging, intermediate and peripheral neoliberalism. In P. Bond & A. Garcia (Eds.), *BRICS: An anti-capitalist critique* (pp. 70–93). Jacana Media.

Katz, C. (2022). The Imperial System in crisis. *LINKS – International Journal of Socialist Renewal.* Retrieved March 1, 2025, from https://links.org.au/imperial-system-crisis

Kenway, P. (1990). Realization problem. In J. Eatwell, M. Milgate, & P. Newman (Eds.), *Marxian economics* (pp. 326–329). The Macmillan Press Limited.

Lenin, V. I. (1950). Imperialism, the highest stage of capitalism. In *Selected works* (Vol. I). Foreign Languages Publishing House. first published in Russian 1917.

Li, Z., & Kotz, D. M. (2021). Is China imperialist? Economy, State, and Insertion in the Global System. *Review of Radical Political Economics, 53*(4), 600–610.

Liu, Z. L. (2023). *Sovereign funds: How the communist party of China finances its global ambitions.* Harvard University Press.

Luce, M. (2015). Sub-imperialism, the highest stage of dependent capitalism. In P. Bond & A. Garcia (Eds.), *BRICS: An Anti-capitalist critique* (pp. 27–44). Jacana Media.

Lumumba-Kasongo, T. (2011). China-Africa relations: A neo-imperialism or neo-colonialsim? A Reflection. *African and Asian Studies, 10*(20), 234–266.

Mao, Z. (1959). Mao Zedong, Outline for a Speech on the International Situation. Wilson Center Digital Archive. Mao Zedong's Manuscripts since the Founding of the People's Republic of China. Vol. 8 (Beijing: Zhongyang wenxian chubanshe, 1993), 599–603. Translated by David Wolff. https://digitalarchive.wilsoncenter.org/document/118893

Marini, R. M. (1972). Brazilian Subimperialism. *Monthly Review, 23*(9), 14–24. https://doi.org/10.14452/MR-023-09-1972-02_2

Mastro, O. (2017). China's Antiaccess-Area Denial (A2/AD) capabilities: Is the U.S. rebalancing enough? In W. H. Natter III & J. Brooks (Eds.), *American strategy and purpose: Reflections on Foreign Policy and National Security in an era of change* (pp. 118–140). Lexington.

Ministry of Commerce of China. (2023). *Statistical bulletin of FDI in China.* China Commerce and Trade Press.

Moyo, S., & Yeros, P. (2014). Rethinking the theory of primitive accumulation: Imperialism and the new scramble for land and natural resources. In *Paper presented to the 2nd IIPPE Conference, 20–22 May 2011*, Istanbul, Turkey.
Moyo, S., & Yeros, P. (2015). Scramble, resistance and a new non-alignment strategy. In P. Bond & A. Garcia (Eds.), *BRICS: An Anti-Capitalist Critique* (pp. 246–250). Jacana Media.
Moyo, S., Yeros, P. and Jha, P.(2011). Rethinking the Theory of Primitive Accumulation: Imperialism and the New Scramble for Land and Natural Resources. Paper presented to the 2nd IIPPE Conference, 20–22 May 2011, Istanbul, Turkey
Nkrumah, K. (2004). *Neo-colonialism: The last stage of imperialism*. Panaf.
Noonan, M.(2017). *Marxist Theories of Imperialism: A History*. I.B. Taurus.
People's Daily (n.d.). *Chairman Mao's Theory of the Differentiation of the Three Worlds is a Major Contribution to Marxism-Leninism*. Retrieved September 18, from https://www.marxists.org/history/erol/ncm-5/theory-3-worlds/section1.htm
Poulantzas, N. (1976). *Classes in contemporary capitalism*. NLB.
Pye, L. W. (1976). Mao Tse-tung's leadership style. *Political Science Quarterly, 91*(2), 219–235.
Ray, R. (2023). "Small is beautiful" A new era in China's overseas development finance? *Global China Initiative (GCI). Policy Brief, 017*, 1–41.
Satgar, V. (2020). *BRICS and the new American imperialism: Global rivalry and resistance*. Wits University Press.
Sautman, B., & Yan, H. (2007). Friends and interests: China's distinctive links with Africa. *African Studies Review, 50*(3), 75–114.
Sautman, B., & Yan, H. (2008). The forest for the trees: Trade, investment and the China-in-Africa Discourse. *Pacific Affairs, 81*(1), 9–29.
Schindler, S., Alami, I., DiCarlo, J., Jepson, N., Rolf, S., Bayırbağ, M. K., et al. (2023). The second cold war: US-China competition for centrality in infrastructure, digital, production, and finance networks. *Geopolitics, 29*(4), 1083–1120.
Schram, S. R. (1969). *The political thought of Mao Tse-Tung*. Praeger.
Schurmann, F. (1968). *Ideology and organization in communist China*. University of California Press.
US Department of Commerce. (2022). *Commerce Implements New Export Controls on Advanced Computing and Semiconductor Manufacturing Items to the People's Republic of China (PRC)*. Press Release.Office of Congressional and Public Affairs.
Uysal, G. (2021). Turkey's sub-imperialism in Sub-Saharan Africa. *Review of Radical Political Economics, 53*(3), 442–461.

Vines, A. V., Butler, C, & Yu, J. (2023). The response to debt distress in Africa and the role of China: Exploring solutions to African debt distress through multilateral cooperation. Research Paper. Chatham House.

Wallerstein, I. (1974). *The modern world system*. Academic Press.

Wallerstein, I. (1979). *The capitalist world economy*. Cambridge University Press and Editions de la Maison des Sciences de 17Homme.

Wood, E. M. (2003). *Empire of capital*. Verso.

Wood, E. M. (2006). Democracy as ideology of empire. In C. Mooers (Ed.), *The new imperialists: Ideologies of empire* (pp. 9–23). Oneworld.

Wu, J. (2005). *Understanding and interpreting Chinese economic reform*. Thomson/South-Western.

Wu, J. (2013). *Wu Jinglian: Voice of reform*. The MIT Press.

Yue, J. (2024). *Crony comprador capitalism: The institutional origins of China's rise and decline*. Palgrave Macmillan.

Zemin, J. (2016). *On socialist market economy*. Central Party Literature Press.

Deconstructing 'Chinese' Debt Trap Diplomacy in Africa-China Relations

Kwaku Obeng Effah and Lloyd G. Adu Amoah

Introduction

The idea of 'Chinese' debt trap diplomacy has lingered on for years, often lacking objectiveness in its application and usage. The propagation of this notion has not only undermined Africa-China engagements, but recent scholarship also highlights how this narrative has been leveraged and co-opted as populist rhetoric, in some instances subtly stoking Sinophobic sentiments in countries like Zambia and Nigeria (Adunbi & Stein, 2019; Agubamah, 2014; Hess & Aidoo, 2014; Obiezu, 2022; Siribi, 2021). Given these ramifications, a constructive approach for assessing the actual dynamics of debt relations remains necessary, among other reasons, to

K. O. Effah (✉)
Department of Government and International Affairs, Lingnan University, Hong Kong, China
e-mail: kwakuobengeffah@ln.hk

L. G. Adu Amoah
Department of Political Science, University of Ghana, Accra, Ghana

Centre for Asian Studies (CAS), University of Ghana, Accra, Ghana
e-mail: alloydgeorgeadu@ug.edu.gh

L. G. Adu Amoah (ed.), *Africa-China Relations*,
https://doi.org/10.1007/978-981-95-4370-0_3

avert potential diplomatic fallout and socio-political consequences. Amid increasing claims of hidden and high indebtedness to China (Brown, 2023) the notion of 'Chinese' debt trap diplomacy undoubtedly necessitates an objective deconstruction. By employing the concept of debt peonage, this work challenges the conventional use of 'Chinese' debt trap diplomacy, arguing that the veracity of debt entrapment must go past the speculated intent of the creditor [China], to holistically include a critical examination of the debtor's role, surrounding conditions and the contract terms for which a financing deal is entered into. Theoretically, this study engages the Resource-financed Infrastructure (RFI) model as a key theoretical framework central to teasing out (by bringing it into conversation with the debt peonage concept) the potentiality of debt entrapment (or otherwise), particularly associated with huge Chinese-financed development projects in Africa. Methodologically, this chapter is anchored in a critical engagement of the Africa-China debt literature directed at concept building.

On Africa-China Relations

China's engagement with Africa has deep historical foundations, dating back to antiquity. Evidence of early interactions suggests two key points of reference. According to Amoah (2016), initial Africa-China contact occurred during late antiquity (third–fifth century), primarily through trade at Alexandria, a critical commercial hub in Egypt's Nile Delta (Filesi, 1972). Material evidence such as Chinese porcelain and coins along Africa's eastern coastline supports this claim (Amoah, 2016, p. 239). However, Shinn (2019) marks the medieval period (fifth–fifteenth century) as the beginning of significant interactions. Despite these differing views, both scholars recognize the Ming Dynasty's exploratory voyages, particularly those led by Admiral Zheng He, as a crucial historical milestone for Africa-China relations (Shinn, 2019).

Following these early interactions, Africa-China relations seemingly stagnated for centuries, only resurfacing in the nineteenth century with the movement of Chinese labourers to Africa (Shinn & Eisenman, 2012). The earlier Ming and Sung dynasty interactions failed to evolve into sustained political or economic ties (Shinn, 2019). Snow (1988) attributes this stagnation to China's retreat from maritime trade, driven by disappointing economic returns, leading to prolonged isolationism. Additionally, European imperial expansion between 1700 and 1899 further constrained

Africa-China interactions, disrupting African trade networks and delaying potential cooperation (Yu, 1966; Amoah, 2016).

By the mid-twentieth century, the African independence movement created renewed momentum for Africa-China relations. Amoah (2016) highlights China's active support for African liberation movements, aligning itself ideologically and materially with anti-colonial struggles. During a diplomatic mission to Conakry in the 1960s, Chinese officials emphasized the similarity between Africa's anti-colonial struggles and China's own revolutionary history, underscoring that Africa's liberation should primarily be driven by Africans themselves, with external support as secondary (Adie, 1964, p. 178). This anti-imperialist stance was a core aspect of China's policy engagement with Africa during the 1950s and 1960s (Oqubay & Lin, 2019a).

The 1955 Bandung Conference and Africa's support for China's re-admission to the UN Security Council notably strengthened diplomatic ties. The Bandung Conference represented China's first major political engagement in Africa, with Premier Zhou Enlai advocating principles such as territorial integrity, non-interference, and mutual benefit (Shinn, 2019, p. 63). Within the same decade, China expanded economic and military aid to African states, demonstrated especially through infrastructure projects like the Tanzania-Zambia railway and various medical and military assistance initiatives (Shinn, 2019).

However, early post-independence Africa-China relations faced challenges, partly due to China's ideological stance (Barnouin & Changgen, 1998). Chairman Mao's Great Proletarian Cultural Revolution aimed at preserving communism and eradicating Western influence (Philips, 2016), negatively affected China's budding engagements with Africa at the time (Ogunsanwo, 1974). In several cases, Chinese backing of revolutionary movements resulted in political instability, such as the toppling of governments in the Central African Republic and present-day Benin. The Ghanaian government expelled Chinese personnel amid political tensions, further underscoring these strains (Barnouin & Changgen, 1998). Ismael (1971) notes that by 1964, several African leaders—including those of Niger, Ivory Coast, and Upper Volta (Burkina Faso) denounced China due to its alleged involvement in coup attempts and radical leftist influence.

Despite these initial setbacks, post-Cold War Africa-China relations significantly intensified, evolving into formalized economic partnerships by the 1990s (Alden, 2012; Amoah, 2016; Brautigam & Xiaoyang, 2009). Currently, China has the largest diplomatic presence on the African continent, and economic ties have grown dramatically (Taylor, 2019). In 2021 alone, Chinese aid inflows to Africa totalled $3.18 billion, and bilateral trade reached $251 billion (China-Africa Research Initiative (CARI), 2023). Between 2000 and 2020, China provided African governments and enterprises with loans amounting to approximately $160 billion, predominantly for infrastructure projects such as Kenya's Standard Gauge Railway, the Addis Ababa-Djibouti railway, and various energy and road networks in Ghana, Nigeria, Ethiopia, and Angola (Monyae & Chapotera, 2023; Global Development Policy Centre, n.d.).

Nevertheless, China's growing financial involvement in Africa has sparked fears of 'debt trap diplomacy'. Critics argue that China's opaque lending practices risk driving African nations into unsustainable debt, potentially leading to asset seizures or undue leverage (Chellaney, 2017; Michael, 2022; Soy, 2023). These concerns keep resurfacing with high debt distress levels and reports of hidden loans owed to China (Horn et al., 2021). Oqubay and Lin (2019b, p. 310) argue that much of this discourse is shaped by Western scepticism, noting that the "myth surrounding China-Africa cooperation has intensified", leading to the widespread notion of[Chinese] debt entrapment. The frequently cited example of Sri Lanka's Hambantota Port, allegedly taken over by China after debt default, amplifies concerns that similar outcomes may emerge in Africa (Al-Fadhat & Prasetio, 2022).

Clearly, Africa-China relations have evolved significantly—from early historical trade and ideological support to contemporary complex economic partnerships. It remains contested whether China's lending strategy constitutes a deliberate debt trap or is part of a broader development model that aligns with Africa's infrastructural and economic aspirations. More often than not, the discourses that speculate debt entrapment tend to oversimplify the contemporary complexities of Africa-China relations, reducing it to binary narratives of exploitation and gain. Such interpretations fail to account for two critical factors: (a) Chinese lending agencies, much like Western financial institutions, require financial sustainability and expected returns on disbursed loans, and (b) African countries exercise some agency however severely constrained in financial negotiations, engaging with China based on strategic economic interests.

Rethinking [Chinese] Debt Trap Diplomacy

Through its $1 trillion 'one belt, one road' initiative, China is supporting infrastructure projects in strategically located developing countries, often by extending huge loans to their governments. As a result, some of these countries are becoming saddled with debt, leaving them even more firmly under China's thumb.

—Remarks from Brahma Chellaney (2017), foremost promoter of the notion of debt trap diplomacy

As could be induced from the above quote and the rhetoric of the writer in general, the notion of debt trap seems to have been outrightly associated with China from the outset, sparking up media spins propagated mostly by the Western media (Brautigam, 2020; Singh, 2020). Per its evolution, the concept of debt peonage could be perceived as a derivative of the initial notion of debt trap diplomacy and its related corpus of writings on debt entanglements. Notwithstanding the indication that debt peonage could be deemed as having been extracted from debt diplomacy, it departs from and is not dependent on the connotations or interpretations of debt diplomacy; its usage by the Sino-Africa expert, Amoah in the call for book chapters[1] in 2023 (as well as earlier in 2022) is a case in point. Before examining debt peonage, debt diplomacy[2] is briefly assessed for the purposes of contextualization. Debt diplomacy is said to have made headway into academia through a publication by graduate students from Harvard University intimating [China's] 'Debt book diplomacy' (Parker & Chefitz, 2018). Brautigam (2020) examines the concept of debt diplomacy and demystifies its 'Chinese-origin intendedness' as she considers it as a meme.

According to Brautigam, debt diplomacy borders on the "claim that China deliberately seeks to entrap countries in a web of debt to secure some kind of strategic advantage or an asset of some kind" (Brautigam, 2020, p. 2). Whilst the writer is not explicit in presenting an operational definition for debt diplomacy, she unearths what accounts for why the concept of debt diplomacy is associated with China. In her view, the negative bias of the West in reaction to China's role in Africa and other developing countries since 2006 is attributable for the rise of the 'Chinese debt diplomacy' tag (Brautigam, 2020). Brautigam avers that "at a time when the rest of the international community had turned away from infrastructure finance, the Chinese were primarily building...Western countries and politicians…began to perceive China as threat, labelling it as new imperial power" (Brautigam, 2020, p. 3). The Western disdain for China's development infrastructure financing in developing countries and the subsequent claim that it uses loans to entrap states, as Singh (2020) explains, comes on the back of China's pursuit of the massive Belt and Road Initiative (BRI). To an extent, these offer insights into why 'the threat of China and Chinese debt diplomacy' seem to dominate coverage in the Western media and is championed by some scholars and even statesmen (Brautigam, 2020; Singh, 2020).

Mlambo (2022, p. 2) explains that "the magnitude of China's lending to African countries as well as China's motives has been labelled as 'debt trap diplomacy'. China's debt trap diplomacy is often labelled as a long-term aim to trap African countries into debt commitments they cannot fulfil and eventually leverage that pretext to obtain African resources or important assets". A similar proposition by Brautigam (2020, p. 8) also contends that "claims about China's debt trap diplomacy unquestioningly assume that China's own economic and geostrategic interests are maximized when its lending partners are in distress". Joining up these two propositions and those of Chellaney (2017) and Parker & Chefitz (2018), the idea 'debt trap diplomacy' as described, is seen to harbour a 'motive-driven' component which implies [China] the creditor wittingly sets out to strategically offer loans to developing countries in order to entrap them and obtain an advantage of some sort.

Debt Peonage: Conceptualizing Beyond Debt Trap Diplomacy

Contrary to the stylized connotations of 'debt trap diplomacy', this study does not only depart from the use of 'debt trap' tagged to China in a possessive sense [i.e., China's], but replaces the idea of 'debt trap' with 'debt peonage'; indicative of the fact that the borrower[s] can of their negligence be entrapped in debt and not necessarily because the creditor planned it so [as was the case of 'motive-driven' definitions previously rendered]. A new construct is needed because the previous connotation is shot through with intractability and is essentially speculative (Brautigam, 2020). For example, how does a researcher concretely prove that China intends to entrap Angola, Africa's largest loan ($42.6billion) debtor to China?[3] Singh (2020) also discredits the use of the term [debt diplomacy] having assessed the cases of some developing countries from Africa and Latin America in respect of debt entrapment.

Drawing from the traditional understanding of peonage (Francis & Rael, 2018; MacLeod, n.d.), two aspects of debt peonage are perceptible; either the creditor wilfully aims to entrap the debtor or conditions beyond the debtor subjects her to the dictates of the creditor's repayment conditions. Based on these reflections and within the context of the study we describe debt peonage as a state of affairs, typically associated with collateralized development financing agreements, wherein (a) official creditors exploit the inability of debtors to repay as leverage to advance unfair advantages/predatory interests, and [or] (b) where certain compelling conditions force debtors to succumb to stricter, unfavourable, and self-serving interests of the creditor, whether by design or oversight of the agreement terms in question. To this end, either compelling conditions or the creditors' deliberate efforts seeking to 'enslave' the debtor, become the plausible elements of debt peonage.

Turning to the plausible elements of the debt peonage conceptualization, this study draws on Brautigam (2020), Brautigam and Kidane (2020), Chellaney (2017), Parker and Chefitz (2018), and Singh (2020), building particularly upon Singh (2020) to present the following conceptual map anchored on what we describe as causalities taking inspiration from Fodor (1994). Causalities for us refer essentially to the triggers that point to the emergence of debt peonage as we construe it in this work. The conceptual map (Fig. 1) is structured to caution about conditions precedent and intentionality in the analyses of the political economy of Africa-China debts.

Drawing from the occurrence of an unforeseen circumstance like that of the Covid-19 outbreak, the concept of *force majeure* becomes a critical aspect of consideration under the 'conditions-driven causalities' of the debt peonage conceptual map sketched above. Within this study's context, the concept of *force majeure* refers to an uncontrollable and unforeseen event or circumstance that may disrupt the contract terms and obligations of parties in a contract, likely shifting or even exonerating the burden of debtor's liability (McKendrick, 2013). Katsivela (2007, p. 110) describes *force majeure* as "extraordinary events independent of the parties' will, that cannot be foreseen or averted by them with due diligence, being beyond their control and preventing the contracting party from fulfilling the obligation undertaken in the contract". Instances of *force*

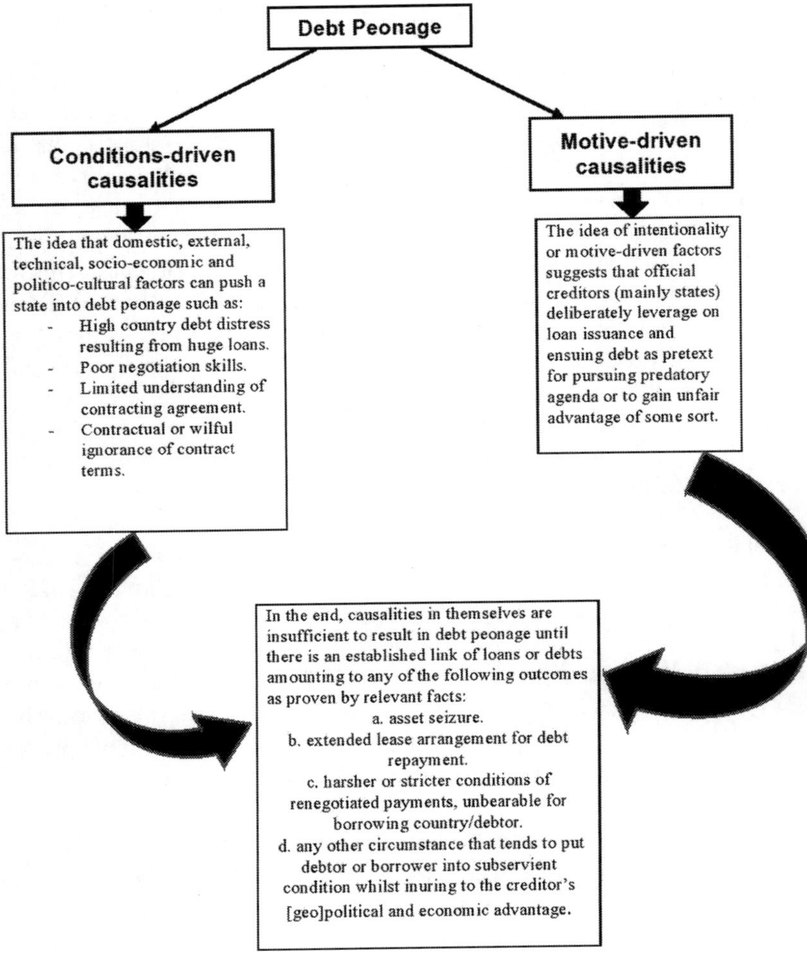

Fig. 1 Conceptual map for analysing debt peonage

majeure include war, explosions, pandemics, unexpected climatic changes, which can significantly disrupt contractual obligations (McKendrick, 2013).

To this end, it is worth questioning whether *force majeure* qualify as 'conditions-driven' causalities of debt peonage in a loan contract or otherwise. The question is whether the occurrence of a *force majeure* affecting [or stalling] the debtors ability to service debts is enough to push the debtor into debt peonage? Deducing from the analysis of Katsivela (2007) and McKendrick (2013), the idea that a *force majeure* may shift the burden of liability from the debtor to the unforeseen orchestration, [hampering the repayment of loans for example] is dependent and relative. Hence, the occurrence of a *force majeure* during the period of indebtedness cannot, in itself, qualify as debtor's default of repayment, nor automatically justify asset seizure or the imposition of exorbitantly adjusted interest rates, which may ultimately amount to debt peonage. This is so because it would depend on a) the contractual provisions or clauses on *force majeure*, [in the absence of such clauses on *force majeure*], then, b) the terms and outcome of re-negotiation may inform the likely determination of debt peonage, c) failure of coming to terms of re-negotiation at the instance of a *force majeure*, a dispute resolution mechanism outlined in the agreement or a court of public international law jurisdiction may determine the ambiguities of burden or excuse of liability (Katsivela, 2007; McKendrick, 2013). Therefore, classifying the concept of *force majeure* as a probable condition leading to debt peonage would require careful scrutiny of contract provisions of the specific loan agreement in question.

Debt Trap Diplomacy: Reality or Hoax?

Amidst the speculations and seeming rebuttals to the concept and practice of debt trap, this section starts off with an analysis of Brautigam (2020) remarks. This analysis would be critical to validating the propositions made in the analytical model above. Essentially answering to the reality or hoax of debt trap, Brautigam responds:

> China has been involved in the construction or operation of 116 overseas ports in 62 countries. Of these projects, that in Hambantota, Sri Lanka, is the only one cited as an actual instance (rather than projected possibility) of debt trap diplomacy as, following an election upset, the highly indebted Sri Lanka conceded control of a port to a Chinese company on a 99-year lease. The New York Times (2018) characterized this as 'China got Sri Lanka to cough up a port'. Is there evidence that China planned matters in this way? Did China deliberately set a debt trap? Was this an asset seizure for non-payment? (Brautigam, 2020, p. 8).

First, this extract of her work clearly affirms the reality of debt entrapment, adding that Sri Lanka's case was indeed '*an actual instance (rather than projected possibility)*'. Invoking her description and critique of 'debt trap diplomacy', there should exist a deliberate motive that drove[4] China in the first place to give over $1billion to Sri Lanka (Moramudali, 2020) with the purpose of entrapment. Whilst no such motive is established as could be inferred, on what grounds then is Sri Lanka's Hambantota case presented as an actual instance of debt entrapment? Was it really a set trap or certain conditions rather handicapped the debtor to give up its assets? No, it was not a trap by China, it happened "following an election upset" (Brautigam, 2020). Simply put, the political condition compelled Sri Lanka to lease its assets and not because China meant it as such. There is no evidence to prove otherwise thus far. In essence, debt peonage could be rather said to have manifested on account of Sri Lanka's political and economic conditions instead of the actuality of debt trap in the conventional sense. To this end, it is not out of place for this study to postulate that certain conditions (as depicted in the analytical model) give borrowing countries and debtors up [Sri Lanka in this case] to unfavourable repayment conditions. The proposed 'condition-driven' approach ensures a means of assessment unlike merely arguing that an official creditor intended to put the borrower in an uncomfortable position for self-serving interest. In this way, debt peonage can be subject to assessment on two comparative premises: a) assessing affecting conditions [technical, political, socio-cultural, and economic] of the country, and b) comparing it with the terms of financial agreement in question, in light of repayment.

Within the African context, countries such as Kenya, Ethiopia, Djibouti, Nigeria, Zambia, Uganda, Ghana, and Cameroon have been highlighted as either vulnerable to or allegedly entangled in [Chinese] debt entrapment (Al-Fadhat & Prasetio, 2022; Monyae & Chapotera, 2023; Ogwang & Vanclay, 2021; Purwins, 2023). Generally, scholarly assessments on China's lending practices in Africa and its broader economic engagements within the continent remain divergent on whether these yield mutual benefits or reinforce asymmetrical dependencies. While Oqubay and Lin (2019a) argue that it is premature to indicate the relationship as either good or bad due to its evolving nature, scholars like Alden (2012), Amoah (2016), and Cheru and Oqubay (2019) frame the scholarship on assessments within positive-negative paradigms. Alden (2012, p. 701) classifies these perspectives into "advocates" and "alarmists", while Amoah (2016, p. 240) refers to them as "fear factor" and "new possibilities frontier". Similarly, Cheru and Oqubay (2019, p. 283) distinguish between "alarmists" and "cheerleaders". Despite variations in terminology, these frameworks share a common binary analytical lens.

The alarmist perspective views China as a neo-colonial power, exploiting Africa's resources for global influence (Moyo, 2013; Southall & Melber, 2009). Such scholars highlight concerns over opaque agreements, resource extraction, and debt accumulation, which, they argue, place Africa in a position of economic subordination (Alden, 2012). Events such as anti-Chinese riots in Zambia and China's role in Sudan's Darfur crisis reinforce this narrative (Taylor, 2019, p. 120). In contrast, advocates see China as a development partner offering an alternative to Western hegemony (Brautigam, 2009; Mohan & Power, 2008). This school of thought credits China with providing infrastructure, investments, and industrial support without the conditionalities imposed by Western financial institutions (Alden, 2012).

Beyond these polarized positions, Alden (2012) introduces a third category: analysts, who assess Africa-China relations based on empirical realities rather than conjectures or ideological biases. Analysts emphasize the role of African agency, governance structures, and the terms of engagement in shaping the outcomes of Africa-China cooperation. Ultimately, the literature suggests that Africa's engagement with China is far from monolithic, reinforcing the argument that country-specific analyses are crucial. Given the variance in bilateral agreements, contract terms and distinct economic climates, it is essential to evaluate individual country experiences rather than generalizing the continent's relationship with China.

The Case of Kenya's Standard Gauge Railway (SGR) Loan

Sino-Kenyan relations have experienced substantial financial engagements with a total of 48 loan agreements between 2000 and 2023, amounting to approximately $9.6 billion across various sectors (Global Development Policy Centre, n.d.). Among these projects, the 472.3km Standard Gauge Railway (SGR) connecting Mombasa to Nairobi stands as the largest Chinese-financed infrastructure project in Kenya. Again, the railway accounts for more than 50% of all transportation projects in the country financed by China presently (Global Development Policy Centre, n.d.), making it a significant landmark in Kenya's infrastructure development. However, the financing and alleged collateralization of the Mombasa Port for the construction of the SGR has often featured in discussions on Chinese debt and financial entrapment. The primary concerns and fears stem[med] from potential asset seizure in the event of loan default, particularly against the backdrop of claims that the Mombasa Port was used as collateral (Office of the Auditor General, 2018). While much of the debt entrapment discourse has been speculative or media-driven, official documentation lends weight to these concerns. In Section 1.4, Paragraph III of the Auditor General's Report on Kenya Ports Authority (KPA), the report explicitly acknowledges the risk of the port's asset takeover by Chinese lenders in the event of repayment default (Office of the Auditor General, 2018).

Despite subsequent denials by both the Kenyan and Chinese governments, and the later clarification that the Auditor General had erroneously classified KPA assets as being at risk of Chinese takeover upon default of the SGR loan repayment (Brautigam et al., 2022), the validity of debt entrapment claims remains a crucial subject for empirical analysis. Consequently, this study applies the debt peonage analytical model as a robust and objective tool for assessing the extent to which Kenya's SGR loan arrangement aligns [or not] with the conventional claims of 'Chinese' debt trap diplomacy. Two key questions emerge from this discourse. First, do motive-driven indicators substantiate (or refute) the claim that China deliberately structured the SGR loan to place Kenya at a strategic disadvantage, either by facilitating the seizure of critical national assets or imposing subjugating repayment conditions upon default? Second, to what extent do structural or condition-driven factors increase the likelihood of Kenya experiencing debt distress, thereby rendering the country susceptible to [Chinese] debt trap as a direct consequence of the SGR loan?

While motive-driven analyses may leave room for subjective contestations, several factors rationally mitigate the claim that China deliberately structured the SGR loan to entrap Kenya in a debt crisis. First, the historic nature of Sino-Kenyan relations suggests a framework of cooperation rather than predatory financial engagement. Second, the operational model of the lending institution—China EXIM Bank—aligns with standard profit-oriented practices of global credit agencies, including Western counterparts, rather than exhibiting predatory intent. Third, Kenya's demonstrated part-payment commitments, coupled with China's due diligence of requiring Kenya to secure insurance through Sinosure as a risk-mitigation mechanism (Brautigam & Kidane, 2020), further reinforce the fact that the creditor in question was arguably more mindful of repayment and not to scheme an asset take over. Additionally, China's broader posturing in debt relief initiatives and renegotiations across multiple debtor nations suggests a pragmatic approach to credit risk management rather than a deliberate strategy to seize sovereign assets. In the case of Kenya, even beyond the assessment of the SGR deal, our analysis finds the claim that China intends to entrap Kenya in a debt crisis for imperialist pursuits is not supported by empirical debt distribution patterns. Of Kenya's total external debt stock of $35 billion, China holds approximately 29%, compared to the 48% owed to Multilateral Development Banks (MDBs) and 20% owed to bondholders (Boston University Global Development Policy Centre, 2024). Moreover, between 2024 and 2028, an estimated 17% of government revenues are projected to be allocated to debt servicing, with 5% directed toward bondholder repayments, 5% toward MDBs, and 5% toward China (Boston University Global Development Policy Centre, 2024). Given this debt distribution, it is statistically untenable to attribute Kenya's debt vulnerabilities solely to China, which holds a minority share of the country's total external public debt. Although the debt owed China is non-negligible, the assertion that China alone possesses the capacity or indeed sought to drive Kenya into a debt quagmire is, therefore, not supported by current financial data.

China's participation in the Debt Service Suspension Initiative (DSSI), particularly the suspension of approximately $378 million in Kenya's debt servicing obligations to China Exim Bank in 2021, alongside other instances of deferred payment renegotiations (China-Africa Research Initiative, 2023), challenges the notion that China harbours an intent to seize strategic assets. If Chinese creditors were motivated by debt entrapment strategies, they would have likely exploited such periods of financial distress by rejecting renegotiation efforts to advance self-serving interests. Furthermore, no documented case exists—either within Sino-Kenyan relations or within broader Sino-African engagements—where China has pursued legal arbitration in an international financial institution to enforce asset seizure as collateral upon loan default. "We have not yet seen cases in Africa where China Exim bank [CHEXIM] or Sinosure have used courts to arbitrate sovereign loan defaults" Brautigam and Kidane (2020, p. 3) underscore this argument. These factors further weaken claims that China deliberately engineers debt distress to exert control over borrower nations.

Besides assessing the motive-driven aspects of debt peonage, it is essential to examine the conditions-driven dimensions: whether certain socio-political, economic, or contractual conditions could lead to debt entrapment. This study finds that at the macroeconomic level, Kenya's debt sustainability at the time of the SGR loan agreement in 2012 mitigates concerns over debt entrapment as debt distress risks were minimal. External debt had decreased by 9.65%, thus, Kenya was arguably not in a precarious fiscal position at the time of borrowing, thereby reducing the likelihood of debt distress triggered by the SGR loan (World Bank, 2023). Put simply, Kenya's SGR financing was not predicated on an unsustainable debt framework but largely on an economically viable fiscal outlook at the time of contracting.

A detailed examination of Kenya's SGR financing structure reveals several risk mitigation measures that challenge prevailing debt trap narratives. First, the hybrid lending model structure comprising a Buyer's Credit Loan (BCL) and a Preferential Buyer's Credit (PBC) incorporates both market-based and concessional lending terms, with interest rates and grace periods comparable to international development finance standards. Observably, CHEXIM bank structured the financing in a way that prioritizes project sustainability rather than immediate financial leverage over Kenya. Additionally, the inclusion of Sinosure credit insurance, covering a significant portion of the loan, serves as a financial buffer against default risks, reducing the likelihood of an aggressive debt recovery approach by CHEXIM bank. Furthermore, Kenya's counterpart financing commitment—covering 10% of the project cost—aligns with global best practices, ensuring that the borrower retains domestic accountability and ownership of the infrastructure project rather than being entirely dependent on external financing.

Beyond loan structuring, the revenue-backed repayment model embedded in the agreement significantly reduces the risk of sovereign financial distress. The Take-or-Pay Agreement between Kenya Railways Corporation (KRC) and Kenya Ports Authority (KPA) ensures a minimum guaranteed freight volume, while the Railway Development Levy (RDL)—a 1.5% tariff on imports—creates an additional buffer to cover potential revenue shortfalls. *Ceteris paribus,* these mechanisms shift repayment obligations from the national budget to the railway's own commercial viability, ensuring debt servicing remains independent of broader fiscal constraints. Further reinforcing this structure, the 2014 Escrow Account Agreement mandates that loan repayments be prioritized through pre-designated revenue and payment accounts, preventing default-induced fiscal strain. Unlike conventional collateralized loans that place sovereign assets at risk, the SGR financing is secured through project revenues rather than direct sovereign guarantees, with structured safeguards ensuring consistent repayment before funds can be diverted elsewhere.

Others like Brautigam and Kidane (2020) have examined the technical and legal conditions of the SGR contract, particularly the sovereign immunity waiver, which has been alleged to permit asset seizure by China. Their analysis establishes that, given the function of sovereign immunity waiver and the contractual structure, such concerns are unwarranted by the actual loan documentation and contract conditions. Conversely, the analysis by Al-Fadhat and Prasetio (2022) fundamentally neglects detailed empirical investigation into the specific terms and contractual conditions of individual loan agreements, relying instead on theoretical propositions of structural power. By simply invoking the existence of asymmetric creditor-borrower relationships, they assert that Zimbabwe, Cameroon, and Djibouti are ensnared in a Chinese debt trap. However, their analysis lacks the empirical specificity and analytical depth required for definitive conclusions regarding debt entrapment. After all, similar power asymmetries exist between African countries and Western creditors, not exclusively China. Therefore, their assertion that China's engagements inherently result in debt traps necessitates further rigorous and evidence-based analyses, such as the motive-driven and conditions-driven assessments employed by the debt peonage model, which has demonstrated its potency as an analytical tool in the case of Kenya's SGR, to accurately evaluate the reality of debt entrapment claims.

In Conversation: The Resource-Financed Infrastructure (RFI) Model and Debt Peonage

RFI model offers useful explanatory and empirical perspectives for concerns about natural resource collateralised financing mechanisms being used as a tool for debt peonage (Halland et al., 2014). Just like the Public-Private Partnership Model and the traditional Government Infrastructure Purchasing Model for example, the RFI model is also another type of development financing model adopted by [most developing] states in recent times to finance infrastructure projects in their countries (Halland et al., 2014). The RFI model could be basically bundled up as a development financing model by which countries access loans or development assistance of some sort such that a) natural resources are exchanged [barter] for the loan, or b) expected natural resource revenues are used for repayment, or c) natural resources are used as collateral to hedge against financial risks or payment defaulting (Halland et al., 2014; Mihalyi et al.,

2020). Halland et al. (2014) are thorough in describing the application and characteristics of RFI as follows:

> …is a mechanism through which a government can obtain essential infrastructure without it having to produce sufficient revenues to support its financing. It will work when a government wants to involve the private sector in the project, and also wants the project to be built with limited or nonrecourse financing to protect the national treasury from credit exposure. It will work when a government does not have funds available to invest currently and cannot borrow on a sovereign basis perhaps due to covenants with the International Monetary Fund (IMF) or other donor agencies. It will work when a government has a resource that it licenses for development and production to a private developer, and as part of that licensing process, or potentially in tandem with or following the grant of the license, the government can borrow against its expected revenue stream from the resource development project. (Halland et al., 2014, p. 31)

The RFI model of development financing is traceable to the mid-nineteenth century when Peru paid Britain off its investment ventures with proceeds from guano fertilizer[5] mined from the Islands of Peru (Mihalyi et al., 2020). Besides the Latin American country, sub-Sahara's Angola marked Africa's first major archetype of an RFI deal with China (Zongwe, 2010) where Angola used crude oil as repayment for Chinese loans acquired (Taylor, 2006). Angola's case was later framed by the World Bank as the Angola Model (Purwins, 2023). The RFI model is one model with a triad coverage and clarification for the financial, operational and structural aspects of infrastructure development financing (Halland et al., 2014). The RFI model, with its intricate components and processes, offers a rigorous theoretical framework for analysing debt peonage.

Additionally, the 'nonrecourse financing' proposition within the RFI model provides insights into understanding the financial dynamics at play in a given contract and disentangling the tendencies or actualities of debt entrapment. By the element of 'nonrecourse financing', the creditor has the leeway to claim or seize the lender's asset set aside as repayment guarantee to offset debts owed (Clark, 2023). Given that asset seizure is characteristic of debt peonage, particularly in contexts where collateralized loans, such as those often seen in Africa-China development assistance deals, are involved, the RFI model remains a potent framework. It provides a robust interpretative basis for understanding resource-financed agreements between African countries and China, which have frequently been labelled as cases of debt entrapment. Risks associated with waiver of sovereign immunity, loss of resource control, and debt distress become more tangible and explicable when examined through the RFI lens as it offers a rigorous basis for evaluating the financing and repayment flows.

Applying the RFI model to Ghana's $2billion loan agreement with Sinohydro in 2018 for instance clarifies the financing and repayment mechanisms detailed in the contract terms. Concerns about debt entrapment, often tied to fears of losing control over Ghana's bauxite resources in the event of default, are alleviated by the fact that revenues from bauxite sales, rather than the resources themselves, serve as collateral. This distinction underscores the RFI framework's utility in unravelling the structural and financial conditions of such agreements, offering a nuanced understanding of associated risks and safeguards. The application of the RFI framework to Kenya's SGR project exonerates it from the potential for asset confiscation tied to resource collateralization, as the loan repayment does not require an explicit resource-backed element. However, in the event that the non-recourse aspect of the RFI model is broadly applied in respect of valuable assets [resource-based or physical] set aside as collateral, only revenues generated from the railway's operations, held in an escrow account as collateral, may be enforced as repayment.

Beyond individual cases, the RFI model's applicability extends to Africa's broader political economy context, where limited access to international financial markets necessitates innovative financing mechanisms like resource-financed agreements and all the dangers these portend. Purwins (2023) and Ogwang & Vanclay (2021) utilized the RFI model to assess Ghanaian and Ugandan deals with China, demonstrating how it reveals the potential for debt peonage or otherwise by examining structural conditions like resource collateralization and mutual interest alignment. Lin and Wang (2016) underscore the RFI model's relevance in understanding China's strategic interests in Africa's infrastructure financing and Africa's preference for Chinese assistance. Thus, the RFI model remains crucial for examining the dynamics of resource-financed [and collateralized] infrastructure projects, tendencies for high indebtedness and potential manifestations of debt peonage as a against the intuited and merely speculative claims of debt trap diplomacy.

Conclusion

The term "debt trap diplomacy", often invoked in discussions about China's financial engagements in Africa, has garnered substantial attention but lacks the analytical rigor required to comprehensively assess the complex debt dynamics at play. Rather than accepting this notion, which frequently oversimplifies and politicizes the motivations behind China's lending practices, this chapter has argued for the adoption of a more nuanced framework: debt peonage. Debt peonage shifts the focus from the purported intentions of the creditor (China) to a thorough examination of the debtor's political, economic, and social conditions, alongside the specific terms of the financial agreements and the facts triggered by debt defaults. By re-reading debt entrapment within the broader spectrum of structural vulnerabilities that borrower countries face, the debt peonage framework provides a more sophisticated and empirically grounded understanding of Africa-China financial relations. It transcends the binary and often reductionist interpretations of good versus bad engagement, thereby offering objective and constructive lenses through which the implications of these financial interactions can be critically assessed. This reframing undoubtedly advances a more balanced scholarly discourse and informs policy responses that better reflect the complexities of Africa-China engagements.

Abbreviations

BCL	Buyer's Credit Loan
BRI	Belt and Road Initiative
CARI	China-Africa Research Initiative
CHEXIM	China Exim bank
DSSI	Debt Service Suspension Initiative
IMF	International Monetary Fund
KPA	Kenya Ports Authority
KRC	Kenya Railways Corporation
MDBs	Multilateral Development Banks
PBC	Preferential Buyer's Credit
RDL	Railway Development Levy
RFI	Resource-financed Infrastructure
SGR	Standard Gauge Railway

Notes

1. Refer to Call for Chapters for the publication of the book captioned "*Africa-China Relations: Partnership, Peonage or Pawnage?*" Accessible at: https://www.ug.edu.gh/cas/blog/africa-china-relations-partnership-peonage-or-pawnage on 30/08/2023.
2. The coinage that arguably informs[ed] the development and conceptual unpacking of debt peonage following objective analysis.
3. Boston University Global Development Policy Centre
4. Indicative of the "motive-driven" component illustrated by this study.
5. Peru Guano Trade: https://americanhistory.si.edu/norie-atlas/guano-trade

References

Adie, W. A. C. (1964). Chou En-lai on Safari. *The China Quarterly, 18*, 174–194. https://doi.org/10.1017/S0305741000041953

Adunbi, O., & Stein, H. (2019). The political economy of China's investment in Nigeria Prometheus or Leviathan? In A. Oqubay & J. Y. Lin (Eds.), *China-Africa and an economic transformation* (pp. 192–215). Oxford Univeristy Press.

Agubamah, E. (2014). Bilateral relations: Periscoping Nigeria and China relations. *European Scientific Journal, 10*(14), 63–70.

Alden, C. (2012). China and Africa: The relationship matures. *Strategic Analysis, 36*(5), 701–707. https://doi.org/10.1080/09700161.2012.712365

Al-Fadhat, F., & Prasetio, H. (2022). How China's Debt-trap diplomacy works in African Countries: Evidence from Zimbabwe, Cameroon, and Djibouti. *Journal of Asian and African Studies, 59*(5), 1463–1483. https://doi.org/10.1177/00219096221137673

Amoah, L. G. A. (2016). China, architecture and Ghana's spaces: Concrete signs of a soft Chinese imperium? *Journal of Asian and African Studies, 51*(2), 238–255. https://doi.org/10.1177/0021909614545854

Amoah, L. G. A. (2023). Call for book chapters: Africa-China relations: Partnership, peonage, or pawnage? Retrieved August 30, 2023, from https://www.ug.edu.gh/cas/blog/africa-china-relations-partnership-peonage-or-pawnage.

Barnouin, B., & Changgen, Y. (1998). *Chinese foreign policy during the cultural revolution*. Routledge. https://doi.org/10.4324/9780203039090

Brautigam, D. (2009). *The dragon's gift: The real story of China in Africa*. Oxford Univeristy Press.

Brautigam, D. (2020). A critical look at Chinese 'debt-trap diplomacy': The rise of a meme. *Area Development and Policy, 5*(1), 1–14. https://doi.org/10.1080/23792949.2019.1689828

Boston University Global Development Policy Center. (2024). *Sovereign Debt and Environment Profiles (SDEP) Database*. Boston University Global Development Policy Center. from http://www.bu.edu/gdp/sovereign-debtenvironment-profiles-database.

Brautigam, D. A., & Xiaoyang, T. (2009). China's Engagement in African Agriculture: "Down to the Countryside". *The China Quarterly, 199*, 686–706. https://doi.org/10.1017/S0305741009990166

Brautigam, D., Bhalaki, V., Deron, L., & Wang, Y. (2022). *How Africa borrows From China: And why Mombasa Port is not collateral for Kenya's Standard Gauge Railway*. China Africa Research Initiative (CARI), School of Advanced International Studies (SAIS), Johns Hopkins University. http://www.sais-cari.org/publications-policy-briefs

Brautigam, D., & Kidane, W. (2020). *China, Africa, and Debt Distress: Fact and Fiction about Asset Seizures*. Johns Hopkins University, School of Advanced International Studies (SAIS), China Africa Research Initiative (CARI). https://ideas.repec.org/p/zbw/caripb/472020.html

Brown, K. J. (2023). Why hide? Africa's unreported debt to China. *The Review of International Organizations*. https://doi.org/10.1007/s11558-023-09513-4

Chellaney, B. (2017, January 23). *China's debt-trap diplomacy*. Project Syndicate. https://www.project-syndicate.org/commentary/china-one-belt-one-road-loans-debt-by-brahma-chellaney-2017-01?barrier=accesspaylog

Cheru, F., & Oqubay, A. (2019). Catalysing China-Africa ties for Africa's structural transformation: Lessons from Ethiopia. In A. Oqubay & J. Y. Lin (Eds.), *China-Africa and an economic transformation* (pp. 282–309). Oxford University Press.

China-Africa Research Initiative (CARI). (2023). *Data on Chinese loans, investment and aid to Africa*. The John Hopkins School of Advanced International Studies. http://www.sais-cari.org/data-chinese-global-foreign-aid

Clark, K. (2023). *Recourse vs. Non-recourse loan: What's the difference?* Investopedia. https://www.investopedia.com/ask/answers/08/nonrecourse-loan-vs-recourse-loan.asp

Filesi, T. (1972). *China and Africa in the middle ages*. Frank Cass.

Fodor, J. (1994). Concepts: A potboiler. *Cognition, 50*(1–3), 95–113. https://doi.org/10.1016/0010-0277(94)90023-X

Francis, L. T. T., & Rael, P. (2018, October 4). *Mentha Morrison: A story of debt peonage in Jim Crow Georgia*. Black Perspectives: African American History Intellectual History Society. https://www.aaihs.org/mentha-morrison-a-story-of-debt-peonage-in-jim-crow-georgia/

Global Development Policy Centre. (n.d.). *Chinese loans to Africa database*. Boston University. https://www.bu.edu/gdp/chinese-loans-to-africa-database/

Halland, H., Beardsworth, J., Land, B., & Schmidt, J. (2014). *Resource financed infrastructure: A discussion on a new form of infrastructure financing*. The World Bank. https://doi.org/10.1596/978-1-4648-0239-3

Hess, S., & Aidoo, R. (2014). Charting the roots of anti-Chinese populism in Africa: A comparison of Zambia and Ghana. *Journal of Asian and African Studies, 49*(2), 129–147.

Horn, S., Reinhart, C. M., & Trebesch, C. (2021). China's overseas lending. *Journal of International Economics, 133*, 1–32. https://doi.org/10.1016/j.jinteco.2021.103539

Ismael, T. Y. (1971). The People's Republic of China and Africa. *The Journal of Modern African Studies, 9*(4), 507–529. https://doi.org/10.1017/S0022278X00052782

Katsivela, M. (2007). Contracts: Force Majeure Concept or Force Majeure Clauses ? *Uniform Law Review - Revue de Droit Uniforme, 12*(1), 101–120. https://doi.org/10.1093/ulr/12.1.101

Lin, J. Y., & Wang, Y. (2016). New structural economics and resource financed infrastructure. *Pacific Economic Review, 21*(1), 102–117. https://doi.org/10.1111/1468-0106.12154

MacLeod, Murdo J. (n.d.). *Debt Peonage*. Encyclopedia of Latin American History and Culture. https://www.encyclopedia.com/humanities/encyclopedias-almanacs-transcripts-and-maps/debt-peonage

McKendrick, E. (2013). *Force majeure and frustration of contract*. Informa law from Routledge.

Michael, P. (2022, August 23). *Don't lose Africa*. Geopolitical Intelligence Service. https://www.gisreportsonline.com/r/africa-china-russia/

Mihalyi, D., Adam, A., & Hwang, J. (2020, February). *Resource-backed;loans: Pitfalls and potential*. National Resource Governance Institute. https://resourcegovernance.org/sites/default/files/documents/resource-backed-loans-pitfalls-and-potential.pdf

Mlambo, C. (2022). China in Africa: An Examination of the Impact of China's Loans on Growth in Selected African States. *Economies, 10*(154), 1–27. https://doi.org/10.3390/economies10070154

Mohan, G., & Power, M. (2008). New African choices? The politics of Chinese Engagement. *Review of African Political Economy, 35*(115). https://doi.org/10.1080/03056240802011394

Monyae, D., & Chapotera, K. (2023). China's Africa debt trap question: Ethiopia and Kenya infrastructure case studies. In B. Ndzendze & D. Monyae (Eds.), *Perspectives on Africa-China infrastructural and industrial cooperation* (pp. 209–228). Springer International Publishing. https://doi.org/10.1007/978-3-031-38395-3_12

Moramudali, U. (2020). The Hambantota port deal: Myths and realities. *The Diplomat*. https://thediplomat.com/2020/01/the-hambantota-port-deal-myths-and-realities/

Moyo, D. (2013). *Winner take all: China's race for resources and what it means for us*. Allen Lane & Penguin Books.

Obiezu, T. (2022, January 7). Nigerian authorities search for abducted Chinese nationals, others. *VOA News*. https://www.voanews.com/a/nigerian-authorities-search-for-abducted-chinese-nationals-others-/6641593.html

Office of the Auditor General. (2018). *Kenya Ports Authority: Report of the Auditor-General on the financial statements for the year ended 30 June 2018*. https://www.oagkenya.go.ke/wp-content/uploads/2021/09/Kenya-Ports-Authority-2017-2018.pdf

Ogunsanwo, A. (1974). *China's policy in Africa 1958–1971*. Cambridge University Press.

Ogwang, T., & Vanclay, F. (2021). Resource-financed infrastructure: Thoughts on Four Chinese-Financed projects in Uganda. *Sustainability, 13*(6), 3259. https://doi.org/10.3390/su13063259

Oqubay, A., & Lin, J. Y. (Eds.). (2019). *China-Africa and an economic transformation* (1st ed.). Oxford University Press. https://doi.org/10.1093/oso/9780198830504.001.0001

Oqubay, A., & Lin, J. Y. (2019a). Introduction to China–Africa and an economic transformation. In A. Oqubay & J. Y. Lin (Eds.), *China-Africa and an economic transformation* (pp. 1–15). Oxford University Press.

Oqubay, A., & Lin, J. Y. (2019b). New trajectory and possibilities. In A. Oqubay & J. Y. Lin (Eds.), *China-Africa and an economic transformation* (pp. 310–324). Oxford University Press.

Parker, S., & Chefitz, G. (2018). *Debtbook diplomacy*. Belfer Centre for Science and International Affairs, Harvard Kennedy School. https://www.belfercenter.org/publication/debtbook-diplomacy

Philips, T. (2016, May 11). The cultural revolution: All you need to know about China's political convulsion. *The Guardian*. https://www.theguardian.com/world/2016/may/11/the-cultural-revolution-50-years-on-all-you-need-to-know-about-chinas-political-convulsion

Purwins, S. (2023). Same same, but different: Ghana's Sinohydro deal as evolved 'Angola model'? *Insight on Africa, 15*(1), 46–70. https://doi.org/10.1177/09750878221114381

Shinn, D. H. (2019). China-Africa ties in historical context. In A. Oqubay & J. Y. Lin (Eds.), *China-Africa and an economic transformation* (Vol. 1, pp. 61–83). Oxford University Press.

Shinn, D. H., & Eisenman, J. (2012). *China and Africa: A century of engagement* (1st ed.). University of Pennsylvania Press.

Singh, A. (2020). The myth of 'debt-trap diplomacy' and realities of Chinese development finance. *Third World Quarterly, 42*(2), 239–253. https://doi.org/10.1080/01436597.2020.1807318

Siribi, H. (2021). Present and emerging issues detrimental to Ghana-China relations. In L. G. A. Amoah (Ed.), *Sixty Sixty years of Ghana-China relations: Friendship, friction and the future* (pp. 145–164). University of Ghana Press.

Snow, P. (1988). *The star raft: China's encounter with Africa*. Weidenfeld and Nicolson.

Southall, R., & Melber, H. (Eds.). (2009). *A new scramble for Africa? Imperialism, investment and development*. University of KwaZulu-Natal Press.

Soy, A. (2023, March 26). Kamala Harris Africa trip: Can US charm offensive woo continent from China? *BBC News*. https://www.bbc.co.uk/news/world-africa-65062976

Taylor, I. (2006). China's oil diplomacy in Africa. *International Affairs, 82*(5), 937–959. https://doi.org/10.1111/j.1468-2346.2006.00579.x

Taylor, I. (2019). The institutional framework of Sino-African relations. In A. Oqubay & J. Y. Lin (Eds.), *China-Africa and an economic transformation* (pp. 98–125). Oxford University Press.

World Bank. (2023). *Kenya economic update. Open Knowledge Repository*. World Bank. https://openknowledge.worldbank.org/server/api/core/bitstreams/45abb6f7-7c7c-53bb-a04d-93b26f6e11e9/content

Yu, G. T. (1966). China's failure in Africa. *Asian Survey, 6*(8), 461–468. https://doi.org/10.2307/2642472

Zongwe, D. (2010). *On the road to post conflict reconstruction by contract: The Angola model*. Social Science Research Network (SSRN). http://www.ssrn.com/abstract=1730442

Chinese Finance for African Infrastructure: Credit enhancements as means for doing business or politics?

Katja Kalkschmied and *Fathia Lawal*

Introduction

Since 2016 and as a result of the rise of China as a global economic powerhouse, Chinese capital flows to the world have been increasingly presented as a security threat (Meunier, 2019; Rogelja & Konstantinos, 2020). The United States and the European Union have tightened measures to keep Chinese finance out of their *critical infrastructures* (The White House, 2022; European Parliament, 2021) and warned the governments of Global South countries to not be lured into seemingly beneficial investment deals for they are used as foreign policy tools to trap countries in economic dependence on China (Blinken, 2021).

Since 2000 with the establishment of the *Forum on China-Africa Cooperation* (FOCAC) and after 2013 within the *Belt and Road Initiative*, development cooperation with China has become a welcome alternative

K. Kalkschmied (✉) • F. Lawal
Vienna School of International Studies, Wien, Austria
e-mail: katja.kalkschmied@da-vienna.ac.at; fathia.lawal@da-vienna.at

L. G. Adu Amoah (ed.), *Africa-China Relations*,
https://doi.org/10.1007/978-981-95-4370-0_4

to Western initiatives with which African countries were largely dissatisfied. Moreover, Chinese development finance has targeted large-scale infrastructure projects that Western financiers were at that time no longer willing to bankroll anymore (Nugent, 2018) although underinvestment in physical infrastructure continued to be seen as major bottleneck for the development of African economies (World Bank, 2019; Chinzara et al., 2023). As African countries' debt levels increased, China's state-capitalist mode of infrastructure financing has come under heightened scrutiny and critiques from Western rivals and also from recipient countries. The critiques focus on non-compliance with international standards for environmental protection and human rights as well as the use of development finance to promote Chinese official strategic interests abroad (Dreher et al., 2022).

This chapter aims to evaluate the latter accusation and, specifically, the existence of what has been termed *debt-trap diplomacy*. Introduced in 2017 by a think tank in Northern India, the term was popularised in Western academia and media within a short period of time (Brautigam, 2020). It accuses China of deliberately entrapping recipient countries in a web of debt to control foreign assets and markets and influence the decision-making of foreign state actors at various scales. A critical pillar of this alleged strategy is that China will seize strategic assets within so called *debt-to-equity swaps* once a borrowing government becomes heavily indebted. Credit enhancements such as government guarantees and collaterals are thereby described as key elements within the toolbox of China, the *predatory lender* (Singh, 2020). This chapter critically evaluates the means of using credit enhancement as a tool for conducting a debt-trap diplomacy and proceeds as follows:

In Section "Literature Review and Methodology", we discuss the use of credit enhancements as means for securing business versus political leverage. We refer to the relevant literature and outline the conceptual basis for our analysis. In Section "Chinese Capital Flows to Africa and African Governments' Indebtedness", we present a quantitative descriptive analysis of Chinese-financed projects in Africa broken down for different regions, sectors and finance types and provide statistics on the usage of credit enhancements. In Section "Case Studies", we present three case studies and in Section "Comparative Analysis of the Cases", we analyse them comparatively to infer the motives for using credit enhancements in Chinese lending for African infrastructure. In Section "Summary and Conclusions", we summarize and conclude.

Literature Review and Methodology

Credit enhancements are common tools in the banking industry to secure economic transactions with borrowers that have poor creditworthiness. They are especially used when paying higher interests to meet higher risks is not feasible due to borrowers' financial constraints as well as adverse impacts on borrowers' credit ratings (Freixas & Rochet, 2023). Yet, Chinese extensive use of credit enhancements to back loans for large-scale infrastructure projects have not been seen as means to strike business deals in risky lending environments; they have been interpreted as means of doing politics. Collaterals allow access to strategic assets in the case of repayment default. These assets can be used to pursue political interests if lenders are official bodies or related to such. Ferchen (2018) and Singh (2020) argue that claims about China's debt-trap diplomacy build on the idea that China's lending activities have the *official intention to bring its lenders into financial distress.* Jones and Hameiri (2020) add that China is portrayed as luring especially resource-rich poor countries into agreeing to unsustainable loans in order to seize their resources and related strategic assets upon default.

This accusation presumes that China, as lender, is a consistent actor pursuing state interests. The methodological nationalism (Lee, 2018) inherent in the narrative of China as predatory lender has been criticized in a growing body of literature that points to the significant heterogeneity and diversity of Chinese capital investments abroad (Lamarque & Nugent, 2022; Chen, 2021): Chinese capital has come as official bilateral aid and debt, as private and state companies' foreign direct investment (FDI) and within private-public partnerships, from syndicates, from multilateral development banks, within joint ventures with local firms, to different shares in different sectors, in different countries and in different regions (Nugent, 2018). Even if one moves away from the idea of the monolithic state agent, to be able to realize a debt-trap strategy, it requires the Chinese national government to have the power to set the development agenda in recipient countries and to have the capacity to coordinate the key actors involved in planning and implementing development projects for its national interests.

The close control of Chinese economic agents by the national government has been challenged. In an ethnographic study, Chen (2021) finds that the Chinese national government provides limited targeted support to the *going out* of Chinese private firms, which navigate through heterogeneous foreign market and institutional environments at various levels. Chinese private firms are frequently required to improvise and create their own business strategies and bargaining mechanisms (Chen, 2021, pp. 219ff). Lee (2018) proposes the concept of *varieties of capital* that differentiates the aims and logics of Chinese private versus official capital. Lee (2018) studies Chinese state-owned companies, which are potentially subject to a political agenda and monitored more closely by the Chinese government. Relatedly, Su and Lim (2023) discuss how contemporary Chinese capitalism encompasses variegated accumulation processes and spatial development strategies. Gallagher and Irwin (2015) emphasize the profit-seeking motives for Chinese private and state-owned firms' activities abroad, the stringent financial frame within they need to operate and the complex and dynamic relationships they have with each other, competing for some and co-operating for other projects across time and space. Taken together, the studies point to heterogeneous, decentralized, and at times spontaneous decision-making processes within Chinese business activities abroad.

Literature on African agency challenges narratives of portraying African states as passive actors or mere recipients of external influence. Corkin (2016) underlines that African actors are in the driver seats for setting their development agenda although they face external and internal limitations to initiate structural change. Important limitations include African countries' subordinate position in the globalized capital system (Taylor, 2007; Carmody, 2017), inefficient administrative capacity (Zajontz, 2024; Nugent, 2018) and the capture of political and economic opportunities by domestic elites (Gambino, 2022; Wolf, 2024; Mohan et al., 2018; Mohan & Lampert, 2013).

We base our analysis of credit enhancements as tools for doing business or politics on the concepts of variegated capitalism and assemblage thinking (Müller, 2015; McFarlane & Anderson, 2011). We thereby move away from a functional view of China as a coherent official lender and focus on the dynamic relations among a complex set of diverse actors and interests involved in the planning, implementation and operation of large-scale infrastructures. We follow Schaefer and Mohan (2024) and integrate the study of shifting assemblages of actors with the study of structures and hierarchies that fortify or shift power relations among actors. Moreover, we integrate the study of territorialities that give the political and economic contexts in which the key actors navigate in concert and on different scales.

Within our study, we combine a quantitative macro-level analysis with a qualitative project-level analysis to capture different aspects and scales relevant for the realization of large-scale infrastructure projects. Within the former, we relate the amount and structure of Chinese finance inflows to African governments' indebtedness. Within the latter, we use the method of comparative case studies to understand the decisions and actions taken by the key actors over time and in their specific contexts. Our primary interest lies in understanding whether the decisions are consistent with motives for either pursuing economic interests or exerting political influence from the Chinese side. Throughout the analysis, we identify the key actors, their (power) relations and track events within and around the projects to infer on the motives for using credit enhancements in the respective cases. This includes studying: (i) the parties of project initiation and their interests, (ii) the choice among different types of finance and credit enhancements, (iii) the evolution of African governments' debt levels and changes in credit spaces, (iv) the presence and time points of debt-to-equity swaps and regulatory amendments in the institutional environments of the projects at the various administrative levels, (v) the presence of debt reliefs and debt renegotiations and (vi) the direct and indirect role of the Chinese national government in the decision-making within the projects and in shaping the context in which the projects take place.

Chinese Capital Flows to Africa and African Governments' Indebtedness

AidData provides information on 20,985 overseas development finance projects of Chinese official institutions committed in the period 2000–2023.[1] 45 per cent of these projects with a total value of 326.06 billion USD took place in Africa. Figure 1a shows the distribution of Chinese development finance across African countries. 65.1 billion (20.0 per cent of the total finance) went to Angola. A significant amount of Chinese capital also went to Ethiopia and South Africa (each country receiving 21.4 billion), Sudan (18.9 billion), Egypt (15.4 billion), Nigeria (14.7 billion), Zambia (14.0 billion), the Democratic Republic of Congo (13.7 billion), Kenya (13.2 billion) and Ghana (10.4 billion). Figure 1b shows African governments' indebtedness, which determines their creditworthiness on international capital markets. The level of financial distress

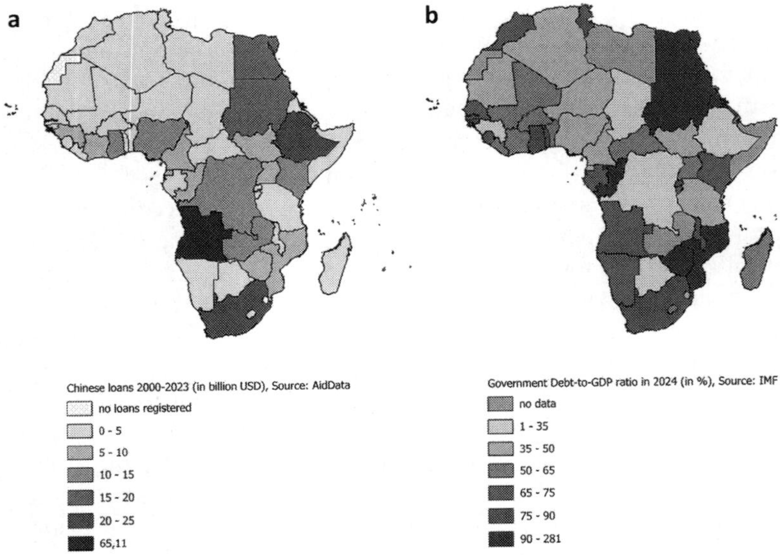

Fig. 1 **a** Sum of Chinese loans to African countries over period 2000–2023. **b** Indebtedness of African governments in 2024

is measured by the government debt-to-GDP ratio using data from the International Monetary Fund (IMF).[2] Among the top three recipient countries, Angola is considered as being at the edge to financial distress, South Africa as being in financial distress and Ethiopia as being one among five African countries with low risk of default.

As we go down the list of countries comparing total amount of Chinese capital inflows with the level of financial distress, we continue finding mixed results. While there are country examples with substantial finance inflows from China and a high default risk (Angola, South Africa, Sudan, Egypt, Kenya, Ghana), there are other examples with high financial inflows and no serious indebtedness (Ethiopia, Nigeria, the Democratic Republic of Congo).

Table 1 allocates Chinese development finance to different regions. The central African region has received a third of Chinese finance to Africa, driven by flows to Angola. With respect to sectors, roughly 50 per cent of the project finance went to infrastructure projects which entails projects in the energy, transportation, storage and production (industry, mining, construction) sectors. The majority of Chinese-financed infrastructure

Table 1 Average government indebtedness and Chinese loan information for the five African regions

	Central	*Eastern*	*Western*	*Northern*	*Southern*
Average debt-to-GDP ratio	50.7	69.5	63.3	114.4	51.82
USD Total value of Chinese loans	110.2 billion	85.9 billion	60.7 billion	37.8 billion	26.1 billion
% for transport projects	19.4	29.8	26.4	14.1	14.4
% for energy projects	30.8	18.8	24.8	20.0	33.4
% for production projects	12.5	16.8	15.3	12.5	14.2
Number of projects	305	320	220	75	96
% credit enhancements	53.4	29.4	30.5	45.3	16.7
% OOF finance	83.0	80.5	78.8	76.0	69.0

projects came as debt finance, i.e. Other Official Flows (OOF), at or close to private market terms (69–83 per cent across the African regions). A substantial portion of infrastructure projects came with credit enhancements (collaterals, government guarantees, loan insurances), which underlines the significance of our research endeavour. In accordance with the previous finding, there is no evidence that regions with more inflows of Chinese finance tend to be regions with a higher average indebtedness of African national governments.

Case Studies

In this section, we present in-depth case studies of Chinese-financed infrastructure projects in Angola, Kenya and Ethiopia.[3] We chose the cases to strike a balance between capturing the diversity of Chinese lending for African infrastructure while retaining the ability to make a comparative analysis on the key actors and interests, the usage of credit enhancements, the role of the Chinese national government and the obstacles to project realization and effectiveness for growth. The chosen projects are of particular large sizes, ensuring their relevance for development on a larger scale and the presence of political interests. The projects are in different sectors and regions, which results in larger differences in the contexts in which they took place.

The Sonangol Project

The Sonangol project has seen the largest sum of capital inflows from Chinese banks among all projects AidData recorded for Africa. All recorded Chinese capital for the project came as debt financing. The loans were provided by Export–Import Bank of China (Eximbank) and China Development Bank (CDB). They were secured by proceeds from oil sales by the borrowing Angolan Sonangol Finance Limited to China International United Petroleum & Chemicals Co. Ltd (UNIPEC), which is part of Sinopec group. Moreover, loan insurances were issued by China Export & Credit Insurance Corporation (Sinosure). All key actors involved in the financing decisions were state-owned companies or state-owned policy banks.

The project was initiated by the Angolan government in response to its economic crisis and hardships following the Angolan civil war. In 2004, Angola's government and Chinese banks signed a 2 billion USD Master Loan Facility Agreement (MLFA) to finance Angola's post-war reconstruction. Sonangol obtained further loans from banks in Brazil and Europe, also posing oil sales as collaterals (Hackenesch & John de Sousa, 2010). In November 2009, the Angolan government and Eximbank signed another MLFA worth 6 billion USD. The MLFA constituted another oil prepayment facility with borrowing terms at market rates. The collateralized proceeds from the oil sales were deposited in an Angolan Ministry of Finance account at Eximbank (AidData, n.d.). The prices for future oil sales were agreed to be set at future market prices, allowing the Angolan government to benefit from increases in oil prices.

Sonangol Finance Limited is the largest company in Angola. It dominates the country's oil and gas sector, which is the backbone of the country's economy and contributing to around 90 per cent of export revenues and a third of its GDP (International Trade Administration, 2024). Sonangol engages in crude oil trading and refined product distribution on international markets and has offices in London, Houston and Singapore. It partners with international oil companies for refineries and infrastructure building and was involved in exploration projects in Mexico and Latin America. Over the years, Sonangol has diversified into the development of Angola's real estate and housing, aviation, banking and finance sectors with the use of Chinese loans that continued to be secured by oil proceeds. Instabilities in the oil and gas markets and inflation have resulted in accumulating debts to China and other bilateral lenders (Brazil, Portugal,

Spain, France), multilateral lenders (IMF, World Bank, African Development Bank) and private lenders (Eurobonds) after 2014. To meet cashflow needs, repay debts and maintain oil production levels, in 2015, CDB granted Sonangol another oil-backed loan at market-rates in the sum of 15 billion USD (Custer et al., 2023; Dreher et al., 2022).

The terms of the 2015 loan stipulated the implementation of the projects with Chinese subcontractors including CITIC Construction Co Ltd., Beijing Urban Construction Group Co., Ltd., China Machinery Engineering Corporation, North China Power Engineering Co, Ltd. and SinoHydro. It also stipulated the use of locally sourced materials and 20 per cent involvement of Angolan companies. Yet, Chinese companies took most of the project tasks and earned most of the proceeds of the Chinese loans taken by Sonangol (Custer et al., 2023; Dreher et al., 2022; de Carvalho et al., 2022). The appointment of ex-president José Eduardo dos Santos' daughter, Isabel dos Santos, as chair of Sonangol in 2016 heightened concerns over nepotism. In 2017, Angola's new president, João Lourenço, dismissed Isabel dos Santos from Sonangol and launched anti-corruption investigations targeting the family's assets (Garside et al., 2020).

Throughout Angola's engagement with Chinese loans, there have been no reported cases of debt-to-equity swaps. In 2016, when Angola experienced hitches in debt settlement to the CDB, there was no push from China for a debt-to-equity swap either. Instead, China authorized an additional 10 billion USD loan to Angola towards alleviating repayment duties and refinancing Sonangol. Again, in 2020, China committed to revising the terms of the 15 billion USD loan from 2015 due to Angola's inability to settle it. This followed the decision of the Angolan government to participate in the G20's Debt Service Suspension Initiative, which allowed Angola to suspend its debt payments and redirect funds towards mitigating the pandemic's health, economic and social impacts. After this recapitalization, Sonangol significantly reduced its external debt, however, only to be effectively moved onto the government of Angola's balance sheet.

To date, Angola continues to face significant debt repayment challenges despite recent economic recovery. In 2024, 59 per cent of Angola's national budget was earmarked for debt servicing. High levels of external debt exacerbated by lower oil revenues, currency devaluation and reduced Chinese oil demand are straining the country's finances and availability to meet repayment obligations further and particularly toward Chinese creditors who hold around 50 per cent of the country's debt. The deteriorated financial situation of Angola has discouraged new sources of funding.

The Kenya Standard Gauge Railway Project

The Kenya Standard Gauge Railway (SGR) project ranks among the biggest infrastructure development projects in East Africa and is the single largest project in Kenya. The SGR aimed at reforming Kenya's railway network to cut down the cost of transit and facilitate trade among Kenyan cities, importantly between its capital, Nairobi, and Mombasa, which hosts Kenya's biggest commercial port. The SGR was borne out of Kenya's Vision 2030 Development plan and initiated by the Kenyan government, which set up the Kenya Railways Corporation to own and operate the railway system. Having failed to acquire finance from the World Bank, IMF, African Development Bank and private investors, the Kenyan government turned to Chinese banks.

According to AidData, in 2014, Eximbank issued a 1.903 billion USD buyer's credit loan at a LIBOR market rate of 3.6 per cent and a 1.6 billion USD preferential buyer's credit at a concessional interest rate of 2 per cent to finance the Phase 1 of the project. For the credit loan, a 0.75 per cent management fee and a 0.75 commitment fee were charged. The preferential buyer's credit came on the condition to use Chinese companies' equipment and technology in the implementation process, mainly from China Road and Bridge Corporation (CRBC). In 2015, another $1.39 billion buyer's credit loan at market terms followed for Phase 2A. This loan was secured by Sinosure and future project revenues plus a government guarantee. 90 per cent of the SGR's total costs were financed from the loans of Eximbank. The remaining 10 per cent came from the government of Kenya (Custer et al., 2023; Dreher et al., 2022).

For the securitization of the principal, fees and interest payments of the loans, the state-owned Kenya Railway Corporation and Kenya Ports Authority (KPA) entered a *Long Term Service Agreement*, which specified a guarantee of receipts from charges of rail freight that had to be put on an escrow account by the rail operator for debt repayment. This includes a *Take or Pay* clause that defined a minimum volume of freight to be transported from the Mombasa port to the Embakasi Inland Container Depot via the SGR. Moreover, the agreement specifies that Kenyan authorities had to issue preferential policies, regulations and approvals to ensure loan repayment (Custer et al., 2023; Dreher et al., 2022).

Repayment issues occurred after the implementation of Phase 1 in 2017 and also after Phase 2A in 2019. Despite reduced travel times between Mombasa and Nairobi, freight volume fell short of projections in feasibility studies due to higher transportation costs by rail compared to road transport. Being committed to the long-term service and preferential credit agreements, the government of Kenya made the transport of freight from the port to the inland depot via rail compulsory, passing on the cost differentials to local and international businesses. In 2018, the project became the target of an anti-corruption drive by Kenya's department of public prosecutions. Atanas Kariuki Maina, managing director of Kenya Railways Corporation, was arrested along with other Kenyan officials for fraudulently handling compensation claims for land claimed for the SGR. The public increasingly pressured the government to lay out the details of the loan contracts with Eximbank and the long-term service agreement, which have only partially been released to the public until today (Wilson-Andoh, 2022).

From its inception, the SGR project was publicly praised for its prospects of reducing travel times, increasing employment and fostering trade. However, the project was running at a deficit and, within the span of three years, it had built up over 200 million USD debt due to increased costs of building materials, exaggerated profit projections, the deterioration of the Kenyan Shilling and the financial ramifications of the COVID-19 outbreak (Wilson-Andoh, 2022). Over the course of 2014–2019, Kenya's indebtedness to China increased by 750 per cent. Since the loan contract required Kenya to allocate 42.06 per cent of the income derived from the project into the escrow account, the utilization of the project revenues was severely constrained (Custer et al., 2023; Dreher et al., 2022).

While the legal authority over the project lay with the Kenya Railway Corporation, the CRBC was taking on staffing and procurement decision-making during implementation and post-completion phases to secure the economic feasibility of the SGR.[4] The CRBC's project feasibility study became a source of controversy due to inconsistent conclusions with previous studies undertaken by the World Bank and a Canadian consultancy firm. Despite a signed agreement with China Communications Construction Company (CCCC) for the extension of the railway from Kisumu to Malaba, a 2019 request by the Kenyan president for another 3.7 billion USD to finance the new section was turned down by China Eximbank due to active corruption investigations and concerns about the government's loan repayment capacity.

Public discourse around the possibility that the Port of Mombasa could be transferred to Chinese banks if loans are not repaid indicated heightened scepticism and a lack of confidence in the project among the population. President Kenyatta dismissed the idea that the Kenyan government had mortgaged the Port of Mombasa to Beijing as “pure propaganda”, referring to a sovereign immunity waiver in the loan contract (Wilson-Andoh, 2022). No debt-to-equity swaps have taken place until today. Debt repayments continue to be an issue. According to Kell (2023), Chinese loans make up 64 per cent of Kenya’s bilateral debts and 17 per cent of its total foreign debts in 2023.

The Ethiopia-Djibouti Gas Pipeline Project

The Ethiopia-Djibouti Gas Pipeline is the largest project AidData recorded for Ethiopia. It is of transnational scope. To finance the construction of a 767 km pipeline from the gas field in Ethiopia’s Somali region to the Port of Djibouti on the Red Sea and to build a LNG plant in Damerdjog (Djibouti), in 2018, Eximbank, CDB and the Industrial and Commercial Bank of China provided a 2.576 billion USD syndicated loan to POLY-GCL Petroleum Group Holding Limited (POLY-GCL), a special purpose vehicle jointly owned by state-owned China Poly Group Corporation and privately-owned Hong Kong-based Golden Concord Group Limited (GCL). Before, POLY-GCL signed a production-sharing agreement (PSA) with the Ministry of Mines of Ethiopia in 2013, a cooperation framework agreement with the Ministry of Energy and Natural Resources of Djibouti in 2014 and a memorandum of cooperation with China Petroleum Pipeline Bureau. also in 2014 For the syndicated loan, no credit enhancement was issued.

The project calculated at 3.68 billion USD total costs was partly equity-financed by POLY-GCL with an agreed ratio of 70:30 debt-to-equity. The 3 billion USD investment of POLY-GCL was amended by a 200 million USD equity investment of the China-Africa Capacity Cooperation Fund. The subscription and shareholders agreement between representatives of POLY-GCL and China-Africa Capacity Cooperation Fund was signed in 2016. Besides the acquisition of funding, POLY-GCL’s key task was to meet and coordinate among representatives of the governments of Ethiopia and Djibouti, the National Bank of Ethiopia and Chinese financial institutions to implement several consensuses and agreements for strategic cooperation over the period 2014-2018 (Custer et al., 2023; Dreher et al., 2022). POLY-GCL awarded a 313 million USD two-year contract to China Oil HBP Group for taking charge of surface construction at the Calub and Hilala gas fields in Ogaden basin and to build long-distance gas pipelines. Also, in 2019, the chairman of Poly-GCL, the General Manager of CCCC and the Deputy Chief Engineer of Zhejiang Energy Group signed a letter of intent for equity investment and LNG purchase. Ethiopia's parliament approved the pipeline's construction in December 2019 and in early 2020 POLY-GCL signed an operation and management agreement for the Ethiopian oil and gas field with PetroChina's Xinjiang Oilfield Company. By then, the ownership structure of POLY-GCL had changed with private GCL and its affiliates increasing their stakes and state-owned Poly Group reducing its stakes.

Under the PSA between POLY-GCL and the Ethiopian Ministry of Mines and Petroleum, the Ethiopian government benefits from royalties, production shares and taxation of POLY-GCL. The percentage of revenue that the government obtains from POLY-GCL varies among subagreements for subprojects. The Ethiopian government expected that the project will enhance Ethiopia's energy security, boost natural gas exports, generate foreign exchange earnings and spur industrial development. To make the project operable, Ethiopia's Prime Minister Abiy Ahmed lifted restrictions imposed by the National Bank of Ethiopia compelling international oil and gas companies to hold a local foreign currency account.[5] POLY-GCL was pushing for a revision of the regulation by National Bank of Ethiopia and the Ministry of Finance. This push was supported by other foreign oil and gas companies interested in the Ethiopian market, including New Age, Africa Oil, Gazprom and Delenox Energy (Tadesse, 2019).

Despite successful exploration works and pilot production trails in 2018, the construction of the production site and pipelines had not commenced until 2022, when the Ethiopian government cancelled its contract with POLY-GCL for failing to meet deadlines in developing the gas field and complying with terms related to POLY-GCL's financial capability. In 2022, 80 per cent of POLY-GCL's shares were sold to Kingdom Investment Corporation Limited, a privately-owned Hong Kong-based company which operates through subsidiaries and special purpose vehicles across various jurisdictions, including Hong Kong, Singapore, Dubai, the European Union and several African countries.

In 2024, following a due-diligence study on POLY-GCL and negotiations with the Chinese government, the government of Ethiopia backtracked on its decision to strip POLY-GCL of the natural gas concession and allowed it to resume its work. The due-diligence study revealed that several legal pieces needed for the development of the natural gas industry including natural gas development policy and related proclamation, regulations and directives have not been finalized by the Ethiopian government and were slowing down the process of project implementation.

The start of construction work was further hindered by disagreements between the government of Ethiopia and POLY-GCL on the utilization of the gas. While the government of Ethiopia aspired to use the natural gas for energy and fertilizer input to support the development of local industries, POLY-GCL expressed the intention to export the natural gas to foreign markets. The usage of the gas was not specified in the PSA. Until today, the Ethiopian government and the Chinese oil and gas company have not reached a consensus on the usage of the gas. The implementation of the project and the realization of anticipated benefits for both sides (Endale, 2024).

Comparative Analysis of the Cases

The described projects were crucial for the countries' prospects of ensuring energy security (Angola, Ethiopia) and encouraging trade (Angola, Ethiopia, Kenya). They were priorities on African governments' development agendas and aimed to push the development of domestic industries via integration into global production and trade networks. Finding local and foreign investors was difficult due to the financial risks of the large-scale investments for both the borrowers and the lenders. The use of credit enhancements as well as coordination and cooperation between Chinese investors, insurance and construction companies and institutional as well as financial facilities provided by the Chinese national government allowed Chinese investors to hand in proposals for project financing.

The projects were of economic and political significance throughout the scales. All key decision-makers were state actors or closely related to them. The Chinese state-owned policy bank Eximbank became lender to Angolan state-owned Sonangol, state-owned Kenya Railways Corporation and partly state-owned POL-GCL. African borrowers were required to provide oil collaterals (Angola) and insurance and government guarantees (Kenya) as credit enhancements for their debt financing. Chinese borrowers were required to provide equity finance and cooperation agreements with African governments. Chinese borrowers were supported by additional finance from the China-Africa Capacity Cooperation funds equipped by the Chinese national government and a diplomatic intervention after the government of Ethiopia seeked to terminate the collaboration with the Chinese investors. In all cases and irrespective of the borrowers' identity, a significant portion of the provided finance was used to subcontract Chinese companies for project implementation.

In the three presented cases as well as in the broader study of Chinese projects in the top ten African recipient countries, we find no instance of debt-to-equity swaps that would follow the logic of, or serve as a clear evidence for, a dominant debt-trap diplomacy motive in Chinese lending for African infrastructure. Rather than growing out of African governments' indebtedness and following a series of unrepayable loan contracts, we find equity-for-infrastructure deals as an alternative financing and investment security strategy. In accordance with the variegated capitalism literature, this hints to different accumulation modes that African countries employ. Countries like Angola, Kenya and Ghana employ more debt financing-based accumulation modes, while countries like Ethiopia and the Democratic Republic of Congo rely on FDI inflows to finance infrastructure development. The strategies of Chinese actors, their interests within the projects, their efforts and leverage for pushing regulatory amendments in African countries as well as their usage of and choice among credit enhancements differ vastly with whether the finance comes as loan or as FDI. Which finance type is used, in turn, is shaped by historically evolved national contexts as well as the political and economic struggles on the national international sphere within which the key actors operate.

Sonangol obtained Chinese debt finance at market rates and retained the management of infrastructure decisions and operations throughout the project phases. The Angolan state actors were not only ultimately owning but also privately profiting from managing Sonangol's operations. They were willing to back the loans with future oil proceeds to remain in control and expand the profit opportunities of Sonangol at home and abroad. No notable regulatory amendments in the institutional framework relevant for the project were recorded. During the implementation phase of the debt-financed project in Kenya as well as the equity-financed project in Ethiopia, changes in the broader regulatory setup instead played a crucial factor: The long-term service agreement between Kenya Railway Corporation and Kenya Ports Authority was set up alongside the financial agreement with Eximbank already when the project was initiated and long before its economic viability was questioned and the government of Kenya forced businesses to transport goods via rail. FDI inflows in Ethiopia's oil and gas industry required a revision of regulationsby the National Bank of Ethiopia and the Ministry of Finance. The regulatory changes were not only pushed by the Chinese investors but also by English, Canadian and Russian oil and gas companies looking for FDI opportunities in Ethiopia. Acknowledgements that delays in regulatory reforms slowed project implementation helped POLY-GCL to be reinstated as the concession holder alongside diplomatic talks with the Chinese government and improvements in POLY-GCL's financial capacity. In the case of POLY-GCL, it was the government of Ethiopia that pressured Chinese investors to ensure financial stability.

Besides the shared dissatisfaction with the slow progress in the development of the gas factory and pipeline infrastructure, relations between the government of Ethiopia and the Chinese POLY-GCL are strained by disagreements concerning the sale of the produced gas on local versus global markets, which was not specified in prior agreements. Disagreements among Kenyan and Chinese state actors also continue to obstruct the railway project as of the time of writing, whereas Eximbank refuses to issue another loan to the Kenyan government until corruption investigations around the railway have been completed and concerns about Kenya's loan repayment capacity are resolved. The relationship of the Angolan government with Chinese banks remains tense, as it does with South African, Egyptian, French and English banks from which Sonangol has also borrowed. Unfavourable developments in national and international markets have exacerbated financial issues in all three cases.

Summary and Conclusions

Large-scale international lending has a political dimension because it creates financial dependencies that give the lenders leverage to access resources and push for regulatory changes in recipient countries. If the lenders are state actors or linked to the state, international lending can become a powerful policy tool to pursue national strategic interests abroad. What ultimately differentiates lending for doing business versus politics is whether economic motives of investing banks and firms or political motives of their home countries' governments prevail in the lending decisions. In this chapter, we analysed the events that happened within and around three large-scale infrastructure projects from the lenses of assemblage thinking to learn about the underlying motives of Chinese lending. We found that the Chinese national government supported Chinese banks and firms in doing business abroad. We also found that the large-scale projects have strained the financial stability of African and Chinese borrowers, Chinese banks demanded securities for loans, Chinese investors pushed for regulatory changes to improve their business environment and large parts of the loan proceeds were used to subcontract Chinese construction firms. We found no evidence of debt-to-equity swaps but occasional events of debt rescheduling, Chinese banks' refusal to issue further loans, African governments' dismissal and reinstatement of Chinese investors as well as rearrangements of Chinese investors and subcontractors on their own initiatives.

Our analysis suggests that the successes of the projects were foiled by high codependencies of key actors which frequently had conflicting interests and insufficient capacities to fulfil their project tasks in the given economic, political and regulatory contexts. Halted, delayed, cancelled and downgraded projects have been costly for all parties, preventing access to assets and markets by anyone. Economic opportunities were seized by Chinese firms and African elites who used the integration into the global capitalist system to reinforce existing state-society relations and exclusive political and economic structures at home. Instead of following a series of loan repayment defaults, we identified equity finance as an alternative financing strategy that characterizes a distinct capital accumulation mode. While debt-based accumulation burdens governments' balance sheets, equity-based accumulation does not. Consequently, African countries with higher Chinese financial inflows do not necessarily have higher government debt. This finding is in accordance with the variegated capitalism literature and encourages further investigations into the determinants, characteristics and paths alongside which debt-based versus more equity-based accumulation modes evolve.

Our analysis suggests that investors were the key decision-makers and profits were their central motives for infrastructure lending on the Chinese side. Chinese investors were supported by the Chinese national government, which relies on the success of its firms in the global market to maintain legitimacy of ruling at home and expand its political power abroad. The governments of Angola, Kenya and Ethiopia have manoeuvred their countries into a situation of financial and economic dependency on Chinese banks and firms. While we dismiss the idea of this to be the outcome of a centrally organised plan by Chinese authorities, African governments are severely constrained in their contemporary financial, production, and political manoeuvring space and Chinese authorities can exploit the evolved dependencies on Chinese banks and firms to structure bilateral relations and demand support in international fora if needed. That win-win situations and symmetric economic and political partnerships for infrastructure development have not been realized in Africa-China relations is a persistent phenomenon in development cooperation within a dynamic global capitalist system, in which a multitude of diverse actors are entangled in constant struggles over profits and power.

Over the last 25 years, by learning from project failures and responding to changing contexts, Chinese and African actors have adapted their strategies in cooperation for infrastructure development to increase their shares in profits and power, respectively. Moreover, aid financing was gradually replaced with debt financing. More recently, and answering climate crises and rising debt defaults, a green and more sustainable financing agenda was established with smaller-scale projects being prioritized. Africa-China relations today are critically structured by unfolding US-China rivalry for global influence. It is unclear whether African actors can use these great power struggles to increase their bargaining position vis-à-vis both powers or whether they are torn apart in wars over resources, infrastructure, and markets. Banks and businesses cooperating and competing over infrastructure development in Africa will continue to be key actors at the forefront of these wars.

Competing Interests The authors have no conflicts of interest to declare that are relevant to the content of this chapter.

ABBREVIATIONS

CCCC	China Communications Construction Company
CDB	China Development Bank
CRBC	China Road and Bridge Corporation
Eximbank	China Export Import Bank
FDI	Foreign direct investment
GCL	Golden Concord Group Limited
IMF	International Monetary Fund
KPA	Kenya Ports Authority
MLFA	Master Loan Facility Agreement
OOF	Other Official Flows

POLGY-GCL	POLY-GCL Petroleum Group Holding Limited
PSA	Production-sharing agreement
Sinosure	China Export & Credit Insurance Corporation
SGR	Standard Gauge Railway
UNIPEC	China International United Petroleum & Chemicals Co., Ltd

Notes

1. The dataset can be accessed here: https://www.aiddata.org/data/aiddatas-global-chinese-development-finance-dataset-version-3-0. AidData compiles and cross-references information on Chinese finance flows from publicly available sources, mainly reports. It has substantial overlaps with similar datasets including SAIS-CARI but has a larger coverage. For our analysis, we rely on AidData having identified all major projects in Africa. To reduce the bias in the selection and presentation of events happening within the projects, we restrict ourselves to presenting hard facts, cross-check with and add information from other sources in our case studies.
2. The IMF and the World Bank consider countries with a debt-to-GDP ratio below 35 per cent at low risk, 35–55 per cent at low moderate risk, 55–70 per cent at a high moderate risk of debt default and countries above 70 per cent in severe financial distress.
3. We started our research with ranking African countries based on the total value of Chinese finance inflows and screened projects in the top ten recipient countries. Besides projects in the countries of our selected cases, we studied projects in South Africa, Sudan, Egypt, Nigeria, Zambia, the Democratic Republic of Congo and Ghana.
4. Although the Kenya Railway Corporation was tasked with supervising project implementation and post-completion management, its jurisdiction was limited to establishing regulatory compliance and coordinating local legal approvals such as modifications to land procurement protocols, permit acquisition and expedition of bureaucratic standards to ensure that the project did not encounter systemic hurdles.
5. The directive required oil and gas companies to open a local foreign currency account to improve financial management and prevent money laundering. Companies were frustrated by the directive as it made borrowing from international creditors difficult and caused bureaucratic hurdles and delays in awarding contracts.

References

AidData. (n.d.). *CDB provides $10 billion to Government of Angola to recapitalize Sonangol and prepay outstanding debts.* https://china.aiddata.org/projects/53063/

Blinken, A. J. (2021, November 19). The United States and Africa: Building a 21st century partnership. Speech delivered in Abuja, Nigeria. U.S. Department ofState.https://www.state.gov/the-united-states-and-africa-building-a-21st-century-partnership/

Brautigam, D. (2020). A critical look at Chinese 'debt-trap diplomacy': The rise of a meme. *Area Development and Policy, 5*(1), 1–14.

Carmody, P. R. (2017). *The new scramble for Africa.* John Wiley & Sons.

Chen, W. (2021). *The dynamics of Chinese private outward foreign direct investment in Ethiopia: A comparison of the light manufacturing industry and the construction materials industry* (Doctoral dissertation, SOAS University of London).

Chinzara, Z., Dessus, S., & Dreyhaupt, S. (2023). *How institutional reforms can attract more private investment* (Working Paper, February 2023). International Finance Corporation, World Bank Group.

Corkin, L. (2016). *Uncovering African agency: Angola's management of China's credit lines.* Routledge.

Custer, S., Dreher, A., Elston, T. B., Escobar, B., Fedorochko, R., Fuchs, A., Ghose, S., Lin, J., Malik, A., Parks, B. C., Solomon, K., Strange, A., Tierney, M. J., Vlasto, L., Walsh, K., Wang, F., Zaleski, L., & Zhang, S. (2023). *Tracking Chinese Development Finance: An application of AidData's TUFF 3.0 methodology.* AidData at William & Mary.

de Carvalho, P., Kopiński, D., & Taylor, I. (2022). A marriage of convenience on the rocks? Revisiting the Sino–Angolan relationship. *Africa Spectrum, 57*(1), 5–29. https://doi.org/10.1177/00020397211042384

Dreher, A., Fuchs, A., Parks, B. C., Strange, A., & Tierney, M. J. (2022). *Banking on Beijing: The aims and impacts of China's overseas development program.* Cambridge University Press.

Endale, A. (2024, June 1). Chinese Poly GCL regains natural gas concession in Somali region. *The Reporter.*

European Parliament. (2021). *European Parliament resolution of 16 September 2021 on a new EU-China strategy (2021/2037 (INI)).*

Ferchen, M. (2018). *China, Venezuela and the illusion of debt-trap diplomacy.* Carnegie-Tsinghua Center for Global Policy. https://carnegietsinghua.org/2018/08/16/chinavenezuela-and-illusionof-debt-trap-diplomacy-pub-77089

Freixas, X., & Rochet, J. C. (2023). *Microeconomics of banking* (3rd ed.). MIT press.

Gallagher, K. P., & Irwin, I. (2015). China's economic statecraft in Latin America: Evidence from China's policy banks. *Pacific Affairs, 88*(1), 99–121. https://doi.org/10.5509/201588199

Gambino, E. (2022). Corridors of opportunity? African infrastructure and the market expansion of Chinese companies. In *Transport Corridors in Africa* (pp. 286–316). James Currey.

Garside, J., Pegg, D., & Osborne, H. (2020, January 19). Revealed: How Angolan ruler's daughter used her status to build $2bn empire. *The Guardian*. https://www.theguardian.com/world/2020/jan/19/isabel-dos-santos-revealed-africa-richest-woman-2bn-empire-luanda-leaks-angola

Hackenesch, C., & John de Sousa, S.-L. (2010). *New actors, old problems: Implications of Chinese and Brazilian engagement in Angola*. German Development Institute. The Current Column, March 29, 2020. https://www.idos-research.de/fileadmin/migratedNewsAssets/Files/Column_Hackenesch.John_de_Sousa_29.03.2010.pdf

International Monetary Fund. (2024). *World economic outlook (April 2024)*. Retrieved August 29, 2024, from https://www.imf.org/external/datamapper/GGXWDG_NGDP@WEO/OEMDC/ADVEC/WEOWORLD

International Trade Administration. (2024). *Angola: Oil and gas*. U.S. Department of Commerce. Retrieved November 20, 2024, from https://www.trade.gov/country-commercial-guides/angola-oil-and-gas#:~:text=Downstream%20activities,50%20service%20stations%20across%20Angola.

Jones, L., & Hameiri, S. (2020). *Debunking the myth of 'debt-trap diplomacy': How recipient countries shape China's Belt and Road Initiative*. Chatham House Research Paper.

Kell, F. (2023). *Kenya's debt struggles go far deeper than Chinese loans*. Chatham House.

Lamarque, H., & Nugent, P. (2022). *Transport corridors in Africa*. Boydell & Brewer.

Lee, C. K. (2018). The specter of global China: Politics, labor, and foreign investment in Africa. In *The Specter of Global China*. University of Chicago Press.

McFarlane, C., & Anderson, B. (2011). Thinking with assemblage. *Area, 43*(2), 162–164.

Meunier, S. (2019). Beware of Chinese bearing gifts: Why China's direct investment poses political challenges in Europe and the United States. In *China's international investment strategy: Bilateral, regional, and global law and policy* (pp. 345–359). Oxford University Press.

Mohan, G., Asante, K. P., & Abdulai, A. G. (2018). Party politics and the political economy of Ghana's oil. *New Political Economy, 23*(3), 274–289.

Mohan, G., & Lampert, B. (2013). Negotiating China: Reinserting African agency into China–Africa relations. *African Affairs, 112*(446), 92–110.

Müller, M. (2015). Assemblages and actor-networks: Rethinking socio-material power, politics and space. *Geography compass, 9*(1), 27–41.

Nugent, P. (2018). Africa's re-enchantment with big infrastructure: White elephants dancing in virtuous circles? In *Extractive industries and changing state dynamics in Africa* (pp. 22–40). Routledge.

Rogelja, I., & Konstantinos, T. (2020). Narrating the China threat: Securitising Chinese economic presence in Europe. *The Chinese Journal of International Politics, 13*(1), 103–133.

Schaefer, F., & Mohan, G. (2024). Conceptualising Chinese transnational infrastructure projects in Europe and beyond. *Progress in Human Geography, 48*(6), 805–825.

Singh, A. (2020). The myth of 'debt-trap diplomacy'and realities of Chinese development finance. *Third World Quarterly, 42*(2), 239–253.

Su, X., & Lim, K. F. (2023). Capital accumulation, territoriality, and the reproduction of state sovereignty in China: Is this "new" state capitalism? *Environment and Planning A: Economy and Space, 55*(3), 697–715.

Tadesse, F. (2019, June 15). Premier permits gas companies to hold offshore accounts. *Fortune Post, 20*(998). https://addisfortune.news/premier-permits-gas-companies-to-hold-offshore-accounts/

Taylor, I. (2007). *China and Africa: Engagement and compromise*. Routledge.

The White House. (2022). *Biden-Harris White House National Security Strategy, October 2022*. Collections, 10–12.

Wilson-Andoh, P. (2022). *China's Belt and Road Initiative in Kenya*. Foreign Policy Research Institute. https://www.fpri.org/article/2022/05/chinas-belt-and-road-initiative-in-kenya/

Wolf, C. (2024). Construction as a Springboard for Industrialisation: Chinese Overseas Construction Projects and Structural Transformation in Angola, Ethiopia and Nigeria. *The European Journal of Development Research, 36*(3), 639–667.

World Bank. (2019). *Beyond the gap: How countries can afford the infrastructure they need while protecting the planet*. Washington, DC.

Zajontz, T. (2024). Seamless imaginaries, territorialized realities: The regional politics of corridor governance in Southern Africa. *Territory, Politics, Governance, 12*(8), 1073–1094.

From the University of African Future to the Museum of Black Civilizations: Imagined and Constructed Visions of China-Africa Relations

Lou Mo

Introduction

From the middle of the twentieth century to first quarter of this century, Africa's relation to China went through some major shifts with the evolution in global geopolitics. The mid-twentieth century international political ambience was strongly marked by the struggle for independence and the effervescence inspired by Third World Solidarity, launched at the 1955 Bandung Conference, an ideology apparent in both communist-lead mainland China and African states' attitude and aspirations, though the same cannot be said about Taiwan. The Chinese Nationalist Party (Kuomingtang, KMT), defeated in the Chinese civil war, retreated to the island of Taiwan in 1949 under the sigil of the Republic of China, remains closely associated with the United States. During the Cold War period,

L. Mo (✉)
Independent Curator, Ivry-sur-Seine, France

L. G. Adu Amoah (ed.), *Africa-China Relations*,
https://doi.org/10.1007/978-981-95-4370-0_5

China and Taiwan competed for diplomatic allies on the African continent, resulting in the ultimate exclusion of the latter from the United Nations (UN) in 1971 signalling its gradual decline in influence. If national political stability and economical futures were uncertain seven decades ago, from the end of the last century to the beginning of this one, we have certainly witnessed Beijing's rise and increasingly imposing presence on the African continent, receiving as much praise as criticism. The lens through which China perceives its position in the world and that of its African partners has altered as it gained economic and political clout in the international arena, and this is manifested in the China Aid projects dotting the African landscape.

Dakar, the administrative heart of Francophone West Africa and Senegal's capital since its independence in 1960, has been home to many ideologically significant and architecturally distinct higher education and museum institutions since the colonial period, such as École normale William Ponty, Université Cheikh Anta Diop, Musée Théodore Monod, Musée Dynamique, Université des Mutants, and more recently Université Amadou-Mahtar Mbow. Bringing together pan-African ambition, modernist or post-modernist design, pedagogical or museological innovation, these projects from different periods testify to the importance of postcolonial rethinking of learning and cultural spaces in Senegal and for Africa, where founding President Senghor's emphasis on cultural policy and Négritude philosophy greatly influenced subsequent national cultural and identity development. These institutions are also reminders to the country's post-independence ambitions.

This chapter focuses on the unfinished and now demolished University of African Future (L'Université du futur africain, UFA), and the recently opened Museum of Black Civilizations (Musée des civilisations noires, MCN) to trace Senegal's relations with the two Chinas throughout the broader context of their diplomatic competition in Africa. The UFA was in part financed by Taiwan, representing the Republic of China government and the MCN was financed and built by the People's Republic of China under Beijing's Belt and Road Initiative (BRI). These grand projects of public cultural infrastructure nature and utopian aspirations were developed against a metamorphosing political backdrop and demonstrative of a continuous negotiation process of ideals and identity to project for the future. They show that the Senegalese state never ceased trying to promote pan-Africanism.

The UFA was a higher educational project undertaken during the Wade administration in the 2000s that took the form of a trans-African partnership project promoted by New Partnership for Africa's Development (NEPAD). Supported by a number of African states as well as Taiwan as part of its race against China for diplomatic allies on the continent, the campus was designed by star Senegalese architect Pierre Goudiaby Atepa to be a grandiose site attracting students from all Africa. Construction was suspended in 2005 after Senegal ended its partnership with Taiwan for the third time and began new diplomatic ties with the People's Republic of China. This rupture is representative of Taiwan's slow and languishing diplomatic failure on the African continent and globally, its retreat from the international scene.

The MCN is another large-scale cultural infrastructure project that has been awaited since the early days of the country's independence, as a new definition of what an African museum should be. There was an unrealized first architectural proposition made under the supervision of United Nations Educational, Scientific and Cultural Organization (UNESCO) and the Senegalese government. The project was led by Swiss ethnologist Jean Gabus and Mexican architect Pedro Vázquez in the 1970s. The museum was finally inaugurated in 2018 with substantial financial support from the Chinese government and designed by the Beijing Institute of Architectural Design. Both the location and the design of the MCN have changed, not to mention our understanding of what the function of a postcolonial museum is in today's world. Shadowed by the growing presence of China in Africa, the tricky position a museum such as the MCN occupies is also examined under the lens of African states' relations with China and the West.

Through both projects, a strong pan-African identity and mission is articulated. However, this identity is also constantly negotiated in its specific geopolitical context locally and internationally. China, as a distant partner, changes signifier and shape. The African and Asian states, partners with benefits, are mutually observed through visions they make of each other.

Senegal and the Two Chinas

Senegal switched diplomatic partners a few times between Republican China and Communist China since its independence in 1960. According to the 2004 Republic of China (ROC, Taiwan) Ministry of Foreign

Services Almanac, listed fifth under its summaries of foreign relations with African countries, the two states first established diplomatic relations in September 1960, shortly after Senegal's declaration of independence in August of the same year. These ties were severed in 1964, resumed in 1969, and again broken off in 1971, the same year the Republic of China lost its seat at the UN to the People's Republic of China (PRC). The ROC embassy closed in the following year. Taiwan and Senegal reestablished diplomatic relations for a third time in 1996, but this final alliance ended in October 2005, during President Abdoulaye Wade's first term, when Senegal switched recognition back to the PRC. The 2004 edition of the ROC's Ministry of Foreign Services Almanac was the last to include a summary of relations with Senegal. Meanwhile, Beijing first established diplomatic relations with Senegal in December 1971, shortly after Taiwan was replaced at the UN. These ties were cut in 1996 when Senegal recognized Taiwan, but were restored in 2005. In 2016, China and Senegal elevated their relationship to a "comprehensive strategic cooperative partnership" (Ministry of Foreign Affairs of the People's Republic of China, 2024).

It is interesting to note that Taiwan and Senegal's first establishment of diplomatic relations (1960–1964) is often ignored (Veney, 2022). The limited declassified documentation accessible at Taipei's Academia Historica include a short notice on this matter (Legislative Yuan funds, 1964) stating that Senegal declared unilaterally its intention to break off relation with Taiwan in September 1964, and the Taiwanese chargé d'affaires *persona non grata*. A new promise of more technical aid, mediation by the United States, Côte d'Ivoire and Upper Volta all amounted to nothing. During that time, the Taiwanese agricultural mission continued its work in Senegal. The Republic of China Ministry of Foreign Services eventually officially declared the rupture of Taiwan-Senegal diplomatic relation in November 1964. This short rupture remains enigmatic, as Senegal resumed relation with Taiwan in 1969 and did not establish official diplomatic relation with Beijing for the first time until 1971. Senegal's 1964 decision to break ties with Taiwan was unlikely an arbitration between which of the two Chinese governments it would rather ally with, but reflected either a desire to follow France's lead after it recognized the PRC that same year, or a domestic political compromise during the Cold War to balance goodwill among internal factions adhering to different ideological camps.

Returning to the 2004 Taiwan Foreign Services Almanac, we can notice that only seven African countries maintained diplomatic relation with Taiwan then, and that number would dwindle down to only Eswatini in 2024. The Almanac also details the total trade between Taiwan and Senegal in 2004 amounted to approximately 12 million USD, with double the import from Senegal (8 million) than export to (4 million). Agricultural missions and aid based infrastructure projects, such as the Thiès to Sindia road, remained the core of Taiwan's achievements in Senegal, marking the asymmetrical nature of their partnership.

With China, we are talking about numbers in a completely different ballpark. For 2023 (Ministry of Foreign Affairs, The People's Republic of China), Chinese statistics announce export to Senegal have reached 5.23 billion USD, and import from Senegal 340 million USD. Still, these numbers would appear modest compared to China's trade values with petrol states such as Angola. China-aided infrastructure projects are numerous in Senegal such as the Léopold Sédar Senghor Stadium dating from the 1980s and the more recent National Wresting Stadium, and still others are large-scale cultural infrastructure projects, such as the Museum of Black Civilizations and the Grand National Theatre.

In fact, until as late as the 1990s, the field was not so clearly marked. At that time, Taiwan still had relative economic advantage to pursue diplomatic allies in Africa, as we would see with the case of the University of African Future. Backed by the United States, there were many endeavours made since the 1950s–1960s, such as "Operation Vanguard," that utilized a combination of aid and technological transfers through Taiwan via diplomacy or non-profit organizations in order to dissuade and influence Southeast Asian and African countries from associating too closely with the communist camp (Chu, 2023). However, the balance has been tipping towards PRC ever since Taiwan's exclusion from the UN in 1971. The two Chinas competed for diplomatic allies and UN votes as did the two Koreas, but unlike the fact that some countries and the UN recognize both North and South Korea, PRC has made One China principle a fundamental part of a partner's pledge. With the PRC, ironically, what started as an ideological alignment with African countries in the rhetoric of Third World Solidarity and anti-imperialism, became essentially a financial incentive as its economy grew, displacing Taiwanese representation as the legitimate China with the same method of carrot and sticks that the former had also employed, giving in order to receive favours and occupy the dominant position.

With China's economic development and increasing investment and influence in Africa since the twenty-first century, Senegal is one of many countries to have switched sides many times, and this change in allegiance is less about making a choice of which ideological Chinese partner to pick than about gaining an ally with the possibility of playing checks and balances with Europe and the United States. As Wade stated in this case (Correia, 2011; Taiwan Info, 2005): "States do not maintain friendships with each other, but pursue their own interests." PRC now undeniably has the upper hand, and Taiwan is at clear disadvantage and seems to have lost interest in actively pursuing partners, even informal, on the African continent.

The University of African Future

The UFA project[1] was activated by President Abdoulaye Wade soon after he took office in 2000, and was anticipated to be one of his grand visionary outputs. In fact, this idea predates his presidency. In 1996, as a minister in President Abdou Diouf's government, Wade had already proposed to construct the UFA (AEF info, 2000). The school was to bear his name and embody his legacy. In May 2001, it was announced that Taiwan would partly finance this project for the amount of 14 million dollars (AEF info, 2001).

On 28 June 2004, President Abdoulaye Wade and King Mohammed VI of Morocco laid down the first stone of Amphitheatre Hassan II on the UFA campus where construction had already been ongoing for about a year. King Mohammed VI named the Amphitheatre in honour of his father. Several heads of state promised to support the building of structures associated with their nations, such as Pavillon Jacques Chirac or the Equatorial Guinea House (De Jong et al., 2014). This monumental reverse pyramid shaped edifice was meant to become an emblem of the university and according to President Wade a 'temple of knowledge, of know-how, and know how-to-be. (Cissé, 2004)' The project, already considered half way through construction, was estimated to cost 27 billion CFA francs, with the first phase financed mainly by Taiwan (Cissé, 2004). Wade's ambition for UFA to be an internationally recognized higher educational institution at the cutting edge of technology is apparent. The UFA would become a new model institution showcasing the possibilities and unity of Africa and to keep its brains at home (Tall, 2005).

In an interview Wade gave in 2005 (Tall), when asked to enumerate his achievements in economic growth and poverty reduction, Wade mentioned the importance of creating new opportunities and illustrated what he said with the cases of UFA for higher education and urban development at Diamniadio, which was also the site he chose for the university. The village of Diamniadio, in the Rufisque department, was chosen as the site for the university. It is located some thirty kilometres from Dakar. The capital city Dakar is shaped like a hand axe protruding from the west coast of Africa into the Atlantic Ocean, surrounded by water. Limited by its geography, the idea of expanding or building a new capital inland, or at least a capital administrative area, dates back to the 1960s during President Senghor's time and comes back as a topic of discussion during each of his successor's mandates. Dakar as the hub of economic activities, industries, social and commercial facilities faced increasing demographic pressure as urban population continued to spike. Different sites around Dakar, such as Diamniadio or Thiès, were proposed as candidates, the latter being where the new Blaise Diagne International Airport is now located.

Under the close instruction of President Wade, his advisor the architect Pierre Goudiaby Atepa undertook the responsibility of designing the UFA campus masterplan and overseeing the design of its main structures with the help of other architects from his firm (Mourtada Gueye, phone conversation with the author, December 27, 2024).[2] The plan was laid out on a regular and symmetrical grid, expanding towards the four cardinal points, with the Amphitheatre on the central axis just beyond the main gate, in the style of a triumphal arch in reference to Roman antiquity (Sénéplus, 2021). The pyramid shape of the Amphitheatre, symbolic of spiritual elevation and the triumph of pan-Africanism, is iconic in Atepa's architectural language, as seen in the building of his own architecture firm or the Centre Africain d'Études Supérieures en Gestion (CESAG) office he designed, both in Dakar. Several UFA buildings, such as the Amphitheatre and a few other administrative buildings, were already under construction before the project came to a halt after 2005. They would never be used.

In October 2005, Senegal chose to embrace Beijing and broke off diplomatic relation with Taipei. *Taiwan Info* (2005), a multilingual news platform managed by the Republic of China Ministry of Foreign Services, reported on this matter a few days later. The article states that Taiwan's considerable efforts to win over Senegal, such as bilateral collaborations for Les Cases des Tout-Petits modern kindergartens or agricultural missions, which were also mentioned in the Foreign Services Almanacs, were only effective for stalling, and Senegal's turn towards Beijing was inevitable. Both Taiwanese and Senegalese press picked up on the fact that Taiwanese funding for the construction of the University of African Future would surely stop and its future unclear, and this was in fact what happened.[3] Diamniadio was considered an accessible site for UFA at the time due to its inhabitants been more willing to accommodate the project than those of Lac Rose, but the swampy soil found there is not adapted for construction, and would have required much more costly foundation preparations than what the Wade administration could afford if the buildings standing on them were to last (Mourtada Gueye, phone conversation with the author, December 27, 2024). Over the years, the buildings deteriorated quickly.

In 2021, the Sall administration announced that UFA, which cost 25 billion CFA francs (Sénéplus, 2021), would be demolished to make place for the National Institute of Petrol and Gas (Institut national du pétrole et du gaz, INPG). The ruins of UFA no longer exist, but the INPG is yet to appear. Another feature story in Senegal's *Le Quotidien* (2021) reported that in 2005 Senegalese Foreign Services Minister Cheikh Tidiane Gadio had tried to secure funding for UFA from the Chinese to continue where the Taiwanese left off, but this was not confirmed by Gadio. In addition, the Office of the State Inspector General (Inspection générale de l'Etat, IGE) reported unfair competition from the Atepa firm as well as the construction and technical control companies associated with the UFA project. Trouble-ridden, UFA is thus buried for good. Instead, Sall chose to establish the Université Amadou-Makhtar Mbow which was inaugurated in 2022, always in Diamniadio, and named after Senegalese politician Amadou-Makhtar Mbow who became the first African Director-General of UNESCO. The Plan Sénégal Émergent (PSE) which was only officially launched in 2014 focuses partly on developing alternative urban agglomerations to ease congestion in Dakar and this includes the creation of two new "urban hubs" in Diamniadio and Lac Rose (Schlimmer, 2022). The New Urban Hub of Diamniadio became a flagship project under Wade's successor President Macky Sall, who continued to devote to large-scale infrastructural projects placed directly under presidential guidance. However, due to the lack of convenient public transportation, housing options, commercial and entertainment venues, even though many ministries have relocated to Diamniadio, it has yet to permanently attract inhabitants.

Incidentally, both UFA and Université Amadou-Makhtar Mbow are located not far from Sébikotane, where the young Wade himself was educated at the École normale William Ponty, founded during the French colonial period. A number of post-independence African leaders were students at Ponty, demonstrative of its regional reach and elite status. UFA was his way to reinvent a place where this dream of pan-Africanism and the ambition of creating a prosperous Africa can be reborn (De Jong et al., 2014). Both Diamniadio and Sébikotane dotted the path planned for road construction expanding from Dakar. The Senegalese capital itself is known for higher education institutions it already harbours, such as Université Cheikh Anta Diop, bearing the name of the famous Afrocentrist historian and anthropologist, or the more ephemeral but no less idealist Université des Mutants on Gorée Island (Kajman, 1979). Building a pan-African university had always been a Senegalese, if not African, dream. For instance, the Africa Union launched the Pan-African University in 2011, a consortium including five institutes in Algeria, Kenya, Nigeria, Cameroon, and South Africa, representing all five regions from the continent. The Pan-African University's mission is promote quality higher education and encourage intra-African exchanges in order to become competitive at the international level (Duchamp, 2010). If colonial education once endeavoured to produce a small local administrative elite in West Africa, formal education in Senegal today has expanded to a larger part of the population, though there is still much room for more inclusion (Kuenzi, 2011).

The Museum of Black Civilizations

On the MCN's official website presentation page (Musée des civilisations noires, 2024), the museum emphasizes its anti-colonial and pan-African ideological origin since Senegal's independence as well as its current mission to celebrate black civilizations and its diasporas. The story started in 1966, when the first World Festival of Negro Arts (Festival mondial des arts nègres) was held under President Senghor. The MCN was first envisioned as an heir to the Musée Dynamique which was specifically launched for the festival. A few years later in 1974, the Senghor administration further declared that a design for the museum had been made and it would be built along Dakar's Corniche Ouest, on the Soumbedienne Bay. This project was placed under the tutelage of UNESCO but lost steam in the following decade and was never accomplished. With a great leap forward in time, the MCN finally opened in 2018. The lost decades were not accounted for, nor was the Chinese involvement.

In a report dated October to November 1974 (file no. 543, Musée des civilisations noires Dakar fonds at Musée d'ethnographie de Neuchâtel in Switzerland)[4], French museologist Georges Henri Rivière, a permanent advisor to International Council of Museums (ICOM), introduced and outlined the MCN project, including how it should approach its different roles (i.e. anthropological, ideological, sociological, etc.) and a rough inventory of its present and future assets (i.e. such as the statement that the MCN should inherit the collection of Musée Théodore Monod). Mexican architect Pedro Ramírez Vázquez and Swiss museologist Jean Gabus, the two experts designated to head the project, had previously collaborated on the National Museum of Anthropology in Mexico City (Moura, 2021). Plans and budgets were made starting from 1975 until 1979, when the MCN should open, for detailed work schedules including that for construction and personnel recruitment (file no. 541, Musée des civilisations noires Dakar fonds). In July 1974 (letter from Pedro Ramírez Vázquez to Jean Gabus, July 14, 1974, file no. 561, Musée des civilisations noires Dakar fonds), Vázquez had already delivered a general plan for the MCN and its grounds rimming the Soumbedienne Bay, featuring a very modern layout including a main architectural structure with rectangular halls lining a circular open space, with different spaces intended for exhibition, research, or public events. The museum was as much for display as a cultural centre for people to engage in activities. However, as early as March 1975, the project's Dakar-based associate architect Thierry Melot (letter from Thierry Melot to Jean Gabus and Pedro Ramírez Vázquez, March 17, 1975, file no. 561, Musée des civilisations noires Dakar fonds) spoke of budget limitations and the necessity to revise and reduce the scope of Vázquez's first layout. The project gradually lost steam and the museum was never built the way the renowned Mexican architect imagined it. Senegalese curator and art critic Ery Camara, who studied in Mexico, was associated with this project, and was consulted when Wade revived the idea of the MCN in 2003. According to Camara, the quandary on whether Vázquez or Atepa was the architect of the original plan was the main reason why it was abandoned in favour of a Chinese plan (Moura, 2021).

The Shanghai Construction Group signed an agreement with Senegalese authorities in November 2011 for the building of the museum, financed by China at a cost of 37 million US dollars (ThePaper, 2022). In addition, the Shenyang Engineering Supervision & Consultation company lists the MCN as an example of a project they supervised, with the Chinese Ministry of Commerce as commissioning client and the Beijing Institute of Architectural Design as design partner (Shenyang Engineering Supervision & Consultation Co., Ltd., 2024). It is not uncommon for different Chinese government-affiliated entities (Xue et al., 2019) to undertake the design, construction, and supervision roles separately in a single China Aid project abroad, and the level to which work efforts are coordinated is often unclear. The Shanghai group broke ground in December 2013 and mustered 300 workers, both Chinese and Senegalese, to work on the MCN site (Shanghai Construction Group, 2015). Indeed, for labor day of the following year, *Phoenix New Media* (2014) published a touching story telling how Chinese carpenter Gu Changfeng spent the day on the MCN construction site, of his life experiences working on Chinese aid projects abroad, and why he thought it is more meaningful to teach Senegalese apprentice carpenters a trade than simply handing out tasks. In each of the reports or news releases issued by the Chinese, the term "aid project" (*yuanjian* 援建) remains omnipresent. The Beijing Institute of Architectural Design, the entity responsible for the architectural plan of the museum, did not release any particular information or showcase the MCN on their website portfolio. However, the China Engineering and Consulting Association includes the museum as an example in an article dedicated (China Engineering and Consulting Association, 2023) to enumerate Beijing Institute of Architectural Design's many contributions to the BRI, in the form of architectural projects abroad. In the case of Senegal, both the Grand National Theatre and the MCN were designed by the Beijing-based institute. The Grand National Theatre is cited as the first major China aid project in Senegal after diplomatic relation resumed in 2005. It would seem that these monumental projects also stand as symbols to outshine previous proposals made by Taiwan, as was the case in Costa Rica (Guzmán, 2020).

The MCN opened December 6, 2018, with a ceremony attended by Chinese Minister of Culture and Tourism Luo Shugang and Senegalese President Macky Sall. The Chinese Minister of Culture and Tourism's news release (Ministry of Culture and Tourism, The People's Republic of China, 2018) states that the MCN is a symbol of friendship between the Senegalese and Chinese peoples, and on the occasion of the museum's opening China also sent twenty sets of masks and costumes from the collection of the Guizhou Museum of Ethnology to present in the inaugural exhibitions. In April 2019, Chinese ambassador Zhang Xun, Senegalese Minister of Culture and Communication Abdoulaye Diop, and MCN's director Hamady Bocoum were all present at a ceremony at the museum where the Chinese donated a number of equipment, such as glass display cases, LED screens, and sound systems to the museum (Ministry of Foreign Affairs, The People's Republic of China, 2019). The existence of this donation ceremony and its documentation in Chinese press also reminds the author of the conspicuous large red spray-painted simplified Chinese characters on garbage cans and fire extinguishers at the museum. One would wonder if Chinese labels on objects in a mostly French and Wolof speaking country are truly useful. The presence of China's aid is certainly felt strongly in the imperfect sensorial experience that the MCN creates.

The MCN sits in the Plateau area in the heart of Dakar between the train station and the Grand National Theatre, and is predated in the capital by Musée Théodore Monod and Musée Dynamique. The Musée Théodore Monod opened in 1961, long after its superintending organization the French Institute of Black Africa (Institut français d'Afrique noire, IFAN) was founded in 1936 for ethnographic, aesthetic, and crafts research, and by that time, committing to ethnographic studies encompassing the French West African federal region from a colonial perspective does seem outdated and has lost its appeal (de Suremain, 2007). This offset in the IFAN museum's positioning is inherited by the newly independent Senegalese republic and remains a challenge for the museum which continues to try to inscribe its collection, mission, and relevance in the country today (Ndiaye & Chérel, 2020). The Musée Dynamique, overlooking the Soumbedienne Bay and featuring a minimalist colonnaded facade, was conceived by Senghor and Gabus, and has been the centre of contemporary art exhibitions in Dakar since its opening in 1966, presenting the works of famous international artists such as Pablo Picasso and Pierre Soulages. As an air-conditioned modern space meeting exhibition requirements that the Musée Théodore Monod cannot, the Musée Dynamique was conceptualized as a museum without a collection, but always in creation of new meanings (Murphy & Vincent, 2019). It switched identity from a museum to a dance school under Senghor, exemplary of how presidential opinion can have a direct and immediate impact on cultural institutions in Senegal, and again as a museum, but transitioning gradually in its last years to a focus on showcasing contemporary Senegalese art creation before it finally closed in 1988 under President

Abdou Diouf, to become the new Palais de Justice. Coincidentally, the former Palais de Justice now serves as the main venue for the official selection of the Dakar Biennial, the longest running and a prestigious contemporary art biennial in Africa.[5]

The MCN as it stands now is an architectural structure stylistically more evocative of Chinese social realist convention halls and stadiums abroad than its Senegalese predecessors in town, and seems slightly out of place in Dakar. It is an immense circular shape building with 14000 m^2 of space on four levels and a large circular indoor open space in the centre. According to the first director of the MCN, professor Hamady Bocoum (Bocoum, 2018), the design of the MCN recall many African traditions, such as the Grand Zimbabwe ruins, the round houses with impluvium from the Bandial Kingdom of Casamance, and that of the Penc—a Wolof word designating an open public gathering place. Despite those claims, it does not seem that Senegalese architects were closely involved in this design. In that same interview (Bocoum, 2018), Bocoum reaffirms that the museum in not only a Senegalese but a pan-African project, carefully debated and studied at its international prefiguration conference in 2016 to give shape to its universal vocation. In the words of Senegalese philosopher Souleymane Bachir Diagne (Diagne, 2020), the question we have to ask ourselves today is about the restitution of African art objects, which have mutated due to their long exile in exogenous contexts, and to reimagine the role an African museum hosting these mutants should have on the continent and internationally. The MCN inherits the dynamism of its forerunner the Musée Dynamique in focusing on events and temporary exhibitions, instead of fixed displays or acquiring a permanent collection. It has also became one of the main venues of the Dakar contemporary art biennial which attracts artists and curators from all over the world.

Cultural Infrastructure and Its Gaps

Soon after MCN's inauguration when Guizhou masks were exhibited, China National Arts Fund and Shanghai University Fine Arts College co-organized an exhibition at MCN about "the emergence of the Chinese countryside through development" in 2019 (ThePaper, 2022). In 2023, the Chinese embassy in Senegal co-organized another exhibition at the museum entitled "Looking at Each Other Across the Ocean—China under the brush of African painters" (Xinhuanet, 2023). It would seem that the exhibition themes and artworks proposed by Chinese authorities are rather scattered and out of touch with pressing trends and issues in international and African museological and contemporary art debates, such as questions of how to decenter postcolonial institutional discourse and restitution of African objects in Western collections.[6] Their cursory and self-congratulatory choice of topics are professedly more targeted towards the Chinese bureaucracy and audience at home. These discrepancies are interesting, in that they show that the Chinese and Senegalese project very different visions unto the same cultural infrastructure born out of aid.

It seems appropriate to circle back to the notion of public cultural infrastructure projects mentioned at the beginning of this chapter to define the shared qualities of UFA and MCN to better discern the China-Africa dynamics at play in their genesis, realization, and usage. An infrastructure project is a sum of many subordinate parts organized in a system or network suggesting a relationship of depth or hierarchy to support a higher order, and not all parts are physical, for they can be abstract ideas as well (Carse, 2017). Though the idea of infrastructure cannot be disassociated from notions of participation in a progressive modernity and growth by answering to the moral obligation of helping the less fortunate or a government's duty towards its people, it is helpful here to outline what Brian Larkin (2013) defines as the technopolitical value of infrastructure. Infrastructure exists beyond its technical functioning and is capable of embodying other deeply political emotions such as pride or frustration. UFA and MCN have many traits in common, in that they are both meant to be public, provided by the state for the non-profit purpose of offering accessible and impressive spaces to welcome people who would come to acquire cultural or scientific knowledge and content. The spaces are meant to be experienced and repeatedly over time. As both names indicate, African agency is of eponymous importance, and this aspiration transcends that of the Senegalese nation.

If we understand the idea of infrastructure as a hierarchical system, then the most salient way these aid associated cultural infrastructure projects can emancipate from the generosity of the donor is by playing with the gaps, both physical and abstract, of the system. When the system is unstable, negotiation becomes possible. One of the sponsor's intentions is to offer a physical structure in a very particular style reminiscent of its largesse to the receiver. However, the receiver is determined to offer a pan-African legacy through the same physical structure. China focuses on the building, the controllable and most visible feature. Senegal has reins on the program, and through this component the material part can be made more invisible. The selection of the building becomes strategic. China does not have a stake in pan-Africanism. It is also interesting to note that art museums built recently in China almost all call upon Western or Japanese architectural firms for their own design, such as Steven Hall Architects for the Shenzhen Art Museum and Library or Tadao Ando for the private He Art Museum in Foshan, both in Guangdong province. These infrastructure projects are also political projects built by architects and project managers who do not have a shared historical or cultural background with its end users, the public. In fact, they may never meet. The receiver, the Senegalese state, inherits this hybrid physical structure not fully in its image and offers it to its public.

The stillborn UFA project may vehicle deception and frustration, both for Wade, Taiwan, and the inhabitants of Diamniadio, but it keeps in line nonetheless with what Senegal had always advocated for in cultural policy, albeit forever in the long shadow of Senghor. This Senegalese pursuit of historical continuity is unlike other China Aid projects parachuted in Africa in that Senegal does not forget to place and gain its own tokens in a long game. In the same way, both Chinas, even though Beijing is definitely more successful than Taipei with the achievement of building the MCN as a lasting landmark in Dakar and a marker of triumph in China Senegal relation, remain a somewhat disengaged partner once the accoutrements are accomplished. Durational custodianship takes over. On the MCN website, the Chinese have been written out completely.

We might ask if these are *in fine* Chinese or Senegalese projects. The gaps in how each tries to position these structures make them chimeric. If the motives for China to build and for African countries to accept grand stadiums can be questioned in terms of what each partner obtains from the exchange, such as raw materials (Dubinsky, 2021), at least the construction of the MCN does seem to accomplish a clear and historical goal on the Senegalese side, that is the delivery of the long awaited pan-African museum. After the nearly forty year break before it finally opened in 2018, the definition of the MCN evolved with the people working within its walls, and it is no longer an ethnological, anthropological, or subaltern museum (Kimeria, 2019) though it does not yet venture to question China's complex role in Africa. If it is always difficult for an institution bearing such heavy symbolic weight to clearly define what it is, at least there is profound and ongoing reflection at the MCN on what it should not be. Even though not all sections of the museum are occupied, not all displays perfect, nor all objects that should be restituted returned, and the Chinese inscriptions on equipment keep luring visitors out of focus, the MCN manifests the ambition to steer its own path and discourse.

Conclusion

China was the recipient of aid from the Soviet Union in the 1950s and Japan in the 1970–80s, and learned how to be a donor through the lens of a receiver (Guzmán, 2020). In turn, the Chinese have been actively acting as patrons of infrastructure projects in Africa, Southeast Asia, and South America since the late 1950s (China Engineering and Consulting Association, 2023). Chinese architects had to overcome challenges when planning and surveying on unfamiliar terrains to invent new methods to resolve technical difficulties often faced in the development of tropical modernist architecture such as temperature and humidity (Liu, 2020). Overcoming most of these issues, China is most often regarded as a provider of technical expertise and loans (Amoah, 2016). Over recent years, other than projects that are rarely frequented and experienced by the public such as dams or power plants, China has also financed a number of theatres and stadiums abroad. This demonstrates China's keen awareness of the multilayered meanings and durational capacity of cultural infrastructure projects.

In the case of Senegal with the two cultural infrastructure projects discussed in this chapter, both Chinas do not seem able to sway the host of its original pan-African intentions. However, aid always comes with conditions. Taiwan's financial withdrawal from UFA after its diplomatic rupture with Senegal contributed to the university project's suspension. The subsequent change of administration left UFA standing hollow until its demolition, stranded in time and aspiration, alienated from its fast developing surroundings. Like the much criticized African Renaissance Monument, which is a combination of Wade's ambition, a Romanian sculptor's design and North Korean production, the MCN is also a hybrid simulacra (De Jong & Foucher, 2010) that escapes from all historical and aesthetic references of the land it stands on. This kind of glitch between materiality and ideology is a jarring reminder of their chimeric nature. This hybridity is also the incongruous site of constant negotiation. As we see through the cases analyzed here, this instability is a challenge that some African institutions face. This type of negotiation should not be ignored as it can be a meaningful way to generate pertinent debate on institutional positioning and the future.

Notes

1. The author would like to thank artists Stéphane Verlet-Bottéro and Hamedine Kane for first introducing her to this project.
2. The author would like to thank curator Oulimata Gueye for the introduction to her brother Mourtada Gueye, a Dakar-based architect who worked at the Atepa firm.
3. There were close to no Taiwan-based Chinese language news reports about the financing of the UFA. One report titled "Republic of China and Senegal Five-Year Collaboration Agreement on the Promotion of Senegalese Socio-Economical Development" dated 2 August 2001 came up with the research keyword 'The University of African Future' and is listed in the online catalogue of the National Archives Administration under National Development Council as belonging to Presidential Palace Archives. The author has requested access to this 21-page report but has not obtained access until the date of this chapter's submission. The author has also requested interviews from Taiwanese diplomats who were posted in Senegal during the time of UFA's genesis but have not been able to secure any. This is consistent with the author's observation from other research projects that Taiwan's diplomatic failure in Africa is still profoundly stigmatized and involved parties generally prefer to stay silent on the matter.
4. The author would like to thank Mr. Daniel Sciboz (Haute école d'art et de design, Geneva, Switzerland) for directing her towards the Musée d'ethnographie de Neuchâtel archives.
5. The author would like to thank Dakar-based curator Idrissa Diallo for taking the time to clarify the chronology and uses of the two Palais de Justice for her.
6. China was also invited to present a national pavilion at the MCN as a part of the 2022 Dakar biennial. The author thinks that the selection of artworks presented and the curatorial concept developed are consistent with her judgement of other Chinese exhibitions aforementioned, meaning that it seems more mindful of its political mission than its quality and relevance as a contemporary art presentation in an international biennial. Due to the limited text length allowed in this chapter, the 2022 Chinese national pavilion exhibition will not be discussed in detail, but it certainly merits a more in-depth analysis.

References

Amoah, L. G. A. (2016). China, architecture and Ghana's spaces: Concrete signs of a soft Chinese imperium? *Journal of Asian and African Studies, 51*(2), 238–255.

Bocoum, H. (2018). Le Musée des Civilisations Noires: une vision d'avenir. *Présence Africaine, 197*, 185–194.

Carse, A. (2017). Keyword: Infrastructure: How a humble French engineering term shaped the modern world. In P. Harvey, C. B. Jensen, & A. Morita (Eds.), *Infrastructure and Social Complexity: A Companion*. Routledge.

China Engineering and Consulting Association. (2023). Beijing Shi jianzhu sheji yanjiuyuan youxian gongsi yong sheji zhuli guojia 'yidai yilu.' [Beijing Institute of Architectural Design Co., Ltd. uses design to help the country's "Belt and Road" initiative.] https://www.chinaeda.org.cn/contents/243/7451.html?id=7451.

Chu, L. (August 2023). With and against the grain: The Asian vegetable research and development center and modest narratives of green revolution in Taiwan, 1963–2002. *Agricultural History, 97*(3), 373–404. https://doi.org/10.1215/00021482-10474447

Cissé, I. (2004, June 29). Sénégal: début de la construction de l'Université du Futurafricain. *AEFinfo*. https://www.aefinfo.fr/depeche/416705-senegal-debut-de-la-construction-de-luniversite-du-futur-africain.

Correia, P. (2011). Dakar-Pékin: une réconciliation opportuniste mais problématique. *Outre-terre, 4*(30), 351–358.

De Jong, F., Quinn, B., & Bach, J.-N. (2014). Ruines d'utopies: l'École William Ponty et l'Université du Futur africain. *Politique africaine, 135*, 71–94.

De Jong, F., & Foucher, V. (2010). La tragédie du roi Abdoulaye ? Néomodernisme et Renaissance africaine dans le Sénégal contemporain. *Politique africaine, 118*, 187–204.

de Suremain, M.-A. (2007). L'IFAN et la « mise en musée » des cultures africaines (1936–1961). *Outre-mers, 94*(356–357), 151–172.

Diagne, S. B. (2020, July–August). Musée des mutants. *Esprit, 466*, 103–112.

Dubinsky, I. (2021). China's Stadium Diplomacy in Africa. *Journal of Global Sport Management, 9*(4), 761–778.

Duchamp, C.(2010, September 6). Création d'une « université panafricaine » programmée dès la rentrée 2010 par l'Union africaine. *AEF info*. https://www.aefinfo.fr/depeche/261262-creation-dune-universite-panafricaine-programmee-des-la-rentree-2010-par-lunion-africaine.

En realpolitik, pas d'amitié qui tienne. (2005, November 1). *Taiwan Info*. https://taiwaninfo.nat.gov.tw/news.php?post=67869&unit=75,81,90,182.

Financement de l'Université du futur africain: Près de 25 milliards enterrés. (2021, January 30). *Le Quotidien (Sénégal)*. https://lequotidien.sn/financement-de-luniversite-du-futur-africain-pres-de-25-milliards-enterres/.

Geyang xiangkan - feizhou huajia bixia de zhongguo huazhan zai dakaer kaimu. [Looking at Each Other Across the Ocean - China under the brush of African painters exhibition open in Dakar.] (2023, May 15). *Xinhuanet*. www.news.cn/shuhua/20230515/1b1152e9cec84741aaa000b2de843c3d/c.html?page=1.

Guzmán Verri, V. (2020). Gifting architecture: China and the National Stadium in Costa Rica, 2007–11. *Architectural History, 63*, 283–311.

Kajman, M. (1979, February 26). L'Université des mutants de Gorée, inventer l'Afrique de demain. *Le Monde*. https://www.lemonde.fr/archives/article/1979/02/26/l-universite-des-mutants-de-goree-inventer-l-afrique-de-demain_3056608_1819218.html

L'INPG sur le site de l'Université du futur africain. (2021, January 30). *Sénéplus*. https://www.seneplus.com/politique/linpg-sur-le-site-de-luniversite-du-futur-africain

Musée des civilisations noires Dakar fonds. Musée d'ethnographie de Neuchâtel, Neuchâtel, Switzerland.

Kimeria, C. (2019, January 28). In conversation: The director of the museum of black civilizations. *Okayafrica*. https://www.okayafrica.com/in-conversation-hamady-bocoum-museum-of-black-civilizations/.

Kuenzi, M. T. (2011). *Education and democracy in Senegal*. Palgrave Macmillan.

Larkin, B. (2013). The politics and poetics of infrastructure. *Annual Review of Anthropology, 42*, 327–343.

Legislative Yuan (Republic of China). (1964). Xingzhengyuan huiyi yishilu tai di 230 ce 891 zhi 893 [Proceedings of Legislative Yuan Meetings vol. 230 no. 891–893], December, Legislative Yuan fonds. Academia Historia, Taipei, Taiwan.

Liu, Y. (2020, March 1). "Re-functioning "tropical architecture": Anti-colonial constructions in Chinese-Built architecture in Africa, 1960s–1970s. *Mediapolis*. https://www.mediapolisjournal.com/2020/03/refunctioning-tropical-architecture/.

Ministry of Culture and Tourism The People's Republic of China. (2018). Saineijiaer heiren wenming bowuguan juxing kaiguan yishi. [Opening ceremony of the Museum of Black Civilizations in Senegal.] https://www.mct.gov.cn/whzx/whyw/201812/t20181207_836436.htm.

Ministry of Foreign Affairs Republic of China (Taiwan). (2004). Woguo yu feizhou diqu guojia guanxi. [The Relationship between our Country and Africa Region Countries]. https://multilingual.mofa.gov.tw/web/web_UTF-8/almanac/almanac2004/08/08_01_03.htm.

Ministry of Foreign Affairs The People's Republic of China. (2024). Zhongguo tong saineijiaer de guanxi. [The Relationship between China and Senegal.] https://www.mfa.gov.cn/web/gjhdq_676201/gj_676203/fz_677316/1206_678404/sbgx_678408/.

Ministry of Foreign Affairs The People's Republic of China. (2019). Zhu sai nei jia er dashi zhang xun chuxi yuanzhu heiren wenming bowuguan wuzi jiaojie zhengshu qianzi yishi. [Zhang Xun, Ambassador to Senegal, attended the ceremony for the delivery of equipment aid to the Black Civilizations Museum]. https://www.fmprc.gov.cn/web/gjhdq_676201/gj_676203/fz_677316/1206_678404/1206x2_678424/201904/t20190423_9323470.shtml.

Murphy, D., & Vincent, C. (2019). Inside Dakar's Musée Dynamique: Reflections on culture and the state in postcolonial Senegal. *World Art, 9*(1), 81–97.

Moura, S. (2021). The museum of black civilisations, between history and Utopia. *Zeitschrift für Kulturwissenschaften, 15*(2), 107–122.

Musée des civilisations noires. (2024). A propos du Musée des Civilisations noires. https://mcn.sn/apropos/.

Ndiaye, E. H. M., & Chérel, E. (2020). Entretien avec El Hadji Malick Ndiaye, Conservateur du Musée Théodore Monod d'art africain (IFAN, université Cheikh Anta Diop). *Trouble dans les collections, 1*, hal-03339469.

Qu zhiminhua lixiang yu zhongguo yuanzhu: sai neijiaer heiren wenming bowuguan. [The ideal of "decolonization" and Chinese aid: The Museum of Black Civilizations in Senegal.] (2022, March 1). *ThePaper*. https://www.thepaper.cn/newsDetail_forward_16868902.

Schlimmer, S. (2022). Building a city from scratch? The Limits of top-down urban policy making in the case of the 'new urban hub' of Diamniadio, Senegal. *Megatrends Policy Brief* no. 6. 10.18449/2022MTA-PB06.

Shanghai Construction Group. (2015). Jituan chengjian de saineijiaer heiren wenming bowuguan jijiang jungong [The Museum of Black Civilizations in Senegal that the Group undertook for construction is nearing completion]. https://www.scg.com.cn/scg_jtyw/2015-12-15/Detail_197228.htm.

Shenyang Engineering Supervision & Consultation Co., Ltd. (2024). Yuan saineijiaer heiren wenming bowuguan xiangmu [Chinese Funded Museum of Black Civilizations in Senegal Project]. http://www.syjlzx.com/productshow.php?com=3&cid=8&nid=32.

Taïwan offre 14 millions de dollars à l'université du futur africain. (2001, June 16). *AEF info*. https://www.aefinfo.fr/depeche/442600-taiwan-offre-14-millions-de-dollars-a-luniversite-du-futur-africain-rdc-lunion-europeenne-offre-30000-ouvrages-scolaires-senegal-15-eleves-admis-dans-les-cpge-francaises.

Tall, M. M. (2005). Il faut assurer une croissance qui ne laisse pas les pauvres sur le bord de la route. *Echos de la Banque Mondiale*, May.

Une université du futur africain: l'un des grands projets du président Abdoulaye Wade. (2000, May 23). *AEF info*. https://www.aefinfo.fr/depeche/450880-une-universite-du-futur-africain-lun-des-grands-projets-du-president-abdoulaye-wade.

Veney, C. R. (2022). The switching of sides by Senegal and Nigeria. In S. O. Abidde (Ed.), *Africa-China-Taiwan relations, 1949–2020*. Lexington Books.

Xue, C. Q. L., Ding, G., Chang, W., & Wan, Y. (August 2019). Architecture of "stadium diplomacy" - China-aid sport buildings in Africa. *Habitat International, 90*, 101985.

Zai heiren wenming bowuguan gongdi shang guo "Wu Yi" de ren [People who spent "Labour Day" at the construction site of the Museum of Black Civilizations]. (2014, May 2). *Phoenix New Media*. https://news.ifeng.com/a/20140503/40132095_0.shtml.

Is It Really About China? Heterogeneous Partnership Configurations in Sino-Ghanaian Infrastructure Projects

Costanza Franceschini

Introduction

"Is it really about China?" asks Iginio Gagliardone (2019) in one of the last chapters of his book *China, Africa, and the Future of the Internet*, which investigates whether and how China is influencing the shaping of information societies in Africa. The same question can be asked regarding China's presence in African infrastructure development. The answer will probably be the same: no, or better, not only. Infrastructures are generally planned, designed, built, funded and desired by people with very different interests: politicians, government administrators, company managers, engineers, construction workers and local residents (Mains, 2019). China's involvement in Africa's infrastructure development is situated within a complex network of global flows of capital, goods, and people (Anthony, 2019, p. 108). While Chinese-financed and -constructed projects are

C. Franceschini (✉)
Institute of Cultural Anthropology and Development Sociology, Leiden University, Leiden, Netherlands
e-mail: c.franceschini@fsw.leidenuniv.nl

L. G. Adu Amoah (ed.), *Africa-China Relations*,
https://doi.org/10.1007/978-981-95-4370-0_6

generally framed by Chinese actors within the discourse of China's infrastructural development cooperation, and various subjects driven by disparate objectives tend to emphasise their "Chineseness" (Pasquali & Franceschini, 2024), these projects could be better described as global assemblages.

The assemblage thinking, originally developed by Deleuze and Guattari (1987), and widely employed in the anthropological and geographical literature on infrastructure, including with Chinese participation (Han & Webber, 2020; Rogelja, 2020), emphasises how infrastructure projects form along the interplay of diverse elements and multiple local and international actors. In the context of Chinese infrastructure projects overseas, in particular, it illuminates how these projects "emerge from the particular ways infrastructures assemble agents and how these in turn relate to each other via the design, construction, and use of those infrastructures" (Oakes, 2024, p. 85). It therefore elucidates that the "infrastructural power" of Chinese projects is inherently "place-bound", meaning that it is highly vulnerable to local—and global—contingencies (ibid.). At the same time, it raises a troubling political issue (Harvey et al., 2017) as the responsibility for the production of unforeseen and unwanted effects is frequently hidden behind or diluted in the assemblages and "assemblages of assemblages" (Delanda, 2016) that shape the projects.

In November 2018, an agreement was signed between the Government of Ghana and the China Development Bank (CDB) for a of USD 185.57 million loan to finance the construction of the Ghana Coastal Fishing Ports and Fish Landing Sites Project (hereinafter referred to as the GFPLS Project). The project encompassed twelve localities, comprising small towns, fishing villages and fishing localities situated within larger urban contexts along the Ghanaian coast. Its objective was twofold: firstly, to enhance the safety and working conditions of local fishermen; and secondly, to promote economic activities related to the fishing industry in those localities. Although sea fishing is the most important economic activity in the entire coastal region of Ghana, it has recently faced significant challenges, largely due to the effects of climate change, overfishing (Ayilu, 2023) and the expansion of oil extraction facilities (Owusu, 2019). This has had a considerable impact on the fishing community, with a notable increase in youth unemployment. The construction of marine infrastructure, including breakwaters and quay walls, and land-based facilities, such as ice-making plants, fishing markers, workshops, net repair facilities, day-care centres, washrooms and power stations, as part of the GFPLS

Project, was aimed at fostering the local fishing industry and providing employment opportunities.

The project was completed in little more than three years and was presented by Chinese actors and media outlets through the lens of China's infrastructural development cooperation, particularly at the outset of the implementation phase (Embassy of the PRC in the Republic of Ghana, 2019). Conversely, subsequent to its completion, the Ghanaian state's narrative on the project has become increasingly detached from China. This chapter presents an examination of the history, discourses and issues associated with the GFPLS Project. In particular, drawing on the suggestion of "thinking through heterogeneous infrastructure configurations" (Lawhon et al., 2018), it addresses the *heterogeneous partnership configurations* that form within Sino-African infrastructural assemblages. Indeed, if Ghana-China relations in the domain of infrastructure development can be described as a partnership, this is, in reality, part of broader configurations. These emerge from a multifaceted division of labour as well as contradictory systems of cooperation, competition, and (inter)dependence that encompass not only African and Chinese actors, but also multinational companies and financing institutions.

The study is grounded in extensive ethnographic fieldwork research. For the present project, the author has spent a total of thirteen months in Ghana between October 2021 and December 2022, conducting participant observation, informal conversation and semi-structured interviews with various individuals involved in different ways and at various levels in the GFPLS Project. Specifically, the author spent a period of four months at three of the project's construction sites, observing everyday dynamics and interactions related to labour issues as well as project development. Informal conversations were also conducted on a daily basis with the staff employed at the sites, including construction workers, supervisors, site managers, and engineers. Furthermore, the author conducted over 30 interviews with government officials and technicians in relevant ministries in Ghana, company managers, local residents, and traditional authorities. Informal conversations were also engaged in with a similar range of actors in the different localities involved in the project. This chapter addresses the following questions: (i) What is the role of Chinese actors in projects labelled as "Chinese"? (ii) What are the local and global dynamics that shape Chinese infrastructure projects in Ghana? (iii) What insights do Sino-Ghanaian infrastructural assemblages and heterogeneous partnership configurations provide into the nature of contemporary China-Africa relations?

Building as Many Fish Landing Sites as Possible: Ghanaian Infrastructural Politics and Chinese Funds

During his speech to the Parliament on 8 March 2023, the President of Ghana, Nana Addo Dankwa Akufo-Addo, declared: "I would like to state categorically that this Government has built [...] more fish landing sites than any other government in the Fourth Republic" (Presidency of the Republic of Ghana, 2023). Many of the fish landing sites mentioned in the President's speech have been constructed as part of the GFPLS Project, which was strongly promoted by the government, playing a central role in the local poetics and politics of infrastructure development (Larkin, 2013). In Ghana, promising infrastructure is part of the currency of national politics (Nugent & Lamarque, 2022, p. 18). However, rather than being something exceptional or new, infrastructure construction in Ghana has always been part of the conduct of the (post-)colonial politics, and it is firmly rooted in the (real or imagined) connection between infrastructure construction, modernity and economic growth. Since the realisation as well as the promise of infrastructure legitimises state authority (Foli, 2023) and generates political support, infrastructure projects are generally announced during the electoral campaign. Moreover, if the party that announced it wins, the project must be completed before the end of the mandate. A project started by one legislature is unlikely to be continued by a legislature led by a different party, and thus projects started by a certain party will have to wait until that party is re-elected before they can be completed. With respect to electrification projects in Ghana, for instance, Briggs (2021) illustrates how party rotations cause large shifts in the location of the projects due to the different voter-targeting strategies.

In light of their political significance, projects are presented in a manner that aligns with a specific political narrative. Upon the conclusion of the GFPLS Project, the Ghanaian government placed considerable emphasis on the successful construction of numerous coastal infrastructure projects for fishermen, while strategically avoiding any mention of the adverse effects that the project had at the local level. Moreover, the role of Chinese funding was not included in the narrative. Indeed, as evidenced by interviews conducted with officials from the Ghanaian government, while China may provide loans for implementation, African governments actually are (and depict themselves) as the ideators and owners of infrastructure projects (Pasquali & Franceschini, 2024). This was frequently highlighted by my interlocutors as a means of emphasising the pivotal role of the African state agency in shaping the trajectory of their country's infrastructural development (Chiyemura et al., 2023).

It is also worth noting that the GFPLS Project did not involve Chinese actors from the outset. The project commenced prior to Chinese involvement, when the Government of Ghana contracted a European company in 2006 to conduct a survey, feasibility studies and technical designs for the construction of a number of fishing harbours and fish landing sites in selected fishing communities along the Ghanaian coast. However, the lack of funds, coupled with a change in the ruling party—in December 2008, the New Patriotic Party (NPP), which initiated the project, lost the elections—resulted in the project's suspension for a considerable period of time. In December 2011, the President of Ghana, Atta Mills, signed a Master Facility Agreement (MFA) in Beijing, thereby securing a loan of USD 3 billion from the China Development Bank. This loan was earmarked for a number of projects, including the construction of the GFPLS Project. In accordance with the stipulation that Chinese-financed construction projects must be undertaken by Chinese state-owned enterprises (SOEs), the Government of Ghana entered into a contract with a Chinese central SOE in July 2012 for the construction of the GFPLS Project. Nevertheless, the project failed to materialise. In July 2014, the Government of Ghana proceeded to cancel half of the USD 3 billion loan, along with all associated infrastructure projects (Chen, 2016). In 2016, almost ten years after the project began, the NPP won elections again and, aiming to complete the project, in 2018 borrowed additional funds from China to finance the project. The Chinese construction SOE that was appointed in 2012, which in the meantime had entered the Ghanaian construction sector and was working on the construction of another port project, took on the project as the main contractor.

Before his inauguration, in March 2012, Akufo-Addo declared that Chinese grants and credit lines are "very welcome" and that "the Chinese interest in our country is a very healthy one, it's one that all of us are very comfortable with in Ghana" (BBC News, 2012). As various online news report, during the years of his mandate, the President of Ghana and its establishment have repeatedly supported the importance of Chinese loans and investments in Africa, especially in the field of construction. According to Amoah (2020), it was starting from the NPP government under the president Akufo-Addo that Ghana began to define a Ghanaian policy towards China and the Chinese presence in the country. In the past (and partly still today), Ghana's relations with China have been mostly characterised by a high level of personalisation (Amoah, 2020, p. 131). For instance, it was thanks to personal relationships established between the Ghanaian President Atta Mills and the former Chinese president Hu Jintao that, during Atta Mills' presidency (2009–2012), Ghana maintained good relations with China and was able to secure a USD 3 billion loan from CDB for infrastructure development. In turn, this meant that Ghana for a long time was unable to formulate a Ghana–China strategy, relying solely on the presidents' personal ties with the Chinese administration, thus allowing Ghana's relationship with China to mutate beyond the capacity of the Ghanaian state to handle (ibid., p. 183). Amoah's analysis echoes what Achille Mbembe (2001, p. 78) describes as the privatisation of sovereignty in the African states. As Mbembe underlines, this practice can be observed across a wide range of personal relations established between African politicians and bureaucrats and international actors, including private firms, aid agencies, non-governmental organisations, transnational corporations and many others.

As the GFPLS Project was financed by China, it was incorporated into the Chinese discourse on China's infrastructural development cooperation. This is evidenced by a report on the website of the Embassy of the People's Republic of China (PRC) in the Republic of Ghana (2019), which states that following the groundbreaking ceremony for the commencement of construction of the project, Ambassador Wang made a speech in which he stated that the construction of the project represents another major achievement of Sino-Ghanaian cooperation.

Despite the Chinese ambassador to Ghana presenting the project as a significant accomplishment of the China-Ghana partnership, in interviews, Ghanaian state officials placed emphasis on the Ghanaian ownership of Chinese-funded projects, portraying China as a lender among a wide range of financial contributors.

> We have our priority list. The Chinese give us grants, they give us concessional loans, they give us buyer's credits. [...] For the concessional loan, we have our priority list. And for the buyer's credit component also, we have our priority list. [...] We determine what is our priority at any point in time.

> [...] For instance, the Ministry of Transport identifies a project and the amount of money to involve on it. It would be difficult for the Government of Ghana to readily provide the funds. We do what we call sourcing for funds. We look at the development partners and the multilateral organizations like the World Bank, African Development Bank, Asia Infrastructure Development Bank, and the European Union, and then the bilateral organizations, the major OECD countries and some other countries that provides support for us. Most of the countries have their areas of competitive advantage. For instance, China has a competitive advantage in the construction sector. (Interview, Government Official, State Ministry, Accra, 2 August 2022)

The descriptions provided by the bureaucrats working for the Ministry of Finance challenge the assumption that the high dependence on aid and foreign financing for infrastructure construction necessarily limits the state's capacity of acting and exercising influence during negotiations with China (Soulé-Kohndou, 2019, p. 189). The officials and technicians working for the Ghanaian Ministries that I interviewed stressed both the role played by bureaucrats in loan negotiations and the political will to implement the projects. Therefore, although African states and their technical and bureaucratic elites are often identified as weak and subservient to the expansionist and colonialist aims of foreign states and multinational companies, the narratives "from within" seem to reveal a different picture. Although it cannot be said that global processes and the neoliberal economy have not partially taken away decision-making power from states, these narratives at least define the room for manoeuvre within which some state actors can transpose processes of globalisation into the national arena. Randeria (2003), focusing on the bargaining strength of the borrowing states and the extent to which they are able to circumvent policies negotiated under conditions of unequal power, uses the notion of the "cunning state" in referring to states' capacity to negotiate with powerful international financial institutions.

At the same time, Ghana's reliance for infrastructure development on external funding and investments, in moments of economic crisis such as the one Ghana has experienced since December 2022, call into question the political and anti-political forces that shape Ghana's infrastructure development. The sustainability of Chinese loans and their implications for African countries are being widely debated by politicians, scholars and the media both in Africa and in Western societies. Even if there are no examples in which China has deliberately "trapped" another country in debt and then used that debt to obtain unfair or strategic advantages (Brautigam, 2020, p. 6), the issue of loan repayments remains a matter of concern. Many scholars and policymakers have already called for a sustainable plan for Chinese loan repayment in Ghana (Graham, 2021, p. 186). Ghana's declaration of default on its external debts in December 2022 provides clear evidence of this issue.[1] Although China is not solely and directly responsible for this situation, Ghana, as well as many other African countries, faces massive debt, aggravated by loans taken to finance its infrastructure-led development. This situation, however, is promoted not only by China but also by a wider "global growth coalition" formed by international financial institutions, the African Union, donors, neoliberal consultancies, investment banks, powerful states and African governments (Zajontz, 2022, p. 178).

Ghana's debt default, which commenced in December 2022, led to the suspension of all ongoing infrastructure projects funded by foreign lenders, including China. The sudden interruption of construction projects not only resulted in the loss of many jobs, the disruptions of mobility in areas where construction sites were located and the risk that, if the works are restarted, the costs could increase and some parts of the work might need to be reconstructed, but it has also demonstrated how these projects could be transformed from "politics" to "anti-politics" machines (Ferguson, 1990). As infrastructure projects become increasingly financially dependent, the decision to implement or continue a project no longer falls to politicians but to lenders. In the current situation in Ghana, for instance, the International Monetary Fund (IMF), to which Ghana has asked help for debt restructuring, will be likely the one to decide which projects can be restarted and under what conditions and which ones will have to wait or be abandoned. The situation that followed Ghana's declaration of default on its external debt demonstrated that Chinese projects in Africa are also subject to the politics of infrastructure suspension and incompleteness (Kovač, 2023). Moreover, it elucidates the extent to which African state actors and local and global infrastructural politics influence the terms and conditions of "Chinese" infrastructure projects on the continent.

A Project Assemblage: Bridging Politics, Multinationals' Business, and Uneven Chinese Infrastructural Development Cooperation

In 2006, the Government of Ghana selected a European international engineering and consulting firm to undertake the feasibility studies and preliminary design for the marine and land infrastructure components of the GFPLS Project. Later on, when Ghana received funds from China for project construction, the Ghanaian government hired a Chinese SOE as main contractor, while it employed the European design and consulting firm to supervise the project. As described by Thierry Pairault (2020) in his analysis of French and Chinese business cooperation in Africa, African governments often drive a sort of "division of labour" between Chinese and European companies, hiring Chinese contractors to undertake the heavy-duty construction work, due to their cheaper, faster and more efficient performance[2] and employing European companies to undertake design and technical tasks, assuming the task will be achieved according to European technical and quality standards.

This division of labour between Chinese and European firms describes neatly the joint operation of the GFPLS Project between the European consulting and design firm and the Chinese construction company. Despite the division of labour between the client, financier, designer, consultant and contractor representing a defining feature of international construction projects, at times African state actors strategically leverage projects to diversify partnerships and extract additional benefits. This approach reflects their efforts to recalibrate power asymmetries and navigate external dependencies (Kaag et al., 2021). This dynamic underscore the multifaceted nature of infrastructure development, where global and local agendas, financial constraints, and strategic manoeuvres converge to shape outcomes—often extending far beyond the scope of Chinese involvement. It is therefore within this context that the heterogeneous partnership configurations emerge—collaborations that are either fostered, imposed or discretionary—and which exert a substantial influence on the trajectories and outcomes of the projects.

As a result of the division of labour, the design of the GPFLS Project was entirely developed by the European company. Nevertheless, the design of the marine infrastructures has resulted in a multitude of challenges. These can be attributed to deficiencies in the design phase, coupled with the absence of comprehensive feasibility studies prior to the commencement of construction. Indeed, as underlined by some engineers working for the Ghanaian Ministries interviewed, the difficulty in finding the feasibility studies lies not only in the fact that the preparatory studies and projects were done a long time ago but also in the fact that many studies never took place or were later modified in order to satisfy political interests and decisions, such as the addition of sites at the last minute, with the primary objective of constructing as many fish landing sites as possible.

The first project design realised for tender between 2007 and 2008 involved 12 localities. In the contract signed with the Chinese SOE, however, only 11 localities were listed. In 2018, when the new financing agreement was signed between the Government of Ghana and CDB, the project included 10 localities. One of the fishing harbours was taken off from the list since China conceded a grant to Ghana for the realisation of the project, whose construction was started in 2020 by another Chinese SOE. Finally, when the project was already ongoing, another locality was also removed from the GFPLS project since the government of Ghana secured additional funds from Belgium. Consequently, following the securing of financial backing for a number of the initially proposed fishing harbour projects, the government opted to expand the scope of the GFPLS Project to encompass three additional locations, a decision that was met with scepticism, particularly from GPHA technicians, given the questionable and questioned procedural approach employed.

> The Government wants to carry out these projects to obtain votes from the communities. The Ministers travel to the various communities and promise them they will do this and that… When we advised them [the Ministers] not to build all these ports but to focus only on few of them, they replied to us: "people want this project, and we will do it for them". (Interview, Engineer, State Authority, Accra, 7 October 2022)

In interviews with engineers employed by the Ghanaian Ministries, it was asserted that the European company's collaboration was instrumental in facilitating this outcome. Additionally, several government technicians posited that the involvement of foreign engineers, who assumed roles more akin to politicians than engineers, contributed to the emergence of this situation.

> The consultants, they are politicians. They act as politicians, not as engineers. Instead of discussing the project with us, they went straight to talk

> with the Ministers. Instead of giving them [the Ministers] technical opinions and suggestions based on their engineering skills they pander to politicians' wishes and tell them that certain projects are feasible even if they are not. The Ministers went to them and said: "We would like to build a port here, is it possible?" And they immediately replied: "Yes, of course, we can do it." Without even having conducted a feasibility study or having considered the economic budget available. (Interview, Engineer, State Authority, Accra, 7 October 2022)

As Daniel Mains (2019, p. 71) points out, while engineering is generally portrayed as an apolitical field, often the success or the failure of a project depends on local political elites and, as in the case of the GFPLS project, on the relationship and intersections between political promises and engineering projects. As Harvey and Knox (2015, p. 9) observe, in the context of infrastructural projects, engineers are regarded as "expert par excellence". However, this expertise is perceived as problematic precisely because it is exercised as "a managerial practice" and is imbued with "a hubristic moral force" (ibid.). However, in the case of the GFPLS project, the engineers employed by the European company "emerge as the villains" in the story (ibid.), not as hubristic technical experts but as subjects who acted not following "technical" accurate and informed choices and approaches and as "politicians" who acted following politics and not engineering. It is political action, guided by politics, according to many of my interlocutors, that has positioned these subjects as "villains" and that has caused the negative consequences for the project—this, of course, without diminishing the technical errors made and the inability to fix them by a more diverse range of actors. In this context, the Chinese state-owned contractor was frequently required to navigate and negotiate between a multitude of interests and rationalities, including political, geopolitical, and engineering considerations.

In the field of international infrastructure construction, Chinese SOEs combine cooperation and business. Often, construction projects financed by China constitute the first projects carried out by Chinese SOEs, allowing them to enter the market and establish their business operations overseas, as in the case of the Chinese company that built the GFPLS Project. However, to remain and expand their activities in the sector, companies need to adopt a wide range of embeddedness strategies (Gambino & Franceschini, 2025). In this scenario, it is of the utmost importance to achieve a balance between competing interests and to consolidate strategic actions. The GFPLS Project encountered significant challenges during its construction phase. These challenges included the failure of the infrastructure project, discontent among local communities, and tensions with various project partners. These difficulties could have jeopardised the company's interests, particularly in terms of maintaining a presence in the local construction sector and forging productive partnerships with both the political counterpart and numerous other international companies involved in infrastructure development projects in the country and the region. Moreover, since the project was financed by China and presented at its inauguration under the umbrella of Chinese cooperation, its failure could easily result in a negative image for Chinese infrastructure development projects in Africa. The Ghanaian government's rebranding of the project, in which the Chinese presence disappeared from the narrative after the project's completion, could therefore be motivated not only by a declaration of ownership by the Ghanaian state actors, but also by an attempt on the part of the Chinese actors to withdraw from a situation with possible negative repercussions.

Therefore, beyond Chinese discourses on win-win cooperation and mutual benefits, it is not always evident that China benefits from these projects. The advantages of involvement in particular projects are contingent upon a number of variables and may vary during the different phases of the project. This is because Chinese-financed projects are not solely of Chinese origin, but rather manifest a "dilution of Chineseness" (Goodfellow & Huang, 2021). The assemblages and heterogeneous partnership configurations that shaped the GFPLS Project, for instance, demonstrated that the project was primarily driven by local political interests and the involvement of transnational corporations and, consequently, that the "Chineseness" of the project was less crucial than the socio-political dynamics within the host country (Wang & Wissenbach, 2019).

"Build What Is on the Drawing, Even If It Is Wrong": Uneasy Heterogeneous Partnership Configurations

Although infrastructure, and engineering projects in general, are commonly perceived as infallible, errors occur at various stages of the project, and particularly in the project design and are more frequent than expected. According to Love et al. (2013, p. 676), errors have become an inherent aspect of the design process in construction and engineering. The design of the GFPLS Project was flawed for a number of reasons, primarily due to the dominance of political rationalities over engineering ones and the exclusion of local knowledge and expertise regarding the areas where the project was to be constructed. As described by numerous interlocutors with whom I conducted the research, including local fishermen and residents, as well as European, Chinese, and Ghanaian engineers and managers involved in the project, the incorrect construction of the breakwaters in almost all locations involved in the project had the greatest impact on the places and caused major problems. These issues manifested in a number of ways, including sedimentation and coastal erosion, flooding, and the absence of water in the harbour. As several interlocutors observed, there was a dearth of consideration for historical precedents and scientific studies on the subject in the context of the coastal infrastructure race along the Ghanaian coast, that was mainly driven by desires, promises and expectations of modernity (Ferguson, 1999).

In West Africa, coastal erosion is a major problem that is increasingly responsible for the loss of coastal land and significantly affects the human and non-human communities inhabiting those places. In Ghana, the coastline is eroding at an alarmingly high rate. It therefore becomes necessary to find ways to protect coastal communities against coastal hazards. Nevertheless, the construction of grey coastal infrastructures, despite their beneficial purpose, do not improved but rather negatively increase coastal erosion migration, complicating coastal management (Charuka et al., 2023). This phenomenon is not new. As reported by Akyeampong (2001), for instance, in Ghana, in the colonial period, the construction of the Takoradi Port drastically altered the coastal landscapes and induced coastal erosion in many localities around Accra, Ada and Keta. The Anlo, in particular, have attributed the phenomena of intense erosion along the coast and the decline in both lagoon and maritime fish stocks to the construction of the deep-water harbours in Takoradi and Tema. Nevertheless, it is frequently the case that the significance of development projects, such as harbours, to national governments leads to a reduction in awareness of the detrimental impact at the local level (ibid., p. 160). This results in a somewhat paradoxical dynamic whereby politicians are eager to construct an increasing number of fish landing sites in order to gain political consensus in as many localities as possible yet, this ultimately has the opposite effect, leading to contestations, disaffection, and a reduction in political support.

During the construction of the GFPLS Projects, the Ghanaian politicians and ministers who had promoted the development of the project never visited the sites in person, thereby failing to become aware of the technical and environmental problems that the project was facing. Similarly, the technicians of some Ghanaian Ministries involved were unaware of the project's evolution, despite their nominal participation (Interview, Government Official, State Ministry, Accra, 28 February 2022). Moreover, the engineers and designers of the European company, which had subcontracted the entirety of the supervision work to a local company, did not undertake any visits to the sites during the entire period of project planning and implementation. Additionally, when new locations were incorporated into the plan, no preliminary feasibility studies were conducted.

Conversely, the Chinese company's engineering personnel and those representing the Ghana Port and Harbours Authority (GPHA) were aware of the problems that the project was causing. Nevertheless, during interviews, GPHA technicians asserted that they lacked the capacity to engage in negotiations and project modifications. Indeed, although Ghanaian political and bureaucratic elites played a pivotal role in the planning, negotiation, and influencing of the GFPLS Project, the client side of the project was comprised of numerous entities, institutions, and subjectivities, each with their own perspectives and agendas, and with varying degrees of negotiation power—and shifting partnerships amongst them.

> When we heard that they wanted to build an additional landing site we said "no", we expressed our disagreement with it. But they didn't listen to us. When we said "no", the Ministers went to talk to the consultants and they said: "Yes, sure, we can do it." And so they did it. We have advised the government against it many times. And when we finally saw the drawings and realised what they were doing, we told them that there was something wrong. We told them it would never work. But the consultants bypassed us and interfaced directly with the Ministers and got the approval to proceed. (Interview, Engineer, State Authority, Accra, 7 October 2022)

The engineers and managers of the Chinese company were aware of the project-related issues and frequently expressed criticism of the operations of the design and consulting company. On occasion, they displayed a notable degree of despondency regarding the manner in which the project was being managed. As a European engineer employed as a consultant by the Chinese company attested:

> The consultants [...] had not designed the ports. What they have done is they have taken an aerial photograph, and they have said, "oh, it might be nice if we built a breakwater like that, and like that. Oh no, we don't have enough money. Let's do it a little bit shorter". Yeah. "But that will cause siltation and erosion change the current". "Oh, don't you talk to us, we are the designer. We're experts in design. You are just a contractor. You do what we tell you". So, all the 10 ports, now only three of them work. Because the idea was that you would have in many of the ports, if here is the land looking down in the field, the boats used to come in here in the beach and the waves generally come in this direction [he draws it]. So, what the designer did was they said "okay, well it needs a breakwater like this" [he draws it], but then they discovered that there wasn't enough money because the job had been agreed back in 2012 at a fixed amount of money. So the designer then went, "okay, well, we will just build a breakwater like that." So then, as soon as I came on the job, because this is something I spent a lot of time doing, I saw that this, the current is this direction [he draws it] and there is always lots of sand in the current. If you block it, if you do don't go out to deep enough water, blocking it here, what happens is the sand which is going on here, sweeps around, like that [he draws it], and just deposit it here. And that is exactly what has happened at several of the sites and is happening at the new ones that we have built. (Interview, Engineer and consultant, Chinese SOE, Accra, 13 January 2022)

The observation of the situation, in the ports and locations involved in the project by the engineers employed by the Chinese company, however, was accompanied by a defence of the Chinese firm, deemed not responsible for what happened. As I had been told, they had to "build what was on the drawing, even if it was wrong". Based on the terms of the contract, indeed, the Chinese company's only duty was to execute the work as designed by the European engineers, and so it did. In part because of this, but also because of a typical Chinese approach aimed at avoiding disputes and open conflict, the Chinese company has never explicitly raised the issue of the European firm's design errors. Instead, the primary concern of the Chinese company's employees was the potential impact of the project's failure on the company's reputation. Nevertheless, prior to the conclusion of the project, the Chinese company entered into two new contractual agreements with the Government of Ghana for the construction of two additional port projects within the country.

After the completion of the GFPLS Project, local residents expected that the project would be inaugurated. In fact, in Ghana, as can be seen not only by reading the newspapers but also by following the social pages of the various Ghanaian Ministries, such as the Ministry of Transport, the Ministry of Roads and Highways and GPHA, infrastructure projects are generally inaugurated shortly after their completion with large commissioning ceremonies. As in most countries around the world, the aim of these ceremonies is to show the local population and the country as a whole the infrastructure works carried out by the government, in order to win the votes and the consensus of the political leaders who promote these initiatives and successes. However, since the GFPLS Project was not a real success, and the government feared that the inauguration ceremony would be more of a showcase for protests than an occasion to celebrate the government's efforts in pursuing the country's infrastructure development, it was never inaugurated.

Initially, this led to the bizarre situation where the marine infrastructure that had caused and continues to cause most of the problems for local fishermen was navigated due to the lack of real alternatives and the impossibility of removing it, while the land infrastructure, such as the structures built to host cold storage facilities, school, offices, public toilets, were not used since they were not inaugurated. Over time, despite the absence of an official inauguration, some of these structures—such as the structures built to host covered fishing markets and covered mending nets sites—have been gradually brought into use. At the time of writing, the project has not yet been inaugurated. Nevertheless, it has been incorporated into the government's account of the number of fish landing sites constructed during its administration. It is likely that the project has also been added to the statistics on the number of projects financed and built by China in Africa, and in Ghana in particular. Moreover, the project marked the Chinese construction company's inaugural venture in Ghanaian markets, paving the way for subsequent projects funded by other sources.

Conclusion

Rather than representing an exceptional or isolated case, the GFPLS Project serves to highlight the dynamics that are typical of contemporary Chinese (and non-Chinese) construction projects in Africa. As the anthropological literature on infrastructure has extensively emphasised, infrastructures are not simply material objects; they are complex assemblages capable of illuminating social, economic and political relations. In this context, Chinese involvement in Africa's infrastructure development should be considered not only in terms of China's (and Chinese state-owned companies') economic and political ambitions but also in terms of private interests and African political elites' desires (Goodfellow & Huang, 2021). The construction of infrastructure is, in fact, the engine of political imaginaries and promises and a source of consensus.

This study discusses the heterogeneous partnership configurations that shape Sino-African infrastructure cooperation projects. This is not to suggest that China has little impact on infrastructure development in Africa, but rather to provide a more nuanced and detailed analysis of what actually happens on the ground (Oakes, 2024). In response to the initial questions posed at the outset of this chapter, the narrative of the GFPLS Project illustrates, in particular, how, (i) while China may serve as the financier of infrastructure projects, African governments assert their ownership of those projects as a means of fostering political consensus. Furthermore, Chinese contractors, when not responsible for the project design, lack both the formal authority and the capacity to influence the projects' outcomes. (ii) Chinese infrastructure projects in Ghana are shaped by a complex interplay of global and local dynamics, including the division of roles between Chinese and non-Chinese companies, and the pivotal role of local infrastructural politics. (iii) Sino-Ghanaian infrastructural assemblages demonstrate that the mutual benefits derived from these projects are highly variable and contingent upon changes that occur during the different phases of the projects.

This analysis illuminates the nature of the partnership that characterises China-Ghana infrastructure development cooperation, while also prompting significant reflections on the issues of ownership and responsibility in projects with heterogeneous partnership configurations. Project ownership varies in terms of narratives—with projects being appropriated or distanced according to convenience—and management—depending on the prevailing partnerships (e.g. between ministries) at a given time. Responsibility for project failures or problems is also very variable and ultimately vague. The ambiguity surrounding the methods, rationales, and procedures that inform certain decisions often gives rise to a lack of clarity regarding the specific responsibilities of the involved parties. This is, in essence, also connected to the nature of the partnerships in question. The reluctance to jeopardise certain relationships, in terms of both the rhetoric of cooperation and economic interests, frequently results in the failure to take appropriate measures to address issues, consequently leading to their unresolved state. Nevertheless, this is not only, but also about China (and Sino-African projects).

Notes

1. On 19 December 2022, the government of Ghana announced that it would no longer make payments on its external debt, declaring that it wanted to default on its sovereign debt. In the meantime, the government of Ghana also declared that it was already in the process of negotiating a debt restructuring agreement with the International Monetary Fund (IMF).
2. This is particularly the case for projects not funded by China. In the case of Chinese-funded projects, this is also a consequence of the above-mentioned requirement of employing Chinese SOEs to obtain Chinese funding.

References

Akyeampong, E. K. (2001). *Between the sea and the lagoon. An eco-social history of the Anlo of Southeastern Ghana c. 1850 to recent times.* James Currey.

Amoah, L. G. A. (2020). *Five Ghanaian Presidents and China: Patterns, pitfalls, and possibilities.* University of Ghana Printing Press.

Anthony, R. (2019). "China in Africa" in the Anthropocene: A discourse of divergence in a converging world. In C. Alden & D. Large (Eds.), *New directions in Africa–China Studies* (pp. 104–117). Routledge.

Ayilu, R. K. (2023). Limits to blue economy: Challenges to accessing fishing livelihoods in Ghana's port communities. *Maritime Studies, 22*(11), 1–16.

BBC News. (2012, March 5). Interview with Nana Akufo-Addo on BBC Hardtalk: China's investment in Ghana is "very welcome". *Hardtalk.* Retrieved November 27, 2024, from https://bit.ly/44qafSq.

Brautigam, D. (2020). A critical look at Chinese "debt-trap diplomacy": The rise of a meme. *Area Development and Policy, 5*(1), 1–14.

Briggs, R. C. (2021). Power to which people? Explaining how electrification targets voters across party rotations in Ghana. *World Development, 141*, 1–11.

Charuka, B., Angnuureng, D. B., & Agblorti, S. K. M. (2023). Mapping and assessment of coastal infrastructure for adaptation to coastal erosion along the coast of Ghana. *Anthropocene Coasts, 11*(6), 1–16.

Chen, T. (2016). What happened to China Development Bank's USD 3 billion loan to Ghana? *China Africa Research Initiative (CARI) Policy Brief* 10: 1–4.

Chiyemura, F., Gambino, E., & Zajontz, T. (2023). Infrastructure and the politics of African state agency: Shaping the Belt and Road Initiative in East Africa. *Chinese Political Science Review, 8*, 105–131.

Delanda, M. (2016). *Assemblage theory.* Edinburgh University Press.

Deleuze, G., & Guattari, F. (1987). *A thousand plateaus: Capitalism and schizophrenia.* University of Minnesota Press.

Embassy of the PRC in the Republic of Ghana. (2019). H. E. *Ambassador Shi Ting Wang attends the ground breaking ceremony of Axim Fishing Port.* Retrieved November 27, 2024, from https://bit.ly/3NZFrSb

Ferguson, J. (1990). *The anti-politics machine: Development, depoliticization, and bureaucratic power in Lesotho.* Cambridge University Press.

Ferguson, J. (1999). *Expectations of modernity: Myths and meanings of urban life on the Zambian Copperbelt.* University of California Press.

Foli, A. (2023). The heterogeneous politics of infrastructure: Claims of authority in Accra's drainage. *Environment and Planning C: Politics and Space, 41*(7), 1459–1473.

Gagliardone, I. (2019). *China, Africa, and the future of the internet.* Bloomsbury.

Gambino, E., & Franceschini, C. (2025). Flexible embeddedness: How Chinese lead firms internationalise in Africa. *Review of International Political Economy*, 1–31. https://doi.org/10.1080/09692290.2025.2538187

Goodfellow, T., & Huang, Z. (2021). Contingent infrastructure and the dilution of "Chineseness": Reframing roads and rail in Kampala and Addis Ababa. *EPA: Economy and Space, 53*(4), 655–674.

Graham, E. (2021). A discourse on sixty years of China-Ghana developmental partnership and some contemporary limitations. In L. G. A. Amoah (Ed.), *Sixty years of Ghana-China relations. Friendship, friction, and the future* (pp. 165–195). University of Ghana Printing Press.

Han, X., & Webber, M. (2020). From Chinese dam building in Africa to the Belt and Road Initiative. Assembling infrastructure projects and their linkages. *Political Geography, 77*(102102), 1–12.

Harvey, P., Jensen, C. B., & Morita, A. (2017). Introduction. Infrastructural complications. In P. Harvey, C. B. Jensen, & A. Morita (Eds.), *Infrastructures and social complexity* (pp. 1–22). Routledge.

Harvey, P., & Knox, H. (2015). *Roads. An anthropology of infrastructure and expertise.* Cornell University Press.

Kaag, M., Khan-Mohammad, G., & Schmid, S. (2021). Destination Africa: Contemporary Africa as a Centre of Global Encounter. In M. Kaag, G. K. Mohammad, & S. Schmid (Eds.), *Destination Africa: Contemporary Africa as a Centre of Global Encounter* (pp. 1–28). Brill.

Kovač, U. (2023). Suspension as politics: A stadium and its ruins in Northwest Kenya. *Ethnos, 90*, 1–27.

Larkin, B. (2013). The politics and poetics of infrastructure. *Annual Review of Anthropology, 42*, 327–343.

Lawhon, M., Nilsson, D., Silver, J., Ernstson, H., & Lwasa, S. (2018). Thinking through heterogeneous infrastructure configurations. *Urban Studies, 55*(4), 720–732.

Love, P. E. D., Lopez, R., & Edwards, D. J. (2013). Reviewing the past to learn in the future: Making sense of design errors and failures in construction. *Structure and Infrastructure Engineering, 9*(7), 675–688.

Mains, D. (2019). *Under construction. Technologies of development in urban Ethiopia*. Duke University Press.

Mbembe, A. (2001). *On the postcolony*. University of California Press.

Nugent, P., & Lamarque, H. (2022). Introduction. Transport corridors in Africa: Synergy, slippage and sustainability. In H. Lamarque & P. Nugent (Eds.), *Transport Corridors in Africa* (pp. 1–34). James Currey.

Oakes, T. (2024). Global China and infrastructure power: The technopolitics of the 'China Model' of development. *Georgetown Journal of Asian Affairs, 10*, 84–93.

Owusu, V. (2019). Impacts of the petroleum industry on the livelihoods of fisherfolk in Ghana: A case study of the Western Region. *Extractive Industries and Society, 6*(4), 1256–1264.

Pairault, T. (2020). French and Chinese business cooperation in Africa. *China Africa Research Initiative (CARI) Policy Brief, 50*, 1–4.

Pasquali, P., & Franceschini, C. (2024). Defining Chineseness in Chinese infrastructure projects in Africa: The Case of Ghana. *China Perspectives, 139*, 59–69.

Presidency of the Republic of Ghana. (2023). *Message on the state of the nation by the President of the Republic, Nana Addo Dankwa Akufo-Addo, on Wednesday, 8th March 2023, at Parliament House, Accra*. Retrieved November 27, 2024, from https://bit.ly/3qBRNYJ

Randeria, S. (2003). Cunning states and unaccountable international institutions: Legal plurality, social movements and rights of local communities to common property resources. *European Journal of Sociology, 44*, 27–60.

Rogelja, I. (2020). Concrete and coal: China's infrastructural assemblages in the Balkans. *Political Geography, 81*, 1–10.

Soulé-Kohndou, F. (2019). Bureaucratic agency and power asymmetry in Benin–China relations. In C. Alden & D. Large (Eds.), *New directions in Africa-China Studies* (pp. 189–204). Routledge.

Wang, Y., & Wissenbach, U. (2019). Clientelism at work? A case study of Kenyan Standard Gauge Railway project. *Economic History of Developing Regions, 34*, 1–20.

Zajontz, T. (2022). Debt, distress, dispossession: Towards a critical political economy of Africa's financial dependency. *Review of African Political Economy, 49*(171), 173–183.

Projects and Polls: Chinese Infrastructural Engagement and African Political Cycles

Elisa Gambino

Introduction

Chinese funding for Africa's infrastructures has dried up. After decades of sustained lending, Chinese funding commitment to transport infrastructure projects in Africa—which accounted for close to USD 50 billion between 2000 and 2019—have dropped to a mere USD 1 billion in 2020, further decreasing in 2021 and 2022 (BU Global Development Policy Centre, 2024). This has marked a shift away from previous decades' large-scale financial commitments, reflecting a broader trend in China's global lending patterns. Indeed, this downturn in Chinese-backed infrastructure funding is taking place against the background of China's domestic economic slowdown, exacerbated by the COVID-19 pandemic, and debates around the rising debt of provincial governments. Additionally, growing concerns around the sustainability of loan repayments amongst African countries also contributed to this shift, as some borrowing countries are under severe debt distress (i.e. Kenya) or have already begun debt

E. Gambino (✉)
Global Development Institute, University of Manchester, Manchester, UK
e-mail: elisa.gambino@manchester.ac.uk

L. G. Adu Amoah (ed.), *Africa-China Relations*,
https://doi.org/10.1007/978-981-95-4370-0_7

restructuring negotiations (i.e. Zambia). The retrenchment of Chinese funding represents a shift from over two decades of Chinese engagement in African infrastructure development strongly supported by Chinese state-backed funding. Now, capital-intensive 'vanity projects' are indeed less frequent, while—in accordance with the 'small and beautiful' approach that emerged on the cusp of the COVID-19 pandemic—smaller projects are increasingly becoming the new normal in China-Africa infrastructural engagement. Although infrastructure has returned as a priority during the Forum on China-Africa Cooperation (FOCAC) 2024, these financial commitments remain distant from the previous focus on large transport infrastructure projects.

The end of the Chinese-backed infrastructure cycle in Africa offers a great opportunity to take stock of what the implications of China-Africa infrastructure engagement in the twenty-first century have been. Lively debates have ensued around the ramifications of Chinese funding for African nations' debt (Carmody et al., 2022) and industrialisation (Tang, 2023). Many have emphasised Chinese projects' contributions to improving connectivity and creating employment, while concerns have been raised about growing debt dependency and the questionable transfer of skills and technology, which often fail to support broader structural transformation in African economies. Very little attention, however, has been paid to the ways in which Chinese engagement intersects and entangles with African political cycles—as highlighted by Nantulya (2021). African leaders have often timed the announcement, commencement, and completion of large-scale infrastructure projects to harness political capital in the face of re-election pressure or against rising public discontent. As suggested by Burgess et al. (2015), elections increase the focus on delivering visible public goods (see also Mani & Mukand, 2007), suggesting that infrastructural provision is intimately connected to the positioning of infrastructure projects within specific political agendas.

This chapter explores the interactions between infrastructure development with Chinese participation and African political cycles. Specifically, it investigates how infrastructure projects and the politics surrounding their planning, development, and governance can craft or challenge political legitimacy, effectively becoming a form of political capital for different actors. The chapter suggests that Chinese infrastructure projects in Africa can be understood as both tools for political legitimacy and instruments of political contestation. In other words, they can become visible and potent reminders of leaders' time in office, but projects raising (financial) sustainability challenges or having poor outcomes also offer opposition candidates instruments to criticise incumbent governments. This review and agenda-setting chapter identifies a crucial future trajectory of research resting on the analysis of the relationship between infrastructure projects and political cycles (with a focus on when and where projects are built).

This chapter is based on a combination of secondary materials and reflections emerged from a broader project on the internationalisation of Chinese state-owned construction companies in Kenya, for which fieldwork was conducted between 2018 and 2019. The research processes involved extended periods of qualitative data collection through semi-structured interviews and ethnographic observations in construction sites. The example of Kenya is nested within a range of cases drawing from different African contexts to broaden the scope of the review and support the identification of a wider research agenda.

The chapter proceeds as follows. First, it contextualises infrastructure development in broader debates on China-Africa engagement. Second, it offers an overview of Chinese engagement with African politics at different scales, such as diplomatic engagement at the bilateral level and the everyday politicisation of infrastructure projects with Chinese participation. Third, the chapter explores the relationship between Chinese infrastructure and African political cycles, outlining the ways in which infrastructure are both tools for political legitimacy and instruments of political contestation. Finally, the chapter proposes a research agenda centred around the intersection of Chinese participation to African infrastructure development (focused on when and where projects are implemented) and political cycles on the continent.

China-Africa in Context: Infrastructure as Political Capital

Sino-African engagement in infrastructure development has prompted a lively scholarly debate in International Relations and International Political Economy. Some have argued that China's engagement in Africa is 'neo-colonial' in nature (Tull, 2006), as the financing and construction of transport infrastructure is considered to be a means to securing and retaining access to natural resources (Carmody & Owusu, 2007). This perspective echoes current discourses in media and policy circles, where the support from the Chinese state through preferential financial incentives aimed towards internationalisation has quickly fed into the so-called China Inc. narrative (Fishman, 2006), according to which Chinese firms' engagement on the African continent not only supported by the Chinese state, but also orchestrated and guided by it. As a result, Chinese companies' overseas engagement is often portrayed as "an extension of government economic policy" (Robins, 2013, p. 526), and thus seen as fitting within a broader (and supposedly coherent) geopolitical agenda.

According to this zero-sum stream of literature, China is attempting to build its position as a new 'imperial' power through the promotion of the so-called China model or Chinese 'state capitalism' (Davies, 2008, 2010; as also discussed in Pairault, 2019; Brautigam, 2020). The perspective of an all-coordinated 'grand strategy' was further fuelled by rising debt distress in many borrowing African countries, which prompted a re-evaluation of the modalities of engagement and further investigations on the actors involved. Indeed, many scholars have refuted the argument of an overarching and coordinated 'Chinese strategy', highlighting the diverging interests of myriad of actors—what Taylor and Xiao (2009) refer to as multiple 'Chinas'—involved in developing Chinese foreign policy and disbursing loans or other financial incentives (see Jones & Zeng, 2019; Brautigam, 2020).

As relations amongst China and "many African countries are maturing and moving beyond state-to-state deals, implicating many more actors" (Mohan & Lampert, 2013, p. 100), the scope of research has moved beyond the narrative of China steering the engagement with African nations. Indeed, Chinese-funded and Chinese-built infrastructure projects are not being developed on a 'blank slate', but are instead are processes shaped by many Chinese and African actors, which cannot be reduced to one-to-one interactions. A rapidly growing body of literature—which Alden and Large (2019, p. 13) refer to as the "African agency turn" in the study of China-Africa engagement—has highlighted the heterogeneous nature of Sino-African interactions (Corkin, 2013; Soulé-Kohndou, 2019b; Chiyemura et al., 2023). Scholars have suggested that the extent to which African agency shapes Sino-African interactions has "as much to do with African politics as it does with the politics of China-Africa relations" (Mohan & Lampert, 2013, p. 93; see also Cheru, 2016; Procopio, 2019).

This chapter builds on this line of enquiry, which foregrounds the agency of an array of African actors in shaping Sino-African encounters. Specifically, it seeks to combine this stream of literature with critical infrastructure studies, which understands infrastructure not only as 'material' or 'technical' objects, but also in light of their symbolism and visibility, as well as their role in projecting state capacity and their mobilisation within political strategy and state-building (Mitchell, 2002; Carse, 2012; Larkin, 2013, 2018; Harvey & Knox, 2012, 2015; Easterling, 2014; Harvey et al., 2017; Lesutis, 2019; Aalders, 2020; Chome et al., 2020). Infrastructure not only connect (and disconnect) places and people, but they also remain closely linked to the rationales for their provision, as well as the coexistence of different agendas that emerge and come into conflict around these projects.

The study of Chinese-funded infrastructure has largely been dominated by discussions around their (often questionable) outcomes, the rising debt levels of African borrowing countries, and the geopolitical implication of growing Chinese presence in the African infrastructure sector. However, as this chapter suggests, Chinese infrastructure projects in Africa are far from being a mere manifestation of the growing capital flows from Chinese sources to African economies. Instead, the process of Sino-African infrastructure development is profoundly embedded in the political contexts in which these projects take place. Infrastructure can indeed become a form of political capital that both crafts and challenge the political legitimacy of those in office. It is thus crucial to the study of China-Africa encounters to understand how and why infrastructure's political nature comes into being within specific political economies.

Chinese Engagement and African Politics

China-Africa relations have consistently deepened since initial engagement in the 1950s. Africa's place in Chinese foreign policy has evolved together with the changing role of China in the international arena, reflecting changes in both the Chinese domestic sphere and across the political economies of African nations. For the better part of the second half of the twentieth century, China was heavily focused on building durable bilateral diplomatic relations with African nations, contingent on the recognition of the People's Republic of China (PRC) over the Republic of China (ROC) as prescribed by the 'One China Policy'. Currently, the Kingdom of eSwatini is the only African country with formal diplomatic relations with Taiwan, down from five countries in 1979.

These configurations, however, can be transitory or unstable. For example, Liberia has long fluctuated between recognising the PRC and the ROC. After first recognising the PRC in 1977, Liberia once again recognised the ROC in late 1989, and in 1997 then President Charles Taylor attempted to recognise both, prompting the PRC to halt all diplomatic relations (Moumoni, 2014). It was only in 2003 that Liberia negotiated the re-establishment of diplomatic relations with Beijing, a policy later made irreversible under the government of President Ellen Sirleaf. Soon thereafter, in 2005, the country received the first loan from a Chinese state-bank (USD 5 million) to refurbish the Samuel Kanyon Doe Sports Complex and other projects (BU Global Development Policy Centre, 2024).

China-Angola relations have similarly been witnessing a reshaping due to the severe economic crisis caused by the drop in oil prices began in 2014 (Corkin, 2017) and the stepping down of late President Dos Santos in 2017 (after 39 years). After a long period of economic engagement with China through different channels, Angola's approach to Chinese lenders and leadership shifted. Indeed, new President João Lourenço, quickly "sought to diversify [the country's] international ties, arguably at the expense of closer ties to China" (de Carvalho et al., 2021, p. 9). In 2018, Angola negotiated a loan facility with the International Monetary Fund (IMF), which included a total of USD 3.7 billion to support the country's economic reform programme (IMF, 2018). This points to a shift towards in the country's economic policy, now moving towards fostering sustained recovery as opposite to the previous infrastructure-led post-conflict reconstruction efforts (see Roque, 2021, pp. 169–202).This suggests that shifts in policy direction in the aftermath of political leadership changes can have implications for Chinese economic actors' prominence, presence, and operations in specific African contexts.

Another key aspect characterising the evolution of Sino-African political engagement is the evolution of party-to-party relations. Under Xi Jinping's rule, party-to-party engagement has intensified, with visits from African delegations reaching their highest frequency right before COVID-19, to then move online and become more sporadic in their bilateral encounters (Shinn & Eisenman, 2023, p. 86). As Shinn and Eisenman (2023, p. 327) outline, Chinese actors—ranging from party to state-owned companies—have "created partnerships with more African elites across a broader range of political and security sectors than ever before." The range of events and meetings organised has also significantly increased, thus having a larger scope both in terms of participation across the political spectrum and with regards to their policy implications (Benabdallah,

2021). This resonates with Kathy Lam's findings (2017, p. 55) on the engagement of Chinese state-owned enterprises with political parties in Ghana, which she states highlight the necessity to "balance and maintain relationships with all of the political parties, not only those in power" (see also Gambino & Franceschini, 2025).

Finally, since political cycles can lead to the swift reorganisation of how decision-making powers are distributed in African nations, these transition—both in the form of democratic elections or through coup d'états—have concrete effects on the engagement of Chinese actors. As an instance of this, the Chinese-backed Bagamoyo Port project in Tanzania was suspended after the election of former President Magufuli. His concerns revolved around the unfavourable contract conditions proposed by China Merchants Port (CMPort), which he believed would be only appealing to "a madman" (Musungu, 2019). Magufuli's move to suspend this project was part and parcel of "the gradual transformation of Tanzania into an autocratic developmental state" during his time in office (Chiyemura et al., 2023, p. 117) and a broader pattern of transformation of the Tanzanian state's approach towards external partners and international investors (Jacob & Pedersen, 2018). Magufuli concentrated on curbing opposition figures and diminishing the space for political contestation (Collord, 2022; see also Paget, 2017, 2021). This trickled down to institutional structures beyond the presidency, thus ensuring his government's (hostile) negotiation trajectory with Chinese counterparts was, for the most part, shielded from critiques.

In another prominent example, relations between Chinese actors involved in the transport and export of oil from Niger through Benin and political leadership in Niger shifted quickly after the most recent coup d'état. In July 2023, the newly-formed presidential guard, led by General Abdourahamane Tchiani, detained then President of Niger Mohamed Bazoum and proclaimed themselves the new leadership of the country, now governed by a military junta. After the coup, Chinese state-owned company China National Petroleum Corporation (CNPC), which has been involved in the extraction oil in Niger's Agadem reserves, signed a further agreement with the military junta in April 2024. This speaks to the previous discussion on how Chinese actors develop and sustain relations with political actors across the political spectrum, although these can, at times, be characterised by instability and uncertainty. In the case of post-coup Niger, CNPC committed USD 400 million for the commercialisation of crude oil to be exported through the Beninese port of Seme

(Neema, 2024). Initially, this agreement was considered as a breath of fresh air for this West African country, which had been increasingly isolated after the military junta had taken power. However, in June 2024, an attack on the pipeline transporting crude oil from Niger to Benin took place, rendering the pipeline unusable (Le Monde and AFP, 2024). This attack, combined with rising tensions between Niger and Benin—as the Nigerien leadership considers Benin's relations to former colonial power France as being too close for comfort—resulted in CNPC closing their operations in Niger until the situation around the pipeline is resolved (Koné & Diallo, 2024).

In short, politics in African nations significantly influence their interactions with both state and commercial Chinese actors. The above-mentioned examples from Liberia, Angola, Tanzania, and Niger highlight how political shifts—whether through elections or coups—can reshape national policies and, in turn, impact relations with Chinese actors. As political cycles unfold, the context in which Chinese investment and lending are taking place also evolve, bringing to the forefront the relationship between political cycles and the economic activities of Chinese actors. Below, I further explore these dynamics through the case of Chinese-backed infrastructure projects.

Chinese-Backed Infrastructure and Electoral Cycles

The deployment of infrastructure as political and electoral prompts not only indicates that these projects serve political objectives (Van Der Westhuizen, 2007), but also that their implementation is closely linked to political cycles (as also observed by Lakmeeharan et al., 2020). This phenomenon is not unique to infrastructure with Chinese participation. For instance, in Zambia, Masaki (2018) observed that projects financed by Western international financiers were directed towards areas where opposition candidates enjoyed more support. Nevertheless, Chinese (financial) participation has not only been crucial to the development of African infrastructure, but has also been the subject of much public controversy and political debate. On the one hand, many infrastructure projects that have received public funding might not have been built without the support of Chinese financiers as they had already been refused by other lenders (Feyissa, 2011; Soulé-Kohndou, 2019a). On the other hand, the financial sustainability and the negative externalities that have been associated with Chinese-funded and -built projects notwithstanding rising Corporate Social Responsibility (CSR) activities undertaken by Chinese companies (Tan-Mullins & Mohan, 2013).

Below, I outline two key roles played by infrastructure with Chinese participation in the context of African politics. The first is infrastructure as tools for political legitimacy. Political legitimacy is here understood as the acceptance and recognition of political leadership resting on what Nugent (2019) terms *productive social contract* in the (often infrastructure-led) development agendas of African states, namely a relationship "where the legitimacy of the state rests on the delivery of certain social goods, or at least the performance of an enabling function" (p. 32). This section highlights how infrastructure with Chinese participation have been used as backdrops for campaign speeches and electoral announcements, but how their deployment to harness political capital can easily backfire depending on shifts in the political context at hand. Second, I explore how infrastructure projects with Chinese participation have also been used as instruments of political contestation, particularly in contexts characterised by rising debt burden and highly competitive elections. Political contestation refers to the challenges and controversies emerging around the legitimacy of the ruling groups, often driven by opposition factions or civil society organisations. This section shows how infrastructure projects with Chinese participations have often raised public discontent and criticisms around project governance—often targeted at those who initiated and promoted their realisation.

Infrastructure as a Tool for Political Legitimacy

The concrete and visible nature of transport infrastructure offers an excellent opportunity for political campaigning, pointing to the ways in which infrastructural provision is intimately linked with specific political agendas. Projects with Chinese participation have indeed been shown to "create novel linkages to broader accumulative processes" of African elites (Reboredo, 2021, p. 16). This trend can be traced to the previous infrastructural boom across the African continent in the 1960s and 1970s, whereby infrastructure projects "generated prestige, personal funds and clients" for African elites "whose authority and legitimacy rested on the display of wealth and the capacity to distribute sinecures [to their associates]" (Dimier, 2014, p. 137). In other words, infrastructures—and the rents they generate—can be deployed to promote specific configurations of power relations within polities, as well as to garner support for capital-intensive development visions underpinned by the pursuit for enhanced connectivity.

The case of the Chinese-funded and -built Nairobi-Mombasa Standard Gauge Railway (SGR) in Kenya is arguably the most straightforward example of this. The SGR Phase I—financed by China Export Import Bank (China Exim Bank) and constructed by the Chinese state-owned enterprise China Road Bridge Corporation (CRBC)—was inaugurated by then President Uhuru Kenyatta during a speech to the nation on the anniversary of the country's independence—Madaraka day. In his 2017 speech, Kenyatta reiterated the relevance of the SGR (also known as Madaraka Express) to Kenya's national development agenda and the country's position in the region, pointing to the competition with neighbouring countries. Most importantly, however, he seized the opportunity to bring the country's attention to his candidacy for a second term, less than two months before election day.

> Madaraka Express, Ladies and Gentlemen, is a true living symbol of the journey we are undertaking together. It is the foundation for better incomes for our farmers, manufacturers, and other businesses. On it rests our dominance as a regional hub, opening up opportunities for new markets for our goods and services, and letting us compete against other ambitious countries for the manufacturing investment that will bring jobs for our sons and daughters. [...] This is a moment for boldness: henceforth, our politics must be shaped by a desire to take Kenya forward to prosperity for all. Brothers and Sisters, on Monday, I submitted my application to serve you for another term, in preparation for that day in August when the future of your motherland will lie in your hands. (Kenyatta, 2017)

The ceremony took place in Mombasa, an opposition stronghold, signalling an interest in 'deploying' infrastructure to raise consensus for the incumbent. In a similar fashion, as Kenyatta's last term was concluding ahead of the general elections of August 2022, he reportedly compelled Chinese contractors to speed up the completion of infrastructure located in the broader coastal region (Olander, 2021), which is historically associated with the opposition party. Kenyatta's latest attempt to mobilise infrastructure with Chinese participation for political purposes thus appears to be both an effort to sediment the electoral foundations of his party and his own legacy. This resonates with the findings of Harvey and Knox (2015, p. 194) in Peru, where the inauguration ceremonies of road infrastructure were not mere "rituals that mark the completion of an infrastructure, but rather political punctuations in a longer trajectory of infrastructural emergence". Indeed, in the Kenyan context, infrastructure-led development has been at the core of the country's development agenda *Kenya Vision 2030*.

In a similar fashion, Chinese infrastructure projects were often used as the backdrop of campaign speeches during the last Zambian elections. Since the early 2000s, Zambia's relations to China have been at the forefront of debates concerning the impacts of Chinese lending for borrowing African countries. Accelerating substantially in 2012, Zambia's external public debt was estimated to be around USD 12.7 billion in 2021 (Hill & Mitimingi, 2021). Out of the total external debt, estimates based on data released by the Lungu administration placed debt to Chinese public lenders at around USD 3 billion (Mfula, 2021), and new estimates suggest that total debt to Chinese lenders—public and private—might be around USD 6.6 billion (Reid & Mfula, 2021).

In the runup to the August 2021 elections, incumbent Edgar Lunga heavily relied on showcasing several Chinese-backed projects. He personally inaugurated the Chinese-funded Kafue Gorge Lower hydropower project (The Africa Report, 2021; Xinhua News, 2021), welcomed a shipment of Chinese vaccines (China Daily, 2021), and ensured the construction of the Simon Mwansa Kapwepwe International Airport was completed ahead of schedule (Construction Review, 2021). The brand-new airport terminal—financed through a loan disbursed by China Exim Bank for a total of USD 400 million and constructed by China Jiangxi Corporation—undoubtedly made an apt backdrop to launch Lungu's final week of campaigning. However, after Lunga lost the election to sixth-time opposition candidate Hokainde Hichilema, this airport project has become a potent reminder of Zambia's debt to Chinese lenders.

Infrastructure as an Instrument of Political Contestation

Close to national elections, the potentialities associated with the politicisation of infrastructure appear, at least in the eyes of prominent political figures, to trump the risks connected to (purposedly) positioning these projects in the limelight. Placing the political spotlight upon projects with Chinese participation could arguably be a 'risky business', as these can be easily leveraged by the opposition or by competing intra-party factions. For instance, Sibiri (2020, p. 8; see also Hess & Aidoo, 2015) highlights how "the growing negative perception of China has created a conducive environment or become an easy target for some political actors to ride on anti-Chinese rhetoric". Indeed, political opponents can readily place Chinese engagement at the centre of inflammatory statements targeting—or even mudslinging—political opponents.

In the runup to the 2018 elections in Zimbabwe, for example, opposition candidate Nelson Chamisa, who later lost the elections, promised that if elected he would "call the Chinese and tell them the deals they signed are unacceptable, and they should return to their country" (BBC, 2018). In a similar fashion, while on the campaign trail in Kenya, now President William Ruto vowed to expel Chinese people whose jobs can be done by Kenyans. Ruto also stated he would publish all government contract with Chinese companies (Houreld & Miriri, 2022), directly referencing the long controversy surrounding the lack of transparency commonly associated with Chinese-funded infrastructure projects, as well as Chinese funding more broadly. In December 2018, a summary of the privately negotiated contract for the Nairobi-Mombasa SGR was leaked to the press.

The leaked note suggested that Mombasa port had been agreed as a guarantee in case of loan repayment default on the part of the Kenyan government (Wafula, 2018). This reading—according to which the country's largest port could be appropriated by the funder China Exim Bank–caused widespread public discontent and prompted loud cries for increased transparency. Then, Kenyan President Uhuru Kenyatta stated he would publish the agreement to put rumours to rest. When this did not happen, activists Khelif Khalifa and Wanjiru Gikonyo petitioned the government to release the agreements signed in relation to the SGR, bringing several state ministries to court. A ruling by the High Court of Mombasa[1] in May 2022 ordered that the government disclose said documents, only to be quickly appealed by the Kenyan Attorney General (Muyanga, 2022).

Ruto's campaign remarks follow years of animated debates around the operations of Chinese companies in Kenya, which are considered to have large financial capabilities and unfair advantages that do not allow for fair competition with Kenyan businesses across different sectors (see for instance, Parliament of Kenya, 2022). In the construction sector, Kenyan firms have demanded increasing protection from the government, arguing that Chinese companies' bidding practices are driving local contractors towards severe financial losses. In 2018, a member of the Kenyan

Parliament stated he would propose a bill to prevent foreign contractors to participate in government-issued EPC tenders valued less than USD 1 million (Otieno, 2020).

In Zambia, presidential hopeful Sata from the Patriotic Front centred his 2006 campaign around harsh critiques of Zambia-China relations under previous presidents. He began by targeting increasing Chinese engagement to the country's development agenda and extractive sectors in his political speeches. For instance, in 2010 he stated that Chinese companies were involved in "slave labour" (Cropley, 2010), criticising the often poor working conditions associated with Chinese companies (Jauch & Sakaria, 2009; Akorsu & Cooke, 2011). Then, while on the campaign trail in 2011, he stated that "Zambia has become a province of China" and that "the Chinaman is coming just to invade and exploit Africa" (French, 2011). After the elections, President Sata's anti-Chinese rhetoric—which tapped into widespread anti-Chinese sentiment (Hampwaye & Kragelund, 2013)—turned out to be nothing more than empty words.

Once elected, his "position shifted immediately [...] as he was structurally enrolled and inducted into the elite actor network" (Carmody & Kragelund, 2016, p. 12), characterised by the seeming convergence of elite interests and those of Chinese actors. During Sata's time in office, began in 2011 and ended upon his death in 2014, loan commitment from Chinese lenders amounted to a total of USD 2 billion (BU Global Development Policy Centre, 2024), of which the largest share were in the transport sector. When Sata's presidency began, Zambia's external debt amounted to around 8.4 per cent of GDP (Ofstad & Tjønneland, 2019), and, as heavy borrowing (both from Chinese and Western lenders) continued under his successors, the country's total external debt reached nearly USD 27 billion—almost 115 percent of GDP—in 2021 (Reuters, 2021).

Towards a Future Research Agenda on Chinese Infrastructure and African Politics

This chapter puts forward a future research agenda focused on the relationship between infrastructure project cycles and electoral cycles, supported by a framework that positions infrastructure as tools for political legitimacy and instruments for political contestation. Since African political leaders often time the announcement, construction, or completion of large-scale infrastructure projects to coincide with electoral cycles, using them as visible demonstrations of their ability to deliver on electoral promises, create employment, and stimulate economic growth. Beyond their timing, infrastructure location can also offer insights into the priorities of different political candidates and their willingness to harness support in specific regions or constituencies. In this regard, future research could explore the location of infrastructure in relations to electoral constituencies and voter behaviour, the likelihood of infrastructure project announcements or fast-tracking during periods of political contestation and competition (i.e. campaigns), and the extent to which perceived failures in the delivery of (financially) sustainable infrastructure projects are leveraged by opposition parties.

This could be done both through a qualitative case study approach, for example focusing on specific countries or infrastructure projects, or through a mixed-method approach that combines the analysis of electoral behaviour data (i.e. through surveys conducted by institutions such as Afrobarometer) and the geolocalisation of infrastructure projects with Chinese participation undertaken through the support of GIS software. Similar work has been undertaken to bring to light the relationship between Chinese development finance and popular protests. Iacoella et al. (2021) mapped the number of protests and contestation across geographical units of the continent and evaluated their correlation with the presence of Chinese projects, finding that higher concentration of Chinese financed projects leads to more protests.

Indeed, infrastructural provision has historically been linked to state legitimacy, which often relied on the provision of tangible benefits to the population. The contemporary focus on developing African infrastructures is similarly characterised by the strengthening of (centralised) forms of state governance which are reframing domestic and regional power relations (Wethal, 2019; Péclard et al., 2020). State-driven infrastructure development efforts—even those financed by external founders such as Chinese policy banks—consistently intersect with enduring modalities and practices characterising territorial politics in African nations. The projection of state power and the degree to which states are willing or able to do so vary significantly across African contexts. As Boone (2024, p. 237) notes, in addition to being crucial to states' territorial strategies, large-scale infrastructure projects also "generate intense political churn around the apportionment of costs and benefits, both at local and national level". Therefore, a geographically sensitive analysis of the intersection between infrastructural provision and voter behaviour is crucial to understanding the impact and influence of the Chinese-backed infrastructure boom on African polities.

Conclusion

This chapter focused on the infrastructure sector to explore the political significance of Sino-African engagement and investigate Chinese actors' entanglements with shifting political patterns in African contexts. The politicisation of infrastructure with Chinese participation finds its origin in the historical trajectories and the renewed centrality of infrastructure development to African development. Initially built to serve the interests of colonial powers, infrastructures are now back at the forefront of the continent's development agenda, prompting the resurgence of political debates around the ways in which infrastructure are built, their long-term sustainability, and their contribution to the structural transformation of African economies.

Over the past 20 years, large amounts of infrastructural investment and funding have been directed towards/deployed on the African continent. Amongst the many external actors involved, Chinese financiers and contractors have gained considerable foothold. Through their rapid expansion, Chinese funders and construction companies have become increasingly embedded in specific African political economies (Gambino and Franceschini, 2025), which has resulted in the growing politicisation of Chinese engagement with African nations. Indeed, as discussed in this chapter, Sino-African engagement increasingly features political debates and electoral campaigns, leading to the need to further investigate the relationship between infrastructure development with Chinese participation and African politics.

As Chinese engagement in African infrastructure enters a new phase due to the sharp reduction in state-backed funding and the shift towards 'smaller' strategic projects, it is crucial to further evaluate the intersection between Sino-African infrastructure projects and the political lives of African nations. Due to rising debt levels, questionable project outcomes, and opaque contracts, Chinese infrastructure projects can readily be politicised and become centrepieces of political debates. This chapter suggests that infrastructure projects with Chinese participation are a form of political capital, which can be leveraged by both ruling and opposition factions for the pursuit of their political agenda, namely crafting or contesting political legitimacy.

The politicisation of infrastructure not only reveals how African leaders and opposition movements strategically deploy Chinese projects, but also how these projects complicates longstanding dichotomic narratives of 'win–win cooperation' or 'debt-trap diplomacy'. Indeed, the chapter identified two broad trends in the politicisation of infrastructure with Chinese participation. First, infrastructure can feature political campaigns as electoral prompts, whereby they are in the background of electoral speeches and/or function as 'visible' legacies of leaders' time in office. Understood as such, they are tools for political legitimacy and serve to consolidate power or harness support. Second, in light of challenging project outcomes or contestation during project implementation, infrastructure can also become an instrument for opposition candidates to criticise incumbent governments and launch smear campaigns.

In highlighting the ways infrastructures become both assets and liabilities in the pursuit of political legitimacy, this analysis foregrounds the evaluation of what two decades of large-scale infrastructure development have meant for African politics. In doing so, it proposes an avenue for future research based on the exploration of whether project location, timing, and schedule is influenced by political cycles (election in particular), with specific attention paid to mapping where and when projects are built. Doing so would allow future researchers to build on this preliminary analysis to take stock of two decades of China-Africa engagement largely centred around infrastructure development to gain lessons for the next stage of Chinese participation in African political economies.

Note

1. Republic of Kenya in the High Court of Kenya at Mombasa, Constitutional and Judicial Review Division, Constitutional Petition n E 032 of 2021.

Bibliography

Aalders, J. T. (2020). Building on the Ruins of Empire: The Uganda Railway and the LAPSSET Corridor in Kenya. *Third World Quarterly, 42*, ahead of publication, 1–18.

Akorsu, A. D. and Cooke, F. L. (2011) 'Labour Standards Application among Chinese and Indian Firms in Ghana: Typical or Atypical?', *International Journal of Human Resource Management, 22*(13), pp. 2730–2748.

Alden, C. and Large, D. (2019) 'Studying Africa and China', in Alden, C. and Large, D. (eds) New Directions in Africa-China Studies. Abingdon: : Routledge, pp. 3–35.

BBC. (2018). Zimbabwe opposition MDC 'will expel Chinese investors'. *BBC News*. Retrieved June 13, 2021, from https://www.bbc.com/news/world-africa-43973908

Benabdallah, L. (2021, October). Ties that Bind: China's Party-to-Party Diplomacy in Africa. *Konrad Adenauer Stifung*. Retrieved January 12, 2025, from https://www.kas.de/en/web/medien-afrika/einzeltitel/detail/-/content/ties-that-bind.

Boone, C. (2024). *Inequality and political cleavage in Africa: Regionalism by design*. Cambridge University Press.

Boston University (BU) Global Development Policy Centre. (2024). Chinese loans to Africa Database. Retrieved November 14, 2024, from https://www.bu.edu/gdp/chinese-loans-to-africa-database/

Brautigam, D. (2020). A critical look at Chinese "debt-trap diplomacy": The rise of a meme. *Area Development and Policy, 5*(1), 1–14.

Burgess, R., Jedwab, R., Miguel, E., Morjaria, A., & Padró i Miquel, G. (2015). The value of democracy: Evidence from road building in Kenya. *American Economic Review, 105*(6), 1817–1851.

Carmody, P., Taylor, I., & Zajontz, T. (2022). China's spatial fix and 'debt diplomacy' in Africa: Constraining belt or road to economic transformation? *Canadian Journal of African Studies / Revue canadienne des études africaines, 56*(1), 57–77. https://doi.org/10.1080/00083968.2020.1868014

Carmody, P. R., & Kragelund, P. (2016). Who Is in Charge? State power and agency in Sino-African Relations. *Cornell International Law Journal, 49*(1), 1–24.

Carmody, P. R., & Owusu, F. Y. (2007). Competing hegemons? Chinese versus American Geo-Economic Strategies in Africa. *Political Geography, 26*(5), 504–524.

Carse, A. (2012). Nature as infrastructure: Making and managing the Panama Canal Watershed. *Social Studies of Science, 42*(4), 539–563.

Cheru, F. (2016). Emerging Southern powers and new forms of South–South Cooperation: Ethiopia's strategic engagement with China and India. *Third World Quarterly, 37*(4), 592–610.

China Daily. (2021). Zambia receives Chinese vaccines in fight against COVID-19 pandemic. *China Daily*. Retrieved March 06, 2022, from https://bit.ly/3p01koH

Chiyemura, F., Gambino, E., & Zajontz, T. (2023). Infrastructure and the politics of African state agency: Shaping the Belt and Road Initiative in East Africa. *Chinese Political Science Review, 8*, 105–131. https://doi.org/10.1007/s41111-022-00214-8

Chome, N., Gonçalves, E., Scoones, I., & Sulle, E. (2020). "Demonstration fields", anticipation, and contestation: Agrarian change and the political econ-

omy of development corridors in Eastern Africa. *Journal of Eastern African Studies, 14*(2), 291–309.
Collord, M. (2022). Wealth, power and institutional change in Tanzania's Parliament. *African Affairs, 121*(482), 1–28.
Construction Review. (2021). Simon Mwansa Kapwepwe International Airport project in Zambia completed. *Construction* Review. Retrieved May 12, 2022, from https://bit.ly/3JHcJmD
Corkin, L. J. (2013) '*Uncovering African Agency: Angola's Management of China's Credit Lines*'. Farnham: Ashgate.
Corkin, L. (2017). *After the boom: Angola's recurring oil challenges in a new context.* Oxford Institute for Energy Studies Paper, n. 72, May.
Cropley, E. (2010). Zambia opposition slates China, Malaysia investors. *Reuters.* Retrieved June 23, 2022, from https://reut.rs/3QlvApK
Davies, M. (2008). China's developmental model comes to Africa. *Review of African Political Economy, 35*(115), 134–137.
Davies, M. (2010). *How China is influencing Africa's development.* OECD Development Centre.
de Carvalho, P., Kopiński, D., & Taylor, I. (2021). A Marriage of convenience on the rocks? Revisiting the Sino-Angolan Relationship. *Africa Spectrum, 57*(1), 5–29.
Dimier, V. (2014). *The invention of a European Development Aid Bureaucracy.* Palgrave.
Easterling, K. (2014). *Extrastatescraft.* Verso.
Feyissa, D. (2011). Aid negotiation: The uneasy "partnership" between EPRDF and the donors. *Journal of Eastern African Studies, 5*(4), 788–817.
Fishman, T. C. (2006). *China Inc.: The relentless rise of the next great superpower* (2nd ed.). Scribner.
French, H. W. (2011). In Africa, an Election Reveals Skepticism of Chinese Involvement. *The Atlantic.* Retrieved April 13, 2022, from https://bit.ly/3A7ut7M
Gambino, E., & Franceschini, C. (2025). Flexible embeddedness: How Chinese lead firms internationalise in Africa. *Review of International Political Economy,* 1–31. https://doi.org/10.1080/09692290.2025.2538187
Hampwaye, G., & Kragelund, P. (2013). Trends in Sino-Zambian Relations. In S. Adem (Ed.), *China's Diplomacy in Eastern and Southern Africa* (pp. 27–29). Ashgate Publisher.
Harvey, P., Jensen, C. B., & Morita, A. (2017). Introduction. In P. Harvey, C. B. Jensen, & A. Morita (Eds.), *Infrastructures and social complexity* (pp. 1–22). Routledge.
Harvey, P., & Knox, H. (2012). The enchantments of infrastructure. *Mobilities, 7*(4), 521–536.

Harvey, P., & Knox, H. (2015). *Roads: An Anthropology of Infrastructure and Expertise*. Cornell University Press.

Hess, S., & Aidoo, R. (2015). Charting the roots of Anti-Chinese populism in Africa: A Comparison of Zambia and Ghana. *Journal of Asian and African Studies, 49*(2), 129–147.

Hill, M., & Mitimingi, T. C. (2021). Zambia's new president pledges to uncover country's true debt burden. *Bloomberg*. Retrieved May 25, 2022, from https://bloom.bg/3BLSPFe

Houreld, K., & Miriri, D. (2022). Kenyan presidential hopeful Ruto promises to publish contracts with China. *Reuters,* July 20. Retrieved August 01, 2022, from https://reut.rs/3zZ0JZo

Iacoella, F., Martorano, B., Metzger, L., & Sanfilippo, M. (2021). Chinese official finance and political participation in Africa. *European Economic Review, 136*, 103741. https://doi.org/10.1016/j.euroecorev.2021.103741

International Monetary Fund (IMF). (2018). IMF Executive Board Approves US$3.7 Billion extended arrangement under the extended fund facility for Angola. International Monetary Fund. Retrieved February 24, 2021, from https://bit.ly/3JKZmlt

Jacob, T., & Pedersen, R. H. (2018). New resource nationalism? Continuity and change in Tanzania's extractive industries. *The Extractive Industries and Society, 5*(2), 287–292. https://doi.org/10.1016/j.exis.2018.02.001

Jauch, H., & Sakaria, I. (2009). *Chinese investments in Namibia: A labour perspective*. Labour Resource and Research Institute.

Jones, L., & Zeng, J. (2019). Understanding China's "Belt and Road Initiative": Beyond "grand strategy" to a state transformation analysis. *Third World Quarterly, 40*(8), 1415–1439.

Kenyatta, U. (2017). *Speech by His Excellency Hon. Uhuru Kenyatta, C.G.H, President of the Republic of Kenya and Commander in Chief of the Defence Forces During the 54th Madaraka Day Celebrations at Kabiruini Stadium, Nyeri on 1st June 2017, Presidency of Kenya*.

Koné, S., & Diallo, F. (2024, July 23). Pourquoi le chinois CNPC lève le pied au Niger' [Why the Chinese company CNPC left Niger]. *Jeune Afrique*. Retrieved November 02, 2024, from https://www.jeuneafrique.com/1591101/economie-entreprises/pourquoi-le-chinois-cnpc-leve-le-pied-au-niger/

Lakmeeharan, K., Manji, Q., Nyairo, R., & Pöltner, H. (2020) *Solving Africa's infrastructure paradox*. McKinsey. Retrieved May 09, 2021, from https://mck.co/3PbnheS

Lam, K. N. (2017). *Chinese state-owned enterprises in West Africa*. Routledge.

Larkin, B. (2013). The politics and poetics of infrastructure. *Annual Review of Anthropology, 42*(1), 327–343.

Larkin, B. (2018). Promising forms: The political aesthetics of infrastructure. In N. Anand, A. Gupta, & H. Appel (Eds.), *The promise of infrastructure* (pp. 175–202). Duke University Press.
Le Monde and Agence France-Presse (AFP). (2024, June 18). Au Niger, un mouvement rebelle annonce avoir mis « hors d'usage » une partie d'un oléoduc [In Niger, a rebel movemner announces that they have put part of an oil pipeline 'out of use']. *Le Monde*. Retrieved November 09, 2024, from https://www.lemonde.fr/afrique/article/2024/06/18/au-niger-un-mouvement-rebelle-annonce-avoir-mis-hors-d-usage-une-partie-d-un-oleoduc_6241087_3212.html
Lesutis, G. (2019). How to understand a xevelopment corridor? The case of Lamu Port–South Sudan–Ethiopia-Transport Corridor in Kenya. *Area, 52*(3), 600–608.
Mani, A., & Mukand, S. (2007). Democracy, visibility and public good provision. *Journal of Development Economics, 83*(2), 506–529.
Masaki, T. (2018). The political economy of aid allocation in Africa: Evidence from Zambia. *African Studies Review, 61*(01), 55–82.
Mfula, C. (2021). Zambia's new president vows to cut 'unsustainable' public debt. *Reuters*. Retrieved June 05, 2022, from https://reut.rs/3SvU1Cy
Mitchell, T. (2002). *Rule of experts*. University of California Press.
Mohan, G., & Lampert, B. (2013). Negotiating China: Reinserting African Agency into China-Africa relations. *African Affairs, 112*(446), 92–110.
Moumoni, G. (2014, April). China and Liberia: Engagement in a Post-Conflict Country 2003–2013, *South African Institute for International Affairs (SAAIA)*. Retrieved March 12, 2024, from https://cisp.cachefly.net/assets/articles/attachments/49418_saia_sop_182_moumouni_20140503.pdf
Musungu, N. (2019). Africa: Magufuli reveals 'strange' conditions set by investors for African Countries. *Nairobi News*. Retrieved May 25, 2022, from https://bit.ly/3A6LKhp
Muyanga, P. (2022, May 20). Attorney-General appeals court order to make SGR tender public. *Business Daily*. Retrieved May 22, 2022, from https://bit.ly/3QOPaKS
Nantulya, P., (2021, March 2). Reshaping African Agency in China-Africa relations. *Africa Centre for Strategic Studies*. Retrieved March 12, 2024, from https://africacenter.org/spotlight/reshaping-african-agency-china-africa-relations/
Neema, C.-G. B. (2024, April 16). 'La CNPC fait une avance de 400 millions de dollars à la junte au Niger' [CNPC makes a $400 million advance to the junta in Niger], *Le Projet Afrique Chine* [The China Africa Project]. Retrieved November 10, 2024, from https://projetafriquechine.com/2024/04/16/la-cnpc-fait-une-avance-de-400-millions-de-dollars-a-la-junte-au-niger/

Nugent, P. (2019). *Boundaries, communities and state-making in West Africa: The centrality of the margins*. Cambridge University Press.

Ofstad, A., & Tjønneland, E. (2019). Zambia's looming debt crisis – is China to blame? *Chr. Michelsen Institute*. Retrieved June 18, 2022, from https://bit.ly/3BLShiv

Olander, E. (2021). *With an eye on his legacy, Kenya's president pressures Chinese contractors to finish road projects before he leaves office*, The China Global South Project. Retrieved January 05, 2024, from https://bit.ly/3JD8g4l

Otieno, J. (2020, March 15). Protect Kenyan contractors from Chinese — senators. *The Star*.

Paget, D. (2017). Tanzania: Shrinking space and opposition protest. *Journal of Democracy, 28*(3), 153–167.

Paget, D. (2021). Tanzania: The authoritarian landslide. *Journal of Democracy, 32*(2), 61–76.

Pairault, T. (2019). Lin Yifu, l'Afrique et le Modèle Chinois d'émergence [Lin Yifyu, Africa and the Chinese Development Model]. Revue de la Régulation. Capitalisme, Institutions, Pouvoirs, 25. Retrieved February 09, 2021, from https://bit.ly/3u0mqD8

Parliament of Kenya. (2022). *The National Assembly – The Hansard (Wed, 2nd February 2022)*. Nairobi: The Parliament of Kenya. Retrieved June 30, 2022, from https://bit.ly/3p3GdS9

Péclard, D., Kernen, A., & Khan-Mohammad, G. (2020). États d'émergence. Le gouvernement de la croissance et du développement en Afrique [States of émergence. The governance of growth and Development in Africa]. *Critique Internationale, 89*, 9–27.

Procopio, M. (2019). Kenyan agency in Kenya-China relations: Contestation, cooperation and passivity. In C. Alden & M. Power (Eds.), *New directions in Africa-China Studies* (pp. 173–186). Routledge.

Reboredo, R. (2021). Disaggregating development: A critical analysis of Sino-African megaprojects. *Progress in Development Studies, 21*, 86–104.

Reid, H., & Mfula, C. (2021). Zambia's Chinese debt nearly twice official estimate, study finds. *Reuters*. Retrieved April 03, 2022, from https://reut.rs/3P9HOAq

Reuters. (2021). Zambia owes nearly $27 billion in foreign and local public debt. *Reuters*. Retrieved June 12, 2023, from https://reut.rs/3QveOnM

Robins, F. (2013). The uniqueness of Chinese outward Foreign Direct Investment. *Asian Business & Management, 12*(5), 525–537.

Roque, P. C. (2021). *Governing in the shadows*. Hurst Publishing.

Shinn, D. H., & Eisenman, J. (2023). *China's relations with Africa: A new era of strategic engagement*. Columbia University Press.

Sibiri, H. (2020). The emerging phenomenon of Anti-Chinese Populism in Africa: Evidence from Zambia, Zimbabwe and Ghana. *Insight on Africa, 13*(1), 7–27.

Soulé-Kohndou, F. (2019a, January 3). How to negotiate infrastructure deals with China: Four things African governments need to get right. *The Conversation*. Retrieved March 07, 2023, from https://bit.ly/3CsXFWY

Soulé-Kohndou, F. (2019b). Bureaucratic agency and power asymmetry in Benin-China relations. In C. Alden & M. Power (Eds.), *New directions in Africa-China Studies* (pp. 189–204). Routledge.

Tang, X. (2023). China's Belt and Road Initiative and African industrialisation. *Wenhua Zhongheng: Quarterly Journal of Chinese Thought, 1*(3), 30–45. https://thetricontinental.org/wp-content/uploads/2023/10/20231001_WHZH_Vol1_No3_EN.pdf

Tan-Mullins, M., & Mohan, G. (2013). The potential of corporate environmental responsibility of Chinese state-owned enterprises in Africa. *Environment, Development and Sustainability, 15*, 265–284. https://doi.org/10.1007/s10668-012-9409-x

Taylor, I., & Xiao, Y. (2009). A case of mistaken identity: "China Inc." and Its "Imperialism" in Sub-Saharan Africa. *Asian Politics & Policy, 1*(4), 709–725.

The Africa Report. (2021). Zambia: Lungu inaugurates projects ahead of election. *The Africa Report*. Retrieved April 06, 2022, from https://bit.ly/3p8XskZ

Tull, D. M. (2006). China's engagement in Africa: Scope, significance and consequences. *Journal of Modern African Studies, 44*(3), 459–479.

Van Der Westhuizen, J. (2007). Glitz, glamour and the Gautrain: Mega-projects as political symbols. *Politikon, 34*(4), 333–351.

Wafula, P. (2018, December 10). Chinese Firm withholds key detail in SGR deal review. *Daily Nation*.

Wethal, U. (2019). Building Africa's infrastructure: Reinstating history in infrastructure debates. *Forum for Development Studies, 43*(3), 473–499.

Xinhua News. (2021). Zambian leader commissions Chinese-built power plant. *Xinhua News*. Retrieved June 23, 2022, from https://bit.ly/3zJqLPY

Trading Natural Resources for Infrastructure: A Sustainable Approach to Financing Africa's Infrastructure Gap?

Hagan Sibiri

Introduction

One of the core pillars of the African Union's (AU) *Agenda 2063* is infrastructure development, reflecting the continent's persistent and well-documented infrastructure deficit. Africa's infrastructure deficit, widely regarded as a major constraint on investment and economic growth (Signé, 2020), is most pronounced in transport networks, electricity generation and distribution, telecommunications, and water supply, all of which are foundational to sustainable development. Tackling this challenge demands billions of dollars annually yet securing adequate financing remains a major obstacle. Infrastructure development in Africa relies largely on domestic resources, international donor support, and loans from multilateral lending institutions (Gutman et al., 2015). However, domestic financing remains constrained by weak revenue mobilisation, while external resources are dwindling amid aid fatigue and shifting priorities in development cooperation. Moreover, the stringent conditions tied

H. Sibiri (✉)
Africa-China Centre for Policy and Advisory (ACCPA), Accra, Ghana

L. G. Adu Amoah (ed.), *Africa-China Relations*,
https://doi.org/10.1007/978-981-95-4370-0_8

to traditional multilateral financing have discouraged many African countries from fully accessing these resources. The resulting financing gap has opened space for emerging and non-traditional partners to complement ongoing efforts in meeting the continent's infrastructure needs.

China has become a major development partner for Africa, offering an alternative approach to infrastructure financing. Its role in the continent's infrastructure market has reshaped strategies for closing gaps and continues to hold strong appeal for African governments. Africa's turn to Chinese funding models is partly a response to the international donor community's neglect of this sector during the 1990s. Unlike traditional Western donors and Western-led financial institutions, China has offered what is seen as a more flexible and less bureaucratic financing model (Munyati, 2024). Between 2000 and 2010, during a period of intensified engagement, it invested over US$75 billion in more than 1700 projects across 50 African countries (Morlin-Yron, 2016). At the 2018 Forum on China–Africa Cooperation (FOCAC) in Beijing, African leaders welcomed China's approach under the Belt and Road Initiative (BRI). This strategy emphasises alignment with the AU's *Agenda 2063*, particularly its infrastructure and industrial development programmes.

The influx of Chinese financing has enabled African leaders to pursue priority, and at times populist, infrastructure projects, but it has also generated considerable concern among scholars, policy analysts, and critics. Key apprehensions centre on debt sustainability, economic dependency, political influence, and the reinforcement of authoritarian governance in some countries. Zambia's debt trajectory illustrates these risks. By the end of 2021, Chinese creditors held an estimated US$6 billion of its external public debt, about 35% of total external liabilities (Bräutigam & Huang, 2023). This exposure has been a major driver of Zambia's unsustainable debt levels. The country fell into arrears with Chinese creditors as early as 2019, deepening a fiscal crisis after years of being classified at high risk of debt distress. A similar pattern is evident in Angola, China's largest borrower in Africa. Between 2000 and 2019, it accounted for nearly 30% of all Chinese loan commitments to the continent. By 2020, half of Angola's US$40 billion debt stock was owed to Chinese institutions (Bräutigam & Huang, 2023). These cases highlight a critical policy dilemma: how can African countries pursue ambitious infrastructure development while safeguarding fiscal autonomy and mitigating the risks of debt distress?

Amid ongoing debates on infrastructure financing, the 'resources-for-infrastructure' model has resurfaced as a key feature of China's global strategy, particularly in Latin America (Davis et al., 2023) and Africa (Zongwe, 2010). With historical precedents in Japan, India, China, and post-war Southeast Asia (Sudo, 1992; Bräutigam, 2009), the model exchanges natural resources for direct infrastructure development. In practice, resource endowments are leveraged to secure projects without immediate cash outlays or conventional debt obligations. Angola pioneered this approach in Africa through an 'oil-for-infrastructure' deal with China dedicated exclusively to infrastructure financing. Since then, several countries, including Ghana, Guinea, the Republic of Congo, and the Democratic Republic of Congo, have adopted variations. Between 2004 and 2018, about 30 such agreements were signed across sub-Saharan Africa (Mihalyi et al., 2022). Yet a critical question remains: does trading natural resources for infrastructure offer a sustainable solution to Africa's infrastructure deficit while mitigating debt risks? The answer is mixed. While the model provides an alternative to conventional borrowing, it raises concerns over resource sovereignty, value for money, and long-term economic implications (Davis et al., 2023).

This chapter critically examines the Africa–China 'resource-for-infrastructure' model as a long-term mechanism for financing infrastructure in resource-rich African countries. It employs a qualitative approach that combines case studies with a literature review. The analysis focuses on Angola and Ghana, drawing on parliamentary records, government reports, media sources, and publicly available data to assess the governance frameworks underpinning each agreement. These cases highlight contrasting trajectories: Ghana, once regarded as a model economy in West Africa, entered a resource-backed deal amid economic decline, while Angola, a less-studied Lusophone country, presents a different but equally instructive experience. The chapter is structured into four sections. The first analyses Africa's persistent infrastructure deficit, highlighting structural and financial barriers and tracing the evolution of financing models, with a focus on China's growing role. The second critically evaluates existing mechanisms, domestic revenues, foreign aid, multilateral loans, and public–private partnerships, emphasising their limitations and declining efficacy. The third section introduces the resources-for-infrastructure model as a context-appropriate solution for countries with abundant natural resources but limited fiscal space. Using the Angola and Ghana cases, it examines how commodities such as oil and bauxite are exchanged for infrastructure without immediate debt accumulation. Framed by historical experiences from Asia and Latin America, these examples reveal both the model's strategic potential and its risks, including transparency gaps, environmental concerns, and questions of long-term sustainability. The final section assesses the model's effectiveness and governance requirements. It concludes that, while the model offers a valuable alternative for infrastructure financing, it must be implemented carefully and integrated into a broader, diversified strategy aligned with national development priorities.

Africa's Infrastructure Gap And Challenges

Africa's infrastructure deficit is well documented. Road access covers only 34% of the population, compared with 50% in other developing regions, while electricity reaches just 30%, far below the 70–90% seen elsewhere. Only 5% of agricultural land is irrigated despite abundant water resources, and internet penetration remains low compared with other regions (Programme for Infrastructure Development in Africa [PIDA], n.d.). Infrastructure development is therefore widely recognised as a critical challenge for the continent, essential to advancing development and prosperity. Despite measures such as public–private partnerships, the African Development Bank (2023a) estimates an annual financing gap of US$130–170 billion. Urban areas face overcrowding and strained services, while many rural regions lack basic amenities. This widespread deficit constrains growth and intra-African trade, which remains around 15%—well below North America (54%), the European Union (70%), and Asia (60%) (African Development Bank, 2024a).

Africa's infrastructure challenges are complex and deeply structural (Haar, 2023). Financial constraints are central, as many countries struggle to mobilise sufficient domestic resources. This stems from narrow tax bases, large informal economies, and weak public financial management systems (Moore et al., 2018). Illicit financial flows and capital flight, estimated at over US$50 billion annually, further erode national revenues (African Union & United Nations Economic Commission for Africa, 2015). Despite abundant natural resources, revenues are often poorly managed or lost through opaque contracts and corruption, leaving many countries fiscally constrained and dependent on external financing. Political risks and weak legal frameworks deter private investment and complicate project delivery, while limited technical capacity contributes to cost overruns and delays. These challenges are evident in the slow pace of regional integration, partly due to poor coordination of cross-border projects. Climate change adds further pressure, highlighting the need for resilient infrastructure, while rapid urbanisation and population growth intensify demand, underscoring the urgent need for continuous investment.

Efforts to address Africa's infrastructure gap have evolved over time. In the post-independence period, development was largely state led, supported by bilateral aid and multilateral lending. Structural adjustment programmes in the 1980s and 1990s, however, curtailed public investment, creating a growing backlog of unmet needs (Akyeampong & Bates, 2010). In the early 2000s, infrastructure regained prominence through initiatives such as the New Partnership for Africa's Development (NEPAD), launched in 2001 by the AU to promote sustainable development, regional integration, and poverty reduction. A decade later, the Programme for Infrastructure Development in Africa (PIDA) was adopted as a strategic framework for continental infrastructure development. These initiatives sought to coordinate regional projects and attract private-sector investment. PIDA (n.d.) estimates that its programmes will require approximately US$360 billion in funding between 2011 and 2040. The AU's *Agenda 2063*, adopted in 2015, prioritises modern, integrated infrastructure to facilitate the free movement of goods and people (African Union, 2015). External partners, particularly China, have played a significant role in addressing Africa's infrastructure gap, aligning their global BRI with the continent's infrastructure agenda despite concerns about debt sustainability. China is now Africa's largest financier and developer of infrastructure (Bo et al., 2024), delivering over 12,000 kilometres of railways and roads, expanding nearly 20 ports, and constructing more than 80 major power facilities in the past decade. Valued at over US$700 billion (CGTN, 2023), these projects highlight the substantial impact of Chinese engagement on Africa's infrastructure development.

Despite ongoing efforts, Africa's infrastructure gap continues to widen as development fails to keep pace with population growth and urbanisation. The scale and nature of the deficit vary across regions and sectors. In the sub-Saharan region, energy infrastructure is particularly weak, with annual power outages costing some countries 1–2% of Gross Domestic Product (GDP) (Avordeh et al., 2024). Transport deficits are most severe in rural areas, where millions lack reliable road networks. Digital infrastructure shows stark urban-rural divides, while water systems face both quantity and quality challenges due to poor maintenance and inefficiency. These deficiencies have broad economic, social, and developmental impacts. Economically, poor infrastructure raises business costs, reduces competitiveness, and deters investment, with firm efficiency significantly affected in some countries (World Bank, 2024a). Socially, inadequate infrastructure exacerbates inequalities by limiting access to education, healthcare, and employment. Weak transport networks restrict market access, particularly for rural producers, while unreliable electricity stifles industrial growth. Insufficient water and sanitation infrastructure contributes to poor health outcomes. At a regional level, limited infrastructure hampers integration and constrains the benefits of larger, connected markets. Collectively, these challenges continue to slow progress toward the Sustainable Development Goals (SDGs) and the transformational objectives of the AU's *Agenda 2063*.

Overview Of Africa's Infrastructure Financing Landscape

Infrastructure financing in Africa has undergone significant changes in recent decades, with traditional models shaping the continent's development trajectory. Yet these models remain insufficient to meet the demands of rapid urbanisation and sustained economic growth. African governments continue to depend largely on domestic resources, international aid, and multilateral financing, each offering distinct advantages and challenges in closing the continent's persistent infrastructure gap (Gutman et al., 2015). Domestic resource mobilisation through taxation and public savings represents the most conventional financing method. Unlike debt-based mechanisms, it gives governments full discretion over project design and implementation. However, its impact is constrained by limited fiscal capacity and competing public expenditure priorities. The median tax-to-GDP ratio across Africa stands at 16.5%, well below the average of 34.3% in the Organisation for Economic Co-operation and Development (OECD) countries and 23.1% in Latin America and Caribbean (Enache, 2020). This shortfall undermines the ability of governments to generate substantial funding for infrastructure development. Foster et al. (2022) highlight that on-budget infrastructure spending in developing countries, including those in Africa, has averaged just 1% of GDP—or 5% of public expenditure—and has been declining. Between 2010 and 2018, infrastructure investment fell by nearly one-third, with the road sector recording the sharpest decline (Foster et al., 2022). While some governments have turned to domestic financial instruments to mitigate this gap, underdeveloped capital markets across much of the continent have limited their effectiveness.

Official Development Assistance (ODA) has long been a key source of infrastructure financing for African countries, with OECD donors playing a central role. In recent years, however, the predictability of aid flows has diminished, as donor priorities have shifted and funding has become increasingly tied to stringent procurement rules, environmental standards, and political considerations (Usman & Washington, 2024). These changes have reduced the volume of aid available for infrastructure, making it more difficult for African governments to secure sufficient external support and driving them to seek alternative financing options. Multilateral financial institutions such as the World Bank and the African Development Bank remain pivotal in Africa's infrastructure development. Beyond direct funding, they provide technical expertise, policy advice, and mechanisms that help crowd in private investment through credit guarantees and political risk insurance. Yet their financing is often accompanied by strict governance and environmental requirements, which, while important for sustainability, tend to prolong project approval and implementation. Emerging institutions such as the Asian Infrastructure Investment Bank and the New Development Bank offer additional opportunities for African countries to diversify financing sources. Nonetheless, complex application procedures and lengthy approval processes continue to constrain timely access to these funds.

Given fiscal constraints, Public-Private Partnerships (PPPs) have emerged as a viable model for infrastructure investment in several African countries (van Wieringen & Zajontz, 2023; Yescombe, 2017). By leveraging the strengths of both public and private actors, PPPs enhance cost-effectiveness, improve service delivery, and accelerate the implementation and coverage of infrastructure projects. These arrangements allow governments to leverage private-sector expertise and resources while sharing risks and responsibilities. PPPs have achieved moderate success, particularly in telecommunications and energy, where returns are clearer. However, outcomes vary across countries and sectors due to differences in regulatory frameworks, political stability, and market conditions (World Bank, 2024a). Despite the establishment of PPP units and enabling legislation, many African countries continue to face challenges in project design, risk allocation, and contract management. The World Bank's PPP Resource Centre recommends supporting PPPs with guarantees, subsidies, and co-financing to enhance project bankability and attract private investment, while strategically balancing risks and benefits to ensure sustainable and efficient infrastructure development (World Bank, 2024b).

As shown above, traditional infrastructure financing models face significant limitations, resulting in a persistent funding gap. Domestic resource mobilisation is hampered by low tax-to-GDP ratios and large informal sectors, while international aid remains both inadequate and unpredictable. Multilateral financing is often slowed by complex bureaucratic processes, and PPPs demand strong institutional capacities that are frequently underdeveloped. In this context, the search for alternative financing models that better reflect Africa's resource potential has become increasingly urgent. One such approach is the resource-backed infrastructure model, referred to hereafter as the *Resources-for-Infrastructure barter model.* This mechanism allows resource-rich countries with limited fiscal space to leverage natural resources to finance infrastructure projects without requiring immediate cash outflows (Davis et al., 2023).

The Africa–China Resources-For-Infrastructure Barter Model: Old Mechanism, New Terrain

Africa possesses vast reserves of both renewable and non-renewable resources. The continent holds approximately 30% of the world's remaining mineral resources, 12% of global oil reserves, 8% of natural gas, 40% of gold, 90% of chromium and platinum, and the largest global reserves of uranium, cobalt, and diamonds (United Nations Environment Programme, 2021). These resources account for about 70% of Africa's total exports and 28% of its collective GDP, with the extractive sector projected to generate more than US$30 billion in annual revenue for African governments over the next two decades (African Development Bank, 2016). In 2014, for instance, exports of natural resources, including crude oil, natural gas, and metals, contributed an average of 25% of government revenues across the continent (see Fig. 1) (Galeazzi et al., 2020). Such figures underscore the central role of extractive resources as a source of wealth, political influence, and, at times, conflict in Africa. Nonetheless, the sector continues to represent one of the continent's most promising avenues for investment.

Over the years, China has become a leading external investor in Africa's resource sector, particularly in extractive industries. Data from the China–Africa Research Initiative at Johns Hopkins University's School of Advanced International Studies (SAIS-CARI, 2025) show that China's

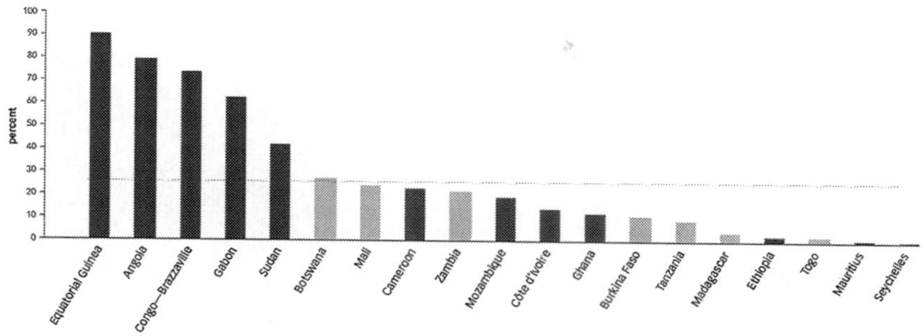

Fig. 1 Share of government revenue from natural resource exports in selected African countries, 2014 (as cited in Galeazzi et al., 2020). Countries where hydrocarbon revenues exceed those from mineral energy materials are highlighted in blue

annual direct investment flows to Africa surged from US$75 million in 2003 to a peak of US$5.5 billion in 2008. Although these flows have fluctuated, falling to US$1.8 billion in 2022, China's cumulative investments have had a profound impact on Africa's economic landscape, consistently exceeding those of the United States until 2022. Notably, Chinese investment has been concentrated in a handful of resource-rich countries, reflecting China's rapid economic expansion and growing demand for raw materials. Between 2006 and 2017 alone, Chinese investment in Africa's mining sector reached an estimated US$33 billion (Ericsson et al., 2020).

While African governments have embraced China's strong interest in the continent's abundant natural resources, a critical question persists: can this engagement help Africa overcome the so-called resource curse? Past evidence shows that many resource-rich developing economies, including those in Africa, have struggled to translate their natural wealth into sustained development and economic growth (Venables, 2016). In response, the AU's *Agenda 2063* outlines a people-centred vision that seeks to harness natural resources to promote inclusive socio-economic development across the continent (African Union, 2015). A flagship initiative under this framework is the Africa Mining Vision (AMV), which calls for transparent and efficient resource governance as a foundation for sustainable growth. The AMV urges African countries to move beyond conventional extractive practices by embedding mineral resource management within broader development strategies, rather than focusing narrowly on maximising fiscal revenues (African Union, 2009). Although implementation has progressed slowly, Oxfam International (2017) views the AMV as a transformative framework with significant potential to advance sustainable development across Africa.

With China's growing interest and dominance in Africa's mineral resources (Benabdallah, 2024; Burrier & Sheehy, 2023), several resource-rich African countries have adopted the strategy of exchanging natural resources for infrastructure projects or financing. While resource-backed transactions are not new globally, Angola was the first African country to implement this approach through an 'oil-for-infrastructure' deal with China (Zongwe, 2010). Since then, variations of the Angolan model have been replicated across the continent, in Ghana, Guinea, Congo-Brazzaville, and the Democratic Republic of Congo, resulting in approximately 30 resource-backed agreements between China and African countries between 2004 and 2018 (Mihalyi et al., 2022; Purwins, 2023).

Globally, resource-backed transaction models have a longer history. Post-war Southeast Asian countries, for instance, benefited from agreements with Japan that exchanged natural resources for industrial products. These arrangements provided Southeast Asian nations with access to Japan's advanced industrial technology and manufactured goods, while ensuring Japan a reliable supply of raw materials to sustain its rapid economic growth (Sudo, 1992). Similar dynamics emerged in Japan's engagements with India and China, albeit with distinct structural features. Beginning in 1958 with India and in 1978 with China, Japan established long-term trade agreements, different from conventional investment contracts, that included resource-backed concessional loans. In China's case, Japan extended low-interest loans to finance a US$10 billion package of industrial technology and materials, which China repaid through exports of crude oil and coal (Bräutigam, 2009). Comparable models have also appeared in Latin America, such as Venezuela's oil-backed deal with China (Mihalyi et al., 2022; Giacalone & Ruiz, 2013). Collectively, these cases illustrate the wider application of resource-backed financing across different historical and regional contexts.

In essence, the resources-for-infrastructure barter model represents both a continuation of historical arrangements in Asia and an adaptation of the traditional barter system to address infrastructure challenges in resource-rich African countries. Historical precedents offer valuable lessons for Africa, particularly in relation to China, which, before reaching its current stage of modern development, exchanged portions of its resource wealth with Japan in return for industrial technology and development materials. Drawing on these past experiences, China has applied similar strategies in its contemporary partnerships with African countries (Bräutigam, 2009; Zongwe, 2010).

The model generally operates through agreements in which host governments commit future natural resource production or revenue streams in exchange for infrastructure development. Instead of relying on immediate cash payments or conventional debt financing, countries pledge a portion of their natural resources, such as oil or minerals, as collateral or repayment (Mihalyi et al., 2022; Venables, 2016; Zongwe, 2010). In the Africa–China context, three main actors are typically involved: the host government, the foreign government or its development bank, and the construction companies implementing the projects. China, through its state-owned banks, provides loans for infrastructure in return for access to mineral resources, while its state-owned construction firms deliver the projects. Repayment is secured through the export of the pledged resources. For instance, Ghana committed part of its bauxite reserves in exchange for US$2 billion worth of infrastructure projects to be developed by China's Sinohydro Corporation Limited. The arrangement includes establishing a domestic bauxite refining industry, with revenues from refined bauxite allocated to repay project costs (Parliament of Ghana, 2018).

In a nutshell, the resources-for-infrastructure barter model is underpinned by several economic theories, including resource-backed development, international trade economics, and development finance. At its foundation, it leverages comparative advantage by enabling resource-rich countries to utilise their natural endowments to address infrastructure deficits (Braun, 2019). It also incorporates principles of project finance, using future resource revenues as collateral for present-day infrastructure investment. This creates a mutually beneficial arrangement: host countries acquire critical infrastructure, while partner countries secure long-term access to strategic resources. Core features of the model include financing structures, resource-backed loans, and project delivery mechanisms (Mihalyi et al., 2022). China, for example, extends export credit lines secured by future resource revenues, with state-owned construction companies tasked with delivering the projects (see Table 1). The type and quantity of resources exchanged are defined in long-term contracts, while project selection, implementation, and monitoring are governed by bilateral agreements spanning government-to-government and commercial contracts. In some cases, the model also incorporates provisions for

Table 1 Basic structure of the resource-for-infrastructure model in Africa

Step	*Action*	*Parties Involved*	*Outcome*
1. Agreement	African countries agree to exchange resources for loans	African countries, China	China provides funds for infrastructure projects.
2. Resource rights	African countries grant China access to minerals or oil	African countries, China	China gets the right to exploit natural resources.
3. Infrastructure development	China sends state-owned companies to build infrastructure	China, Chinese construction companies	Infrastructure projects are built in Africa.
4. Repayment	Natural resources are exported to repay loans	African countries, China	Exported minerals or oil repay the cost of infrastructure.

technology transfer, local content participation, and technical skills development.

Angola's 'Oil-for-Infrastructure' Agreement with China

Angola is richly endowed with natural resources, including crude oil, iron ore, diamonds, and copper. Yet its economy remains heavily dependent on the oil sector, which accounts for more than 90% of total exports and about 60% of government revenues (International Monetary Fund, 2024). This reliance highlights the centrality of oil to Angola's fiscal and external balances. Since the end of its civil war in 2002, Angola has become a key destination for Chinese investment, receiving an estimated US$46 billion through 270 loan agreements between 2000 and 2023 (Boston University GDP Centre, 2025). These loans, primarily resource-backed, have been pivotal to post-war reconstruction, particularly in energy, transportation, and telecommunications.

A turning point in Angola–China relations came in 2004, when the China National Petroleum Corporation established joint ventures with *Sonangol*, Angola's state-owned oil company, to support oil and gas production, industrial petroleum activities, and infrastructure development (Ferreira, 2008). In the same year, China's Exim Bank extended a US$4.5 billion loan in exchange for oil supplies, marking the introduction of the Africa–China resource-for-infrastructure financing model (Alden & Alves, 2009). By 2010, Exim Bank had provided oil-backed credit lines worth

US$10.5 billion to finance public investment projects in Angola (Corkin, 2011). These agreements, offered at a 1.5% interest rate with a 17-year repayment period and a five-year grace period, stipulated that Chinese companies approved by Beijing would execute 70% of the construction projects, while the remaining 30% of contracts were reserved for the Angolan private sector. In practice, however, local participation often meant the hiring of Angolan labour rather than meaningful involvement of domestic firms (Corkin, 2011).

In 2018, the China Development Bank issued an additional US$2 billion loan for infrastructure projects (CGTN, 2018). Although details of this agreement remain undisclosed, it underscores the entrenchment of resource-backed financing in the Angola–China partnership. According to the China Africa Research Initiative at Johns Hopkins University's School of Advanced International Studies (SAIS-CARI, 2024), Angola received roughly US$43 billion in Chinese infrastructure loan commitments between 2000 and 2018, making it the largest African recipient of such funding.

This Angola–China financing approach, now widely referred to as the 'Angola model', centres on *Sonangol* supplying crude oil in exchange for infrastructure financing for housing, railways, and roads. While the model facilitated large-scale post-conflict reconstruction and reshaped Luanda's skyline with new infrastructure, it has also been criticised for favouring politically connected elites and producing substandard housing projects (Onishi, 2017; Benazeraf & Alves, 2014).

Ghana's 'Bauxite-for-Infrastructure' Agreement with China

Over the past two decades, Ghana has increasingly turned to Chinese financing to address infrastructure deficits in the energy, transport, and technology sectors, with resource-backed loans emerging as a key strategy. Between 2007 and 2019, Ghana secured at least seven such loans from China (see Table 2) (Agyei, 2023). Among the most notable is the controversial US$2 billion 'bauxite-for-infrastructure' agreement signed in 2018. Under the Master Project Support Agreement (MPSA) between the Government of Ghana and *Sinohydro* Corporation Limited, a Chinese state-owned construction firm, Sinohydro committed to independently finance and deliver infrastructure projects, including roads, interchanges, housing, and hospitals, worth US$2 billion. In return, Ghana pledged repayment through proceeds from refined bauxite, alumina, or

Table 2 Ghana's resource-collateralised loans from China: 2007–2019

Year	*Amount (US$ million)*	*Collateralised Resource*	*Purpose*	*Sector*
2007	306	Cocoa export	Bui hydropower project (400 MW)	Energy/ power
2012	151	Cocoa export	1st and 2nd Additional finance for Bui Hydropower (400mw)	Energy/ power
2013	850	Oil export	Western Corridor Gas Infrastructure Project (Jubilee Oil Field)	Energy/ power
2013	150	Oil export	Integrated National Security Communications Enhancement Network (ALPHA) project	ICT
2019	186	Oil export	Eleven coastal fishing landing site construction projects	Agriculture
2019	211	Oil export	Accra Intelligent Traffic Management system and road completion	Transport
2019	550	Bauxite export	Construction and rehabilitation of selected roads and interchanges (Phase 1 of MPSA)	Transport

aluminium, with extraction linked to deposits in the ecologically sensitive *Atewa* forest reserve (Parliament of Ghana, 2018).

A distinctive feature of the MPSA is its emphasis on value addition. Sinohydro was not granted rights to mine or export Ghana's bauxite. Instead, the Ghana Integrated Aluminium Development Corporation (GIADEC) was established to oversee the development of bauxite mines and refinery operations. Revenues from processed products were intended to service the repayment, thereby advancing local industrialisation. While the deal was structured to limit debt exposure through a special-purpose vehicle, concerns have persisted regarding transparency, environmental risks, particularly mining in *Atewa* forest reserve, and Ghana's growing dependence on Chinese financing.

By 2021, three years after the agreement, only US$100 million had been disbursed, with no projects fully completed (JoyOnline, 2021). Some progress has since been made, including the completion of the Tamale Interchange in 2022, the first road interchange in Ghana's Northern Region, alongside other ongoing works. However, delays in establishing bauxite processing facilities, coupled with broader economic challenges, have significantly impeded implementation. For instance, construction of the three-tier road interchange in Sekondi-Takoradi, the first of its kind in the Western Region, has come to a complete halt. These setbacks have been compounded by Ghana's economic crisis, which forced the government to seek an International Monetary Fund (IMF) bailout. The bailout conditions, which require the renegotiation of earlier agreements such as the MPSA, have further complicated implementation. Consequently, the rollout of the MPSA has diverged substantially from its original vision (Adams, 2023).

The Promise and Pitfalls of Trading Natural Resources For Infrastructure

The replication of the resources-for-infrastructure barter model in Africa represents a major shift from conventional infrastructure financing approaches on the continent. Unlike credit facilities in global bond markets, aid, or public–private partnerships, this model directly links the utilisation of natural resources to the delivery of infrastructure projects. It offers several advantages: countries can fast-track priority infrastructure without immediately increasing foreign debt or depleting foreign exchange reserves (Braun, 2019), while also reducing reliance on traditional multilateral institutions by accessing more affordable financing, particularly valuable for nations with limited entry to global financial markets (Mihalyi et al., 2022).

Yet these benefits are accompanied by significant risks. Potential challenges include the misvaluation of resource assets, reduced fiscal flexibility, and the possibility of long-term resource lock-in (Benefo & Addaney, 2021). Other concerns centre on opaque contracting, environmental damage, and the overall sustainability of such arrangements (Mihalyi et al., 2022; Purwins, 2023; Ding et al., 2021; IMANI Africa, 2018). The danger of resource depletion is particularly acute, as repayment schedules often incentivise accelerated extraction, which can deplete resources prematurely, leaving countries with infrastructure but diminished natural wealth (Rönnbäck, 2020). Moreover, while distinct from traditional debt, these arrangements still raise debt sustainability concerns. Long-term resource commitments can become onerous if commodity prices fall or extraction costs rise. They may also erode sovereignty, constraining policy options through binding resource-backed obligations. These risks are compounded by the frequent opacity of agreements and the lack of public oversight. Reflecting these concerns, the African Development Bank (2023b) has sharply criticised resource-backed loans, warning they are 'a disaster for Africa' because of their secrecy and potential to create unsustainable debt burdens. Its President, Akinwumi Adesina, has further stressed that Africa's US$824 billion debt load is aggravated by non-transparent resource-based loans, which undermine long-term development prospects and weaken public trust (African Development Bank, 2024b).

Notable, the resource-for-infrastructure model has yet to demonstrate effectiveness as a driver of broad-based economic transformation (Acheampong & Mensah, 2018). While it has accelerated infrastructure development, its contributions to industrial growth, job creation, and economic diversification remain limited. Its long-term viability will depend on balancing immediate infrastructure needs with sustainable resource management, fair resource valuation, environmental safeguards, and meaningful technology and skills transfer. To maximise developmental impact, infrastructure projects must be embedded within coherent national strategies that strengthen linkages with local industries and align with broader development goals. This will likely require reforms such as expanding local participation, ensuring practical skills transfer, and enhancing connections to domestic economic activities. The model's continued relevance will also hinge on its adaptability to emerging priorities, including climate change adaptation and digital infrastructure. As Konijn (2014) observed, a point still pertinent today, the sustainability of the approach remains uncertain without critical reforms to ensure inclusive and transformative development outcomes.

Angola and Ghana provide valuable early lessons in the use of resource-backed financing. While such agreements are often associated with raw material exports, Ghana's bauxite-for-infrastructure deal, explicitly linked to local value addition, illustrates how the model can be aligned with Africa's industrialisation agenda. Realising this potential, however, requires a deliberate shift toward beneficiation, technology transfer, and economic diversification in line with the Africa Mining Vision and broader Pan-African development frameworks. Moreover, Angola's longer experience with the model underscores the importance of diversifying both funding sources and repayment mechanisms, an insight that should guide other African countries considering similar strategies.

Having outlined the potential benefits and pitfalls of the resource-for-infrastructure model, its applicability to other resource-rich African countries depends on several critical factors, notably the quality of natural resources and the strength of institutional frameworks. Countries with substantial reserves of strategic minerals may stand to benefit the most, particularly when access to traditional financing is limited or prohibitively expensive. However, successful implementation requires more than resource endowment: it hinges on strong negotiating capacity, effective legal and governance systems, and mechanisms that guarantee value-for-money and efficient project delivery. Evidence from Ghana and Angola demonstrates that resource wealth alone is insufficient; institutional capacity is indispensable for managing these complex arrangements effectively (Purwins, 2023). This conclusion is reinforced by the World Bank's Independent Evaluation Group (2023), which finds that international partnerships underpinned by stronger institutions tend to yield better outcomes and higher success ratings across Africa. Thus, while the model could theoretically be applied across resource-rich countries, its success is far more likely in contexts with well-established institutional frameworks capable of negotiating, implementing, and overseeing such agreements.

All in all, despite its appeal, the resource-for-infrastructure barter model has attracted significant criticism. Past experiences suggest that it can deliver critical infrastructure without immediate fiscal strain, but only under specific conditions, robust resource management, transparent contracts, and strong governance. Its long-term viability, therefore, depends less on the model itself and more on the institutions and safeguards governing its execution. Rather than being treated as a panacea for Africa's infrastructure deficit, the model should be integrated into a diversified financing strategy. This would involve evolving toward more flexible arrangements that blend resource-backed financing with conventional funding mechanisms, thereby enhancing risk management and adaptability to shifting economic conditions. Such an evolution is particularly urgent in light of implementation challenges. Done effectively, the model could provide resource-rich African countries with a more sustainable framework for leveraging their extractive industries to advance long-term development goals.

Conclusion

This chapter has examined the Africa–China resource-for-infrastructure barter model, underscoring its significance as a long-term financing mechanism for resource-rich African countries. The model is situated within China's evolving resource-backed financing strategy and Africa's broader ambition to convert natural wealth into sustainable development. Angola pioneered the approach through its oil-for-infrastructure agreement, explicitly directed toward public infrastructure delivery. Since then, several countries, including Ghana, Guinea, the Republic of Congo, and the Democratic Republic of Congo, have adopted variations, demonstrating its diffusion across the continent.

Strategically, the model serves both China and its African partners. For China, it guarantees access to critical resources while advancing commercial and geopolitical interests under the BRI. For African countries with limited access to conventional credit, it provides a context-specific alternative for financing infrastructure without immediate fiscal strain. Yet, as the cases of Angola and Ghana demonstrate, the model's effectiveness depends less on resource endowments than on governance quality, institutional oversight, and alignment with national development priorities. While it offers opportunities for fiscally constrained but resource-rich states, it also carries risks: fiscal opacity, limited domestic value addition, environmental degradation, and missed opportunities for skills transfer and technological upgrading. Reliance on Chinese firms and labour often undermines local participation, while the resource-intensive nature of agreements can accelerate unsustainable extraction.

To mitigate these risks, revenues from resource-backed deals must be channelled into diversified sectors through local-content provisions, sovereign wealth funds, industrialisation policies, human capital investment, and rigorous environmental safeguards. Institutional capacity, transparent negotiations, and effective contract enforcement are pivotal in ensuring long-term benefits. Furthermore, growing interest from other external partners, such as India, Russia, and Turkey, though currently modest, provides African states with an opportunity to diversify partnerships, reduce dependency, and strengthen bargaining leverage. Regional coordination can also enhance negotiating power, promote best practices, and align infrastructure projects with regional integration goals. The Africa Mining Vision (AMV) offers a normative framework for resource governance, but its impact has been constrained by weak institutions and political inertia.

Translating AMV principles into enforceable reforms remains critical, especially in the context of resource-backed deals. Priority measures include standardised contracts, mandatory transparency and disclosure requirements, robust environmental and social impact assessments, technology transfer mechanisms, independent regulatory oversight, and active civil society participation. Advancing these reforms will demand political will and institutional strength, but they are essential for ensuring that resource-for-infrastructure agreements support inclusive, transparent, and sustainable development.

Ultimately, the model should not be treated as a substitute for conventional financing but as one element of a diversified infrastructure financing strategy. Its role within Africa–China relations thus lie at the heart of the broader debate over partnership, pawnage, or peonage. On the one hand, well-governed agreements could foster genuine partnerships, delivering reciprocal benefits through infrastructure development, industrial upgrading, and technology transfer, while safeguarding African agency. On the other hand, poorly governed ones, risk entrenching asymmetric dependencies, reducing African states to pawns in China's strategic calculus, or worse, creating a form of economic peonage in which future resource revenues are mortgaged for short-term gains without achieving long-term sovereignty, diversification, or resilience. The future of this model, and its legacy in Africa–China relations, will therefore depend on whether African states can institutionalise robust governance frameworks, assert negotiation leverage, and strategically blend financing models to advance their development priorities within an evolving global political economy.

Abbreviations

AMV	Africa Mining Vision
AU	African Union
BRI	Belt and Road Initiative
FOCAC	Forum on China–Africa Cooperation
GDP	Gross Domestic Product
GIADEC	Ghana Integrated Aluminium Development Corporation
IMF	International Monetary Fund
MPSA	*Master Project Support Agreement*
NEPAD	New Partnership for Africa's Development
ODA	Official Development Assistance
OECD	Organisation for Economic Co-operation and Development

PIDA	Programme for Infrastructure Development in Africa
PPPs	Public-Private Partnerships
SDGs	Sustainable Development Goals

References

Acheampong, T., & Mensah, K. A. (2018). *Towards an integrated aluminium industry in Ghana: Some policy considerations.* Natural Resource Governance Institute.

Adams, K. A. (2023). Sinohydro abandons projects over IMF deal. *The Chronicle.* https://thechronicle.com.gh/sinohydro-abandons-projects-over-imf-deal-lays-off-304-workers-working-on-tdi-flyover-after-paying-them-three-months-salaries/

African Development Bank. (2016). *African Natural Resources Centre: Catalysing growth and development through effective natural resources management.* African Development Bank.

African Development Bank. (2023a). *Public-private partnerships needed to bridge Africa's infrastructure development gap.* African Development Bank. https://www.afdb.org/en/news-and-events/public-private-partnerships-needed-bridge-africas-infrastructure-development-gap-65936

African Development Bank. (2023b). *Natural resource-backed loans are a disaster for Africa, warn IMF and African Development Bank.* African Development Bank.https://www.afdb.org/en/news-and-events/press-releases/natural-resource-backed-loans-are-disaster-africa-warn-imf-and-african-development-bank-64852

African Development Bank. (2024a). *Integrate Africa.* African Development Bank. https://www.afdb.org/en/the-high-5/integrate-africa

African Development Bank. (2024b). *Africa's $824 billion debt burden and opaque resource-backed loans hinder its potential, African Development Bank President warns.* African Development Bank. https://www.afdb.org/en/news-and-events/press-releases/africas-824-billion-debt-burden-and-opaque-resource-backed-loans-hinder-its-potential-african-development-bank-president-warns-70183

African Union. (2009). *Africa mining vision.* African Union. https://au.int/en/documents/20100212/africa-mining-vision-amv

African Union. (2015). *Agenda 2063: The Africa we want.* African Union. https://au.int/Agenda2063/popular_version

African Union & United Nations Economic Commission for Africa. (2015). *Illicit financial flows: Report of the high-level panel on illicit financial flows from Africa.* AU/ECA.

Agyei, I. K. (2023). *China has access to Ghana's mineral revenue and electricity sales upondefaultof4loans–IMF.* https://www.myjoyonline.com/china-has-access-to-ghanas-mineral-revenue-and-electricity-sales-upon-default-of-4-loans-imf/

Akyeampong, E., & Bates, R. H. (Eds.). (2010). *Africa's development in historical perspective.* Cambridge University Press.

Alden, C., & Alves, A. C. (2009). China and Africa's natural resources: The challenges and implications for development and governance. *Occasional Paper No. 41,* SAIIA.

Avordeh, T. K., Salifu, A., Quaidoo, C., & Opare-Boateng., R. (2024). Impact of power outages: Unveiling their influence on micro, small, and medium-sized enterprises and poverty in Sub-Saharan Africa. *Heliyon, 10(13), 1–13.*

Benabdallah, L. (2024). *China's engagement in the critical minerals landscape in Africa. Policy Brief.* Africa Policy Research Institute.

Benazeraf, D., & Alves, A. (2014). Oil for housing': Chinese built new towns in Angola. *Policy Briefing,* 88, SAIIA.

Benefo, A., & Addaney, M. (2021). Promises and Pitfalls: China's financing of the Atewa Bauxite mining project in Ghana. *Georgetown Journal of International Affairs.* https://gjia.georgetown.edu/2021/07/11/promises-and-pitfalls-chinas-financing-of-the-atewa-bauxite-mining-project-in-ghana/

Bo, H., Lawal, R., & Sakariyahu, R. (2024). China's infrastructure investments in Africa: An imperative for attaining sustainable development goals or a debt-trap? *The British Accounting Review,* https://doi.org/10.1016/j.bar.2024.101472

Boston University GDP Centre. (2025). *Chinese loans to Africa database.* Boston University. https://www.bu.edu/gdp/chinese-loans-to-africa-database/

Braun, T. N. (2019). *Why infrastructure is central to achieving a more resource-efficient future.* SDG Knowledge Hub. https://sdg.iisd.org/commentary/guest-articles/whyinfrastructure-is-central-to-achieving-a-more-resource-efficient-future/

Bräutigam, D. (2009). *The dragon's gift: The real story of China in Africa.* Oxford University Press.

Bräutigam, D., & Huang, Y. (2023). *Integrating China into multilateral debt relief: Progress and problems in the G20 DSSI.* Briefing Paper, No. 09/2023, SAIS-CARI, Johns Hopkins University, Washington, DC.

Burrier, E. A., & Sheehy, T. P. (2023). *Challenging China's grip on critical minerals can be a boon for Africa's future.* The United States Institute of Peace.

CGTN. (2018). Angola secures $2 billion in infrastructure financing from China. https://newsaf.cgtn.com/news/3d3d414e784d7a6333566d54/index.html

CGTN. (2023). Graphics: How Belt and Road has impacted China-Africa cooperation. *CGTN.* https://news.cgtn.com/news/2023-06-29/Graphics-How-Belt-and-Road-has-impacted-China-Africa-cooperation-1l1r5Od5wys/index.html

Corkin, L. (2011). China and Angola Strategic partnership or marriage of convenience? *Angola Brief, 1*(1), 4.
Davis, Z., Boelman, B., & O'Connor, C. (2023). China's infrastructure for resources model: Case studies of Bolivia and Argentina. *Journal of Student Research, 12*(4), 1–15.
Ding, Q., Hubbard, H., Larkin, E., & Shonibare, D. (2021). *Chinese resource-backed infrastructure financing investments: Comparing governance in Guinea and Ghana*. SAIS-CARI, Johns Hopkins University.
Enache, C. (2020). OECD report: Tax revenue in African countries. *Tax Foundation*. https://taxfoundation.org/blog/africa-tax-revenue-oecd-report-2020/
Ericsson, M., Löf, O., & Löf, A. (2020). Chinese control over African and global mining—past, present and future. *Mineral Economics, 33*, 153–181.
Ferreira, M. E. (2008). China in Angola: Just a passion for oil? In C. Alden, R. S. de Oliveira, & D. Large (Eds.), *China returns to Africa: A rising power and a continent embrace* (pp. 297–317). Columbia University Press.
Foster, V., Rana, A., & Gorgulu, N. (2022). *Understanding public spending trends for infrastructure in developing countries*. World Bank Group.
Galeazzi, C., Steinbuks, J., & Cust, J. (2020). *Africa's resource export opportunities and the global energy transition*. World Bank Group.
Giacalone, R., & Ruiz, J. B. (2013). The Chinese–Venezuelan oil agreements: Material and nonmaterial goals. *Latin American Policy, 4*(1), 76–92.
Gutman, J., Sy, A., & Chattopadhyay, S. (2015). *Financing African infrastructure: Can the world deliver?* Brookings.
Haar, J. (2023). Modernising infrastructure vital to fulfilling Africa's promise. *The WilsonCentre*.https://www.wilsoncenter.org/article/modernizing-infrastructure-vital-fulfilling-africas-promise
IMANI Africa. (2018). *Government must clarify a whole lot in the Bauxite-Barter deal with China*. Accra.
International Monetary Fund. (2024). Angola: 2024 First post-financing assessment-Press release; and staff report. *IMF Economic Review*, 2024(224).
JoyOnline. (2021). '$2bn Sinohydro deal: Government justifies non-completion ofsomeroadprojects.https://www.myjoyonline.com/2bn-sinohydro-deal-government-justifies-non-completion-of-some-road-projects/
Konijn, P. (2014). *Chinese Resources-for-infrastructure (R4I) swaps: An escape from the resource curse?* SAIIA.
Mihalyi, D., Hwang, J., Rivetti, D., & Cust, J. (2022). *Resource-backed loans in Sub-Saharan Africa*. Policy Research Working Paper; No. 9923. Washington D.C., World Bank Group.
Moore, M., Prichard, W., & Fjeldstad, O. H. (2018). *Taxing Africa: Coercion, reform and development*. Zed Books.

Morlin-Yron, S. (2016). All aboard! The Chinese-funded railways linking East Africa. *CNN*. https://edition.cnn.com/2016/11/21/africa/chinese-funded-railways-in-africa/index.html?no-st=1535962960

Munyati, C. (2024). Why strong regional value chains will be vital to the next chapter of China and Africa's economic relationship. *World Economic Forum*. https://www.weforum.org/stories/2024/06/why-strong-regional-value-chains-will-be-vital-to-the-next-chapter-of-china-and-africas-economic-relationship/

Onishi, N. (2017). Angola's corrupt building boom: 'Like opening a window and throwing out money. *The New York Times*. https://www.nytimes.com/2017/06/24/world/africa/angola-luanda-jose-eduardo-dos-santos.html.

OXFAM. (2017). From aspiration to reality: Unpacking the Africa mining vision. *OXFAM Briefing Paper*, OXFAM International.

Parliament of Ghana. (2018). Master project support agreement (MPSA) between the government of the Republic of Ghana and Sinohydro Corporation Limited. https://ir.parliament.gh/handle/123456789/170

PIDA. (n.d.). Closing the infrastructure gap vital for Africa's transformation. PIDA-AfDB. https://www.afdb.org/fileadmin/uploads/afdb/Documents/Generic-Documents/PIDA%20brief%20closing%20gap.pdf

Purwins, S. (2023). Same same, but different: Ghana's Sinohydro deal as evolved 'angola model'? *Insight on Africa, 15*(1), 46–70.

Rönnbäck, K. (2020). The business of barter on the pre-colonial Gold Coast. *Economic History of Developing Regions, 35*(1), 123–142.

SAIS-CARI. (2024). *Chinese loans to Africa*. SAIS-CARI. https://www.sais-cari.org/research-chinese-loans-to-africa

SAIS-CARI. (2025). *Data: Chinese investment in Africa, 2003–2022*. SAIS-CARI. https://www.sais-cari.org/s/FDIData_Feb2025.xlsx

Signé, L. (2020). *Unlocking Africa's business potential: Trends, opportunities, risks, and strategies*. Brookings Institution Press.

Sudo, S. (1992). Post-war Japan's Re-entry into Southeast Asia. In *The Fukuda Doctrine and ASEAN: New dimensions in Japanese Foreign policy* (pp. 24–52). ISEAS–Yusof Ishak Institute.

United Nations Environment Programme. (2021). *Our Work in Africa*. United Nations Environment Programme. https://www.unep.org/regions/africa/our-work-africa

Usman, Z., & Washington, T. (2024). *Are the world's largest donors cutting their bilateral aid to Africa?* Carnegie Endowment for International Peace.

van Wieringen, K., & Zajontz, T. (2023). From loan-financed to privatised infrastructure? Tracing China's turn towards public–private partnerships in Africa. *Journal of Current Chinese Affairs, 52*(3), 434–463.

Venables, A. J. (2016). Using natural resources for development: Why has it proven so difficult? *Journal of Economic Perspectives, 30*(1), 161–184.

World Bank. (2024a). *Infrastructure challenges and how PPPs can help*. World Bank Group. https://ppp.worldbank.org/public-private-partnership/applicable-all-sectors/infrastructure-challenges-and-how-ppps-can-help

World Bank. (2024b). *Government support in financing PPPs*. World Bank Group. https://ppp.worldbank.org/public-private-partnership/applicable-all-sectors/government-support-financing-ppps

World Bank Independent Evaluation Group. (2023). *Elements that enhance institutional capacity development in World Bank projects and country partnerships in Sub-Saharan Africa*. The World Bank Group.

Yescombe, E. R. (2017). *Public-private partnerships in Sub-Saharan Africa: Case studies for policymakers*. UONGOZI Institute.

Zongwe, D. (2010). *On the road to post conflict reconstruction by contract: The Angola Model*. SSRN Electronic Journal. https://doi.org/10.2139/ssrn.1730442

Digital Infrastructure and Sino-African Relations: Chinese ICT Companies and African Agency

Maximilian Mayer, Yen-Chi Lu, and Alex Demissie

Introduction

Over the past decade, many African countries have demonstrated a robust commitment to digital transformation,[1] recognising the potential of digital technologies to drive economic growth and enhance access to public services, while the continent remains plagued by uneven access to the Internet and a lack of digital infrastructure. African governments have developed great ambitions. For instance, the Smart Africa Alliance, a commitment from African leaders, has grown its membership from seven countries in 2013 to 40 countries in 2025 (Smart Africa Alliance, 2024, last paragraph). African governments have proactively implemented various policies to promote Information and Communication Technology (ICT) and associated infrastructure development, foster innovation and talent, and attract investment in the ICT sector. For example, Ethiopia introduced the "Digital Ethiopia 2025 Strategy", aiming to identify local

M. Mayer (✉) • Y.-C. Lu • A. Demissie
University of Bonn, Bonn, Germany
e-mail: maximilian.mayer@uni-bonn.de

L. G. Adu Amoah (ed.), *Africa-China Relations*,
https://doi.org/10.1007/978-981-95-4370-0_9

solutions to the country's development challenges (FAO, 2020). Rwanda, another key example, introduced several sector-specific digital strategies that aim at making Rwanda a centre of digital innovation on the African continent (Ministry of Information Communication Technology and Innovation, n.d.).[2] Kenya created a "Digital Economy Blueprint" to transform the entire economy (Republic of Kenya, 2019). In pursuing ICT sector-specific policies, African countries are trying to close the persistent "digital divide" and leapfrog to innovative solutions tailored to the needs of African markets in agriculture, fintech, AI, smart energy, and education, among other fields, impacting the everyday life of their population and defining how the continent's digital future is shaped (Southwood, 2022).

Recognising the increasing importance of Africa's digital economy, global powers such as China and the United States are increasingly competing for control. Chinese and US ICT technology firms have increased their activities in the region's digital sector as commercial providers of both digital infrastructure and cloud services. At the state level, the People's Republic of China (PRC) has been particularly active through the Digital Silk Road Initiative to forge strong ICT-related connections with African governments through loans, while the private sector aimed to expand the market share of Chinese digital technologies in developing countries (Shinn & Eisenman, 2023; Gordon & Nouwens, 2022; Gagliardone, 2019). To counter this trend, in 2022, the United States launched the Digital Transformation with Africa Initiative, which, under the Africa Digital Policy Council, involves over 17 US agencies targeting the areas of digital economy and infrastructure, human capital development, and digital enabling environment (Munga & Monye, 2024).

Such competitive tendencies have led some observers to raise concerns, arguing that Africa is entering a "digital arms race" and that the effects of digital transformation are leading to new inequalities, asymmetric dependencies, and control that resemble "digital colonialism" (Bradford, 2023) or "digital imperialism" (Adu Amoah, 2025). So, empirically, the question is how much digital infrastructure and data ecosystems in Africa are controlled by US or Chinese actors and to what degree African countries demonstrate agency, as they remain active stakeholders in shaping digital infrastructure development in the region based on their national interests. In fact, African countries are active in shaping the regulation of AI and other emerging technologies while maintaining cooperation with China and other countries. At the recent Forum on China–Africa Cooperation (FOCAC), African countries welcomed China's Global AI Governance

Initiative and Global Initiative on Data Security. Conversely, China supports the African Consensus Declaration on Artificial Intelligence, adopted at the High-Level Forum on Artificial Intelligence held in Rabat in June 2024 (Ministry of Foreign Affairs, People's Republic of China, 2024). It is, hence, critical and worthwhile to dive deeper into the ongoing infrastructural power dynamics to understand how African countries can or cannot utilise their agency to shape the future trajectory of digital infrastructure development on the continent (Agbebi et al., 2021). As the need for large-scale public and private investments into critical digital infrastructure, from cloud and hyperscale computing, to Internet access, data centres, and 5G networks, and much more, is growing, African governments have to make difficult choices in identifying the best approach to get what their societies and economies need at affordable prices and suitable scales, affecting their approach to external powers in this critical sector.

Against this backdrop, this chapter examines current trends in the development of digital infrastructure on the continent, with particular focus on the role and growing influence of Chinese firms. Firstly, we explore the increasing significance of Chinese infrastructure projects, digital technologies, loans, as well as investments for digital development. Secondly, we provide a brief overview of national digitalisation strategies, setting the stage for an analysis of the critical importance of Chinese influence by examining who controls the various layers of digital technology ("stack") in Africa (cf. Huang & Mayer, 2023), as well as exploring the potential for the export of digital authoritarianism through the increasing presence of Chinese firms and technologies (Bradford, 2023; Arnold, 2024). Finally, the chapter focuses on Ethiopia, examining the extent to which this large African country can shape its digital sovereignty through its relations with leading technological powers such as China and the United States.

The Role of Chinese Technology and Infrastructure Companies

Chinese telecom and technology companies are becoming crucial in modernising the infrastructural basis of African societies and economies, which have long suffered from the so-called "digital divide" (Fuchs & Horak, 2008) and a long-standing lack of different kinds of infrastructure investments in general. Notably, the presence of Chinese technology in African countries is not new. There is a long tradition of Chinese companies' involvement in constructing critical infrastructure in African countries, including roads, ports, railways, and airports reaching back to the period of decolonisation in the 1960s and 1970s.[3] With the implementation of China's flagship Belt and Road Initiative (BRI) in the last decade, the involvement of Chinese companies in the construction of critical infrastructure increased manifold, including in technological infrastructures, fuelling the next development phase in African countries. While public infrastructure investments are usually initiated by African governments, Chinese policy and commercial banks have provided the necessary capital for these investments to materialise.

Aside from the financial and construction involvement, Chinese activities also have a spatial characteristic. The BRI activities are characterised by an approach that has been analysed as "corridorization". By creating new corridors and linking supply chains, trade networks and transport arteries through new logistical and institutional infrastructure, such as special economic zones, Chinese activities have, among other things, connected hinterlands and changed the location and geography of trade and production (Mayer & Zhang, 2021; Carmody et al., 2022; Aalders et al., 2021). Ethiopia's Industrial Park/SEZ program has had heavy Chinese involvement from the start, which had a profound impact on its development, especially on the textile industry and its modernisation process (Alves & Lee, 2022). In addition, the Addis-Djibouti Railway, as one of the main transport corridors to the port, is servicing SEZ-based companies along the corridor in Adama, Dukem/Mojo, and Addis Ababa.

Although some of these corridors were planned long before the BRI, Chinese loans enabled the acceleration of railway projects and the modernisation of the ports that form a key part of the corridors.[4] According to the former Chinese ambassador to Nigeria, Cui Jianchun, Chinese companies have built around 100 seaports in African countries over the past 20 years (Hellenic Shipping News, 2022), highlighting the importance of Chinese infrastructure companies in the development trajectory of African countries. And, although the construction boom in China has slowed down, Chinese construction companies are enjoying significant success abroad. In 2022, the gross annual revenue of Chinese companies' engineering and construction projects in Africa totalled US$38 billion, accounting for 19.4 percent of the global revenue of these companies (China Africa Research Initiative, 2024).

The role of Chinese firms in information technology projects has become increasingly central, as they are now officially associated with the "Digital Silk Road" and the "high-quality development" phase of the BRI, with its shift from "hard" to "soft" infrastructure (Gordon & Nouwens, 2022; Jie & Hong, 2023). Chinese companies' involvement comes in different forms including through market entry, construction projects, direct investments, or through technology and know-how transfer. Following an approach that has been described as the "integrated investment, construction and operation" model, the Chinese infrastructure industry, financial institutions, and policymakers have been keen on advancing a market-seeking foreign direct investment model, particularly in the ICT sector (Zhang, 2023). Beyond this kind of state-firm coordination, foreign direct investment flows have also increased. Worldwide, greenfield investment from Chinese companies in information technology, communications, and electronic components totalled 17.6 billion US dollars in 2022, six times the value when the BRI was launched (Yasoshima & Nishino, 2023).

Chinese technology companies, such as ZTE and Huawei, have shown interest in entering African ICT markets to increase market share and further develop their in-house technology in line with the needs of consumers in African markets. Strong strategic partnerships with leading African telecom networks and technology companies, a low-price strategy, and preferential loans from Chinese policy banks allow them to gain technical expertise and access to African networks and customer bases (Wen, 2020, pp. 70ff). The flexible mix of business strategies and government support has allowed Chinese ICT companies, such as Huawei, to thrive in African countries, despite US-led sanctions. In fact, Huawei components make up around 70 percent of 4G networks across Africa and are leading the 5G rollout (Ehl, 2022). This trend will likely continue in the coming years due to the affordability and convenience of the equipment and services provided.

From the perspective of African governments, these targeted approaches allow Chinese technology companies to steadily increase their value to African countries by helping to reduce the digital divide and enabling African states to address three fundamental issues: job creation, technology transfer, and production localisation, including in future-oriented areas such as artificial intelligence. With China's changing behaviour focusing more on "small but smart" projects and emphasising the training and retention of highly skilled human resources in African countries,

ICT-related projects by Chinese companies are expected to play a prominent role in shaping the implementation of ICT development strategies of many African countries. For instance, in July 2024, Huawei announced its plans to train 150,000 ICT talents in Sub-Saharan Africa until 2027 under its Leadership Employability, Advancement, and Possibility (LEAP) program, in addition to those 120,000 talents already trained (PR Newswire, 2024). One prominent example is Huawei's "Seeds for the Future" training program, which brings together ICT students from different African countries to provide training sessions focusing on cutting-edge technology and innovation areas, including 5G technologies, the Internet of Things, network, cloud, entrepreneurship, and leadership skills—giving Huawei access to the local talent pool. The company also runs several annual projects, such as ICT competitions and women in tech, to identify and retain talents for its African projects (Xinhua, 2024). In addition, China is already a leading AI technology provider and hosts some of the world's top AI experts. The Chinese leadership sees its increasing influence in AI deployment as part of the objectives of the "Chinese Dream" vision of global influence (Stanford University, 2024; Cheng & Zeng, 2023). Given that African countries are often portrayed as lacking skilled labour, developing access to a well-trained talent pipeline can be a strategic advantage for Huawei. Local talent is cost-effective vis-à-vis hiring foreign experts and allows to provide faster service to clients in African countries. In addition, African countries profit from experienced local professionals who can start building their own businesses and become service providers for Huawei and other ICT companies in the country (Ye, 2024, pp. 23–41).

Infrastructural Statecraft, National Digitalisation Strategies, and State-Firm Cooperation

Mobile connectivity, or the lack of it, continues to drive digital transformation, socioeconomic advances, and societal fashions in African countries today. As Achille Mbembe points out, the mobile phone "is not only a medium of communication. It is also a medium of self-stylization and self-singularization" (Mbembe, 2021, p. 216). Yet, the use of smartphones is still limited, and large segments of existing mobile communication systems remain slow. A great infrastructural leap forward is therefore needed to satisfy the growing demand for faster Internet, especially among younger consumers. According to GSMA, while 3G remains the most dominant technology in the region, the adoption of 4G will more than double to 45 percent over the next five years, with an expected 1.2 billion smartphone connections by 2030 (GSMA, 2023). Infrastructural statecraft is required to meet this demand, and Chinese companies were among the first to recognise the strategic and commercial potential of this transformation. They brought with them the expertise gained from China's own massive infrastructure expansion. Indeed, they have become major suppliers of smartphones to African markets (see Fig. 1) and have played a key role in developing telecommunications networks. Clearly, companies that can provide reliable, fast connectivity are highly valued by African states and will gain more leverage as digital products and services increasingly depend on seamless, equitable Internet access (personal communication, February-March, 2022).

The aim of technological leapfrogging is, however, not merely about faster and more convenient Internet access using smartphones. Improved core connectivity infrastructure (e.g. mobile towers, handsets, etc.) and supporting infrastructure (e.g. power) enable improved access to various critical services, further empowering individuals and communities. Through building the necessary infrastructure in collaboration with companies from China and elsewhere, African countries see digital technology

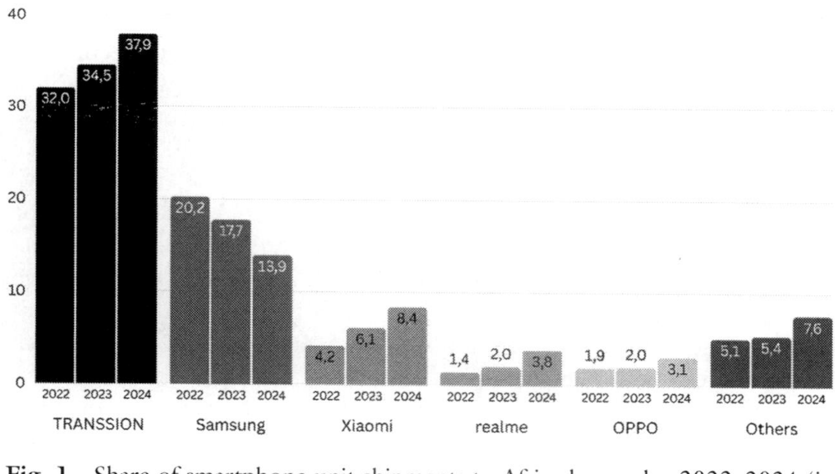

Fig. 1 Share of smartphone unit shipments to Africa by vendor 2022–2024 (in million units). (Note: Transsion brand includes Tecno, Infinix, and iTel; Xiaomi estimation also includes POCO and Redmi. Source: Canalys, 2024)

and AI as an opportunity to drive progress on the most pressing challenges, such as improving healthcare access in remote regions through telemedicine or transforming education by personalising digital learning (Mckinsey, 2023). The effects of the COVID-19 pandemic have significantly accelerated the belief that more emphasis should be given to the advancement of digital transformation, including the digitisation of analogue information and the digitalisation of working processes. Increased smartphone connectivity and enhanced data management capability, including the availability of data infrastructure, such as mobile payment, create an enabling environment to introduce bold policies.

For example, in June 2024, Ethiopia unveiled its first AI National Strategy to provide a framework for further developing this nascent but growing sector. As most of Ethiopia's ICT infrastructure has been constructed by Huawei and ZTE, it is plausible to assume that Chinese enterprises will also support the further development of the Digital sector in Ethiopia. In January 2024, the Ethiopian Government, through its Sovereign Wealth Fund, Ethiopian Investment Holdings, entered into an agreement with Chinese company West Data Group, based in Hong Kong, to "establish cutting-edge infrastructure dedicated to data processing operations and AI training in Ethiopia", especially Bitcoin mining, which is expected to be at the core of the US $250 million project (Resilient Digital Africa, 2024). West Data Group is part of China's Chuan Chu United International Engineering Co. Ltd., specialising in EPC general engineering contracting, including developing cloud intelligent technology applications and data centre development (Chuan Chu, 2024). According to West Data's company profile, the company built several of Huawei's National Data Centers in Ethiopia between 2020 and 2022 (West Data Group, 2024).

Another critical area for the development of African countries is the establishment of functioning online payment systems. The characteristics of "fast infrastructures" (Edwards, 2021), such as technical flexibility and low capital intensity, make fintech platforms another key object for Africa's leapfrogging strategy. African countries can rapidly build their fintech industries by capitalising on the global spread of expertise and open-source software and by taking advantage of the vast and still-growing population demanding financial inclusion. The growth of mobile Internet and mobile phone usage has enabled this trend. For example, M-PESA, launched in Kenya in 2007, reached 9 million customers in three years, or 40 percent of Kenyan adults (Mas & Radcliffe, 2010). M-PESA has expanded its operations across African countries and even beyond the African continent to India (Edwards, 2021, pp. 326–329). In recent years, the emergence of African fintech ecosystems and innovations in countries, such as Nigeria, Ethiopia, Kenya, and others, have made it one of the leading sectors in Africa in terms of startup funding (Resilient Digital Africa, 2022). Despite the prominent activities of Chinese tech companies, many African fintech startups retain close cooperation with US and European companies (personal communication, February-March, 2022).

How Critical Is China for Africa's Digitalisation?

As the influence of leading US tech companies such as Alphabet, Microsoft, and Meta in African countries remains strong (Southwood, 2022, pp. 93–101), how important are Chinese tech companies for the continent? To begin with, the answer to this question varies depending on which sectors and technology areas one looks at. For example, as noted above, the availability of basic telecommunication connectivity through mobile phones is a key issue. Chinese companies such as Transsion, a Shenzhen-based manufacturer of low-cost mobile phones, play a key role here but are often largely unknown in China and the West. Founded in 2006, Transsion was one of the first to take advantage of Africa's technological opportunities, using the African ICT market as a lucrative springboard to increase its visibility and market penetration in China and other emerging markets by introducing market-appropriate ICT products that address specific real-world problems. For example, Transsion was one of the first companies to introduce dual SIM card technology and local language mobile phones to the African market—resulting in an increase in its overall sales in African countries. Today, the company employs more than 10,000 people in 60 emerging markets (Techpoint Africa, 2018).

Based on the total number of smartphones shipped for 2024, Chinese companies dominate the African market, with more than 71 percent of the units shipped—with Transsion controlling almost 51 percent—while the South Korean company Samsung instead had a market share of only 19 percent in shipped smartphones (see Fig. 1). Other companies such as Oppo and Xiaomi have found a growing number of untapped markets in Africa, providing cutting-edge technology at an affordable price for Africa's young population (Williams, 2019; Business Insider Africa, 2024).

In addition to affordable devices, Chinese Lenders, in particular Chinese policy banks, have become crucial in providing loans for ICT projects. From 2000 to 2023, Chinese policy banks provided loans to African countries in the amount of US $15.7 billion for ICT-related projects (Boston University Global Development Policy Center, 2024). Data on Chinese ICT-related lending (Fig. 4) also revealed its critical role in the development of telecommunications infrastructure in Africa. With a total of US $8.1 billion granted (53 loans), Ethiopia, Nigeria, Angola, Cameroon, and Ghana are the top five African recipients of Chinese loans for digital technology from 2000 to 2023. Meanwhile, 57 percent (30) of these loans were for the construction of telecommunications infrastructure. In fact, without both Chinese tech companies and loans, cellular communications in Africa would not be at the same level as they are today: "50 percent of 3G systems used by African telcos were built by Huawei and another 20 percent to 30 percent were built by ZTE, while Huawei has built up 70 percent of 4G networks and is likely to build all 5G networks" (Wright, 2020).

Another key indicator is the number of projects undertaken by leading Chinese high-technology companies in Africa. According to the ASPI data set (see Fig. 2), projects in African countries amounted to 12 percent of their overall projects abroad by 2021. This indicates an outsized interest in and expectation of the continent, given the relatively small share of Africa in Chinese foreign trade. Most of these projects are funded by African governments and implemented by Chinese companies. Among Chinese tech companies active in Africa, Huawei is by far the most prominent. Figure 3 shows that Huawei conducts the largest share of projects of Chinese tech firms in Africa (44 percent), followed by ZTE (18 percent), Uniview (9 percent), and China Telecom (6 percent). This mix indicates that Chinese companies are absolutely critical providers of telecommunication infrastructures in Africa.

In sum, China's Digital Silk Road addresses the need of African countries to invest in and construct massive digital and data infrastructures that are required to run Africa's growing megacities and emerging economic corridors. However, more investment is needed by African countries to continue closing the digital divide. For instance, in sub-Saharan Africa, 43 percent of adults were still not connected to mobile Internet in 2022, while 15 percent lived in a region without mobile Internet coverage (Shanahan, 2024). In September 2024, Xi Jinping offered roughly 360 billion yuan ($50.70 billion) of new funding for the African continent that includes, among other things, 210 billion yuan for credit lines and around 70 billion yuan in "fresh investment by Chinese companies" (Chen &

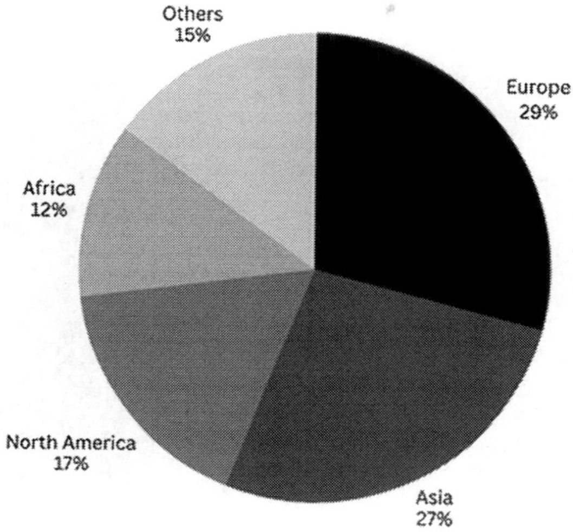

Fig. 2 Distribution of Chinese tech companies' overseas projects 1997–2021 by region. (Source: Calculated and visualised by the authors based on data: https://chinatechmap.aspi.org.au/#/homepage/. Note: The ASPI data on China's overseas technology projects include aid, sales of product and service, investment, and loans

Cash, 2024). In addition, infrastructure, scientific cooperation, and the digital economy feature prominently in the "Forum on China–Africa Cooperation Beijing Action Plan (2025–2027)" (Ministry of Foreign Affairs of the People's Republic of China, 2021). Additional measures strengthening ICT-cooperation to facilitate industrialisation, talent development, and agricultural development have been adopted at the 9th FOCAC meeting in Beijing in September 2024.

The variety of sectors and different uses of digital technologies provided by Chinese tech companies in Africa point to a trend of diversification away from telecommunication infrastructure. As shown by Fig. 4, 43 percent of Chinese ICT loans to the top five African recipients were allocated to digital technologies related to E-Governance, E-Learning, national security, and public security. Figure 5 shows that surveillance (27 percent) and "smart city" projects (30 percent) account for 57 percent of activities. Yet, there are also e-payment ecosystems, biotechnology, cloud technology, artificial technology projects, and increasingly, activities in fintech startups (Nyabiage, 2022). Chinese IT aid projects, perhaps, might

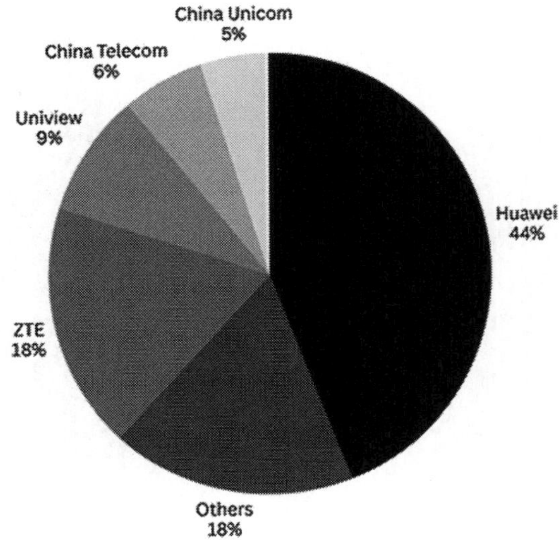

Fig. 3 Overseas technology projects in Africa 1997–2021 by Chinese tech companies. (Source: Calculated and visualised by the authors based on data: https://chinatechmap.aspi.org.au/#/homepage/)

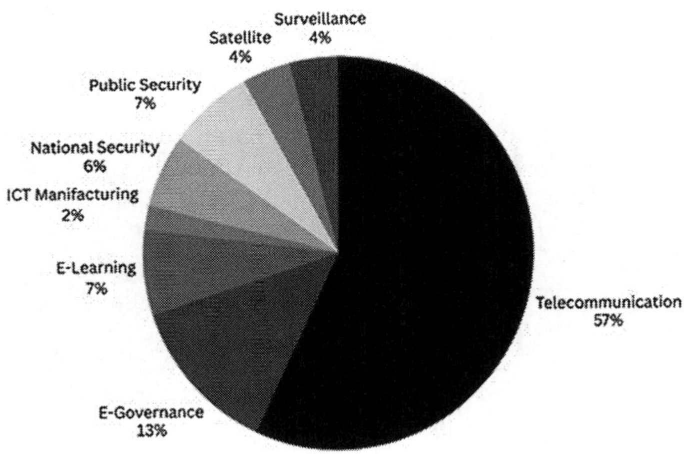

Fig. 4 Chinese loans to top five African recipients by technologies (2000–2023). (Source: Calculated and visualised by the authors based on data: http://bu.edu/gdp/chinese-loans-to-africa-database. Lenders include Chinese policy banks and private companies)

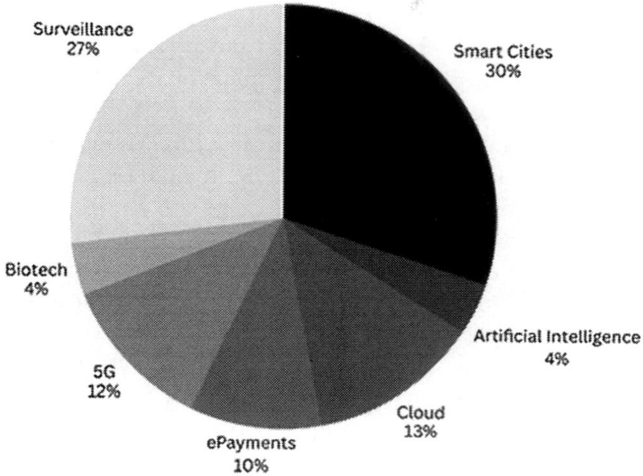

Fig. 5 Chinese tech companies' activities in Africa according to different sectors 1997–2021. (Data source: Gu et al., 2022, p. 33)

add here a transnational network of private and state actors to the picture, which pushes digitalisation in various African countries. In sum, Chinese tech companies have become close to indispensable for Africa's digital transformation, and African governments thus find great difficulties in joining the US-led "Clean network initiative" or a "Clean Energy Supply Chains" (cf. Usman & Csanadi, 2023), which aimed at curbing the influence of firms such as Huawei and ZTE.

Who Controls Digital Infrastructures of African Countries?

The diverse activities of Chinese tech companies result in a unique interplay between Chinese and local actors within the African tech landscape. This interplay, and the changing pattern of dependence and control, require a more nuanced analytical approach than the often one-dimensional understanding of the impact of "Chinese state capitalism" on African economies (Wang et al., 2020). Case studies, for instance, demonstrate that private tech firms and state-owned enterprises adopt different investment, organisational, and engagement strategies and show a variety of interaction and collaboration patterns with local actors (see Lee, 2018). The assertion that Chinese-funded projects and associated loans automatically create "debt traps" in Africa is highly questionable and lacks supporting evidence (Brautigam, 2020, p. 6). Furthermore, African societies and governments can counteract some of the structural limitations of global value chains by skilfully pursuing their developmental interests. For example, Ethiopia's approach to Chinese ICT firms' involvement in the telecommunications sector is a prime example of this (Fei, 2021). However, as China has become the most important trading partner for many African countries, a key economic and developmental concern is the integration of African firms and sectors into global value chains. This would increase the share of higher-value activities in their export structure (Qobo & le Pere, 2017).

A pertinent question to pose at this juncture is whether digital dependencies can be mapped. Chinese firms and institutions have been involved in different aspects of digital infrastructure (Shen, 2018, Heeks et al., 2024). A simple way to distinguish the complexity of digital technologies with different hardware and software systems and layers building on each other is the "stack"—the multi-layered infrastructure assemblage from cables and satellites to cloud platforms and digital interfaces, as well as service applications that are essential for the daily functioning of digitalised societies and the sustainable development of the digital economy (cf. Kagermann et al., 2021). In fact, we find across the levels of the stack a clear trend of increasingly one-sided dependence. While the heterogeneous distribution of actors and agency is a crucial part of the new reality of African technological development (Chen, 2022), dependency on Chinese technologies is growing, as shown below in the case of Ethiopia. Given the cheap and reliable technological solutions offered by Chinese companies, from smartphones and submarine cables to 5G infrastructure and smart surveillance technologies, it is undoubtedly the case that Chinese digital technologies have already become essential components at all levels of the African tech stack.

African stacks are increasingly dependent on Chinese suppliers, especially at the hardware level. According to trade data from UNCTAD (see Fig. 6), African countries collectively imported 57 percent of their total ICT hardware from China in 2023, amounting to US $11.6 billion. When only Sub-Saharan countries are included, China's share increases to 60 percent. African countries that receive Chinese ICT loans are particularly dependent on Chinese hardware. For example, Ethiopia, Nigeria, and

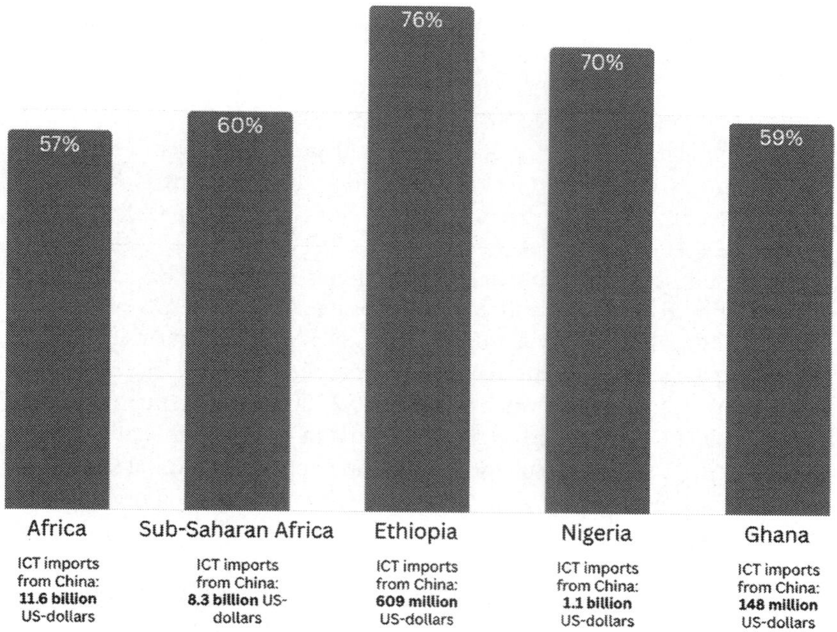

Fig. 6 Share of Chinese products in total ICT goods imports of selected African countries in 2023. (Data source: UN Trade and Development (UNCTAD))

Ghana imported 76 percent, 70 percent, and 59 percent of their ICT hardware from China, respectively, in 2023.

These trends have raised concerns. The involvement of Huawei in multiple "Safe City" projects across African countries has, therefore, led to the assumption that Chinese companies could soon become dominant players in the global South. "After adopting Huawei's equipment, countries may be "locked-in" by high replacement costs. As these economies grow, Huawei is poised to capture market share, spread its standards, and gain access to foreign data to improve its technology" (Hillman & McCalpin, 2019). In some cases, Chinese companies used IT standards for ICT broadband backbone that were only compatible with Huawei routers (Vaidyanathan & Gomera, 2019). Another example is massive Chinese investments in the construction of the new Egyptian capital, which includes urban conglomerations, smart infrastructure, and industrial and special manufacturing zones along the Suez Canal. This will give China a stake in the capital of one of the regionally leading states. Moreover, African experts also warn that the engagement of global tech companies has drawbacks concerning the drainage of data and human capital. Seydina Moussa Ndiaye, for instance, stresses that the vast majority of the data currently generated in Africa is controlled and processed by multinationals "whose infrastructure is developed outside the continent, where most African AI experts also operate. It's a loss of African talent" (UN News, 2024).

As a result, it seems improbable that Chinese firms will have a monopoly on digital technology and control over data in Africa. US companies, including Google, Facebook, and Starlink, also build enormous new infrastructures, including satellite-based Internet access and new sea cables that link Africa with other continents (Wright, 2020). As a result, the digital divide could be further reduced, while African governments are unlikely able to increase their control and ownership over critical digital infrastructure. African countries are, in fact, increasingly dependent on both US and Chinese tech companies, while their soft and hardware infrastructure (stake) entails components from the rivalling technopoles, which implies the growing importance of a binary exclusionary logic (cf. Mayer & Lu, 2023; Mayer & Lu, 2025). As a result, African technology sectors and the infrastructures underpinning them are poised to become a hotbed for geoeconomic competition, which evolves around China's BRI, the EU's global gateway, and a renewed US interest in Africa (Runde et al., 2021). But neither the United States nor China is able to fully dominate African stacks due to the diversification of digital technology suppliers in African countries. Moreover, assuming that African policymakers are unaware of the potential risks to sovereignty and political implications associated with Chinese technology solutions would be an underestimation of the capacity of African countries to shape their digital cooperation with China (anonymous, personal communication, February-March, 2022).

Authoritarian Digitalisation in Africa?

The rise of Chinese digital technology and platform companies in Africa has also raised eyebrows, often linked to the claim that Chinese companies would spread authoritarian models of government (Ross, 2020; Shinn & Eisenman, 2023). The influence of Chinese firms developing digital ecosystems for smart cities and surveillance in African countries has become a concern for US and EU companies, primarily because future market opportunities are locked in, and Western technology providers are left out of potentially lucrative future markets. As the last frontier of development, African countries rapidly integrate digital solutions into their long-term national development plans, and China's digital projects are more affordable for African countries (Hillman, 2021). As the digital realm is closely linked to physical infrastructure, China's technological expertise enables it to promote BRI-related projects in African countries, including those in renewable energy, transportation, infrastructure, power, and healthcare. It also enables China to shape standards and regulatory approaches. However, China's growing influence on standards and regulations raises concerns about the possible deterioration of privacy and data protection regulations in African countries. This could be part of a wider techno-political trend towards authoritarian digitalisation, where the rise of authoritarian government techniques, including censorship and surveillance, and the spread of various digital technologies are mutually reinforcing (for a debate, see: Pearson, 2024).

Given the complexity of technopolitical developments, claims that China is spreading "digital authoritarianism" in Africa need to be scrutinised (Gagliardone, 2019, pp. 114–116, Bagwandeen, 2021). Observers and scholars have noted that some African states are trying to emulate China's approach to Internet governance, including censorship and surveillance techniques. Others have argued that China can export its brand of digital authoritarianism through the use of exported digital information technology and data infrastructure (Shinn & Eisenman, 2023). Moreover, China's approach to cyber governance is attractive to authoritarian regimes. So far, however, there is little evidence that Chinese companies are actually successfully exporting digital authoritarianism. Recent research on the impact of Chinese digital technologies and ICT infrastructure on African countries shows that Chinese companies are primarily profit-seeking rather than exporting "digital Leninism" (Tong, 2021; Bagwandeen, 2021). In most cases, Chinese ICT companies have not yet monopolised the markets, but they still have to compete with other competitors, such as US companies, to maintain or increase market share. This gives African countries bargaining power vis-à-vis Chinese technology suppliers.

Chinese Tech Firms and Ethiopia's "Digital Sovereignty"

With "the Digital Ethiopia 2025 Strategy", Ethiopia aims to create an enabling environment for digital transformation, including reliable energy supply, strong data and telecom infrastructure expansion, cybersecurity, a conducive regulatory framework, strategic engagement with other countries on digitisation projects, and the establishment of dedicated institutions such as the Artificial Intelligence (AI) Institute (Digital Ethiopia, 2025). The comprehensive set of goals inadvertently highlights the major challenges this strategy faces. Official ambitions include digital IDs, the rollout of the mobile payments system, and the provision of reliable electricity supply through the finalisation of the Grand Ethiopian Renaissance Dam. The potential availability of electricity also plays a big role in attracting Bitcoin mining companies to Ethiopia. Since 2024, 19 out of the 21 bitcoin mining firms that have reached agreements with Ethiopia's state power company are headquartered in China (Manning, 2024).

The Ethiopian government views Chinese tech companies as key technology partners to drive economic growth and improve the quality of life for its 126 million people (anonyms, personal communication, 2022). Chinese digital technology is indeed crucial for Ethiopian development on all stack levels. For instance, almost all broadband infrastructure in Ethiopia was built by Huawei and ZTE, who entered the Ethiopian market in 2006. Both companies' vendor financing opportunities enabled the Ethiopian government to expand ICT capability throughout the country. Today, Huawei is a leading provider of telecom infrastructure, controlling the further development of the two important sub-sectors of the digital economy in Ethiopia (mobile money and e-commerce platforms) with access to a growing yet underdeveloped digital market in Ethiopia (anonym, personal communication, February-March, 2022). In space technology, China has provided financial support to Ethiopia and agreed on technology transfer and knowledge sharing. As a result, Ethiopia successfully launched remote sensing satellites in 2019 and 2020 (Space in Africa, 2020). The success of the Chinese-Ethiopian cooperation in satellite technology has reduced Ethiopia's one-sided reliance on foreign satellite data companies and European assistance in space technology.

Today, Chinese companies, such as Huawei, Transsion, and Alibaba, working closely with the Ethiopian government and other companies, are well-positioned to dominate the market in the coming years. Huawei's infrastructural plan for Ethiopia indeed highlights all levels of the stack.[5] As these companies will control the underpinning infrastructure, we must assume that their latent control over Ethiopia's digital future will increase as the country develops its digital economy. For instance, working closely with Ethio Telecom, Huawei has been instrumental in transforming the state-owned carrier from a pure telecommunications provider to a digital solutions provider. By building the cloud infrastructure and offering innovative digital services under the E.M 2.0 model, the collaboration with Huawei has made Ethio Telecom the undisputed market leader in the country, helping it to increase its revenue from new services and market share in mobile money transactions. From a digital sovereignty perspective, Huawei's technology support and cooperation have prepared Ethio Telecom to face competition from new players in a new era of liberalisation of Ethiopia's telecommunications sector for foreign companies. Since 2021, Safaricom Ethiopia has become the second telecom company offering services in Ethiopia. The company is backed by a consortium led by Kenya's Safaricom, Vodafone, and Japan's Sumitomo, with financial support from the World Bank and the US-based Development Finance Corporation.

At the request of Ethio Telecom, Huawei co-developed the leading mobile payment and digital wallet platform, Telebirr, which enables bill payment and instant money transfers in Ethiopia (anonym, personal communication, February-March, 2022). As of August 2024, the Telebirr platform, which has already achieved super-app status, has 48.7 million active users, including 203,000 merchants, with a total transaction value of 2.7 trillion Ethiopian Birr (Ethio Telecom, 2024). The app is an integral part of the daily life of Ethiopians. While Ethio Telecom owns the platform, Huawei is an important partner through a long-standing relationship, maintaining the platform's functionality by providing data centres and maintenance services in the background and especially by targeting the rural population, and providing platforms for Ethiopian entrepreneurs to use digital marketplaces (anonym, personal communication, February-March, 2022).

Similarly, the nascent but growing e-commerce is another sub-sector in which Chinese stakeholders are actively involved. In partnership with the Ethiopian government, Alibaba Group created the Electronic World Trade Platform (eWTP) Ethiopia Hub in 2019 (Fasil, 2019). Linked to Alibaba's Tmall Global, eWTP facilitates exporting agricultural products such as coffee from Ethiopia to China (Johnston, 2021; Mureithi, 2022). In

2024, in partnership with Ethiopian Airlines, the Ethiopian Digital Transformation Association, and private Ethiopian companies, Alibaba Group launched AliExpress, a clear indication of Alibaba's intention to enter the emerging e-commerce space in Ethiopia and beyond. With a dedicated "Africa-first strategy", Ethiopian Airlines provides e-commerce logistics services in Ethiopia and Africa. In addition, the AliExpress platform allows purchases in local currency, Ethiopian Birr, opening up a whole new way of international trade for Ethiopian businesses. AliExpress also plans to integrate Telebirr and other local fintech companies as payment options, enabling millions of Ethiopians to participate directly in AliExpress e-commerce activity. According to the Ethiopian Ministry of Innovation and Technology, creating a functioning digital marketplace is an opportunity to position Ethiopia in international trade (Ministry of Innovation and Technology, 2024).

Based on Huang and Mayer's (2023) data power framework, Chinese digital companies currently control three of the four digital stack layers in Ethiopia: the physical infrastructure, cloud infrastructure, and platform as sectoral applications. Regarding the physical Infrastructure, Ethiopia's backbone and broadband infrastructure are firmly anchored with Huawei and ZTE. New entrants into the market, such as Safaricom, rely on China-made compatible systems to provide services (Swinhoe, 2022). At the cloud infrastructure level, although some new and non-Chinese private market entrants are available at the cloud infrastructure level, Huawei remains the main data centre and cloud ecosystem provider to Ethio Telecom.[6] Besides, new Chinese companies are discussing with Ethio Telecom the building of a hyperscale data centre to service the growing needs of Ethiopian customers, strengthening the latent control over the cloud infrastructure layer in the country (Okorie, 2024). The third layer demonstrating growing control of Chinese stakeholders in Ethiopia's digital ecosystem is the emergence of e-commerce platforms such as Alibaba's AliExpress. These platforms determine the further development of the country's e-commerce capabilities and corresponding sectoral developments from nurturing local digital entrepreneurship, onboarding local mobile payment applications, and developing last-mile logistics delivery. In other words, Ethiopia has simultaneously diversified its options of suppliers and expanded its digital capabilities across multiple digital sectors, thereby strengthening Ethiopia's overall digital sovereignty despite growing dependence.

Conclusion

Digital transformation is a high priority for most African countries. The strategic implications of this transformation are paramount, both in terms of choosing partners to implement projects and in terms of identifying local capabilities and skills that can be enhanced to support the further development of African economies and societies. As shown above, Chinese tech companies are involved at all levels of the stack, from developing physical infrastructure and human resources to providing digital services and creating digital payment ecosystems; they now play an indispensable role in Africa's digital transformation. Returning to the title of this book, "Partnership, Peonage, or Pawnage", we can conclude that Chinese ICT companies are unique in that they operate across all channels of interaction. They act as vendors, constructors, service providers, and investors, and closely cooperate with PRC policy banks and other loan facilitators. While the extent of technology transfer by Chinese ICT companies is still being debated, there is evidence of significant skill and knowledge transfer. Consequently, their comprehensive contribution to Africa's digital transition differs from that of US and European firms, resulting in both greater dependence and greater capacity building, enabling the political agency of African states and contributing to economic development.

In summary, the term "asymmetric partnerships" perhaps best encapsulates the evolving digital relations between China and African countries. Although increased engagement by Chinese and US ICT companies helps to reduce the digital divide in African countries, primarily through the creation of digital infrastructure, African governments are unlikely to be able to reduce their overall dependence on foreign suppliers for critical digital infrastructure. While the Internet policies and infrastructure constellations emerging in African countries suggest a degree of independent local agency that does not reproduce the logic of "neo-colonialism" (Gagliardone, 2019, p. 158), we also see that, as highlighted above in our case study, Chinese digital technologies are critical to Ethiopia's development at all stack levels and will remain so for the foreseeable future. However, this does not mean that Ethiopia is merely a pawn in the further development of its digital transformation. Instead, the case study demonstrates the country's ability to provide the policy parameters and administrative oversight under which foreign companies operate.

While a robust and strategic African agency vis-à-vis Chinese and other ICT companies is urgently needed, above all, the question remains as to who will own and control the vast amount of data generated in the process of building Africa's digital economy and who will be able to analyse it and provide actionable knowledge for the digital development of African countries. While Ethiopia is eagerly seeking partnerships to advance its digital development under its Digital Ethiopia 2025 strategy, it is evident that Chinese companies (and others) are increasingly expanding their infrastructural and productive data power, reshaping the local capabilities, interests, and agency of local actors in Ethiopia. To establish local production and innovation capabilities, Ethiopian stakeholders have to collaborate with Chinese and other ICT providers to develop robust local capabilities. For instance, the Ethiopian government is also keen to have a trained workforce to fuel its future development goals, and it uses strategic partnerships with leading state companies such as Ethio Telecom and Ethiopian Airlines to train its workforce with the help of Chinese companies, such as Huawei and Alibaba. Conversely, Transsion's experience in Ethiopia exemplifies how a Chinese firm can adopt a localisation strategy to meet the needs of African digital consumers.

The increasing risk posed by the geopolitical instrumentalisation of digital technologies is a concern as it could turn African countries and their various economic sectors into pawns in a global economic and technological power play (Zajontz, 2025; Mayer & Lu, 2025). As these countries become more dependent on technology companies from the United States and China, their technology sectors and supporting infrastructures are likely to become breeding grounds for heated competition and even open rivalry. Therefore, it is crucial to further strengthen African knowledge creation and innovation capacity in order to increase strategic agency, self-determination, and influence over the trajectory of Africa's digital development (see Wu, 2025). Further research is also essential into the cross-cutting issues that growing digital dependence and geopolitics could bring to African societies. The more we understand how Chinese and other digital companies operate and impact African digital transformations, the better the business plans, policy choices, and societal responses that can be developed.

Abbreviations

AI	Artificial Intelligence
BRI	Belt and Road Initiative
ICT	Information and Communication Technology
PRC	People's Republic of China

Notes

1. Digital transformation, which describes the holistic integration of digital technologies into all areas of business, fundamentally changing how it operates and delivers value. The focus of digital transformation is the change in business models, operations, and customer experience, but also the provision of public services and the operations of government that influences growth potentials, innovation, and competitiveness in the digital age.
2. Among other ICT-related policies, Rwanda introduced "The National AI Policy", "The National Broadband Policy and Strategy", and "National Digital Talent Policy" to strengthen Rwanda's position as an ICT hub in Africa.
3. A famous example is the construction of a railway line between Tanzania and Zambia (completed in 1976). In 2012, Chinese state-owned enterprises announced that they would build a $1.32 billion rail link between the Lake Victoria port city of Mwanza and the town of Isaka, as part of a 341 km railway infrastructure linking the Indian Ocean port of Dar es Salaam with Tanzania's interior. Chinese companies are also the leading actors in African dam projects (cf. International Rivers, 2012).
4. The Addis Ababa Djibouti rail connection has been funded 85 percent by China EXIM Bank and 15 percent by Ethiopian and Djiboutian Governments.
5. See Huawei's 2.0 model concept with Ethio Telecom: https://www.huawei.com/en/huaweitech/publication/202401/em-2-digital-intelligent-transformation-african-carriers
6. Cloud infrastructure companies such as Wingu Africa, Raxio, and RedFox are active in Ethiopia.

References

Aalders, J. T., Bachmann, J., Knutsson, P., & Musembi Kilaka, B. (2021). The making and unmaking of a megaproject: Contesting temporalities along the LAPSSET corridor in Kenya. *Antipode, 53*(5), 1273–1293.

Adu Amoah, L. G. (2025). Global digital political economy and its concerns: Is digital imperialism the elephant in the room? *Global Political Economy, 4*(1), 89–101. https://doi.org/10.1332/26352257Y2024D000000028

Agbebi, M., Xue, G., & Zheng, Y. (2021). *China-powered ICT Infrastructure: Lessons from Tanzania and Cambodia*. (SAIIA Policy Briefing; No. 252). South African Institute of International Affairs. https://saiia.org.za/research/china-powered-ict-infrastructure-lessons-from-tanzania-and-cambodia/

Alves, A., & Lee, C. (2022). Knowledge transfer in the global South: Reusing or creating knowledge in China's special economic zones in Ethiopia and Cambodia? *Global Policy, 13*(S1), 45–57. https://doi.org/10.1111/1758-5899.13060

Arnold, S. (2024). Africa's roads to digital development: Paving the way for Chinese structural power in the ICT sector? *Review of International Political Economy, 31*(4), 1148–1172. https://doi.org/10.1080/09692290.2023.2297363

Bagwandeen, M. (2021, September 13). *Don't blame China for the rise of digital authoritarianism in Africa*. Foreign Policy Research Institute. Retrieved April 5, 2022, from https://www.fpri.org/article/2021/09/dont-blame-china-for-the-rise-of-digital-authoritarianism-in-africa/.

Boston University Global Development Policy Center. (2024, n.d.). *Chinese Loans to Africa Database*. Retrieved April 26, 2025, from http://bu.edu/gdp/chinese-loans-to-africa-database

Bradford, A. (2023). *Digital empires: The global battle to regulate technology*. Oxford University Press.

Brautigam, D. (2020). A critical look at Chinese 'debt-trap diplomacy': The rise of a meme. *Area Development and Policy, 5*(1), 1–14.

Business Insider Africa. (2024, November 18). *Xiaomi Nigeria announces dual-brand strategy with Xiaomi and POCO, paving the way for the future*. https://africa.businessinsider.com/local/lifestyle/xiaomi-nigeria-announces-dual-brand-strategy-with-xiaomi-and-poco-paving-the-way-for/gtbdbtq

Canalys. (2024, March 4). African smartphone market surges 24% in Q4 2023, despite macro headwinds. Retrieved September 20, 2024, from https://www.canalys.com/newsroom/africa-smartphone-market-Q4-2023

Carmody, P., Taylor, I., & Zajontz, T. (2022). China's spatial fix and 'debt diplomacy'in Africa: Constraining belt or road to economic transformation? *Canadian Journal of African Studies/Revue canadienne des études africaines, 56*(1), 57–77.

Chen, L., & Cash, J. (2024, September 5). China offers Africa $51 billion in fresh funding, promises a million jobs. *Reuters*. Retrieved April 27, 2025, from https://www.reuters.com/world/china-deepen-industrial-agricultural-trade-investment-ties-with-africa-2024-09-05/

Chen, W. (2022, February 21). China and Africa: Ethiopia case study debunks investment myths. *The Conversation*. Retrieved April 5, 2022, from https://theconversation.com/china-and-africa-ethiopia-case-study-debunks-investment-myths-177098

Cheng, J., & Zeng, J. (2023). Shaping AI's future? China in global AI governance. *Journal of Contemporary China, 32*(143), 794–810.

China-Africa Research Initiative. (2024). Data: Chinese contract revenues in Africa, 1998–2023. Retrieved June 20, 2024, from https://www.sais-cari.org/data-chinese-contracts-in-africa

Chuan Chu. (2024, n.d.). *Intro - Chuan Chu United International Engineering Co., Lt.* https://www.ccunin.com/en/about.html

Edwards, P. N. (2021). Platforms are infrastructures on fire. In T. S. Mullaney, B. Peters, M. Hicks, & K. Philip (Eds.), *Your computer is on fire* (pp. 313–336). The MIT Press.

Ehl, D. (2022, August 2). Africa embraces Huawei tech despite security concerns. *Deutsche Welle.* Retrieved June 18, 2024, from https://www.dw.com/en/africa-embraces-huawei-technology-despite-security-concerns/a-60665700.

Ethio Telecom. (2024). *Telebirr statistics.* https://www.ethiotelecom.et/telebirr/

FAO. (2020). Digital Ethiopia 2025: A digital strategy for Ethiopia inclusive prosperity. Retrieved September 14, 2025, from https://faolex.fao.org/docs/pdf/eth215804.pdf.

Fasil, M. (2019, November 25). Alibaba Group to help Ethiopia set up first eWTP hub, the second in Africa. *Addis Standard.* Retrieved April 5, 2022, from https://addisstandard.com/news-alibaba-group-to-help-ethiopia-set-up-first-ewtp-hubthe-second-in-africa/

Federal Democratic Republic of Ethiopia. (2020). *The Digital Ethiopia 2025 - A strategy for Ethiopia inclusive prosperity.* Retrieved July 30, 2024, from https://www.fao.org/faolex/results/details/en/c/LEX-FAOC215804/

Fei, D. (2021). Chinese telecommunications companies in Ethiopia: The influences of host government intervention and inter-firm competition. *The China Quarterly, 245*(March), 186–207. https://doi.org/10.1017/S0305741020000417

Fuchs, C., & Horak, E. (2008). Africa and the digital divide. *Telematics and Informatics, 25*(2), 99–116. https://doi.org/10.1016/j.tele.2006.06.004

Gagliardone, I. (2019). *China, Africa, and the future of the internet.* Bloomsbury Publishing.

Gordon, D., & Nouwens, M. (Eds.). (2022). *The digital silk road: China's technological rise and the geopolitics of cyberspace.* Routledge.

GSMA. (2023). *The Mobile Economy Sub-Saharan Africa 2023.* Retrieved June 20, 2024, from https://www.gsma.com/solutions-and-impact/connectivity-for-good/mobile-economy/wp-content/uploads/2023/10/20231017-GSMA-Mobile-Economy-Sub-Saharan-Africa-report.pdf

Gu, X., Dinkelbach, C., Huang, Y., Ke, X., Ohnesorge, H., Mayer, M., & Heidbrink, C. (2022). *China's engagement in Africa: Activities, effects and trends.* Center for Global Studies (CGS), Chair for International Relations, Rheinische Friedrich-Wilhelms-Universität.

Heeks, R., Ospina, A. V., Foster, C., Gao, P., Han, X., Jepson, N., Schindler, S., & Zhou, Q. (2024). China's digital expansion in the Global South: Systematic literature review and future research agenda. *The Information Society, 40*(2), 69–95. https://doi.org/10.1080/01972243.2024.2315875

Hellenic Shipping News. (2022, November 11). *China has built 100 seaports in Africa-ambassador*. Retrieved September 21, 2023, from https://www.hellenicshippingnews.com/china-has-built-100-seaports-in-africa-ambassador/
Hillman, J. (2021). *The digital silk road: China's quest to wire the world and win the future*. Harper Business.
Hillman, J. E., & McCalpin, M. (2019, November 4). *Watching Huawei's "Safe Cities."* CSIS Center for Strategic and International Studies. https://www.csis.org/analysis/watching-huaweis-safe-cities
Huang, Y., & Mayer, M. (2023). Power in the age of datafication: Exploring China's global data power. *Journal of Chinese Political Science, 28*(1), 25–49.
International Rivers. (2012, November). *The New Great Walls. A guide to China's overseas Dams industry* (2nd ed.). Retrieved April 5, 2022, from https://www.globalccsinstitute.com/archive/hub/publications/162708/new-great-walls-chinas-overseas-dam-industry.pdf
Jie, Z., & Hong, L. (2023). China-ASEAN cooperation on high-quality BRI: Regional experience, order reconstruction and strategic rethinking. *China International Studies, 101*, 53–79.
Johnston, L. (2021). World Trade, E-Commerce, and COVID-19: Role of and implications for China's electronic trade platform (eWTP). *The China Review, 21*(2), 65–86.
Kagermann, H., Streibich, K.-H., & Suder, K. (2021). *Digital sovereignty: Status quo and perspectives [Acatech IMPULSE]*. acatech – National Academy of Science and Engineering. https://en.acatech.de/publication/digital-sovereignty/
Lee, C. K. (2018). *The specter of global China*. University of Chicago Press.
Manning, L. (2024, February 19). Chinese partnership to bring large scale bitcoin mining to Ethiopia. *Bitcoin Magazine*. Retrieved March 18, 2025, from https://bitcoinmagazine.com/markets/chinese-partnership-to-bring-large-scale-bitcoin-mining-to-ethiopia.
Mas, I., & Radcliffe, D. (2010). *Mobile payments go viral: M-PESA in Kenya*. World Bank Group.
Mayer, M., & Lu, Y.-C. (2023). Illusionen der Autonomie? Europas Position in den globalen digitalen Abhängigkeitsstrukturen. *SIRIUS–Zeitschrift für Strategische Analysen, 7*(4), 390–410.
Mayer, M., & Lu, Y.-C. (2025). Global structures of digital dependence and the rise of technopoles. *New Political Economy*. https://doi.org/10.1080/13563467.2025.2497766
Mayer, M., & Zhang, X. (2021). Theorizing China-world integration: Sociospatial reconfigurations and the modern silk roads. *Review of International Political Economy, 28*(4), 974–1003.
Mbembe, A. (2021). *Out of the dark night*. Columbia University Press.

Mckinsey. (2023, March 10). *How digital tools could boost efficiency in African health systems.* Retrieved June 27, 2024, from https://www.mckinsey.com/industries/healthcare/our-insights/how-digital-tools-could-boost-efficiency-in-african-health-systems.

Ministry of Foreign Affairs of the People's Republic of China. (2021, November 30). Forum on China-Africa Cooperation Dakar Action Plan (2022–2024). Retrieved April 5, 2022, from https://www.fmprc.gov.cn/mfa_eng/wjdt_665385/2649_665393/202112/t20211202_10461183.html.

Ministry of Foreign Affairs People's Republic of China. (2024). *Beijing Declaration on jointly building an all-weather China-Africa Community with a shared future for New Era.* https://www.mfa.gov.cn/eng/xw/zyxw/202409/t20240905_11485993.html

Ministry of Information Communication Technology and Innovation (MINICT): Policy Documents. (n.d.). Retrieved June 24, 2024, from https://www.minict.gov.rw/policies.

Ministry of Innovation and Technology (MINT). (2024, n.d.). *Alibaba Group (AliExpress) has announced the launch of an e-commerce market in Ethiopia.* Retrieved December 5, 2024, from http://www.mint.gov.et/w/alibaba-group-aliexpress-has-announced-the-launch-of-an-e-commerce-market-in-ethiopia.

Munga, E., & Monye, E. (2024, March 11). *Tracking progress of the U.S. digital transformation with Africa Initiative.* Carnegie Endowment for International Peace. Retrieved June 29, 2024, from https://carnegieendowment.org/posts/2024/03/tracking-progress-of-the-us-digital-transformation-with-africa-initiative?lang=en.

Mureithi, C. (2022, January 27). African diplomats are live-streaming and making deliveries to China's consumers. *Quartz Africa.* Retrieved April 5, 2022, from https://qz.com/africa/2117788/african-nations-bet-big-on-chinas-e-commerce-market/.

Nyabiage, J. (2022, August 29). Chinese investors are again pouring millions into Africa's fintech start-ups. *South China Morning Post.* Retrieved April 5, 2022, from https://www.scmp.com/news/china/diplomacy/article/3146678/chinese-investors-are-again-pouring-millions-africas-fintech.

Okorie, I. (2024, September 24). Ethio Telecom in talks with a Chinese firm for a hyperscale data centre. *Techpoint.africa.* Retrieved December 1, 2024, from https://techpoint.africa/2024/09/24/ethio-telecom-talks-with-chinese-firm-for-a-hyper-scale-data-centre/.

Pearson, J. S. (2024). Defining digital authoritarianism. *Philosophy & Technology, 37*(73). https://doi.org/10.1007/s13347-024-00754-8

PR Newswire. (2024, July 4). *Huawei to train additional 150,000 people in Sub-Saharan Africa by 2027.* Retrieved October 24, 2024, from https://www.

prnewswire.com/news-releases/huawei-to-train-additional-150-000-people-in-sub-saharan-africa-by-2027%2D%2D302189415.html.

Qobo, M., & le Pere, G. (2017). The Role of China in Africa's industrialization: The challenge of building global value chains. *Journal of Contemporary China, 27*(110), 208–223.

Republic of Kenya. (2019). *Digital economy blueprint: Powering Kenya's transformation.* https://smartafrica.org/wp-content/uploads/2021/08/Kenya_Digital_Economy_2019.pdf

Resilient Digital Africa. (2022, June 29). *Zekarias Amsalu 'The African Fintech ecosystem is undergoing a period of unprecedented exponential growth.'* https://resilient.digital-africa.co/en/blog/tech_voices/zekarias-amsalu-the-african-fintech-ecosystem-is-undergoing-a-period-of-unprecedented-exponential-growth-2/

Resilient Digital Africa. (2024, February 21). *The Ethiopian Government strikes deal with Hong Kong company to establish data center.* Retrieved July 10, 2024, from https://resilient.digital-africa.co/en/blog/2024/02/21/the-ethiopian-government-strikes-deal-with-hong-kong-company-to-establish-data-center/rica.

Ross, A. (2020). The panopticon is already here. *The Atlantic, September.* Retrieved April 5, 2022, from https://www.theatlantic.com/magazine/archive/2020/09/china-ai-surveillance/614197/

Runde, D., Savoy, C. M., & Staguhn, J. (2021). *China and SMEs in Sub-Saharan Africa: A Window of Opportunity for the United States.* Center for Strategic and International Studies. Retrieved April 5, 2022, from https://www.csis.org/analysis/china-and-smes-sub-saharan-africa-window-opportunity-united-states.

Shanahan, M. (2024, April 8). *Despite improvements, Sub-Saharan Africa has the widest usage and coverage gaps worldwide.* GSMA. https://www.gsma.com/solutions-and-impact/connectivity-for-good/mobile-for-development/blog/despite-improvements-sub-saharan-africa-has-the-widest-usage-and-coverage-gaps-worldwide/

Shen, H. (2018). Building a digital Silk Road? Situating the internet in China's Belt and Road Initiative. *International Journal of Communication, 12*, 2683–2701. https://ijoc.org/index.php/ijoc/article/view/8405/2386

Shinn, D. H., & Eisenman, J. (2023). *China's relations with Africa: A new era of strategic engagement.* Columbia University Press.

Smart Africa Alliance. (2024). Who we are. Retrieved June 27, 2024, from https://smartafrica.org/who-we-are/.

Southwood, R. (2022). *Africa 2.0: Inside a continent's communications revolution.* Manchester University Press.

Space in Africa. (2020). *Ethiopia has launched its second satellite, ET-SMART-RSS.* Space in Africa. Retrieved December 06, 2024, from https://africanews.space/ethiopia-has-launched-its-second-satellite-et-smart-rss/.

Stanford University. (2024). *Artificial intelligence index report 2024*. Retrieved June 28, 2024, from https://hai.stanford.edu/assets/files/hai_ai-index-report-2024-smaller2.pdf.

Swinhoe, D. (2022, January 20). *Safaricom to deploy pre-fab data center in Ethiopia*. Data Centre Dynamics. Retrieved December 1, 2024, from https://www.datacenterdynamics.com/en/news/safaricom-to-deploy-pre-fab-data-center-in-ethiopia/.

Techpoint Africa. (2018). 27+ noteworthy facts about Transsion Holdings, the company behind TECNO, iTel and Infinix. Retrieved September 14, 2025, from https://techpoint.africa/general/transsion-holdings-brief-history/.

Tong, A. (2021). China's ICT engagement in Africa: A comparative analysis. *The Yale Review of International Studies, 11*. Retrieved April 5, 2022, from http://yris.yira.org/essays/4702.

UN News. (2024, Febuary 20). INTERVIEW: AI expert warns of 'digital colonization' in Africa. Retrieved December 5, 2024, from https://www.ipsnews.net/2024/02/interview-ai-expert-warns-digital-colonization-africa/.

Usman, Z. & Csanadi, A. (2023). *How Can African countries participate in U.S. clean energy Supply Chains?*. Carnegie Endowment for International Peace. Retrieved December 5, 2024, from https://carnegieendowment.org/research/2023/10/how-can-african-countries-participate-in-us-clean-energy-supply-chains?lang=en.

Vaidyanathan, V., & Gomera, J. (2019). Power and communication infrastructure—Case studies of Mtwara – Dar es Salaam Natural Gas Pipeline Project and National ICT Broadband Backbone (NICTBB). In V. Vaidyanathan (Ed.), *China's infrastructure development in Africa: An Examination of projects in Tanzania and Kenya* (pp. 95–110). Institute of Chinese Studies.

Wang, R., Bar, F., & Hong, Y. (2020). ICT aid flows from China to African countries: A communication network perspective. *International Journal of Communication, 14*, 1498–1523.

Wen, Y. (2020). *The Huawei model. The rise of China's technology giant*. University of Illinois Press.

West Data Group. (2024). *West data center overview*. Retrieved July 11, 2024, from http://www.westdataholding.com/index.html.

Williams, A. (2019, December 12). China is making more of Africa's phones than you think. *Quartz Africa*. Retrieved April 5, 2022, from https://qz.com/africa/1764356/china-makes-majority-of-africas-smartphones/.

Wright, B. (2020, March 23). *Made in China: Africa's ICT infrastructure backbone*. Chief Information Officer. https://www.cio.com/article/193170/made-in-china-africas-ict-infrastructure-backbone.html Last accessed on on April 5, 2022.

Wu, Y. (2025). Mutual accommodation: How do Chinese firms and state agencies adapt to the politics of infrastructure development in Kenya? *Area Development and Policy, 10*(3), 370–387. https://doi.org/10.1080/23792949.2024.2448426

Xinhua News Agency. (2024, July 2). *Ethiopia lauds Huawei's role in talent development in its ICT sector*. Retrieved April 5, 2023, from https://english.news.cn/20240702/f2eded24a20b438e9cf676f971c086dd/c.html

Yasoshima, R., & Nishino, A. (2023, May 6). China's Belt and Road pivots from coal plants to data centers. *Nikkei Asia*. Retrieved April 5, 2023, from https://asia.nikkei.com/Spotlight/Belt-and-Road/China-s-Belt-and-Road-pivots-from-coal-plants-to-data-centers.

Ye, W. (2024). Digital talent development cooperation between China and Africa. In L. G. Adu Amoah (Ed.), *Examining the rapid advance of digital technology in Africa* (pp. 26–44). IGI Global. https://doi.org/10.4018/978-1-6684-9962-7

Zajontz, T. (2025). Locating Africa in the Second Cold War: The geopolitical economy of Kenyan polyalignment. *Third World Quarterly*, 1–21. https://doi.org/10.1080/01436597.2025.2516050

Zhang, H. (2023). *From contractors to investors? Evolving engagement of Chinese State Capital in global infrastructure development and the case of Lekki Port in Nigeria*. Working Paper No. 53. China Africa Research Initiative, School of Advanced International Studies, Johns Hopkins University. http://www.saiscari.org/publications

Africa-China Agricultural Cooperation and the Promises of Modernization

Mariasole Pepa and Paola Minoia

Introduction

> Modernization is an inalienable right of all countries. But the Western approach to it has inflicted immense sufferings on developing countries [...] China and Africa's joint pursuit of modernization will set off a wave of modernization in the Global South
>
> (President Xi Jinping's Keynote speech at the opening of FOCAC 2024)

At the opening ceremony of the 2024 Forum on China–Africa Cooperation (FOCAC), a platform for coordinating economic investments and social development in Africa, President Xi Jinping underscored the centrality of modernization in shaping the future of Africa–China relations. This vision of modernization, at least rhetorically, aims to depart from the constraints of Western paradigms and the long-standing association of modernization with Westernization. Through the "win-win"

M. Pepa (✉)
University of Padua, Padua, Italy
e-mail: mariasole.pepa@unipd.it

P. Minoia
University of Turin, Torino, Italy

L. G. Adu Amoah (ed.), *Africa-China Relations*,
https://doi.org/10.1007/978-981-95-4370-0_10

narrative and "South-South" cooperation rhetoric (Carrozza, 2021), the Chinese government reasserted itself as a cooperative partner distinct from the West.

Modernization also features prominently in the FOCAC agenda on agricultural cooperation—a sector that has been a cornerstone of Africa–China relations since the early 1950s (Jiang, 2020). Notably, China's agricultural engagement in Africa garnered increased attention in the aftermath of the 2007–2008 food and financial crises, which marked a pivotal moment in China's global economic expansion (Cheru & Modi, 2013). This period also witnessed intensified media discourse around a perceived Chinese "Scramble for Africa" (Obeng-Odoom, 2022).

China's diffused presence in African agriculture has led many to ask whether this is a new wave of land grabbing, drawing parallels to historical colonialism, where China's motivations might align with neo-colonial ambitions (Bräutigam & Xiaoyang, 2009). Others have interpreted these developments through a more benign lens, framing them as opportunities to revive the Bandung Spirit (Moyo, 2016). A third perspective foregrounds China's domestic imperatives, emphasizing its pursuit of food security and the externalization of agricultural production to meet the demands of its growing population (Zhang, 2019). These divergent interpretations speak directly to the central analytical concern of this book: do Africa–China relations (in agriculture) constitute a partnership, a form of peonage, or a strategic pawnage? In other words, to what extent does the agricultural cooperation between China and African countries represent an innovative model of international cooperation?

Moreover, dealing with agricultural systems means engaging with a multidimensional world that extends beyond techniques for increasing farming productivity. It encompasses labor, social structures, local knowledge, relationships with forestry and livestock systems, land tenure, access to natural resources, cooperative and/or corporate farming models, and interactions with institutions and political frameworks (Minoia, 2020). Thus, the question is whether Chinese agricultural cooperation intends to address these multiple issues.

To interrogate these questions, this chapter engages with Chinese institutional policy documents concerning its engagement with Africa, with a particular focus on the agricultural sector. A key source of China's programmatic discourse is the body of documents produced through the Forum on China–Africa Cooperation (Cheng et al., 2022). Analyzing these texts allows us to trace how narratives of cooperation have evolved within FOCAC over time (2000–2024), shaped through a process of negotiation between Chinese and African governments. While this approach foregrounds the agency of African states—who actively mediate and negotiate the terms of engagement despite the asymmetries in power relations (Chiyemura et al., 2023)—it also prompts a deeper inquiry into the normative assumptions embedded within FOCAC's vision. What models of development are being advanced? Who stands to benefit from them? And, critically, which voices, lived experiences, and epistemologies are rendered invisible or delegitimized in the process?

In-Between China's Food Security Strategy and African Governments Agendas

Global concerns over China's rising food demand and its economic and environmental impacts are not new. Lester Brown's *Who Will Feed China?* (1995) framed China's food insecurity as a global concern, a theme revisited by Deborah Bräutigam in *Will Africa Feed China?* (2015).

In recent decades, this concern has also become increasingly central to Chinese government policy. Indeed, China's agricultural self-sufficiency has faced significant challenges, with the country's arable land now comprising only 9% of the global total. Decades of industrialization and intensive agriculture have led to soil contamination, pollution, and farmland degradation, undermining China's food production capacity (Li & Pan, 2020; Wan et al., 2018). Urbanization, land conversion, shifting dietary patterns (Zhu et al., 2023), and climate change (Yu & Zhai, 2020) have further destabilized the country's food security. To address these challenges, in September 2024, China issued new guidelines to halt arable land loss, setting a minimum threshold of 124.33 million hectares (Xinhua, 2024).

China's focus on food security stems from a deliberate strategy aimed at diminishing reliance on external providers, achieved in part through the expansion of Chinese global agribusiness endeavors (Zhang, 2019). This trajectory is a direct response to China's aspirations to counterbalance the influence of prominent entities such as the US-based Archer Daniels Midland, Bunge, Cargill, and Netherlands-based Louis Dreyfus, the four biggest controllers of agricultural commodities. In the early 2000s, China launched the *Agriculture Going Out Policy,* which encouraged Chinese enterprises to invest in agricultural ventures abroad. As part of this strategy, China reduced export taxes on fertilizers, facilitating the expansion of Chinese agricultural enterprises overseas; African countries have prominently featured in the execution of this policy (Fiorentini, 2016).

Hence, alterations in China's food strategy have yielded repercussions that extend far beyond its national boundaries. Alongside the reconfiguration of its domestic agricultural system through the Agriculture Going Out Policy, the Belt and Road Initiative (BRI), launched in 2013, has played a pivotal role in expanding China's global agricultural footprint, particularly through infrastructure-led development (McMichael, 2020). Under the BRI, China is attempting to strengthen a "Food Silk Road" based on technology transfer, agricultural infrastructure expansion, and a space of coordinated policies intending to restructure the global food supply chains to serve China's geopolitical interests (Tortajada & Zhang, 2021). The launch of China's Belt and Road Initiative (BRI) has heightened concern among traditional Western powers. In response, the European Union introduced the Global Gateway in 2021, including a €150 billion Africa–Europe Investment Package. This new plan fits into a global dynamic of geopolitical competition between China and the West, with African markets emerging as a pivotal arena for this interaction, and international cooperation turning into another space of competition.

Nevertheless, China's food security strategy, along with its efforts to "fix" agro-technologies in African contexts (Pepa, 2021), constitutes only one dimension of a broader and more nuanced picture. While the Chinese government actively supports the entrance of domestic companies into African markets—often through mechanisms such as FOCAC—many African governments have not only welcomed these investments but have also played an instrumental role in facilitating them. Grand modernist agricultural projects have been promoted by many African governments, often at the direct expense of peasant communities. In Uganda, for instance, Banjwa (2024) explores how Ugandan state actors and Chinese private investors deploy the discourse of "idle land" to legitimize Chinese project implementation. This narrative—long central to both Chinese and Western land rush strategies—opens the door to multiple forms of accumulation (Borras & Franco, 2024). Banjwa (2024) further argues that displacement in this context is not merely a material or territorial process but also a form of epistemic violence, in which local epistemologies and relationality with land are dismissed and overwritten by external logics of land capitalization. Moreover, these processes of expulsion are frequently legitimized through a narrative of "mutuality" and shared anti-colonial struggle, strategically mobilized by both African and Chinese governments to justify the expansion of China's agricultural investments on the continent (Muinga, 2024). Such discourse obscures the underlying asymmetries of power and systematically marginalizes local forms of resistance and contestation.

Another example of African governments actively facilitating Chinese—and more broadly, foreign—investments is Mozambique, where the state enabled land dispossession for a Chinese project by designating the targeted area as "state land" (Ntauazi, 2024). Similarly, in Sudan, the government has long pursued strategies aimed at attracting foreign investment in land and water resources (Pepa et al., 2025). In Tanzania, this dynamic is evident in initiatives such as the Southern Agricultural Growth Corridor of Tanzania (SAGCOT) (Sulle, 2020) and, more recently, the Building a Better Tomorrow (BBT) program, both intended to attract agribusiness investment and foster public-private partnerships to integrate the country into global value chains. In the case of the BBT program, the Tanzanian government's push to attract foreign agribusiness aligns with China's growing interest in soybean production in the country. However, a new report from GRAIN and La Via Campesina (2024) warns that this alignment is likely to trigger a new wave of land conflicts, particularly affecting smallholder farmers and pastoralists.

FOCAC and Its Criticism

The Forum on China–Africa Cooperation (FOCAC) is the main multilateral cooperation mechanism involving actors from China and Africa. FOCAC reflects China's determination to play a prominent role in the development landscape, as well as to challenge the DAC regime promoting South-South cooperation (Domínguez, 2018). Started in the 2000s, FOCAC has been held every three years, hosted alternatively by China and African countries. Since 2006, the centrality of FOCAC in China–Africa relations has grown extensively, with particular attention to agriculture. In this chapter, FOCAC is examined as a tool of soft power, used by China to advance its geopolitical strategies and development ideas in Africa (Nantulya, 2018). Soft power, in this context, refers to noncoercive influence derived from a country's culture, political values, and foreign policies, which counterbalance China's hard power (Nye, 2021). Central to this strategy are selective narratives of "win-win" cooperation, which frame China's interventions as mutually beneficial. These narratives help legitimize China's foreign policy in Africa, presenting them as apolitical rather than part of broader geopolitical objectives (Mohan & Tan-Mullins, 2019). However, as previously observed, these discourses are frequently endorsed by African governments, which strategically attract Chinese investments and loans not merely as economic opportunities but as instruments to diversify their international partnerships, circumvent enduring political marginalization, and assert a more prominent role within global governance frameworks (Soulé, 2020).

Despite the prominence of FOCAC, several analysts have critiqued the nature of China's cooperation. Ibonye (2020) argues that the benefits for Africa in FOCAC negotiations remain limited compared to China's strategic interests. Benabdallah (2021) further notes that African countries are not all treated equally in FOCAC consultations, with the prioritization of certain states based on China's geopolitical considerations. Soulé (2021) critiques FOCAC for its exclusion of non-state actors, calling for a "more hybrid and inclusive form of summitry" that incorporates civil society voices (p. 19). Moreover, the lack of transparency in FOCAC's operations is a significant issue; as Olander (2024) observes, "we know very little about how many of the FOCAC promises made over the past 24 years were ever kept." This lack of accountability underscores the difficulty of evaluating the concrete outcomes of FOCAC agreements. Nevertheless, these discourses are deeply embedded in specific power relations and advance particular visions of development that this research seeks to critically unpack.

Research Methodology

This research focuses on the discursive constructions of agricultural cooperation as articulated in the policy documents of FOCAC. Drawing on discourse analysis in geography and development studies, we engage with critical scholarship that exposes the implicit power relations embedded in development discourses (Waitt, 2010; Ziai, 2016). Following Ziai (2016), we trace specific features of development discourse—such as naturalization, othering, legitimization, hierarchization, depoliticization, and appropriation—that underpin China–Africa agricultural cooperation. Development, framed as a neutral response to poverty or food insecurity, is thereby reduced to a technical domain, devoid of historical and geopolitical specificity (Ferguson, 1994). Through this lens, development interventions become legitimized, even as they reproduce binary distinctions (e.g., developed/underdeveloped) and marginalize alternative epistemologies. At the same time, development discourse is a contested space, where struggles over meaning, agency, and the appropriation of claims persist (Ziai, 2016). As such, discourse analysis offers a powerful tool for deconstructing the assumptions and exclusions inherent in dominant development paradigms (Cornwall & Eade, 2010).

Our analysis is moved by an investigation of discursive structures, and how these formations allow the perpetuation of regimes of truth in the framework of China's official discourse (Dittmer, 2010). This study comprises 23 documents issued by FOCAC from 2000 to 2024. Three types of FOCAC materials were central: the opening speech of China's president or prime minister; the official joint declarations; and the action plans released after each conference. We used the official English version of FOCAC's documents that were retrieved from the institutional website. In the analysis, first, we selected the texts that dealt with agricultural cooperation, and then we identified the most recurrent themes, which we recognized as: technological modernization and green development.

In our analysis, we focus on how China's foreign policies, particularly through FOCAC, construct specific meanings about development and agricultural cooperation. Moreover, we looked for any spaces of agency and resistance that could have been recognized by the programmatic statements but were instead invisibilized (Rose, 2001). Given the generality and vagueness that characterize many Chinese diplomatic texts (Alves & Seungjoo, 2022), we aim to expose the silencing of diverse local experiences and the deliberate omission of alternative visions for agricultural and development practices.

Document Analysis: FOCAC's Vision on Agricultural Development

Agriculture has held a position of prominence within China–Africa relations right from the inception of FOCAC's meetings. Its importance has escalated in recent years, notably highlighted by the establishment of the Forum on China–Africa Cooperation in Agriculture (FOCACA) in 2019. China's engagement in African agriculture encompasses a broad spectrum, ranging from participation in agricultural infrastructure projects tied to the BRI to facilitate new food trade routes, public-private partnerships, agricultural training, backing of Chinese investors in the sector, and, more recently, interventions in land and agricultural policies.

Additionally, beginning with FOCAC 2015, the first under the leadership of President Xi Jinping, a significant emphasis has been placed on the trade of agricultural products between China and Africa, which has consistently increased in the last few years. In November 2023, during the 2nd FOCACA, China announced its intention to boost the trade value of agricultural products with African countries to exceed USD 20 billion by 2030 (Voncujovi, 2024). This reflects a long-term trend of expanding agricultural trade. For instance, between 2000 and 2018, agricultural trade grew from USD 650 million to USD 6.92 billion, representing an average annual growth rate of 14% (Ministry of Agriculture and Rural Affairs of the People's Republic of China, 2019).

As part of this evolving trade and development strategy, during the 2021 FOCAC, China also unveiled plans to establish "green lanes" to facilitate the import of African agricultural products into China (Mlilo, 2023)—a measure reaffirmed at FOCAC 2024. Further reinforcing these efforts, in December 2024, China pledged to expand its 100% zero-tariff policy to encompass 33 of Africa's Least Developed Countries (LDCs), building on an earlier 2003 initiative that had covered fewer countries and a narrower set of products. While framed as a step to share development opportunities (Xinhua, 2024), analysts at Development Reimagined—an African-led international development consultancy—warned of consistent trade imbalances in which the majority of exports to China, for instance, from Angola, Zambia, and Mauritania still consist of oil and minerals.

The following section will analyze how two key themes—*technological modernization* and green development—are presented in the studied FOCAC documents.

Technological Modernization

Technological and modernist narratives are central in agricultural discourse in FOCAC. These narratives have been employed to simplify the complexities of African agriculture in terms of technical deficiencies, e.g., presenting insufficient modern technology or needing hybrid seeds to improve productivity. Consequently, the documents assert the need for the acquisition of direct control of China over emerging agro-technologies as a pivotal aspect of core development processes (Flint & Waddoups, 2019). Yet, Lawther (2017) emphasized that African governments also welcome Chinese partnerships because of the intermediary agricultural technology that China can offer.

Beginning with the 2004–2006 Action Plan, "agro-technological cooperation" emerged as a key pillar of China's soft power strategy in Africa. As it has been observed also by Dibua (2006), the proposed Chinese strategy involves a modernization of production processes based on mechanization, hybridization, the use of Chinese genetically modified crops, pesticides, fertilizers, and intensive land use. Technology transfer in agriculture also involves skills transfer, and the dispatch of Chinese agricultural experts providing technical assistance in Africa.

A key mechanism of this strategy has been the establishment of Agricultural Technology Demonstration Centers (ATDCs), introduced at the 2006 FOCAC summit and now established in more than 25 African countries. These Centers reflect an *aid+business* model through which technology transfer is linked with business opportunities for Chinese enterprises (Jiang, 2020). The kind of modern technologies that are transferred through the ATDCs depends on the specialization of the Chinese companies that manage the Centers since they are appointed from different provincial governments. For instance, in the case of the ATDC in Tanzania, the Center attempted to introduce over 10 varieties of Chinese hybrid rice (Pepa, 2021). In the case of Zambia, there was an attempt to introduce Chinese seeds, especially for mushroom production. Presented as means to contribute to Africa's food security, these centers allow machinery, pesticides, fertilizers, hybrid seeds, etc. to enter from China to various agricultural production systems in Africa, based on a promotion of the Chinese successful farming model. In the Beijing Action Plan (2024–2027), China reaffirmed its commitments to build or upgrade 10 ATDCs.

The 2015 FOCAC represented another turning point in China's increased engagement in agricultural development in Africa. President Xi's 2015 keynote speech introduced new narratives on Africa's industrialization, through capacity building in technological modernization. This strategy was re-emphasized in the Action Plan 2016–2018, as a way to overcome the problem of food poverty in Africa. "In view of the challenges in Africa on food security (…) China supports Africa in enhancing productive capacity in agriculture which comprises promotion of high-tech food production" (3.1.4).

The 2018 and 2021 FOCAC under Xi's leadership reinforced and expanded the narratives of the 2015 FOCAC. In the African context, technology transfer appears through experimental centers that are strategic spaces for opening new markets. A clear example of this strategy is represented by the setup of ATDCs. Training for African officials in China is another important way in which China exercises soft power and promotes new commercial links as part of China's development cooperation strategies. The Dakar Action Plan (2022–2024) and the Beijing Action Plan (2024–2027) give particular attention to the training of African officials and the construction of agro-technology centers in China rather than in African countries, despite certain contestations had already been expressed around the suitability and usefulness of agricultural training in China for the African local context and needs (Tugendhat & Alemu, 2016).

Recent action plans have expanded the scope of China's agro-technological initiatives to include "digital agriculture." The Dakar Action Plan (2022–2024) introduced measures for integrating digital technologies into agriculture, such as a Joint Research Center for Digital Agriculture and a Center for E-commerce in agricultural products. The Beijing Action Plan (2024–2027) reinforces these initiatives, emphasizing the application of agricultural remote sensing, and big data. While these efforts align with broader trends in global agricultural innovation, they raise questions about their adaptability and accessibility for local farmers, as well as the potential reinforcement of dependency on Chinese technology.

Green Development

In his opening speech at the 2015 FOCAC, President Xi emphasized the relevance of the forum's theme, "China–Africa Cooperation for Common Development," for an inclusive and sustainable development of the African continent. This marked the beginning of a heightened focus on sustainability within FOCAC discussions, coinciding with increased global awareness of environmental crises and the outcomes of the 2015 Paris Climate Change Conference. Since then, the discourse around "green, low-carbon, and sustainable development" has become a consistent record.

Officially, China's geostrategic narratives align with the global discussion on ecological transition. In his 2018 keynote speech, President Xi reaffirmed China's commitment to working with Africa to pursue green and sustainable development to "protect our lush mountains and lucid waters and all living beings on our planet." Following this statement, the Action Plan 2019–2021 has posed a special emphasis on "sustainable agriculture and organic farming through enhanced food safety and food security" (3.1.4). However, the Action Plan does not clarify how agricultural modernization and organic farming could possibly coexist and be offered as a model of agricultural development; and how this novel ecological sensitivity for organic farming would be implemented in practice, what farming groups would be involved, and in which countries will be targeted. This lack of specificity persists in subsequent documents. The 2024–2027 Action Plan references China's support for "organic and ecological agriculture" and of "eco-friendly agriculture." Yet, these commitments remain vague, with no clear indication of beneficiaries, project locations, or detailed plans for execution.

A similar trend can be observed concerning "green development" in recent FOCAC Action Plans. The 2022–2024 plan, for the first time, contains a dedicated section on green development, with the term "green" appearing 26 times. This emphasis intensifies in the 2024–2027 plan, where the word is mentioned 36 times, compared to only 11 mentions in the 2019–2021 plan. The increasing frequency of the term across documents underscores a rhetorical commitment to sustainability and environmental considerations. Yet, the term "green" is applied broadly to sectors traditionally associated with high carbon emission and environmental degradation, such as manufacturing, energy, and industrial parks.

Green narratives have become a persistent theme across recent FOCAC Action Plans, culminating in the 2025–2027 document where "industrialization, agricultural modernization, and green development" are emphasized as the pathways to modernization. This continuity suggests an attempt to construct a coherent legacy of green-oriented policies. However, the lack of a clear, actionable definition of "green development" weakens these narratives, leaving questions about the coherence of these commitments. Several questions emerge from this greening turn, especially since the different political documents do not form a coherent whole. For instance, while a sustainability approach would involve social sustainability, FOCAC's documents have never mentioned any local farming knowledge, or the type of local producers' involvement in the agrobusiness they propose to achieve; on the contrary, they have invisibilized farmers groups, including women farmers and environmental activists, from the green transition.

Which Cooperation? Which Agriculture? And Who Will Benefit?

An analysis of the FOCAC documents reveals that Chinese cooperation in Africa is framed within a "win-win" rhetoric (Strauss, 2019), emphasizing the dual goals of improving Africa's food security through technology transfer, intended to enhance productivity and market competitiveness, while simultaneously promoting green solutions and reinforcing China's geopolitical influence on the continent. However, a closer examination reveals that China's discourse on agricultural cooperation closely mirrors earlier European interventions, which have been widely criticized by African communities for contributing to their impoverishment (Bereano, 2017; Boafo & Lyons, 2021; Kansanga et al., 2019). Despite its rhetorical distinctions, China's approach often mirrors Western development models by prioritizing governance frameworks and commercial agendas that align with external interests, frequently sidelining the needs and aspirations of African partner countries (Cheng et al., 2022). China's recent emphasis on environmentally friendly agricultural solutions closely parallels the New Green Revolution funded by the Organisation for Economic Co-operation and Development (OECD) and the Bill and Melinda Gates Foundation under the Alliance for a Green Revolution in Africa, which Mkindi et al. (2020) have criticized as a massive failure. The green transition that is present in FOCAC and other official discourses appears more as a rhetoric compliant with global climate concerns than as an effective policy, especially outside of China's domestic boundaries (Si et al., 2017; Nedopil et al., 2021). Promises of greening the BRI and the overall development cooperation seem more instrumental to advancing market and investments' penetration rather than concrete measures on the ground (Harlan & Lu, 2022), which, on the contrary, show an increase in the use of fertilizers and chemicals in the agricultural model proposed for Africa. Globally, China is assuming a central role in controlling technology and chemical inputs for agriculture, as suggested by ChemChina's acquisition of Syngenta, one of the world's major crop chemical companies (Zhang, 2019). This transfer of chemical-intensive agribusiness from Chinese to African lands changes the global geography of pesticides and questions the sustainability of Chinese agrarian interventions (Schneider, 2017; Shattuck, 2021); nowadays, it is unavoidable to consider China's role when debating the redefinition of the global food regime (McMichael, 2020).

Within this context, Chinese agricultural cooperation appears to reinforce a capitalist logic aimed at restructuring local production systems rather than strengthening land-based knowledge systems and community-driven decision-making (Matunhu, 2011). Far from fostering a distinct "Southern alternative" to agriculture under the framework of South-South Cooperation, China's programmatic discourses are heavily oriented toward technological modernization, commercialization, and digitalization. This approach mirrors the priorities of North-South cooperation and reflects continuity with established development paradigms rather than offering an alternative departure (Giunta & Pepa, 2022). This continuity raises serious questions about the transformative potential of China's engagement in African agriculture and suggests an emergent pattern of dependency. Indeed, within the framing of this volume, it invites a critical reflection on whether these relations constitute, instead of partnerships, forms of "pawnage" or "peonage."

The case of Agricultural Technology Demonstration Centers (ATDCs) provides a telling lens through which to interrogate China's attempt to export its agro-technological model and consolidate new forms of dependency. Despite being repeatedly celebrated in FOCAC documents as flagship projects of agricultural cooperation, their practical impact remains highly contested (Xu et al., 2016). In the case of Zambia, Nalwimba and Mudimu (2024) examine whether ATDCs deliver on their promises of empowerment and food security as promoted by Zambian and Chinese policymakers. Their findings suggest a limited impact on peasant communities, revealing signs of "agro-capitalism." Chinese seeds, fertilizers, and agricultural machinery—rather than locally developed resources—are promoted and tested in the ATDC, further embedding dependencies on Chinese inputs.

This disjuncture between official narratives and ground realities has also been observed by one of the authors during field visits to ATDCs in Tanzania and Sudan. In Tanzania, the center was trialing Chinese hybrid rice seeds despite the widespread use of locally adapted varieties developed by the Tanzania Agricultural Research Institute. As in Zambia, the dominance of imported Chinese agro-inputs risks undermining local seed sovereignty and agronomic knowledge (Pepa, 2021). In Sudan, the ATDC appeared in a state of neglect: Chinese machinery lay unused, and agricultural activities had largely ceased (Fig. 1). Training programs, suspended since 2019 due to the COVID-19 pandemic, had been primarily directed at ministry officials rather than local farmers. When asked why the center

Fig. 1 ATDC in Al-Fao, Sudan, February 2023. (Source: M. Pepa)

remained open despite its inactivity, the Chinese director responded: "Our company, our government, needs to stay here" (Interview, Al-Fao, February 2023).

These examples highlight how the strategic, political, and symbolic imperatives underlying China's presence in Africa can significantly overshadow the stated development objectives of its initiatives and challenge the diffused "win-win" rhetoric.

The question arises spontaneously: who do the Agricultural Technology Demonstration Centers truly serve? While African governments, in various capacities, support the establishment of these centers within their countries, their impact on empowering peasant communities remains limited. Furthermore, Chinese agricultural investments do not happen in a vacuum but must be considered within broader socio-political contexts. A notable example of local resistance is the Wambao Agriculture project in Xai-Xai, Mozambique, where Chinese-led initiatives were implicated in violent land acquisitions, with the complicity of the Mozambican government. Bulldozers were deployed to clear land for large-scale plantations, displacing smallholder farmers and undermining their livelihoods. This action provoked significant opposition from affected communities, who were supported by advocacy organizations such as Justiça Ambiental (Mora, 2016; Wise, 2020). Ntauazi (2024) critically examines this investment, asserting that while rural elites benefited from the project, smallholder farmers were incorporated into exploitative labor practices.

These instances underscore the persistent disconnect between the rhetoric presented at FOCAC and the realities on the ground. A central concern is the absence of robust monitoring frameworks to evaluate the efficacy of FOCAC-related projects. Without such systems, it remains uncertain whether the lofty promises of agricultural cooperation are ever fully realized. This raises critical questions: How many of the projects announced at FOCAC have actually been implemented? What specific activities are being carried out? What management structures are in place, and are they operational? These uncertainties complicate the central inquiry of this work—whether the agricultural cooperation between China and Africa constitutes genuine partnership or perpetuates patterns of dependency and exploitation, thus reinforcing a dynamic of peonage. This highlights the critical importance of field research in bridging the enduring gap between policy narratives and the realities faced by local communities.

Looking at the Margins at FOCAC: Roots for Alternatives

Part of our interest in critically examining the FOCAC documents stemmed from a desire to explore the margins and the silences within these discourses—particularly the voices, actors, and epistemologies that have been persistently excluded from consultations over the past two decades. While African governments have actively supported Chinese investments, often framing these engagements within narratives of mutual benefit, other non-state actors—such as peasant communities and farmer organizations, who we contend should be at the center of these conversations—have been systematically excluded from decision-making processes and forcibly displaced from their land.

While Chinese agricultural technologies and expertise are central to FOCAC's agricultural cooperation framework, these initiatives largely exclude Indigenous knowledge systems, traditional farming practices, and local know-how. This mechanism is not novel; it mirrors approaches previously advanced by Western actors and institutions for the past decades.

Moreover, various social groups that are deeply involved in the agrarian world and often belong to the poorest (e.g., landless farmers, agro-pastoralists, small landowners, members of cooperatives or water user associations, migrants, seasonal workers, etc.) are usually overlooked in FOCAC documents as either co-producers or beneficiaries of any proposed initiatives. This exclusion occurs despite the crucial role agrarian movements have played (Martiniello & Nyamsenda, 2018). Similarly, the role of women in agriculture remains inadequately recognized, despite the pivotal contributions of rural women's movements in safeguarding environmental commons, resisting genetically modified crops (Pereira, 2021), advocating for the preservation of seed diversity, and engaging in land struggles (e.g., the Rural Women Assembly: Andrews, 2019). Significant examples of this resistance include the Green Belt Movement, led by Wangari Maathai, and the WoMIN African ecofeminist alliance, both of which link gender with ecological justice and actively challenge the foundational principles of hegemonic models built on patriarchal capitalist exploitation (The WoMin Collective, 2017). These movements also advocate for alternative approaches to the grand modernist visions of agricultural development, which have proven ill-suited to Africa during the Green Revolution. Similarly, in China—like in the West—unsustainable farming practices have contributed to challenges in food productivity, further highlighting the limitations of these top-down, industrialized models of agricultural development.

Speaking of alternatives, Sustainable Agriculture Tanzania (SAT), located approximately 60 km from the Chinese Agricultural Technology Demonstration Center (ATDC), actively promotes agroecological practices that consider both the social and environmental aspects of agriculture. The organization advocates for agricultural technologies through its Farming Training Center, which shares organic solutions and environmentally friendly methods that align with genuine "green" concerns. These approaches have the potential to contribute to the creation of sustainable livelihoods, offering an alternative to the industrial agricultural models promoted by larger initiatives (Mdee et al., 2018). At a broader scale, the agroecological movement in Africa is gaining momentum through networks such as the Alliance for Food Sovereignty in Africa (AFSA). This coalition, comprising farmers, NGOs, and civil society actors, actively documents and promotes community-led agricultural initiatives across the continent. By centering local knowledge systems, supporting biodiversity, and highlighting practices that mitigate climate change, AFSA challenges dominant development paradigms and advocates for food sovereignty (AFSA, 2016).

Despite their exclusion from institutional discourse and FOCAC consultation mechanisms, grassroots organizations have emerged in various other forms. These include movements for land restitution (Wise, 2020) and opposition to the influx of competitive Chinese products that erode local markets (Aidoo, 2016). Resistance also takes shape in everyday practices that contest racialized labor divisions (Huang, 2021) and in organized actions against illegal mining and extractive industries, which have caused profound environmental destruction, social disruption, and escalated anti-Chinese sentiments in affected areas (Aidoo, 2019; Wameru, 2020; Yi, 2021).

The absence of recognition of these movements testifies to the persistence of the prevailing neoclassical model of economic development and overproduction championed as primary objectives by African state institutions and local elites, supported by international financiers, from either the Global North or the South (Scoones et al., 2016). Chinese interventions, much like their Western counterparts, frequently engage with national elites and private investors in Africa while sidelining grassroots resistance to land grabbing and resource extraction. This marginalization persists even when local agrarian and food sovereignty movements present viable, sustainable alternatives to these conventional models of development (Kuadjovi-Ayedeu, 2021; Merwe et al., 2019).

Conclusion: Between Hopes, Promises, and Silence

This chapter has critically unpacked the dominant narratives of agricultural cooperation promoted through the Forum on China–Africa Cooperation from 2000 to 2024. The analysis reveals that FOCAC, widely embraced by African governments, systematically promotes a narrative centered on Chinese modernization and technologization of agriculture. This narrative—rooted in the belief that the challenges of African agriculture can be resolved through the transfer of external technological solutions—perpetuates a model that has repeatedly proven ill-suited to the socio-ecological realities of the continent. As with prior waves of development intervention, this model is being transposed onto African contexts with minimal regard for local needs, knowledges, or agrarian histories.

FOCAC 2024, rather than signaling a shift toward more inclusive or transformative cooperation, reinforced earlier iterations of modernization-driven visions, closely mirroring the frameworks and logics historically associated with North-South development partnerships. Rather than offering a break from established paradigms, China's agricultural cooperation appears to be entrenching new forms of dependency—on Chinese seeds, fertilizers, machinery, and technical expertise—ultimately deepening Africa's structural reliance (Taylor & Zajontz, 2020).

The central issue is not merely the form of the Africa–China relationship—whether it constitutes partnership, patronage, or peonage—but rather the reproduction of developmental models that systematically marginalize agrarian movements, silence peasant resistance, and ignore viable alternatives. These failures are not incidental but are embedded in the very architecture of agricultural cooperation, which relies on the transfer of economic and technological models conceived outside of African contexts and informed by foreign epistemologies (Obeng-Odoom, 2017).

Returning to the broader framing question of this volume, it becomes clear that there is no singular or definitive answer. The case of agriculture shows that while Chinese companies, African governments, and segments of the rural elite may benefit from these collaborations, these gains are frequently secured at the expense of smallholder farmers and agrarian communities. The more urgent question, then, is not whether Africa–China relations represent partnership, patronage, or peonage, but rather: *who benefits* from these arrangements, and at *what cost*?

As this chapter has shown, the answers lie not in Beijing or in the official discourses of African governments but in the margins—in the testimonies of displaced farmers, in the resistance of agrarian movements, and in the agroecological alternatives already flourishing across the continent. It is in these margins that the possibility of a different agricultural future can still be found—if we are (finally) willing to listen.

Abbreviations

AFSA	Alliance for Food Sovereignty in Africa
ATDC	Agricultural Technology Demonstration Center
BBT	Building a Better Tomorrow
BRI	Belt and Road Initiative
FOCAC	Forum on China–Africa Cooperation
SAGCOT	Agricultural Growth Corridor of Tanzania
SAT	Sustainable Agriculture Tanzania

References

AFSA. (2016). *Agroecology: The bold future of farming in Africa*. AFSA and TOAM.

Aidoo, R. (2016, July 18). Why Anti-Chinese sentiment in Africa is on the Rise. *Sixth Tone*. https://www.sixthtone.com/news/1076/why-anti-chinese-sentiment-africa-rise.

Aidoo, R. (2019). The politics of Galamsey and Anti-Chinese populism in Ghana. In R. Aidoo (Ed.), *The Politics of Economic Reform in Ghana*. Routledge. https://doi.org/10.4324/9781351018982

Alves, A. C., & Seungjoo, L. (2022). China's BRI developmental agency in its own words: A content analysis of key policy documents. *World Development, 150*, 105715. https://doi.org/10.1016/j.worlddev.2021.105715

Andrews, M. (2019). A case study of the Southern African rural women's assembly: 'We can bend the stick.'. *Agenda, 33*(1), 48–58. https://doi.org/10.1080/10130950.2019.1598275

Banjwa, A. (2024). Chinese agricultural investments in Uganda and the paradox of 'idle land'. In F. Mazwi, G. T. Mudimu, & K. Helliker (Eds.), *Chinese investment in Africa* (Economic Geography) (pp. 23–44). Springer. https://doi.org/10.1007/978-3-031-52815-6_2

Benabdallah, L. (2021, July 26). In line for FOCAC 2021: Africa, China, and the others. *ISPI*. https://www.ispionline.it/it/pubblicazione/line-focac-2021-africa-china-and-others-31249.

Bereano, P. (2017). Philanthrocapitalism: The Gates' Foundation's African Programmes are not charity. *Third World Resurgence, 328*(December), 2–5. http://www.twn.my/title2/resurgence/2017/328/eco1.htm

Boafo, J., & Lyons, K. (2021). The rhetoric and farmers' lived realities of the Green Revolution in Africa: Case study of the Brong Ahafo Region in Ghana. *Journal of Asian and African Studies., 57*(3), 406–423. https://doi.org/10.1177/00219096211019063

Borras, S. M., & Franco, J. C. (2024). Land rush. *The Journal of Peasant Studies*, 1–16. https://doi.org/10.1080/03066150.2024.2317961.

Bräutigam, D. (2015). *Will Africa feed China?* Oxford University Press.

Bräutigam, D. A., & Xiaoyang, T. (2009). China's engagement in African agriculture: 'Down to the countryside.'. *The China Quarterly, 199*, 686–706. https://doi.org/10.1017/S0305741009990166

Brown, L. R. (1995). *Who will feed China? Wake-up call for a small planet*. Routledge.

Carrozza, I. (2021). Legitimizing China's growing engagement in African security: Change within continuity of official discourse. *The China Quarterly, 248*(1), 1174–1199. https://doi.org/10.1017/S0305741021000242

Cheng, H., Mawdsley, E., & Liu, W. (2022). Reading the Forum on China–Africa Cooperation (2000–2021): Geoeconomics, governance, and embedding ‘creative involvement. *Area Development and Policy, 8*(1), 60–83. https://doi.org/10.1080/23792949.2022.2092018

Cheru, F., & Modi, R. (Eds.). (2013). *Agricultural development and food security in Africa: The impact of Chinese, Indian and Brazilian Investments.* Zed Books.

Chiyemura, F., Gambino, E., & Zajontz, T. (2023). Infrastructure and the politics of African state agency: Shaping the Belt and Road Initiative in East Africa. *Chinese Political Science Review, 8*(1), 105–131. https://doi.org/10.1007/s41111-022-00214-8

Cornwall, A., & Eade, D. (2010). *Deconstructing development discourse. Buzzwords and fuzzwords.* Practical Action Publishing.

Dibua, J. I. (2006). *Modernization and the crisis of development in Africa: The Nigerian experience.* Routledge.

Dittmer, J. (2010). Textual and discourse analysis. In D. DeLyser, S. Herbert, S. Aitken, M. Crang, & L. McDowell (Eds.), *The SAGE handbook of qualitative geography* (pp. 274–286). SAGE Publications.

Domínguez, R. (2018). China Y La construcción De Un régimen Internacional De Cooperación Sur-Sur. *Carta Internacional, 13*(1). https://doi.org/10.21530/ci.v13n1.2018.737

Ferguson, J. (1994). *The anti-politics machine. Development, depoliticization and bureaucratic power in Lesotho.* University of Minnesota Press.

Fiorentini, M. (2016). How is the Chinese “going out” policy having an impact on agriculture-related trade with Africa *Future Agricultures Working Paper* 134. https://www.future-agricultures.org/publications/working-papers/document/how-is-the-chinese-going-out-policy-having-an-impact-on-agriculture-related-trade-with-africa/

Flint, C., & Waddoups, M. (2019). South-South cooperation or core-periphery contention? Ghanaian and Zambian perceptions of economic relations with China. *Geopolitics, 26*(3), 889–918. https://doi.org/10.1080/14650045.2019.1659781

Giunta, I., & Pepa, M. (2022). Geografie policentriche della cooperazione internazionale Differenze e convergenze fra cooperazione Nord-Sud e Sud-Sud in agricoltura. *Semestrale di Studi e Ricerche di Geografia, 2*, 57–72.

GRAIN, and La Via Campesina. (2024). A new wave of land grabs strikes Tanzania. *La Via Campesina*, February 10. https://viacampesina.org/en/2024/02/a-new-wave-of-land-grabs-strikes-tanzania/

Harlan, T., & Lu, J. (2022). *Green cooperation: Enviromental governance and development aid in the belt and road.* Wilson Center.

Huang, M. (2021). The Chinese century and the city of gold: Rethinking race and capitalism. *Public Culture, 33*(2 (94)), 193–217. https://doi.org/10.1215/08992363-8917178

Ibonye, V. (2020). The forum on China–Africa Cooperation (FOCAC) and knowledge transfer in Sino-Nigerian development cooperation. *Asian Journal of Comparative Politics, 7*(4), 1045–1069. https://doi.org/10.1177/2057891120912333

Jiang, L. (2020). *Beyond official development assistance: Chinese development cooperation and African agriculture*. Palgrave Macmillan.

Kansanga, M., Andersen, P., Kpienbaareh, D., Mason-Renton, S., Atuoye, K., Sano, Y., Antabe, R., & Luginaah, I. (2019). Traditional agriculture in transition: Examining the impacts of agricultural modernization on smallholder farming in Ghana under the new Green Revolution. *International Journal of Sustainable Development and World Ecology, 26*(1), 11–24. https://doi.org/10.1080/13504509.2018.1491429

Kuadjovi-Ayedeu, E. (2021). *Agroecology: Our land is our life*. AFSA. https://afsafrica.org/wp-content/uploads/2021/12/agroecology-our-land-is-our-life.pdf.

Lawther, I. (2017). Why African countries are interested in building agricultural partnerships with China: Lessons from Rwanda and Uganda. *Third World Quarterly, 38*(10), 2312–2329. https://doi.org/10.1080/01436597.2017.1333889

Li, H., & Pan, L. (2020). Expulsion by pollution: The political economy of land grab for industrial parks in rural China. *Globalizations, 18*(3), 409–421. https://doi.org/10.1080/14747731.2020.1724244

Martiniello, G., & Nyamsenda, S. (2018). Agrarian movements in the neoliberal era: The case of MVIWATA in Tanzania. *Agrarian South, 7*(2), 145–172. https://doi.org/10.1177/2277976018779860

Matunhu, J. (2011). A critique of modernization and dependency theories in Africa: Critical assessment. *African Journal of History and Culture, 3*(5), 65–72.

McMichael, P. (2020). Does China's 'going out' strategy prefigure a new food regime? *The Journal of Peasant Studies, 47*(1), 116–154. https://doi.org/10.1080/03066150.2019.1693368

Mdee, A., Wostry, A., Coulson, A., & Maro, J. (2018). A pathway to inclusive sustainable intensification in agriculture? Assessing evidence on the application of agroecology in Tanzania. *Agroecology and Sustainable Food Systems, 43*(2), 201–227. https://doi.org/10.1080/21683565.2018.1485126

Merwe, J. V. D., Bond, P., & Dodd, N. (2019). *Brics and resistance in Africa: Contention, assimilation and co-optation*. Bloomsbury Academic and Professional.

Ministry of Agriculture and Rural Affairs of the People's Republic of China. (2019). *First Forum on China-Africa Agricultural Cooperation Convenes in Sanya*. https://english.moa.gov.cn/news_522/202005/t20200520_299827.html

Minoia, P. (2020). Corporate land grabs: Colonial continuity and space of exception in Kenya. *Land Use Policy, 99*, 104964. https://www.sciencedirect.com/science/article/pii/S0264837719302558?via%3Dihub

Mkindi, A. R., Maina, A., Urhahn, J., Kock, J., Bassermann, L., Goita, M., Nketani, M., Herre, R., Tanzmann, S., Wise, T. A., Gordon, M., & Gilbert, R. (2020). *False promises: The alliance for a green revolution in Africa*. Rosa Luxemburg Stiftung. https://www.rosalux.de/fileadmin/rls_uploads/pdfs/Studien/False_Promises_AGRA_en.pdf

Mlilo, N. (2023, August 25). South Africa deal to export avocados to China. *China Daily*. https://www.chinadaily.com.cn/a/202308/25/WS64e7d949a31035260b81e18d.html.

Mohan, G., & Tan-Mullins, M. (2019). The geopolitics of South-South infrastructure development: Chinese-financed energy projects in the global South. *Urban Studies, 56*(7), 1368–1385.

Mora, S. (2016). China: Cooperación Sur-Sur y land grabbing. Un análisis desde las resistencias sociales al proyecto Xai-Xai en Mozambique. *Conjuntura Austral, 7*(35), 95–113. https://doi.org/10.22456/2178-8839.61260

Moyo, S. (2016). Perspectives on South-South relations: China's presence in Africa. *Inter-Asia Cultural Studies, 17*(1), 58–67. https://doi.org/10.1080/14649373.2016.1138615

Muinga, D. (2024). Problematising the mutuality discourse in Chinese Agricultural Investment in Uganda. In F. Mazwi, G. T. Mudimu, & K. Helliker (Eds.), *Chinese investment in Africa* (Economic Geography). Springer. https://doi.org/10.1007/978-3-031-52815-6_4

Nalwimba, N., & Mudimu, G. T. (2024). Chinese agricultural technology demonstration centre and peasant empowerment in Zambia: Discourse and reality. In F. Mazwi, G. T. Mudimu, & K. Helliker (Eds.), *Chinese investment in Africa. Economic geography*. Springer. https://doi.org/10.1007/978-3-031-52815-6_7

Nantulya, P. (2018, August 30). *Grand strategy and China's soft power push in Africa*. African Center for Strategic Studies. https://africacenter.org/spotlight/grand-strategy-and-chinas-soft-power-push-in-africa/.

Nedopil, C., De Boer, D., Fan, D., & Thang, Y. (2021). What's China new guidelines on 'green development' mean for the Belt and Road. *China Dialogue*. https://chinadialogue.net/en/business/what-chinas-new-guidelines-on-green-development-mean-for-the-belt-and-road/.

Ntauazi, C. (2024). Land Displacements, production relations and resistance in the context of Chinese Investments in Mozambique. In F. Mazwi, G. T. Mudimu, & K. Helliker (Eds.), *Chinese investment in Africa* (Economic Geography). Springer. https://doi.org/10.1007/978-3-031-52815-6_3

Nye, J. S. (2021). Soft power: The evolution of a concept. *Journal of Political Power, 14*(1), 196–208. https://doi.org/10.1080/2158379X.2021.1879572

Obeng-Odoom, F. (2017). The myth of economic growth in Africa. *Review of African Political Economy, 44*(153), 466–475. https://doi.org/10.1080/03056244.2017.1313217

Obeng-Odoom, F. (2022). "China-Africa relations" in the economist, 2019–2021. *Journal of Asian and African Studies, 59*(3), 1000–1017. https://doi.org/10.1177/00219096221125423

Olander, E. (2024, August 27). Without more transparency, FOCAC could become irrelevant. *The China-Global South Project.* https://chinaglobalsouth.com/analysis/without-more-transparency-focac-could-become-irrelevant/

Pepa, M. (2021). Cooperazione agricola Cina-Tanzania: Innovazione o dipendenza? *Rivista Geografica Italiana, 3*, 105–137. https://doi.org/10.3280/rgioa3-2021oa12537

Pepa, M., Pase, A., Bertoncin, M., Ganawa, E. S., Musa, A. E., & Hamed, M. A. (2025). Sudan: A 'picture' of irrigation spaces before April 15, 2023. In A. Pase, A. Kronenburg García, M. Pepa, F. Gianoli, M. Bertoncin, & C. Braga (Eds.), *Water and land in the Sahel mapping the Flow* (pp. 215–243). Routledge.

Pereira, C. (2021). Walking into slavery with our eyes open' – the space for resisting genetically modified crops in Nigeria. *Feminist Africa, 2*(1), 99–125.

Rose, G. (2001). *Visual methodologies: An introduction to researching with visual materials.* SAGE.

Schneider, M. (2017). Dragon head enterprises and the state of agribusiness in China. *Journal of Agrarian Change, 17*(1), 3–21. https://doi.org/10.1111/joac.12151

Scoones, I., Amanor, K., Favareto, A., & Qi, G. (2016). A new politics of development cooperation? Chinese and Brazilian Engagements in African Agriculture. *World Development, 81*(C), 1–12.

Shattuck, A. (2021). Generic, growing, green?: The changing political economy of the global pesticide complex. *The Journal of Peasant Studies, 48*(2), 231–253. https://doi.org/10.1080/03066150.2020.1839053

Si, Z., Scott, S., Schumilas, T., & Chen, A. (2017). Conclusion. In S. Scott, S. Zhenzhong, T. Schumilas, & A. Chen (Eds.), *Organic food and farming in China. Top-down and bottom-up ecological initiatives* (pp. 199–212). Routledge.

Soulé, F. (2020). 'Africa+1' summit diplomacy and the 'new scramble' narrative: Recentering African agency. *African Affairs, 119*(477), 633–646. https://doi.org/10.1093/afraf/adaa015

Soulé, F. (2021). Mapping the future of Africa-China relations: Insights from West Africa. *SAIIA Occasional Paper* 330.

Strauss, J. C. (2019). Layered rhetorics and multiple realities: China and Africa. In C. Hartmann & N. Noesselt (Eds.), *China's New Role in African politics: From non-intervention towards stabilization.* Routledge.

Sulle, E. (2020). Bureaucrats, investors and smallholders: Contesting land rights and agro-commercialisation in the Southern agricultural growth corridor of Tanzania. *Journal of Eastern African Studies, 14*(2), 332–353. https://doi.org/10.1080/17531055.2020.1743093

Taylor, I., & Zajontz, T. (2020). In a fix: Africa's place in the Belt and Road Initiative and the reproduction of dependency. *South African Journal of International Affairs, 27*(3), 277–295. https://doi.org/10.1080/10220461.2020.1830165

The WoMin Collective. (2017). Extractives vs development sovereignty: Building living consent rights for African women. *Gender and Development, 25*(3), 421–443. https://doi.org/10.1080/13552074.2017.1379782

Tortajada, C., & Zhang, H. (2021). When food meets BRI: China's emerging Food Silk Road. *Global Food Security, 29*, 100518. https://doi.org/10.1016/j.gfs.2021.100518

Tugendhat, H., & Alemu, D. (2016). Chinese agricultural training courses for Africa officials: Between power and partnership. *World Development, 81*, 71–81. https://doi.org/10.1016/j.worlddev.2016.01.022

Voncujovi, S. (2024, July 4). Is $20 Billion by 2030 realistic? Evaluating China-Africa agricultural trade ambitions. *The Diplomat*. https://thediplomat.com/2024/07/is-20-billion-by-2030-realistic-evaluating-china-africa-agricultural-trade-ambitions/

Waitt, G. (2010). Doing foucauldian discourse analysis-revealing social realities. In I. Hay (Ed.), *Qualitative Research Methods in Human Geography* (pp. 217–240). Oxford University Press.

Wameru, S. M. (2020). Who is against Sino-African relations? Evolving perceptions on Chinese engagement in Kenya. *Chinese Journal of International Review*. https://doi.org/10.1142/S2630531320500110.

Wan, X., Yang, J., & Song, W. (2018). Pollution status of agricultural land in China: Impact of land use and geographical position. *Soil and Water Research, 13*, 234–242.

Wise, T. A. (2020). *Failing Africa's farmers: An impact assessment of the alliance for a Green revolution in Africa*. Global Development and Environment Institute Working Paper No. 20-01.

Xinhua. (2024). China to enforce strictest possible arable land protection system. September 25. https://english.www.gov.cn/policies/latestreleases/202409/25/content_WS66f34474c6d0868f4e8eb36a.html

Xu, X., Li, X., Qi, G., Tang, L., & Mukwereza, L. (2016). Science, technology, and the politics of knowledge: The case of China's ATDC in Africa. *World Development, 81*, 82–91.

Yi, S. (2021). Kenyan coal project shows why Chinese investors need to take environmental risks seriously. *China Dialogue*.. https://chinadialogue.net/en/energy/lamu-kenyan-coal-project-chinese-investors-take-environmental-risks-seriously/

Yu, R., & Zhai, P. (2020). More frequent and widespread persistent compound drought and heat event observed in China. *Scientific Reports, 10*, 14576. https://doi.org/10.1038/s41598-020-71312-3

Zhang, H. (2019). *Securing the "rice bowl": China and global food security*. Palgrave Macmillan.

Zhu, Y., Wang, Z., & Zhu, X. (2023). New reflections on food security and land use strategies based on the evolution of Chinese dietary patterns. *Land Use Policy, 126*, 106520. https://doi.org/10.1016/j.landusepol.2022.106520

Ziai, A. (2016). *Development discourse and global history: From colonialism to the sustainable development goals*. Routledge.

Mediterranean Africa, China and the European Union

Thierry Pairault

Introduction

Geopolitical and geo-economic literature discussing the relationship between African countries and China often suffers from a double bias. Firstly, the term "Africa" is frequently employed to refer to sub-Saharan Africa rather than the continent as a whole; furthermore, the concept of sub-Saharan Africa is not consistently defined across studies, even within the World Bank. Secondly, these studies tend to emphasise a rivalry between China and "the West, led by the US", to use a Chinese propaganda meme, thereby obscuring the existence of Europe and especially the European Union—among the most recent are Adarkwah et al. (2025), Cabestan (2025), Eickhoff and Thiele (2023), Luo and Li (2024), Olander (2025), Sun (2025), Wang and Zou (2025), Zhang (2024) and others. In order to provide a breath of Europe back into the Afro-Chinese equation, this paper will focus on the African countries bordering the

T. Pairault (✉)
France's National Centre of Scientific Research (CNRS), EHESS Research Centre on Modern and Contemporary China (CECMC), Paris, France
e-mail: pairault@ehess.fr

L. G. Adu Amoah (ed.), *Africa-China Relations*,
https://doi.org/10.1007/978-981-95-4370-0_11

Mediterranean Sea: from east to west, Egypt, Libya, Tunisia, Algeria and Morocco. These five countries will be referred to as "Mediterranean Africa" or "the Five". China does not perceive the Mediterranean in terms of its historical and civilisational centrality, as do the countries bordering it to the north and south do, and so it has never developed any Mediterranean strategy. Rather, there are *ad hoc* cooperation mechanisms—such as the "+1" format—involving either African countries through the Forum on China–Africa Cooperation (FOCAC) or Arab countries through the China–Arab States Cooperation Forum (CASCF) (Ekman, 2014; Pairault & Richet, 2021).

In the first part of this study, we will take stock of Mediterranean Africa's economic relations with China, on the one hand, and the European Union on the other. The aim is to gain a better understanding of the relative roles played by these two powers, if not hegemons. Then, in the second part, we will look at the Chinese strategies at work in the Five and ask to what extent the Chinese presence is not primarily designed to facilitate China's access to the European market. Given the dearth of research papers on Mediterranean-African relations with China, and even more so on the triangular relationship between Mediterranean Africa, China and the European Union (Pairault, 2013, 2015b, 2024; Pairault & Richet, 2021), the main thrust of this research will be to gather and exploit the facts. When studying under-researched and complex topics, description is a choice that focuses on gathering relevant information to provide detailed insights into the phenomena in question. This approach is advocated by Amartya Sen (1980) in "Description as choice" at a time when Deng Xiaoping was proclaiming "Seeking the truth from facts" (Wu, 2019).

Economic Overview

Analysis of Chinese statistical data and that of international institutions reveals that Chinese enterprises in Mediterranean Africa do not operate as investors, as it is often believed or wrongly reported in the media. Instead, Chinese companies in Mediterranean Africa mostly operate as service providers, customers and suppliers of goods. Figure 1 illustrates that in 2022, the volume of commercial activities (services and goods) was 236 times greater than the actual Chinese foreign direct investment in the five countries. During the same period, Chinese direct investment in these countries totalled only 0.2 billion dollars, a very small amount to be shared between the five countries.

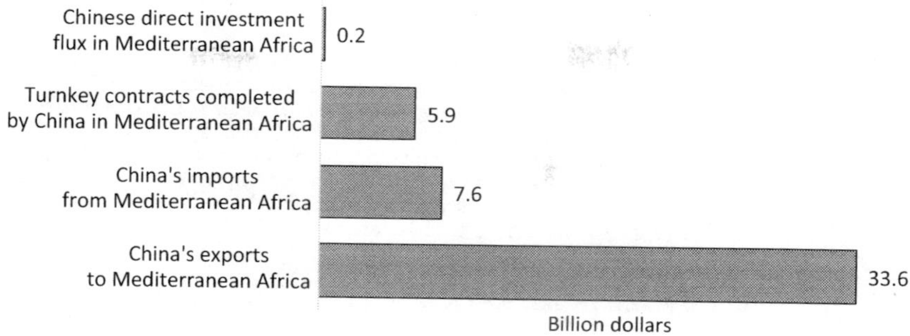

Fig. 1 Mediterranean Africa and China: economic relations in 2022. (Sources: Author's calculations based on Chinese Statistical Yearbook http://www.stats.gov.cn/tjsj/ndsj/, MOFCOM statistical releases http://fec.mofcom.gov.cn/article/tjsj/tjgb/and UNCTAD online database https://unctadstat.unctad.org/datacentre/)

Foreign Direct Investment

It is a common misconception that there are a lot of Chinese investments in Africa. In fact, when we compare them to FDI numbers elsewhere in the world, Chinese FDIs in Mediterranean Africa, similarly to Chinese investments in the rest of Africa, are relatively low. It is important to clarify a common confusion between the terms investment, financing and service provision. To illustrate the discrepancy in numbers between investment and service provision, Figure 2 compares the amount of Chinese investment from 2003 to 2022 with the turnover from Chinese overseas construction contracts in the same years in Mediterranean African countries. Remarkably, in 2022, the turnover generated by Chinese construction companies was almost 30 times the amount which was actually invested by China. This was not an isolated incident, but a recurring pattern. So, China's presence in Mediterranean Africa is one of a services' provider rather than an investor. These statistics also show that Mediterranean Africa is primarily a customer. This means that, despite Algeria's receiving most of Chinese investment in Mediterranean Africa (see Fig. 3), China is only minimally involved in the industrialisation of the region. This is because its investments are in labour-intensive activities, and therefore do not significantly contribute to industrialisation or generate substantial technology transfers.

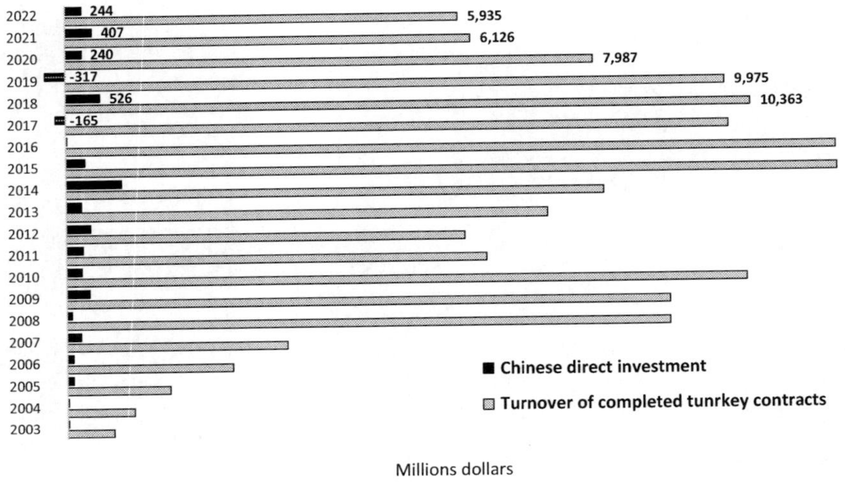

Fig. 2 Chinese FDI flows and contracts turnover in Mediterranean Africa. (Source: See Fig. 1)

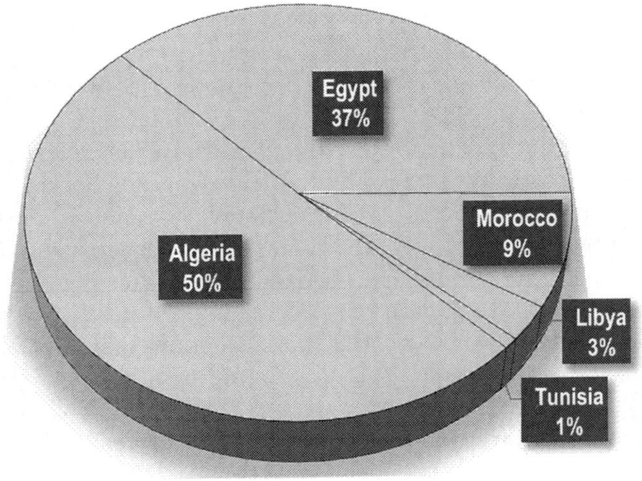

Fig. 3 Mediterranean Africa's FDI Inward Stock (2022). (Source: See Fig. 1)

Since 2003, the Chinese Ministry of Commerce (MOFCOM) has published annual statistics by recipient countries. While the accuracy of Chinese FDI statistics is not inherently inferior to that of statistics produced by international institutions, the data currently available highlight general trends. By 2022, the stock of Chinese FDI in Mediterranean Africa represented just under 0.1% of global Chinese FDI (Africa as a whole representing approximately 1.5%). Thereby, the significance of the Five as a destination for Chinese FDI is relatively limited. But what is China's weight in Mediterranean Africa's economic landscape, vis-à-vis other economies, particularly the European Union (EU)?

In 2022, China and the EU had similar overall economic weights, at 18% and 17% of world GDP, respectively. However, the magnitude of their outward FDI stocks reflected their historical role on the global stage: the EU's stock represented 32% of the global outward FDI stock, compared with just 7% for China. With regard to Mediterranean Africa, the EU accounted for 28.2% of the total stock in the Five, while China represented a mere 0.9% (see Fig. 4). And yet, in spite of its comparatively smaller importance, for some policy-makers in Mediterranean Africa, China is seen as a key economic partner: the more FDIs flow into these countries, the better. The inflow of Chinese FDI represents a chance to diversify their economic relations and enhance their position vis-à-vis other long-standing partners, including France, the United States and others.

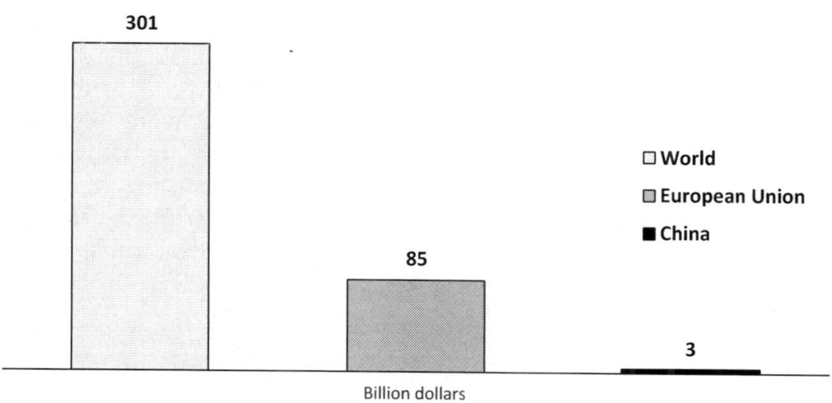

Fig. 4 FDI stocks in Mediterranean Africa (2022). (Sources: See Fig. 1 and OECD online database. https://data-explorer.oecd.org)

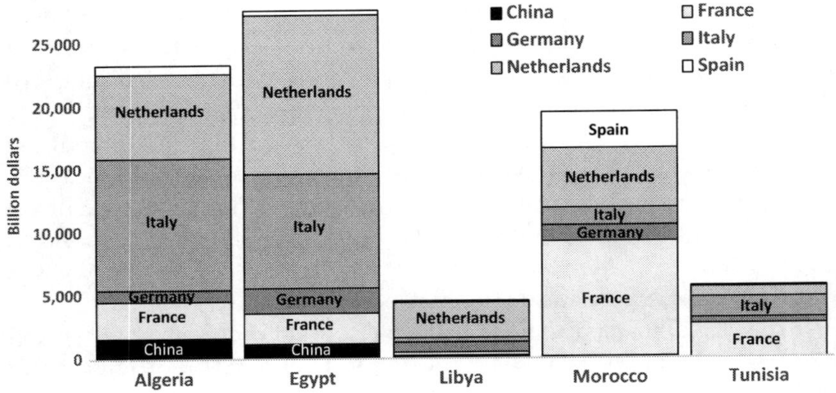

Fig. 5 FDI stocks: China versus major European partners (2022). (Sources: See Fig. 4)

A glance at the FDI stocks of the main European countries investing in Mediterranean Africa reveals unequivocal facts (see Fig. 5). First, the Netherlands has played an important role in this context, especially in Algeria, Egypt and Libya. Until 2022, the Netherlands hosted the headquarters of the Shell Oil Company. It is not surprising that countries with hydrocarbon resources attract investment from such a company. The Netherlands is also a tax haven that attracts companies and capital. Consequently, the stock of Dutch FDI could also include investment from other countries. Secondly, France continues to hold significant historical legacy in the region. However, its current role is much more limited. The challenging relations between Paris and Algiers have indeed led to constraints on French investments. Nevertheless, France maintains a prominent position in Morocco and Tunisia. Thirdly, Italy (investment in hydrocarbons) and the other two large Mediterranean countries in the EU are investing in Mediterranean Africa. The scale of investment in Egypt and Algeria demonstrates the key role played by the hydrocarbon sector, and suggests that Libya could have been an equally significant recipient country had it not been for the civil war.

Service Provision: Turnkey Contracts and Loans

Low levels of Chinese FDI in Mediterranean African countries contrast with high turnover levels generated by Chinese-built infrastructure projects in the same countries. The statistics on such contracts are the result of

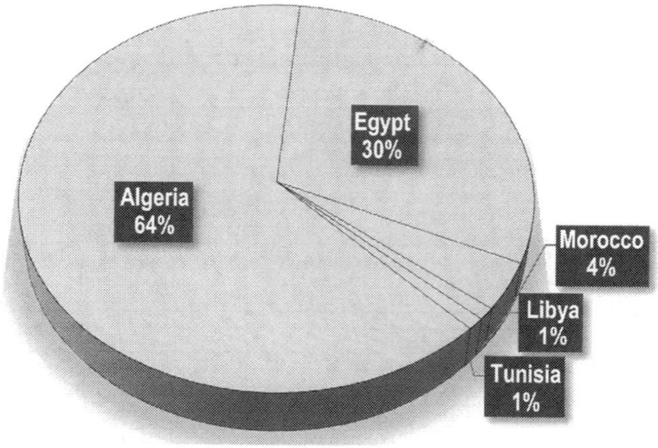

Fig. 6 Completed turnkey contracts (2003–2022). (Sources: See Fig. 1)

Chinese government data collection, which has no equivalent elsewhere. This is probably the result of a highly centralised state with tight control over its state-owned enterprises.

When looking at the distribution of turnover by country over the period 2003–2022, Algeria stands out, accounting for almost two-thirds (64%) of all payments made to Chinese companies for major projects. Egypt ranks second with less than one-third (30%) (see Fig. 6). These statistics result from the Algerian government's policy of building infrastructure to promote social stability. Similarly, Egypt also extensively engaged with Chinese contractors to develop and modernise its infrastructure. In particular, China State Construction Engineering Corp (CSCEC) signed in 2018 a contract with the Egyptian government to build a petrochemical complex. That same year, CSCEC further secured a loan for Egypt, covering 85% of the cost of a project to develop a new political and administrative centre 45 kilometres from Cairo. In addition to that, in December 2020, CSCEC secured another loan from a consortium of Chinese banks to erect a prominent tower (the Iconic Tower), for which it had already received an order.

Except for Algeria, which has historically prioritised self-reliance in financing major projects through oil revenues, securing external financing is a crucial aspect of the completion of these projects. Any country seeking to invest in its infrastructure through Chinese financing has to choose Chinese contractors. Some Western countries, such as France, have a

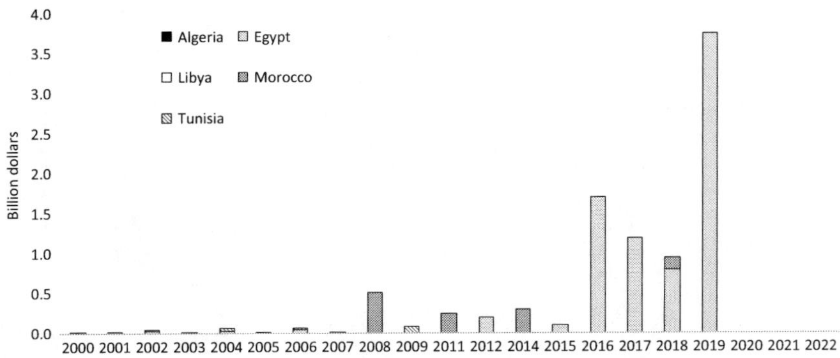

Fig. 7 Chinese loans to Mediterranean Africa (2000–2022). (Chinese Loans to Africa Database, 2023, https://www.bu.edu/gdp/chinese-loans-to-africa-database-data-download/)

markedly restricted practice of tied loans, as shown by the practices of the French development finance institution (AFD, 2025).

So, it is unsurprising that Egypt received by far the highest amount of loans in value terms (86%) from 2000 to 2022, which is the period referenced by the database managed by the Global Development Policy Center at Boston University (see Fig. 7). Looking at lending to Egypt in detail, 47% of the amounts lent went to support Egyptian financial institutions and 42% to operations related to the New City of Cairo project. Morocco ranks second with 12% of total loans by value; a single loan—a buyer credit granted in 2008 by China's Exim Bank for the purchase of unspecified equipment—accounted for 41% of total loans. The available data, as reported above, show that Chinese loans were primarily utilised to support services provided by Chinese contractors rather than contributing directly to the industrialisation of these countries[1]. It is clear that Chinese loans to Mediterranean Africa are of secondary importance, although they are, of course, very welcome.

A close examination of the current sovereign debt[2] levels of the Five reveals that the share owed to China represents no more than 3% of their total sovereign debt, compared with 10% owed to EU countries. From a bilateral standpoint, Mediterranean Africa is more reliant on the EU than on China—to say nothing of that owed to the World Bank IBRD (14%) and even to bondholders (25%). Among the Five, there are several attitudes to sovereign debt at the end of 2022 (see Fig. 8). Algeria has

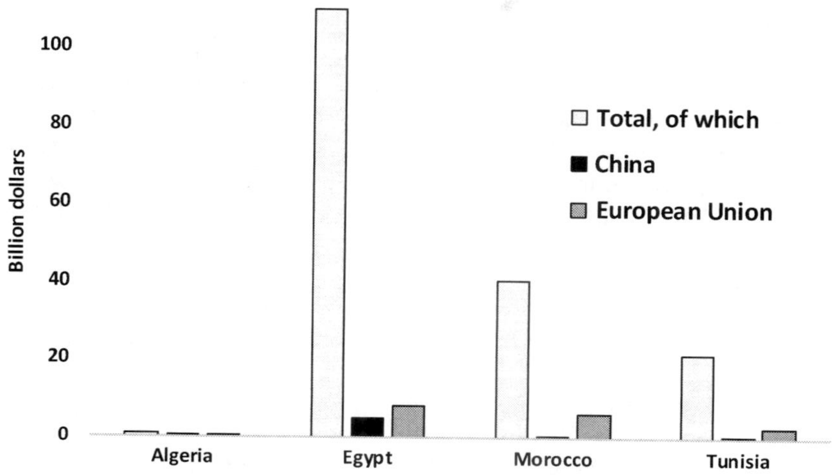

Fig. 8 Sovereign debt: China versus European Union (2022). (Source: World Bank's International Debt Statistics database, https://databank.worldbank.org/source/international-debt-statistics)

consistently refused to engage in debt financing. Egypt, by contrast, accounts for 63% of the total sovereign debt of the Five and has allocated a relatively modest share to China (4.7% of its sovereign debt) and a slightly larger share to the EU (7.7%). Conversely, again based on World Bank data, Morocco and Tunisia, whose ratios of sovereign debt to gross national income[3] are higher than Egypt's (32%, 48% and 24%, respectively) have virtually no debt to China (0.9% and 0.2%) but have relied more heavily on the EU (15.7% and 13.3%). When it comes to financing, Mediterranean African countries are more dependent on the EU and other creditors than they are on China.

In terms of financing, it is extremely challenging to compare the two powers (China and the EU) beyond the respective weight of their contributions (equity and debt). In the case of China, the situation appears relatively straightforward, and its "grand strategy" can be summed up by reference to the New Silk Roads, which we will discuss below. This is not the case within the EU. The EU institutions have their own strategies that are not necessarily aligned with the national strategies of each of the 27 member states. Furthermore, the strategies of EU firms are not automatically aligned with those of the member state in which they are incorporated. To clarify, simply compare Sinopec and TotalEnergies (formerly Total). Sinopec is a state-owned Chinese company that is directly supervised by the Chinese government, and its market is primarily Chinese. In contrast, TotalEnergies has been a private French company since 1991 (with no "golden share"[4]), and its market is mainly global. It plans to move its main listing from the Paris to the New York stock exchange in an attempt to free itself from both French and European control. To refine such comparisons, it would be necessary to move away from a macroeconomic approach and towards meso-economic research. For this reason, we will simply suggest that the EU's financial influence is still potentially more significant than China's to date.

Merchandise Trade

As illustrated above in Fig. 1, the volume of merchandise trade provides an accurate representation of the state of (and, indirectly, the general trend of) economic relations between Mediterranean Africa and China. However, these relations manifest with considerable asymmetries. The initial and most illustrative one is exhibited in the discrepancy between the volume and value of this trade in comparison to the overall trade of each partner (see Fig. 9). The volume of merchandise trade (exports plus imports) with China represents 9.1% of the foreign trade of the Five, which is a relatively significant proportion. Conversely, the volume of

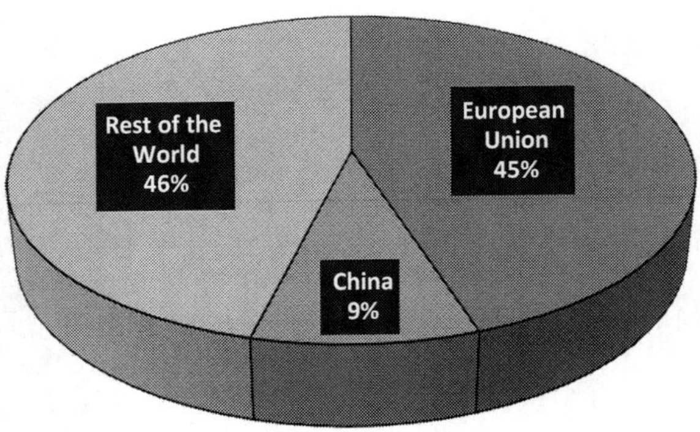

Fig. 9 China and European Union in Mediterranean Africa trade (2022). (Source: Author's calculations based on UNCTAD online database https://unctadstat.unctad.org/datacentre)

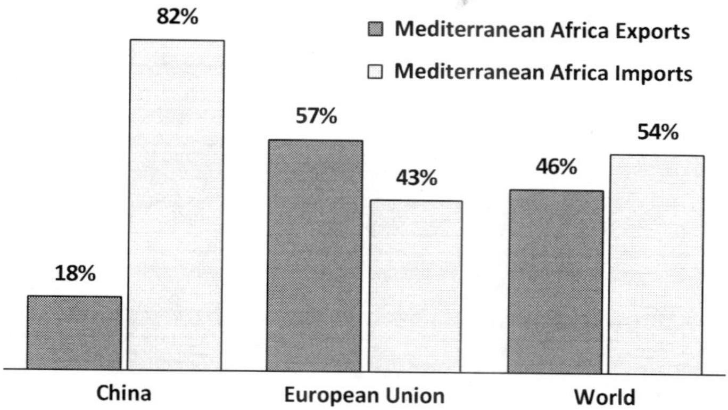

Fig. 10 Mediterranean Africa trade (2022). (Source: See Fig. 9)

China's trade with these countries represents just 0.6% of China's foreign trade. The same imbalances are observed in the relations between the Five and the EU. However, the most striking aspect is the prominence of relations with the EU. The volume of merchandise trade between the Five and the EU represents 44.5% of the Five's total foreign trade, whereas the volume of trade between the EU and the Five represents just 1.6% of the EU's total foreign trade. Asymmetries are also reflected in the structure of trade flows. While a deficit with China exists, a surplus with the EU is recorded (see Fig. 10). The trade with China is almost entirely one-way, as the Five's imports from China account for 82% of total trade with China. In contrast, the trade with the EU is more balanced, with the Five's imports from the EU accounting for 43% of total trade with the EU—share of exports from the Five to the EU: 57%.

The role of the EU is also markedly distinct from that of China, even before considering the composition of imports and exports. Each Mediterranean African country occupies a particular place in the region, and of these, Egypt is distinguished from the others by its unique position. As Table 1 shows, one-third (34%) of the Five's trade with China is with Egypt, which also has the lowest share of total trade with the EU (26%). The four other countries are highly dependent on their trade with the EU, and, in comparison, only slightly dependent on their trade with China. In contrast, Morocco has a relatively high degree of independence from the EU, with a share of only 49%, however, it is Mediterranean Africa's leading partner with the EU (27%).

Table 1 Volume of trade with the Mediterranean African countries (2022).

Countries	*Share of trade within the five*		*Share of trade with each country*	
	China	*European Union*	*China*	*European Union*
Algeria	21%	26%	9%	52%
Egypt	34%	16%	11%	26%
Libya	18%	18%	11%	53%
Morocco	19%	27%	7%	49%
Tunisia	8%	13%	7%	57%
Total/Mean	100%	100%	9%	45%

Source: Author's calculations based on UNCTAD online database. https://unctadstat.unctad.org/datacentre

Looking at exports alone, by 2022, the two oil-producing countries will account for three-quarters of the Five's exports to China (Libya with 50% and Algeria with 24%), but also more than half to the EU (Libya with 21% and Algeria with 34%). With the exception of Libya, where 10% of all exports go to China, the Chinese market is not really important, especially when compared to the size of the EU market (see Table 2). Figure 11 juxtaposes Primary commodities (including fuels) with Manufactured goods. In fact, the structure of trade does not depend so much on the destination of exports as on the strengths of each of the five countries, although exports to the EU are somewhat more diversified than those to China. The Five face a dilemma: either they continue to develop their economic dependence on the EU countries, which is geographically natural, or they try to diversify their "customer base", in the knowledge that one of the most important "customers", China, has never stopped diversifying its suppliers so that suppliers depend on their customers, and not the other way round.

Looking at imports now. On average, imports of Chinese products account for 14% of total imports, while imports of European products account for 35% (see Table 3). All countries import more from the EU than from China, but Egypt and Morocco stand out. Egypt is the biggest importer of Chinese products among the Five (38%), while Morocco is the biggest importer of European products (also 38%). However, Egypt's dependence on China (16% of Egyptian imports) is lower than Morocco's dependence on the EU (45% of Moroccan imports). Nevertheless, Egypt's

Table 2 Exports by the Mediterranean African countries (2022).

Countries	*Share of exports within the five*		*Share of exports by destination*		*EU compared to China (China = 1)*
	China	*European Union*	*China*	*European Union*	
Algeria	24%	34%	3%	64%	22
Egypt	17%	13%	3%	33%	12
Libya	50%	21%	10%	67%	7
Morocco	8%	20%	1%	55%	37
Tunisia	1%	12%	1%	72%	219
Total/ Mean	100%	100%	4%	56%	15

Source: see Table 1

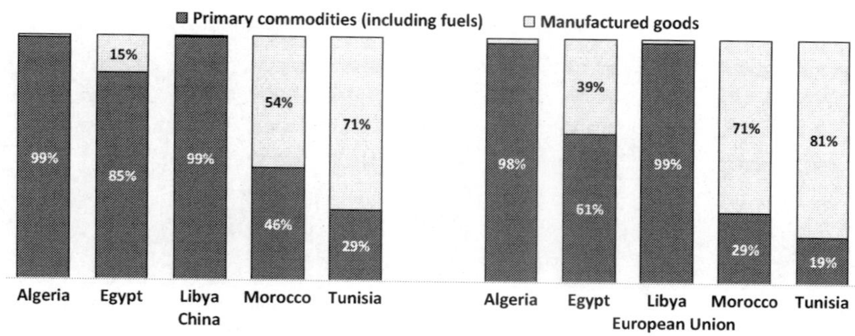

Fig. 11 Structure of exports to China and European Union (2003–2022). (Sources: see Table 1)

dependence on the EU remains higher than its dependence on China (20% versus 16%). The product structure of imports is the opposite of that of exports: Manufactured goods steadily dominate, with more than 90% for imports from China, but to a much lesser extent for imports from the EU (see Fig. 12).

From an economic perspective, and only from that perspective, this overview of economic relations between Mediterranean Africa and China supports two conclusions: Mediterranean Africa as such is of little economic importance to China, and China's economic relations with Mediterranean Africa are still small compared to those with the European

Table 3 Imports by the Mediterranean African countries (2022).

Countries	*Share of imports within the five*		*Share of imports by origin*		*EU compared to China (China = 1)*
	China	*European Union*	*China*	*European Union*	
Algeria	20%	15%	17%	34%	2
Egypt	38%	20%	16%	22%	1
Libya	11%	12%	12%	36%	3
Morocco	22%	38%	10%	45%	4
Tunisia	9%	14%	12%	46%	4
Total/ Mean	100%	100%	14%	35%	3

Source: see Table 1

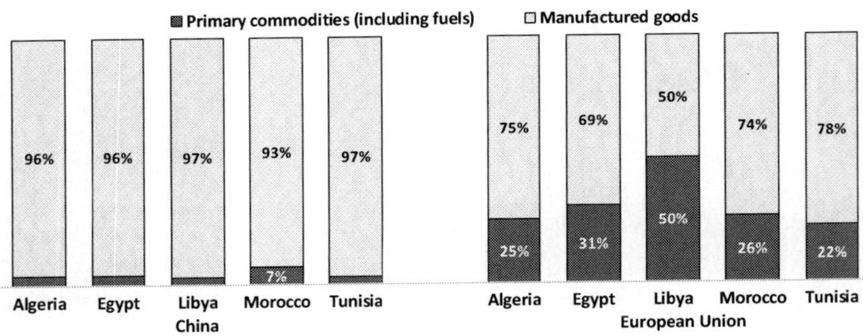

Fig. 12 Structure of imports from China and European Union (2003–2022). (Source: see Table 1)

Union. Conversely, from a political and even geopolitical point of view, economic relations between Mediterranean Africa and China, however limited they may be, can be used by the Five to take advantage of China's growing economic presence to diversify their partnerships, gain negotiating power and pursue development goals, inevitably leading to increased competition and often shifting the balance of influence away from traditional European partners[5].

"New" Maritime Road Towards the European Union

Both the inland and maritime Silk Roads are a legacy of the traditional trade routes between Asia and Europe. The maritime road is the successor of the Ceramics Road that Arab and Indian merchants had been travelling since the ninth century AD, but it was not until the nineteenth century that it evolved into its present form. The CMA–CGM—the world's third-largest container shipping company, based in Marseilles—is a very active player along today's maritime silk road. Its forerunner, created in 1851, operated this maritime road from the opening of the Suez Canal in 1869. It is the initiator of the port of Djibouti (1888) as well as one of the promoters of the Franco-Ethiopian railway from 1897. The company has never stopped trading with China. In fact, it has steadily strengthened its ties with the country. Xi Jinping's New Maritime Silk Road is an epigone of the route created in the nineteenth century and subsequently travelled continuously by the world's leading shipping companies, including the Italo-Swiss MSC, the Danish Maesrk and the French CMA-CGM.

The New Silk Roads Strategy

Prior to its designation as a political "initiative" in 2016, the New Silk Roads project launched in 2013 was primarily an economic strategy designed to facilitate trade. In September 2015, a communiqué published on the Chinese government's information website recalled that the Central Committee and the government endorsed a "strategy" known as "One Belt and One Road" to advance the development of a "New Open Economic System". Since the Asian crisis of 1998, and especially since the early 2000s, Chinese officials have tried, with very limited success, to change the engine of their economy, *i.e.* to replace growth driven by external markets with growth driven by the domestic market. Hence, Xi Jinping's call for liberal globalisation in Davos in 2017 can almost be interpreted as admitting failure. The New Silk Roads strategy is therefore an initiative to better penetrate European markets (mainly the European Union). These are the primary markets for Chinese products, ahead of the countries of South-East Asia (at least at that time) and the United States.

Figure 13 presents a grouping of countries initially involved in the New Silk Roads strategy by region. It shows that Chinese exports to the EU are significantly higher (19.0%) than those to South East Asian countries (11.6%). For the purposes of this analysis, countries bordering the

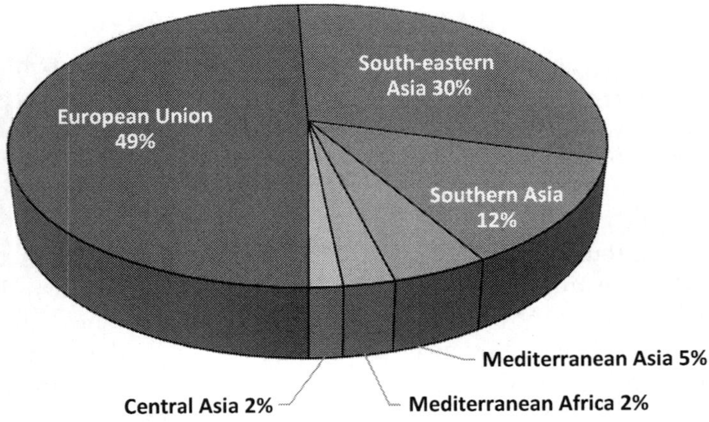

Fig. 13 China and European Union in Mediterranean Africa trade (2022). (Sources: see Table 1)

Table 4 Chinese exports and their transport to the Mediterranean (2021)

Region	*By FOB value*				*By Cargo weight*			
	Air	*Sea*	*Land*	*Total*	*Air*	*Sea*	*Land*	*Total*
European Union	15.5%	22.7%	30.5%	68.6%	2.2%	32.5%	26.6%	61.5%
Mediterranean Asia	3.6%	10.2%	4.7%	18.5%	0.3%	15.2%	4.5%	20.0%
Mediterranean Africa	3.4%	1.9%	7.6%	12.9%	0.3%	5.9%	4.5%	18.5%
Total	22.4%	34.8%	42.7%	100.0%	3.2%	53.8%	43.0%	100.0%

Sources: see Table 1

Mediterranean (other than EU countries) have been grouped into two regions: Mediterranean Africa and Mediterranean Asia. Their role is minimal. Table 4 uses data produced by UNCTAD on an experimental basis to measure the role of different modes of transport in the delivery of China's exports to countries bordering the Mediterranean (*i.e.* those with ports). The data confirms that there is a significant discrepancy between the ratio of the "free on board" (FOB) value to the total FOB value of goods transported by air (22.4%) and the ratio of the weight of these goods to the total weight of goods transhipped (3.2%)[6]. Conversely, for goods transported by ship, the ratio of FOB value is 34.8%, while the ratio of the total weight of goods is 53.8%. Most crucially, however, is the significant role

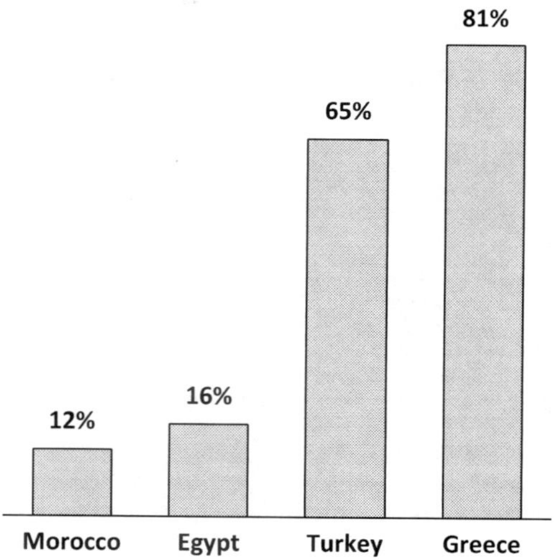

Fig. 14 Share of imports from China arriving by sea (2021). (Sources: see Table 1)

that European and Mediterranean-Asian ports can play in trade with China, compared with Mediterranean-African ports (FOB values of 22.7%, 10.2% and 1.9%, respectively). Clearly, this is bound to affect how the Five can participate in the maritime Silk Road strategy.

Although these data are still experimental, they reveal a significant asymmetry that reflects China's strategic choices regarding the Maritime Silk Road. Figure 14 examines some Mediterranean countries with a high volume of maritime trade, comparing the FOB value of Chinese goods arriving by sea as a proportion of their total imports from China. There is a stark contrast between the two northern Mediterranean countries, where the overwhelming majority of Chinese goods are transported by sea (Greece: 81.0%; Turkey: 65.1%), and the two southern Mediterranean countries, where the proportions are significantly lower (Egypt: 15.9%; Morocco: 11.5%). But what makes the contrast even more striking is the absolute importance of maritime transport, especially northbound: Turkey's trade in Chinese goods arriving by sea is 25 times greater than the same trade in Morocco and 12 times greater than the same trade in Egypt. Similarly, the same trade in Greece is 10 times greater than the same trade in Morocco and 5 times greater than in Egypt. The Maritime Silk Road is primarily aimed at markets north of the Mediterranean, and only incidentally at the southern shores (see Map Fig. 15).

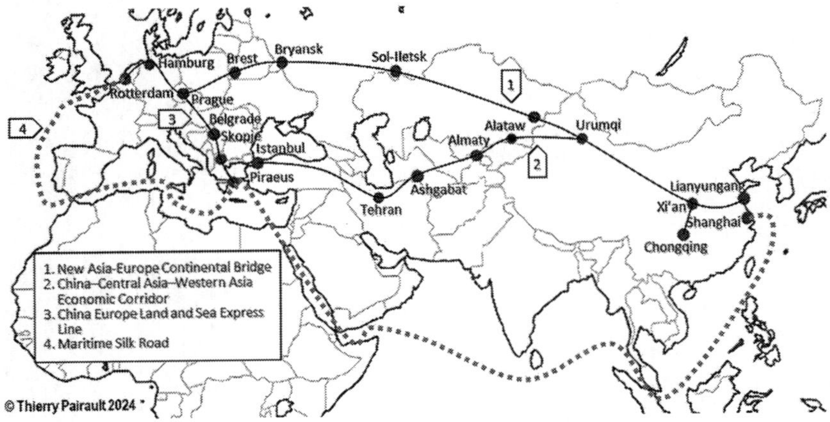

Fig. 15 Map of Maritime Silk Road and other economic corridors

Chinese Operators in Mediterranean Africa Ports

China's port presence in the Mediterranean has given rise to speculation about the "Chinese threat". But, actually, with the exception of the port of Piraeus, Chinese state-owned companies are only involved as terminal operators or port builders (Aurégan, 2023; Pairault, 2019b).

To date, COSCO holds stakes in the management of two Egyptian port terminals. The oldest of the terminals is the Suez Canal Container Terminal, built by the China Harbour Engineering Company (CHEC) in the eastern part of Port Said. In 2004, its operation was conceded to a consortium comprising APM Terminals—*i.e.* a subsidiary of Maersk—(55%), COSCO (20%), the Suez Canal Authority (10.3%), the National Bank of Egypt (5%) and various Egyptian shareholders (9.7%). The most recent terminal, Damietta Container Terminal, is managed by a joint venture financed as follows: 25% by a Kuwaiti operator, KGL International for Ports Warehousing and Transport; 20% by Terminal Link (CMA-CGM allied with China Merchants); and 20% by COSCO. The remainder is split between various investment funds and the public institution that owns and manages the port of Damietta (Pairault, 2023, pp. 37–38).

On 4 March 2025, the Hong Kong-based operator Hutchison announced its intention to sell its shares in subsidiaries managing 43 global ports to a US consortium[7]. At that time, the company was overseeing the operation of five terminals in Egypt. Two of these terminals (one in the Port of Alexandria and the other in the Port of El Dekheila) are managed by a joint venture, Alexandria International Container Terminals. Hutchison currently holds 80% of the capital, while the remaining 20% is held by other investors, namely the Alexandria Port Authority and a Saudi investment fund. In August 2022, three additional container terminal projects were initiated. The first is to be built at the port of El Dekheila in partnership with Luxembourg's Terminal Investment Limited (a subsidiary of the Italian-Swiss company MSC), a second at Ain Soukhna in partnership with CMA-CGM and COSCO, and a third at the Egyptian naval base of Aboukir by a joint venture that will hold a 38-year concession.

As the preceding enumeration of partners suggests, the involvement of Chinese companies in the management of Egyptian container terminals is not indicative of a monopoly, but rather a reflection of their integration into a globalised industry where Western shipping companies have traditionally held a dominant position and are willing to collaborate with their Chinese counterparts. The only other country in Mediterranean Africa where one of the three major Chinese stevedoring companies is involved is Morocco, where China Merchants Port has an indirect presence.

China Merchants Ports is also a company with a long history. Currently, it has a presence in Tangiers through the terminal operator Terminal Link, which is a subsidiary of CMA-CGM. In June 2013, China Merchants Ports purchased 49% of the shares belonging to CMA-CGM. The agreement provides the Chinese operator with access to 14 terminals, including the one managed by Eurogate in Tangiers. Notwithstanding the significance of the port of Tangiers, it is obvious that Chinese shipping companies are not yet as keen on it as they are on Egyptian ports.

The situation in Algeria differs from that in Egypt and Morocco in that no port or container terminal is currently managed by a Chinese company. The Port du Centre project in El Hamdania was conceived with the idea of creating a transhipment hub that would provide a vertical link between the European Union, the Mediterranean and Africa. Such a link could also facilitate the implementation of China's Silk Road strategy in Africa. Algeria's postponement—if not cancellation (Hamill-Stewart, 2025)—of its decision to build the port does not bode well for its involvement in the Maritime Silk Road or in the future vertical link proposed by certain European parties.

Neither in Libya nor in Tunisia are there any Chinese companies managing port terminals. However, there are several instances of Chinese contractors participating in the development of Mediterranean African ports, such as the extension of the container terminals at the ports of Oran and Arzew undertaken by an Algerian-Chinese joint venture in which the aforementioned CHEC played a role. In his study of China's control of African ports, Isaac Kardon's often-quoted work makes reference to the port of Radès in Tunisia and to Huawei's involvement in 2014 (Kardon, 2022). While it is true that Huawei signed a contract to light the port using photovoltaic solar energy, it is inaccurate to suggest that Huawei exerts control over the port as a result.

Special Economic Zones in Mediterranean Africa

The story of China in Mediterranean African ports described above is mirrored by the story of China in the region's special economic zones (SEZs), with the presence of the European Union always in the background. From the outset, participation in SEZs abroad was seen as a powerful tool for the internationalisation of Chinese companies. A project launched in 2005–2006 envisaged the creation of around 50 such zones. Information published by MOFCOM on its website shows that only 20 "Overseas Economic and Commercial Cooperation Zones" have been "certified", of which only four are in Africa (after the declassification of the Jiangling project in Algeria): Ethiopia, Egypt, Nigeria and Zambia (Pairault, 2022, pp. 79–81). Among the five Mediterranean African countries, there are in fact five SEZ experiments: one in Algeria (which failed), two in Egypt and two in Morocco.

The creation of an SEZ in Algeria may have been encouraged by two factors. One is the trans-Saharan road project, which would open up an economic corridor from the Mediterranean to the Gulf of Benin. The second is the EU-Algeria Association Agreement, which was signed in 2002 and came into force in 2005. It aimed to establish an EU-Algeria free trade area, including the complete dismantling of tariffs, by September 2020. Disagreements between the potential Chinese partner and the Algerian government have prevented both parties from benefiting from these two opportunities.

Conversely, the Suez TEDA Sino-Egyptian Economic and Trade Cooperation Zone has been deemed a success in Egypt, becoming the sole Chinese SEZ in Africa to generate profits, as evidenced by Wang Hongyi (2017, pp. 19–24). An initial attempt in 1994 proved unsuccessful. Consequently, a new structure—with a 93-year emphyteutic lease—was devised in July 2008, situated in the Soukhna industrial zone adjacent to the Ain Soukhna port on the Gulf of Suez's western coastline, north of the Red Sea. It is, therefore, a structure that is 90% under the control of the Chinese side and is subject to the supervision of the General Authority for the Suez Canal Economic Zone. For Chinese SMEs that may become clients of the SEZ, their contact is a company (under Chinese law), the Sino-African TEDA Investment Company, 60% owned by TEDA and 40% by the China–Africa Development Fund. The advantage for the SMEs in such a Chinese enclave is twofold. First, they benefit from direct support from the Chinese government. Second, they enjoy the usual privileges of tax exemption that SEZs traditionally offer. Most importantly, they are entitled to market their products as "Made in Egypt". This enables them to benefit from the bilateral free trade or preferential trade agreements that have been signed between Egypt and the European Free Trade Association (EFTA), the United States, the Mercosur countries, Turkey and, last but not least, the European Union.

A second Chinese industrial park is to be constructed under the name of Mankai Textile Park in Sadat City, 95 kilometres from Cairo. The objective of the developer is to attract Chinese textile companies to produce in Egypt, thereby enabling them to benefit from the free trade agreement signed in 2004 with the European Union, under which textiles and clothing can be imported from Egypt duty-free.

In June 2013, the EU and Egypt entered into discussions with a view to deepening their trade and investment relationship through the establishment of a Deep and Comprehensive Free Trade Area (DCFTA) (ECTD, 2024a). This prospective DCFTA would extend beyond the Association Agreement of 2004 to encompass, *inter alia*, trade in services, public procurement, competition, intellectual property rights and investment. It is understandable that Chinese companies are eager to establish a presence in Egypt.

The Chinese government is promoting the establishment of SEZs in Africa to serve as incubators for Chinese companies attempting to internationalise (Pairault, 2018). Morocco has implemented its own SEZ policy that has been both proactive and successful. However, Chinese companies in the automotive sector (as in the aeronautics and other sectors) will not require the support of their national partners in a delocalised bubble. They are much better off with the Western car manufacturers implanted in China, of which they are already the subcontractors. This allows them to gain insight into the demands of the manufacturers, who in turn have a clear understanding of their capabilities.

Renault has been engaged in production activities within the Tangiers-Med zone since 2012. By 2021, the company had achieved a local integration rate of 63%, with an objective of attaining 80% by 2025. In 2019, PSA (Peugeot, Citroën, DS, Opel) commenced production at its Kenitra facility. It is still anticipated that Volkswagen will establish an assembly line in the Kenitra area. With regard to Ford, although it does not intend to invest immediately, it is already utilising the services of subcontractors attracted by the dynamism of the Renault ecosystem in Morocco to supply its Valencia plant in Spain. All of the aforementioned carmakers maintain close relations with Chinese car manufacturers. Ford has formed a partnership with Jiangling, while Volkswagen has established a collaboration with the Shanghai Automotive Industry Corporation (SAIC) and the First Automobile Works (FAW), which are the first and eleventh Chinese manufacturers, respectively. Similarly, Peugeot and Renault have joined forces with Dongfeng, which is the third Chinese manufacturer.

There is therefore a Renault ecosystem, stretching from China to Morocco, which can provide Chinese companies setting up in Morocco under its wing with all the services that MOFCOM requires from special economic zones under its supervision [MOCFOM, 2015]. Peugeot is not lagging behind and is strengthening of its own ecosystem. One of the largest French automotive suppliers, Faurecia, also has an ecosystem stretching from China to Morocco, where it can welcome its Chinese subcontractors. To cite the best-known examples, this is probably how Renault's partner, tyre manufacturer Qingdao Sentury Tyre, has set up in 2023. The same goes for Peugeot's Discatal partners in 2019 and Xiezhong in 2017. What has been the outcome of this policy? In 2023, according to the OICA (International Organisation of Motor Vehicle Manufacturers), Morocco is the leading producer of passenger cars in Africa, ahead of South Africa (OICA, 2024), and, according to UNCTAD, the leading African exporter to the EU (see Fig. 16).

Another Moroccan project—a private one—is the Tangiers Tech Mohammed VI Special Economic Zone. The objective is to consolidate Morocco's presence in the Euro-Mediterranean zone by specifically welcoming Chinese companies. The initial concept was conceived by Othman Benjelloun, a billionaire and the chairman of the Banque Marocaine du Commerce Extérieur (BMCE), which subsequently became the Bank of Africa. The project—in partnership with the China Communications Construction Company and one of its subsidiaries, the China Road and Bridge Company—is scheduled for completion in 2027.

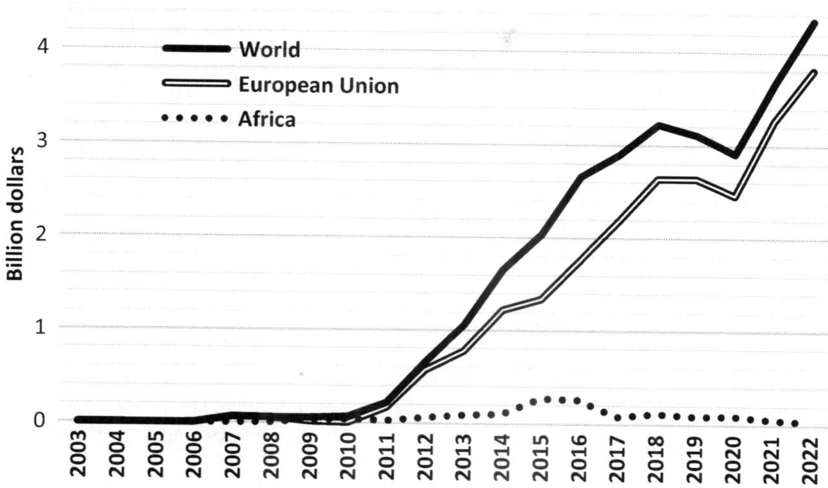

Fig. 16 Morocco's exports of passenger cars. (Sources: UNCTAD online database https://unctadstat.unctad.org/datacentre)

While Morocco, China and the EU are using Morocco's special economic zones as a platform to promote trade, the EU is also denouncing some unfair trade practices by Chinese companies. For example, Dika Morocco Africa SARL—the Moroccan subsidiary of Dicastal (aluminium wheel rims)—has been hit with a 17.5% anti-dumping duty; similarly, PGTEX Morocco SARL—the Moroccan subsidiary of PGTEX China (glass fibre fabrics)—has been hit with a 69% anti-dumping duty (ECTD, 2024a, 2024b). More recently, in March 2025, the European Commission condemned the Chinese company Changshu Longteng (aluminium road wheels), based in Morocco, for receiving direct cross-border financial contributions from China "as part of the new Silk Road cooperation" (ECTD, 2025).

Conclusion

Mediterranean African countries still have closer economic ties with the EU than with China. For straightforward geographical reasons, the European strategy known as Global Gateway is likely to foster even deeper cooperation across the Mediterranean and with the five African Mediterranean countries, despite its whole-of-Africa ambition. Moreover, the evident successes that China has achieved in recent years in the region do not preclude the EU from exerting influence. Conversely, the Global Gateway strategy, by redefining the modalities of cooperation with developing countries, could enhance the EU's credibility, as Wu Hao and Yang Chengyu (2022) explicitly fear.

Commercially, the European Union and China may be in direct competition in Mediterranean Africa. However, the EU remains the Five most important partner. Politically, the competition is not direct. China's strategy of influence is primarily aimed at securing supplies of raw materials (hydrocarbons, copper and phosphates in Mediterranean Africa), but also at providing diplomatic support for the internationalisation of its enterprises. The EU's strategy of influence is different, as it seeks to organise the collective strengthening of security in the region through the promotion of initiatives to combat terrorism and violent extremism, including in cyberspace.

"European diplomacy of values", to quote Wu and Yang (2022, p. 64), is currently giving impetus in China to a normative and ideological crusade to de-Westernise the world. China imbues this confrontation with a quasi-messianic dimension, heralding the establishment of the *sinicised* "Global Civilisation Initiative" that Xi Jinping catechises. How best to capitalise on this "civilisational clash" between the West—here the EU—and China is a challenge for Africa, in particular Mediterranean Africa. Thus, it is up to the African countries themselves to decide on the nature of their relations with China and the EU, and to choose between partnership, peonage and pawnage.

The above observations regarding the relationship between the Five and China, on the one hand, and the Five and the EU, on the other, do not provide any evidence that Mediterranean Africa's relationship with these two powers can be characterised as peonage or pawnage, or that these relations will evolve in these directions in the short term. For instance, until now, the sovereign debt of each of these five countries has never affected their relations with China or European countries. So far, no lender country has requested the enforcement of the sovereign waiver clause or *a fortiori* requested the seizure of assets. The actual question is the nature of any possible partnership with China or the EU. Partnership is a concept that can mean different things, depending on who is claiming it. It often reflects the goals of the party who claims to be working towards them. It is evident that the partnerships between Mediterranean Africa and China and the EU are very imbalanced, as this paper has highlighted.

It appears that the imbalance may be even more pronounced with China than with the EU. It is clear that China's primary objective in Mediterranean Africa is to establish a strategic foothold for its commercial expansion into the European market, rather than seeking to augment its market share in Africa. Conversely, European objectives are likely to be more political, as suggested by the Euro-Mediterranean Partnership (Euromed), which aims at strategic regional cooperation (albeit without much success). But to continue the comparison, another dimension needs to be taken into account. China remains a command economy, while the EU is a market economy. The relationship between politics and economics is very different in these two powers. If a European company were to enter into a partnership with one of the Five, it could completely disregard European partnership strategies, which is hardly conceivable in the case of a Chinese company.

Nevertheless, the greatest risk is the temptation for a country to enter into an unequal relationship with one "partner" in the belief that it is thereby liberating itself from another, which could ultimately lead to a scenario where that country would be beholden to both "partners". As the Burkinabé philosopher Joseph Ki-Zerbo observed, Africa "must not sleep on other people's mats", and must reject "keys-in-hand development, which is false development", and embrace a proactive approach that is "keys-in-head development" (Ki-Zerbo, 1992)[8].

Abbreviations

AFD	Agence française de développement
BMCE	Banque Marocaine du Commerce Extérieur
CASCF	China–Arab States Cooperation Forum
CHEC	China Harbour Engineering Company
COSCO	China Ocean Shipping Company
CSCEC	China State Construction Engineering Corp
DCFTA	Deep and Comprehensive Free Trade Area
ECTD	European Commission's trade department
EU	European Union
Euromed	Euro-Mediterranean Partnership
FDI	Foreign direct investment
FAW	First Automobile Works
FOCAC	Forum on China–Africa Cooperation

GDP	Gross Domestic Product
GNI	Gross National Income
IBRD	[World Bank] International Bank for Reconstruction and Development
MOFCOM	[The Chinese] Ministry of Commerce
OICA	Organisation Internationale des constructeurs automobiles
PSA	Peugeot, Citroën, DS, Opel
SAIC	Shanghai Automotive Industry Corporation
SEZ	Special economic zone
US	United States of America

Notes

1. Dani Rodrik (2017) clearly explains that the structural changes and economic growth induced by large projects are not enough to generate industrialisation in African countries.
2. By "sovereign debt", this study means "External debt stock, public and publicly guaranteed" in current dollars, whose code given by the World Bank is [DT.DOD.DPPG.CD].
3. Gross National Income (GNI) has largely replaced Gross Domestic Product (GDP) in international statistics, as it offers a more precise calculation of national income by considering net receipts from abroad.
4. A "golden share" is a special type of share in a company that grants its holder a veto right.
5. Cf. Pairault (2015a) for specific examples of how Algeria leveraged China. In Mediterranean Africa, the sectors that have seen this competition come to the fore are in particular hydrocarbons, phosphates, armaments, automobiles and pharmaceuticals.
6. Rough calculations indicate that the selling price per kilogram of an iPhone (200 grams, transported by air) is approximately €7500/kg, whereas that of an SUV (2.5 tonnes, transported by sea) is around €40/kg.
7. The negotiation period (145 days) was due to end at the end of July 2025. However, since 11 August, discussions have taken on a new dimension involving the UN Security Council, presided over by Panama (Lederer, 2025).
8. Two books have been published since the final draft of this chapter was written: one in January 2025 and the other in June 2025. These publications could undoubtedly have provided further insights, although neither deals directly with my subject. The first one is a 1250-page book entitled *The Palgrave Handbook on China-Europe-Africa Relations* edited by Li et al. (2025). The second book examines the economic relations between North African countries and China's Zhejiang Province (Lü, 2025).

References

Adarkwah, G. K., Sabel, C. A., & Zilja, F. (2025, February 28). Caught between a rock and a hard place? Africa's position in the US–China strategic rivalry. *AIB Insights*. https://doi.org/10.46697/001c.130834.

AFD [Agence française de développement]. (2025). *Appels d'offres et passations de marchés*. https://www.afd.fr/fr/appels-doffres-et-passations-de-marches.

Aurégan, X. (2023). Déconstruire la cartographie des relations sino-africaines: le cas des ports. *Revue internationale des études du développement, 2023*(252), 29–55.

Cabestan, J.-P. (2025, Janvier–Mars). La Chine en Afrique: une nouvelle hégémonie. *Cahiers de Conflits, 1*, 23–34.

ECTD [European Commission's trade department]. (2024a). *EU trade relations with Egypt. Facts, figures and latest developments*. https://policy.trade.ec.europa.eu/eu-trade-relationships-country-and-region/countries-and-regions/egypt_en

ECTD [European Commission's trade department]. (2024b). *EU trade relations with Morocco. Facts, figures and latest developments*. https://policy.trade.ec.europa.eu/eu-trade-relationships-country-and-region/countries-and-regions/morocco_en.

ECTD [European Commission's trade department]. (2025). *Commission imposes duties on unfairly subsidised imports of aluminium road wheels from Morocco*. https://policy.trade.ec.europa.eu/news/commission-imposes-duties-unfairly-subsidised-imports-aluminium-road-wheels-morocco-2025-03-14_en.

Eickhoff, K., & Thiele, R. (2023, June 15). Debt relief in Africa: Conflicting interests between the West and China Hinder multilateral solutions. *Megatrends Spotlight*, 25.

Ekman, A. (2014). La vision chinoise du Maghreb. In T. Pairault & F. Talahite (Eds.), *Chine-Algérie: Une relation singulière en Afrique* (pp. 171–192). Riveneuve Éditions.

Hamill-Stewart, C. (2025, March 19). Algeria cancels deep-water port project with China. *Arabian Gulf Business Insight*.

Kardon, I. (2022). China's ports in Africa. In N. Rolland (Ed.), *(In)roads and outposts critical infrastructure in China's Africa strategy*. NBR Special Report #98, pp. 9–20.

Ki-Zerbo, J. (1992). *La natte des autres. Pour un développement endogène en Afrique*. Karthala.

Lederer, E. (2025, August 12). China and the US clash at the UN over the Panama Canal, a focus of Trump's attention. *The Associated Press*. https://apnews.com/article/un-us-china-panama-canal-trump-2aafbbfb0d5fdb27ce04c54a0204a10a.

Li, Y., Francisco, J. B., Leandro, S., Tavares, J., & da Silva, C. R. (2025). *The Palgrave handbook on China-Europe-Africa relations*. Palgrave Macmillan.

Lü, Q. (Ed.) (2025). Zhejiang sheng canyu gong jian yidai yilu (beifei guojia juan 2013-2023) [Zhejiang Province's Participation in the Joint Construction of the Belt and Road Initiative (North African Countries Volume 2013–2023)]. Hangzhou [Hangzhou], Zhejiang daxue chubanshe [Zhejiang University Press].

Luo, J., & Li, Y. (2024). Dangqian feizhou dui zhong fei hezuo de renshi yu qidai [Current African Perceptions and Expectations of China-Africa Cooperation]. *Dangdai zhongguo yu shijie [Contemporary China and the World], 04*, 120–126.

MOFCOM [(Chinese) Ministry of Commerce]. (2015). Jingwai jingmao hezuo qu fuwu zhinan fanben [Draft guide to services offered by Foreign economic co-operation zones], November 3. http://fec.mofcom.gov.cn/article/zcfb/jwjmhz/201511/20151101153854.shtml.

OICA [Organisation Internationale des constructeurs automobiles]. (2024). *Production statistics*. https://www.oica.net/category/production-statistics/2023-statistics/.

Olander, E. (2025, January 11). Development finance in Africa, the new terrain for US-China rivalry. *The Africa report*.

Pairault, T. (2015a). *China's economic presence in Algeria*. C.C.J. Occasional Papers n°1, January.

Pairault, T. (2015b). Economic relations between China and Maghreb countries. In J. Wouters, J.-C. Defraigne, & M. Burnay (Eds.), *China, the European Union and the developing world* (pp. 298–324). Edawrd Elgar.

Pairault, T. (2018, July 5). China in Africa: Goods Supplier, Service Provider Rather Than Investor. *Bridges Africa*, 7(5). https://www.ictsd.org/bridges-news/bridges-africa/news/china-in-africa-goods-supplier-service-provider-rather-than.

Pairault, T. (2019b). La route maritime de la soie et les terminaux portuaires en Méditerranée. *Monde chinois, 2*(58), 121–135.

Pairault, T. (2022). Industrial parks in Africa: Building nests for the Chinese Phoenix. In N. Rolland (Ed.), *(In)roads and outposts Critical Infrastructure in China's Africa Strategy*. NBR Special Report #98, 2022, pp. 75–88.

Pairault, T. (2023). L'axe Le Caire-Pékin: une diplomatie de la précaution. *Moyen-Orient, 58*, 36–41.

Pairault, T. (2024). *L'Union européenne face à la Chine en Afrique – Un bilan statistique des relations commerciales en 2023*. Working paper, https://shs.hal.science/halshs-04683276.

Pairault, T. (2013). Booming Sino-Maghreb economic relations: Incentives for a new European partnership. In M. G. Berhe & L. Hongwu (Eds.), *China-Africa relations: Governance, peace and security* (pp. 96–114). Institute for Peace and Security Studies (Addis Ababa University) and Institute of African Studies (Zhejiang Normal University).

Pairault, T., & Richet, X. (2021). *Présences économiques chinoises en Méditerranée*. L'Harmattan.

Rodrik, D. (2017, October 10). Growth without industrialization. *Project Syndicate*.

Sen, A. (1980). Description as choice. *Oxford Economic Papers, 32*(3), 353–369.

Sun, Y. (2025, mars 3). US-China engagement in Africa: A crossroads, Foresight Africa 2025–2030. *Brookings Africa Growth Initiative*, pp. 190–194. https://www.brookings.edu/articles/us-china-engagement-in-africa-a-crossroads.

Wang, H. (2017). Zhong Fei gong jian chanye yuan de xianzhuang, wenti he duice [Status, problems and measures for the industrial parks jointly established by China and Africa]. In Z. Hongming and W. Hongyi (Eds.), *Feizhou fazhan baogao n°19 (2016–2017): Feizhou gongyehua yu zhongguo zai feizhou chanye yuanqu jianshe* [African Development Report n°19 (2016–2017): African Industrialization and China's Construction of Industrial Parks in Africa, pp. 1–28]. Beijing, Shehui kexue chubanshe.

Wang, J., & Zou, X. (2025). "Quanqiu nanfang" yu jing xia zhong fei xieshou xiandaihua zhi lu [China-Africa Partnership for Modernisation in the Context of the 'Global South']. *Xiya Feizhou* [West Asia and Africa]. *02*, pp. 66–87+168–169.

Wu, H., & Yang, C. (2022). Oumeng "quanqiu menhu" zhanlüe ji qi dui "yidai yilu" changyi de yingxiang [The EU's "Global Gateway" Strategy and Its Impact on the "Belt and Road Initiative"]. *Guoji wenti yanjiu* [International Studies], *5*, 58–77.

Wu, J. (2019, July 19). Deng Xiaoping: Shishiqiushi, shi wuchan jieji shijieguan de jichu [Deng Xiaoping: Seeking truth from facts is the foundation of the proletarian worldview]. Deng Xiaoping jinian wang [Deng Xiaoping Memorial Network]. http://cpc.people.com.cn/n1/2019/0719/c69113-31244697.html.

Zhang, B. (2024). Africans in China, Western/White supremacy and the ambivalence of Chinese racial identity. *The China Quarterly, 260*, 932–947.

The Ecological Implications of Africa–China Partnership in the Extractive Sectors of Africa: Lessons from Artisanal and Small-Scale Mining in Ghana

Emmanuel Graham and Asaah Sumaila Mohammed

Introduction and Background

Africa remains a paradox: a continent rich in nearly every natural resource, yet faces severe poverty (Panford, 2017). In demonstrating the wealth of Africa Diop (1987) in his book "*Black Africa: The Economic and Cultural Basis for Federal State*", mentions enormous amount of energy resources in Africa—what he called the "Compendium of Energy Sources". These are "hydraulic energy, solar energy, atomic energy, thermonuclear energy, wind energy, thermal energy of the sea, tidal energy, global heat, volcanic thermal energy and geothermal energy" (Diop, 1987, p. 37). Another source of wealth in Africa is the abundance of minerals such as gold, oil,

E. Graham (✉)
York University, Toronto, Canada
e-mail: graham19@yorku.ca

A. S. Mohammed
CK Tedam University of Technology and Applied Sciences, Navrongo, Ghana

L. G. Adu Amoah (ed.), *Africa-China Relations*,
https://doi.org/10.1007/978-981-95-4370-0_12

diamonds, bauxite, and other precious minerals. Nonetheless, these abundances of resources paradoxically coexist with pervasive poverty, a situation described as the "resource curse" (Auty, 1993). The resource curse essentially suggests that countries rich in natural resources often experience lower or less economic growth, poor developmental outcomes, and conflict compared with countries poor in natural resources (Karl, 1997; Auty, 2001; Sachs & Warner, 2001).

In recent times, China has made strides as an economic powerhouse in the world, which has reshaped Africa's extractive sector. Africa–China relations have expanded rapidly in the last decade, characterized by strong Chinese investment in the extractive sectors of Africa (Asante, 2018). This partnership has brought both opportunity (Chin & Gallagher, 2019) and challenges (Chen, 2016). Boasting a reputation as a leading democratic light on the continent, Ghana has a rich history in gold mining and resources like bauxite, manganese, and, more recently, oil and gas found in huge quantities in the country (Gyampo, 2014; Panford, 2017; Tuokuu et al., 2018). The extractive sector is one of the pillars of Ghana's economy and an important contributor to her GDP, foreign exchange earnings, and employment (Aryee, 2001). Chinese investment in Ghana's petroleum and mining sectors is a prime example of the larger Africa–China relationship, which is characterized by infrastructural development, foreign direct investment, and the setting up of China-led companies that have operations within the boundaries of Ghana (Adjuik & Robert, 2018).

Indeed, a corpus of research has contributed to the discourse on China–Africa relations (Alden, 2007; Cheru & Obi, 2011; Amoah, 2012; Zhao, 2014; Taylor, 2014; Haslam et al., 2009; Chen, 2016; Mlambo et al., 2016; Sibiri, 2021). Others have examined China in specific regions of Africa (Moody, 2011; Sindzingre, 2011; Burgess & Beilstein, 2013; Taylor, 2014). Nonetheless, there are few studies on China's involvement in Ghana's extractive sector (Hilson et al., 2014; Kumah, 2023). Although there have been great economic benefits from Ghana–China partnership, the ecological impact of Chinese nationals in the extractive sector has raised concerns worth investigating, especially Chinese involvement in "galamsey" or Artisanal and Small-scale Mining (ASM). It is from this background that this chapter seeks to examine the ecological implication of Ghana–China partnership in the extractive sector, with a specific focus on the intersection of environmental degradation, governance failures, and local community impacts. Using political ecology as a theoretical framework, the chapter interrogates the structural power dynamic that underpins ecological harm and marginalization. Our central thesis is that, though China may be characterized as a developmental partner of Ghana, the involvement of Chinese nationals in the extractive sectors, who are autonomous from the Chinese state, has led to some ecological implications that are a dent on the Chinese government's partnership with Ghana. Our research questions are: what are the environmental impacts of Ghana–China collaborations in Ghana's extractive sectors, and how does it affect their partnership?

By examining these questions, we aim to contribute to a more nuanced understanding of Africa–China relations, pointing to the urgent need to re-centre ecological justice in the governance of extractive resources. We employ a qualitative methodological approach in this chapter by applying content analysis to both primary and secondary data. For primary data, we relied on documentary evidence, stakeholder statements, reported interviews by government officials, and other officials on the topic available on GhanaWeb, JoyNews, among others. Secondary data are from books, journals, and internet media. We sorted the information by themes and sub-themes through content analysis. The chapter is organized as follows: Section "Introduction and Background" is the introduction and background. Section "Theoretical Framework: Political Ecology and the Extractive Sector" is the theoretical framework, where we discuss political ecology. Section "Ecological Impacts of ASM Activities in Ghana Through the Lens of Political Ecology" is the discussion and analysis. Section "Concluding Remarks" is concluding remarks.

Theoretical Framework: Political Ecology and the Extractive Sector

Political ecology serves as a comprehensive theoretical framework for understanding the ecological and socio-economic implications of the extractive sector's activities. Political ecology is an interdisciplinary framework that looks at relations between politics, society, and the environment. It stresses on the power dynamics and social disparities that mould environmental outcomes, focusing on the ways in which economic, social, and political factors affect decision-making on the environment. This theoretical framework examines change as a function of power relations between actors who have competing interests, with emphasis on how political, economic, and ecological systems intersect to shape or influence social and environmental outcomes (Robbins, 2011; Essah & Andrews, 2016; Kumah, 2023).

A fundamental premise in political ecology is that environmental change cannot be entirely comprehended without considering the political and economic structures within and from which it is embedded (Kumah, 2023; Robbins, 2011). Political ecology highlights the differences between "winners" and "losers" in resource management, revealing hidden costs and the power structures that drive social and environmental inequalities (Bryant, 1997; Robbins, 2011). While political ecology sheds light on structural power imbalances, it also acknowledges the agency of marginalized groups in rejecting environmental injustices. This act of rejecting injustices comes in various forms, including legal challenges and grassroot mobilization and movements against powerful entities (Bryant & Bailey, 1997).

The political ecology framework is relevant when discussing the environmental and social consequences of extractive industries such as mining and the oil and gas sectors. The reason is that extractive industries most of the time involve complicated power relationships between state governments, local communities, multinational firms, and international finance houses. How these relationships pan out often determines the environmental outcomes, which also depend on how the resources are exploited and the groups that benefit from the extracted resources, and how the associated risks are shared. A major contention of political ecology is the fact that exploitative industries are generally mired in social conflict and environmental degradation. Extracting resources from the earth generally leads to deforestation, water pollution, and the destruction of ecosystems, with significant impacts on biodiversity and human health (Bryant, 1997; Bryant & Bailey, 1997; Robbins, 2011). However, the impacts on the environment from resource extraction are not distributed evenly, and political ecology proves that vulnerable communities, mainly local people and rural populations, are disproportionately impacted by the destruction of the environment where the resource is being exploited, while the main beneficiaries of the economic benefits do not feel the negative impact.

Robbins (2011) identifies five central theses in political ecology, two of which are particularly applicable to understanding the ecological and socio-political implications of extractive industries in Africa. The first is the degradation and marginalization thesis: This thesis posits that those external interventions—whether by state actors or global market forces disrupt sustainable local resource management, leading to overexploitation and ecological degradation. In the case of Ghana, state-led policies under the Structural Adjustment Programs (SAP) led to the integration of local economies into the global system, leading to resource extraction at unsustainable levels. These reforms often prioritized large-scale multinational corporations, marginalizing local communities and traditional resource management practices (Hennessy, 2014). The resulting overexploitation of land and mineral resources not only undermined local livelihoods but also exacerbated ecological degradation and resource scarcity.

The second is the conservation and control thesis, which critiques conservation policies that, while aimed at sustainability, often lead to the dispossession of local actors. In Ghana, land previously managed by local communities was reallocated to multinational mining corporations, ostensibly to generate state revenue. This enclosure of communal lands deprived local populations of access to vital resources, disrupting traditional livelihoods and creating long-term socio-economic vulnerabilities (Acheampong et al., 2024). Surface mining operations have degraded large tracts of land, leaving communities with inadequate compensation and limited means of recovery.

The Africa–China partnership in the extractive sectors, particularly in Ghana, underscores the relevance of political ecology. Chinese involvements in ASM have intensified resource conflict, especially in mining communities, highlighting the unequal power dynamics between local actors and Chinese workers. The privatization of mining rights and the expansion of Chinese mining operations have exacerbated land degradation, reduced local resource access, and heightened tensions within affected communities (Kumah, 2023; Acheampong et al., 2024).Over the past few years, Chinese firms have become a major force in the extractive sector in Africa, mainly in mining. In Ghana, Chinese firms have invested a lot in gold mining, which has had a major impact on the environment and the social life of the communities in which they operate (Kumah, 2023). The partnership between national governments in Africa and Chinese firms sets great examples of the power dynamics that political ecology aims to tackle.

To understand the political ecology of the Africa–China partnership in Ghana, one will have to look at the power relations that exist between the Ghanaian government, Chinese firms, and the local communities, and how that affects the environment. The Chinese most of the time work under laxed environmental regulations that allow them to operate in ways that result in forest devastation, water pollution, and land degradation

(Hilson et al., 2014). Even though resource extraction is profitable to these firms, it is the local communities that suffer the consequences of the environmental impacts, mainly due to water contamination and loss of agricultural land.

More so the political ecology framework exposes the role of the Ghanaian government in paving the way for Chinese investments into the mining sector. They often mask these investments as development opportunities that will create jobs, but political ecologists opine that these investments normally come at the expense of environmental sustainability and social equity. In many instances, local people are not consulted about the projects that will be happening in their backyards, and their agitations are not considered or left unattended (Hilson et al., 2014).

The case of Ghana - China partnership also shows the global dimensions of political ecology. Because gold is a highly sought-after commodity in the international market, it pushes the extraction of the resource in Ghana, linking local environmental destruction to international economic processes. Political ecologists say that extractive capitalism in this form buttresses already existing power disproportions between the global north and global south as powerful entities in developed countries reap the rewards from resource exploitation to the detriment of the local people in these resource-rich areas (Bebbington et al., 2008).

To mediate these power imbalances, local communities in Ghana have marshalled resistance movements to challenge the environmental injustices associated with Chinese mining operations. Political ecology acknowledges the importance of these local people in taking on powerful entities and advocating for environmental justice. Many civil society organizations have advocated for stringent environmental regulations, greater community participation in decision-making, and equitable compensation for the environmental and social abuse inflicted by resource extraction operations (Kwofie et al., 2015). All these demonstrate ways through which disadvantaged people can challenge environmental injustices and demand more equity and sustainability in resource management practices.

Ecological Impacts of ASM Activities in Ghana Through the Lens of Political Ecology

The mining sector is one of the most important economic drivers in Ghana, creating jobs and contributing significantly to national revenues. However, it also represents the complex power relations, environmental degradation, and socioeconomic disruptions associated with extractive operations in the Global South. This section investigates the impact of Chinese mining (ASM) operations in Ghana through the perspective of political ecology, assesses the environmental consequences of these activities, and examines the local opposition and power struggles that occurred in this context. It is important to mention that it is not only Chinese who are involved in these illegal mining. The ecological consequences of Chinese involvement in ASM in Ghana are deeply linked with its political and economic arrangements locally and globally. From a political ecological viewpoint, we demonstrate how power relations, regulatory choices, and international partnership affect environmental outcomes, whereby several communities experience the greatest burdens. This is visible in Ghana in the ASM, particularly the involvement of Chinese businessmen who are separate from the Chinese government. Their activities have led to several ecological problems and social inequalities.

Environmental Degradation, China's Role, and Localized Ecological Harm

The environmental impact of mining, particularly illicit small-scale mining, is significant. Ghanaian rich forest ecosystems and water bodies have been among the most severely impacted by these activities. Chinese mining operations (Table 1), which are commonly located near rivers and wetlands, contribute greatly to water pollution by releasing mercury and other hazardous substances. Research conducted by Ofori et al. (2024) helps us to understand that rivers such as the Pra and Ankobra have been severely contaminated, harming aquatic ecosystems and rendering water unfit for home and agricultural use. Another important issue is soil degradation, which has resulted in the conversion of vast areas of agricultural land into mining pits (Kuffour et al., 2018). This not only impacts the local food supply but also causes soil sterility, limiting the opportunity for land rehabilitation. The loss of vegetation cover worsens climatic vulnerabilities (Lal, 2015; Sivakumar, 2007), such as increased erosion risk and

Table 1 Chinese mining operations in Ghana

Aspect	*Details*
Involvement	Over 50,000 Chinese nationals entered Ghana for illegal gold mining between 2008 and 2013 (Aikins, 2024; Global Initiative Against Transnational Organized Crime, 2021).
Key figures	En "Aisha" Huang, known as the "Galamsey Queen", is a prominent figure in illegal mining operations (Africa Defence Forum, 2023).
Mining techniques	The introduction of heavy machinery (excavators, bulldozers) replaced traditional artisanal methods.
Environmental impact	Pollution of major rivers (Pra, Ankobra) and destruction of forests; 34 out of 288 reserves affected (Aikins, 2024; Green, 2024).
Economic effects	Loss of livelihoods for local miners; cocoa production significantly impacted due to land degradation (Aikins, 2024; Green, 2024).
Government response	Multiple crackdowns and deportations; ongoing challenges in enforcement and regulation (Global Initiative Against Transnational Organized Crime, 2021).

Source: Authors' Creation

reduced carbon sequestration potential. Environmental studies of these mining activities usually reveal a disconnect between policy and practice. Despite Ghana's strong environmental laws and guidelines, enforcement is at best sporadic and limited due to corruption, resource limits, and political influence (Teschner, 2012; Ampaw et al., 2023). It is so pathetic that Chinese mining companies, frequently aided by powerful local and international networks (legal loopholes), exploit systemic flaws to continue unsustainable practices (Antwi-Boateng & Akudugu, 2020).

The influx of Chinese miners in Ghana since the 2000s transformed galamsey (ASM) by introducing heavy machinery and advanced techniques. This has outcompeted local miners and increased environmental degradation. Key figures like "Aisha Huang" exemplify the challenges faced by Ghanaian authorities in curbing illegal mining activities in Ghana, which have significantly contributed to environmental degradation and economic disruption (see, Table 1). It is estimated that about 50,000 Chinese nationals came to Ghana to partake in illegal mining from 2008 to 2013 (Aikins, 2024). These operations, as shown in Table 1 and Fig. 1, have caused widespread environmental degradations. The extraction methods used lead to deforestation, water pollution, and soil degradation, severely affecting local ecosystems (Awewomom et al., 2024).

Fig. 1 Kunsu, Ghana, March 20, 2023, rural women in small-scale mining (Galamsey) in Ghana (image credits Green, 2024)

Chinese participation in mining ASM reflects wider geopolitical power structures, whereby on one hand, it depicts a strategic development partnership and on the other, it exemplifies how unequal relationship allow foreign enterprise to exploit resources at the expense of local communities (Kumah, 2023). Although ASM contributes to national economic metrics, mining activities disproportionately harm rural communities, reinforcing cycles of poverty and ecological degradation (Sarpong, 2010). The government has attempted various interventions, but challenges persist due to political influences and ineffective enforcement of regulations (Aziabah & Ayelazuno, 2024). The Ghanaian government frequently places a higher priority on resource extraction than environmental sustainability because of the country's desire for economic growth and foreign investment. Corruption, lax enforcement, and collusion between state authorities and business entities routinely undermine policies and regulations meant to protect natural resources. Global mining and oil corporations have a lot of sway and use their financial might to negotiate advantageous conditions and get around environmental regulations. Rural communities frequently have little influence over decision-making processes (Mohammed et al., 2022), despite being the ones most affected by environmental degradation. These communities often lack the resources and information necessary to hold the government and companies responsible. The displacement and interruption of traditional livelihoods, such as farming and fishing, brought on by extractive operations exacerbate their marginalization (Table 2).

Disproportionate Burdens on Marginalized Communities

Environmental degradation from Ghana's ASM activities has produced unequal effects across different communities. Rural and marginalized communities face disproportionate impacts from mining activities (Oberman, 2023). Mining operations have directly damaged agricultural lands and forest resources on which rural communities depend for their living (Akyeampong & Xu, 2023; Aryee et al., 2003; Hilson, 2002). Polluted rivers can no longer support domestic and agricultural needs, forcing residents to turn to costly or inconsistent water sources (Oberman, 2023).

The combination of destroyed farmland and toxic soil contamination has led to decreased agricultural production, which drives economic distress and creates food supply issues. The appropriation of lands for mining purposes, combined with land infertility, destroys traditional ways of living while increasing social displacement. Health conditions in these regions have experienced significant decline. The local population notes a rise in cases of respiratory diseases, skin conditions, and infections from contaminated water sources due to pollutants from mining operations (Oberman,

Table 2 Negative impacts of illegal mining in Ghana

Impact	*Description*
Environmental degradation	Deforestation, habitat destruction, soil erosion, and biodiversity loss (Aikins, 2024)
Water pollution	Contamination of rivers with heavy metals, affecting drinking water and agriculture (Ofori et al., 2024; Awewomom et al., 2024)
Health risks	Chronic diseases (kidney failure, respiratory issues) among miners and local communities (Aikins, 2024)
Socioeconomic effects	Disruption of livelihoods, especially in agriculture (e.g. cocoa production) (Awewomom et al., 2024)
Regulatory challenges	Ineffective enforcement of mining laws and political interference hinder progress (Aikins, 2024)

Source: Constructed by authors using indicated references

2023). There have been reports of mercury poisoning, which causes severe dangers because it creates persistent neurological and reproductive harm, disproportionately affecting women and children in these communities (Awewomom et al., 2024).

Affected communities endure the majority of negative impacts, but they generally do not possess the political influence or legal knowledge required to seek justice or hold responsible parties accountable. The majority of Environmental Impact Assessments (EIAs) happen without the participation of impacted communities, while any available compensation remains inadequate and is typically provided late. Ghana's development model, which favours external capital and state revenue, functions as both a reason for and an outcome of these communities' marginalization (Fig. 2).

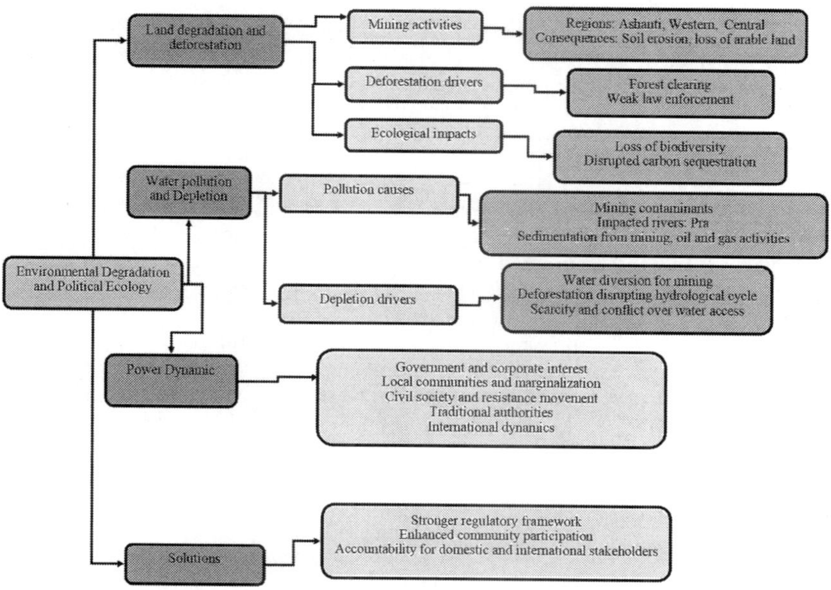

Fig. 2 Environmental degradation and political ecology (Source: Authors)

Biodiversity Loss

Biodiversity in Ghana encompasses a rich variety of flora and fauna, including unique ecosystems that provide essential services such as climate regulation, food production, and cultural value (Osei et al., 2018). However, this biodiversity is under significant threat due to extractive activities (see Table 3), deforestation, agricultural expansion, urbanization, and climate change. Biodiversity loss has far-reaching implications for local ecosystems and livelihoods, reflecting the intersection of ecological degradation and socio-political dynamics. A political ecology perspective reveals the power imbalances and governance challenges underlying these losses while proposing pathways for sustainable conservation.

The impact of biodiversity loss on Ghana's flora and fauna is extensive and alarming. Extractive activities such as mining and oil exploration are primary drivers of habitat destruction, leading to the displacement or extinction of numerous plant and animal species (Scanes, 2018). The impact of biodiversity loss on flora and fauna is extensive and alarming in Ghana (see Table 4).

Table 3 Anti-galamsey organizations and movements in Ghana

Organization/ Movement	*Description*	*References*
Coalition of concerned citizens against galamsey	Organized protests against illegal mining, demanding government action and the repeal of pro-mining legislation.	(AfricaNews, 2024)
Ghana coalition against galamsey	Advocates for stricter enforcement of mining laws and environmental protection, expressing disappointment in government responses.	(Lartey, 2024)
Ghana Water Company Limited	Raised alarms about water contamination due to galamsey, impacting public health and access to clean water.	(Citinewsroom, 2022)
Environmental Protection Agency (EPA)	Involved in monitoring and regulating mining activities to mitigate environmental impacts, although facing challenges.	(Aikins, 2024)
Community-based organizations	Local groups that address land conflicts and advocate for the rights of affected communities against illegal mining practices.	(AfricaNews, 2024)

Source: Constructed by authors using references provided

Table 4 Environmental impacts of illegal gold mining (galamsey) in Ghana

Impact	*Description*	*References*
Deforestation	Galamsey activities lead to significant deforestation as forested areas are cleared for mining operations.	Ofori et al. (2024)]
Habitat destruction	Destruction of habitats results in loss of biodiversity, affecting both plant and animal species.	Ofori et al. (2024)
Water pollution	Use of hazardous chemicals like mercury and cyanide contaminates water bodies, harming aquatic life.	Awewomom et al. (2024)
Soil degradation	Soil quality deteriorates due to mining activities, impacting agricultural productivity and local ecosystems.	Gilbert and Albert (2016)
Biodiversity loss	Many native species face extinctions due to habitat loss from mining, disrupting ecosystem services.	Ofori et al. (2024)
Erosion and land degradation	Removal of vegetation leads to increased soil erosion and degradation of land quality.	Kuffour et al. (2018)
Impact on agriculture	Cocoa farms and other agricultural lands are severely affected, threatening food security in communities.	Osman et al. (2022)

Source: Authors drawing on references provided

Forests in Ghana, especially in regions like the Western and Ashanti areas, have been significantly depleted. The clearing of forest land for mining, agricultural expansion, and infrastructure development results in the loss of endemic plant species (Attuquayefio et al., 2017). Forest reserves, which serve as critical biodiversity hotspots, are often encroached upon by illegal mining operations (galamsey) and logging activities (Tengapoe et al., 2023). This has led to the disappearance of medicinal plants, timber species, and other vegetation essential for ecological balance and human livelihoods.

The cumulative impact of these pressures disrupts the ecological functions of Ghana's ecosystems, diminishing their capacity to support biodiversity and provide essential services to humans and wildlife alike. The loss of forest cover and habitat fragmentation severely affect wildlife populations. Species such as elephants, pangolins, and various primates face declining numbers due to habitat destruction and poaching (Dzakpasu et al., 2024). Rivers and wetlands, vital for aquatic biodiversity, have been degraded by pollution from mining chemicals like mercury and cyanide. Fish species, which are crucial to local diets and economies, have experienced population decline due to polluted and sedimented water bodies.

The degradation of biodiversity has cascading effects on local ecosystems, undermining their resilience and productivity. Biodiversity underpins critical ecosystem services (Elmqvist et al., 2012), such as water purification, soil fertility, pollination, and carbon sequestration. The loss of flora and fauna disrupts these processes (Crooks, 2002), reducing agricultural productivity and increasing vulnerability to climate change. For instance, deforestation in watershed areas exacerbates water scarcity and soil erosion, threatening both human communities and wildlife. The extinction or decline of keystone species destabilizes ecosystems, leading to a chain reaction of negative effects. For example, the loss of pollinators such as bees and butterflies affects crop yields, while the decline of predator species can lead to overpopulation of certain prey species, further altering ecological balances.

Local communities, particularly in rural areas, depend heavily on biodiversity for their livelihoods. Fishing, hunting, and foraging for wild foods and medicinal plants are integral to their sustenance. Biodiversity loss thus not only threatens ecological health but also undermines the cultural and economic well-being of these communities, deepening poverty and social inequality. From a political ecology perspective, biodiversity conservation in Ghana is intricately linked to issues of power, governance, and equity (Ayelazuno, 2014). This framework highlights the socio-political structures and power dynamics that influence resource use and conservation outcomes. The exploitation of natural resources in Ghana is often driven by powerful actors, including multinational corporations, government agencies, and local elites. These stakeholders prioritize short-term economic gains over long-term ecological sustainability, sidelining the interests of local communities. For instance, forest reserves and protected areas are frequently encroached upon for mining and logging, often with tacit approval from political and economic elites.

Community Health and Livelihoods

The environmental impacts of extractive activities in Ghana extend beyond ecological degradation, profoundly affecting the health and livelihoods of local communities (see Table 2 and Table 5). Pollution, displacement, and socio-economic upheavals are persistent challenges, especially in regions

Table 5 Community health and livelihoods in Ghana: a political ecology perspective

Key themes	*Description*
Pollution-related health issues	Extractive activities generate pollutants that severely impact local health, including air, water, and soil contamination.
Air and water pollution	Mercury, cyanide, and Volatile Organic Compounds (VOCs) from mining and oil activities lead to respiratory illnesses, neurological disorders, and cancer risks.
Soil contamination and food security	Heavy metals compromise agricultural productivity and food safety, causing health issues like gastrointestinal disorders and immune deficiencies.
Vector-borne diseases	Stagnant water in mining pits increases malaria and schistosomiasis prevalence, disproportionately affecting vulnerable populations.
Displacement and socio-economic effects	Communities face forced relocations, loss of livelihoods, and social fragmentation due to extractive industry expansion.
Forced relocations	Inadequate compensation, loss of ancestral lands, and cultural heritage erosion occur due to land acquisition for industrial projects.
Loss of livelihoods	Pollution and restricted access to natural resources disrupt farming, fishing, and artisanal mining, leading to economic instability.
Social fragmentation	Displacement weakens community cohesion and traditional support systems, increasing vulnerability to environmental and economic risks.
Power relations and community responses	Government and corporate priorities, marginalization of local communities, and grassroots resistance shape the socio-economic landscape.
Government and corporate influence	Policies often prioritize revenue and foreign investment over community welfare, concentrating benefits among elites.
Marginalization of local communities	Limited political power, legal knowledge, and financial resources hinder communities' ability to advocate for their rights.
Community resistance	Grassroots movements and civil society organizations demand accountability, fair compensation, and environmental justice.
Role of traditional authorities	Traditional leaders act as negotiators or align with corporate interests, reflecting complex power dynamics.
Environmental justice	Efforts focus on amplifying marginalized voices, equitable benefit distribution, and inclusive decision-making processes.

Source: Authors

where mining and oil and gas activities dominate. Examining these issues through the lens of political ecology highlights the underlying power dynamics and structural inequalities that shape community experiences and responses. This section explores the health impacts of pollution, the socio-economic consequences of displacement, and the power relations influencing community resilience and resistance.

Extractive activities in Ghana, particularly mining and oil exploration, generate a range of pollutants that pose severe health risks to local populations. Industrial processes such as gold mining release harmful substances into the environment. Mercury and cyanide, used in mining, contaminate rivers and groundwater, exposing communities to toxic chemicals that can cause neurological disorders, kidney damage, and developmental issues in children (Anim-Gyampo et al., 2021). The leaching of heavy metals into soil near mining sites compromises agricultural productivity and food safety. Crops grown in contaminated soils absorb toxins, which can enter the food chain and impact human health over time (Munishi et al., 2021). This contamination reduces the nutritional quality of food and contributes to long-term health issues such as gastrointestinal disorders and immune system deficiencies.

The creation of mining pits that accumulate stagnant water increases the prevalence of waterborne and vector-borne diseases (Hinwood et al. 2011). These diseases disproportionately affect vulnerable groups, including children and pregnant women, worsening public health challenges in mining regions. The expansion of extractive industries often leads to the displacement of communities, disrupting their social structures and economic activities. In many cases, mining and oil projects require large tracts of land, necessitating the relocation of communities. These forced relocations often result in inadequate compensation, loss of ancestral lands, and the erosion of cultural heritage (Maldonado, 2008). Communities are frequently resettled in areas with limited access to resources, infrastructure, and employment opportunities, deepening poverty and social marginalization.

Traditional livelihoods such as farming, fishing, and artisanal mining are directly threatened by land degradation, water pollution, and restricted access to natural resources. For instance, oil spills in coastal regions have decimated fish stocks, leaving fishing communities without a sustainable income source (Mohammed et al., 2023). Similarly, the conversion of agricultural land into mining zones reduces food production and disrupts rural economies. Displacement and economic instability often lead to social fragmentation, as families and communities are forced to migrate in search of better opportunities. This disrupts community cohesion and weakens traditional support systems, increasing vulnerability to economic shocks and environmental risks.

The impacts of extractive activities on health and livelihoods are shaped by complex power relations involving governments, corporations, and local communities. Multinational corporations (MNCs) wield significant influence in shaping policies and negotiating contracts, frequently sidelining the interests of affected populations. These power dynamics perpetuate systemic inequities, where the economic benefits of resource extraction are concentrated among elites, while local communities bear the brunt of environmental and social costs.

Local communities, particularly those in rural and marginalized areas, often lack the political power and resources to effectively advocate for their rights. For instance, residents of communities along the Pra and Ankobra rivers have been excluded from EIAs and lack the legal literacy to contest land seizures (Ofori et al., 2024). In Ellembelle District, coastal populations displaced by oil activities received little compensation and had no legal recourse due to limited knowledge of Ghana's regulatory framework (Mohammed et al., 2023). Community members in Tarkwa and Kunsu who protested environmental harm or galamsey were often intimidated, arrested, or silenced through state or corporate force (AfricaNews, 2024; Green, 2024). These dynamics—compounded by poverty, exclusion, and institutional bias, highlight the structural constraints facing local resistance efforts and exacerbate their vulnerability to environmental and livelihood harm. Despite these challenges, local communities have increasingly mobilized to resist the negative impacts of extractive activities. Grassroots movements, often supported by civil society organizations and advocacy groups, have emerged to demand greater accountability, fair compensation, and environmental justice. Examples include protests against illegal mining (galamsey) and campaigns for stricter regulations on oil spills and gas flaring.

Traditional leaders play a dual role in these dynamics. In some cases, they act as intermediaries, negotiating with corporations on behalf of their communities. However, others may align with corporate or government interests, prioritizing personal or political gains over community welfare. This duality underscores the complexity of power relations within local contexts. At its core, the struggle to address the health and livelihood impacts of extractive activities is a fight for environmental justice. A political ecology perspective highlights the need to amplify the voices of marginalized communities, ensure equitable distribution of benefits and risks, and promote inclusive decision-making processes.

The health and livelihood impacts of extractive activities in Ghana illustrate the deep interconnections between environmental degradation, socio-economic inequality, and governance challenges. Pollution-related health issues, displacement, and the erosion of traditional livelihoods underscore the urgent need for reforms that prioritize community welfare. By addressing power imbalances, fostering community participation, and strengthening regulatory frameworks, Ghana can mitigate the adverse effects of extractive industries and promote a more equitable and sustainable future.

Synthesis: Structural Violence and the Ecology of Extraction

The preceding analysis has shown that the ecological impacts of extractive activities in Ghana cannot be understood without accounting for the interlocking structures of power, governance, and global capital. These dynamics form a system of structural violence, a condition in which economic and political arrangements create and perpetuate harm manifested in environmental degradation, livelihood loss, and community marginalization (MacNeil, 2018).

Political ecology helps uncover how this structural violence is sustained through asymmetrical relationships between foreign investors, especially Chinese actors, and domestic elites. Ghana's government supports foreign direct investment as an economic development plan but frequently sacrifices both environmental sustainability and social justice in the process. China's mining activities in Ghana demonstrate this contradictory situation. China has established itself as a strategic economic partner through its investments in both infrastructure and energy sectors. Chinese nationals who work beyond formal regulatory boundaries have emerged as key players in unauthorized artisanal mining activities, resulting in extensive environmental degradation and conflicts over resources (Akyeampong & Xu, 2023).

The blurred distinction between officially sanctioned Chinese enterprises and rogue actors permits both to operate without sufficient accountability. The weak regulatory framework in Ghana, combined with legal loopholes and local partnerships, allows Chinese companies to access land and resources without proper environmental safeguards (Ayelazuno,

2011; Debrah & Asante, 2019). The framework of South-South cooperation and development assistance often legitimizes these arrangements while masking their exploitative and unequal characteristics.

What emerges is a dual complicity: Chinese state and private sector entities follow strategic economic agendas while disregarding environmental impacts, but Ghanaian authorities who are driven by political benefits or hide behind institutional stagnation do not carry out legal enforcement or safeguard at-risk populations. Harvey (2003) describes "accumulation by dispossession" as the process where economic growth occurs through the displacement and disenfranchisement of local populations due to this convergence of interests.

The development model prioritizes national economic expansion and treats natural resources as tools for growth instead of recognizing their role in ecological systems or community livelihoods. The focus on GDP growth and export revenue undermines the importance of cultural heritage alongside biological diversity and public health. The drive for national modernization treats communities who depend on natural resources like clean water and fertile land as collateral damage. The relationship between Ghana and China illustrates how powerful countries export environmental risks to weaker nations in the Global South. Resource-rich African nations, including Ghana, participate in an international labour division where they provide raw materials for external consumption and wealth generation. The current geopolitical arrangement maintains historical economic dependencies but operates within today's multipolar world system.

Yet, resistance to this model persists. Civil society organizations, together with local communities and portions of traditional leadership, maintain resistance against state authorities and international entities to secure better accountability and fair distribution of resource-derived wealth. These struggles serve as representative examples of wider environmental justice efforts that work to both reduce harm and change natural resource governance systems.

The extractive industry in Ghana functions as a smaller-scale representation of the worldwide environmental crisis. Political and economic systems, influenced by internal governance issues and external pressures, cause unsustainable practices that worsen social inequality. Solving these problems demands addressing the political roots of environmental damage instead of just technical changes. Foreign partnerships need clear accountability for sustainable development, which becomes critical when engaging with powerful nations such as China. Local communities need legal protections along with participatory governance structures to leverage their ecological knowledge effectively. Ghana must transform its interactions between governmental bodies, foreign investors, and social organizations to transition from harmful extractive practices to environmental fairness.

Resistance and CSOs in Extractive Sector

The unequal distribution of mining-related gains and burdens is a clear indication of power struggles. Even though mining profits boost the country's economy, underprivileged rural areas bear a disproportionate amount of the environmental and social costs (Sarpong, 2010). These communities frequently lack the political clout to hold mining firms or government officials accountable, which feeds the cycles of ecological degradation and poverty.

Nonetheless, there are several ways that people have resisted these injustices. With the help of civil society organizations (CSOs), grassroots movements have come together to oppose illicit mining activities and call for more stringent environmental regulations. Table 3 summarizes the key organisations and their roles in opposing galamsey in Ghana. Given the huge stakes involved in resource wars, local resistance has occasionally turned violent. Furthermore, local government actors and traditional authority have contested both central government programs and foreign miners in an effort to regain control over natural resources.

CSOs and grassroots movements have emerged as critical voices advocating for environmental justice. These groups challenge the prevailing power structures by highlighting the ecological and social costs of extraction, demanding stricter regulations, and supporting community resistance efforts. However, their influence is often constrained by limited funding, state suppression, and the dominance of corporate narratives. Traditional leaders play a dual role in this dynamic. While some act as defenders of community interests, others align with corporate and state actors, trading access to resources for personal or group benefits. This duality underscores the complexity of power relations in resource governance.

Conclusion

As discussed in this chapter, the involvement of some Chinese nationals in ASM has significantly increased the ecological impact of mining in Ghana. This is a major setback to Ghana–China relations, displaying contradictions between the economic promises of foreign partnership and environmental realities in rural communities. While the immediate financial benefits of resource extraction can mask long-term effects, including dwindling agricultural output, health issues, and the destruction of natural ecosystems that sustain life and control the climate, Ghana can safeguard its ecosystems and provide equitable, long-lasting economic gains by including sustainable practices in development planning. By examining the sociopolitical systems and power dynamics that contribute to environmental deterioration, political ecology provides a potent framework for tackling these issues. It shows how unfair decision-making practices frequently result in local populations being marginalized, while corporate and elite interests are given precedence over sustainability. Rethinking resource governance and benefit distribution is necessary to use political ecology for a fair and sustainable future.

The analysis uncovers how decision-making systems that lack equality typically disadvantage local residents while benefiting corporate powers and elite groups. The path to a sustainable and equitable future depends on redesigning current systems of resource management and benefit allocation. To establish ecological sustainability, there is a pressing need to tackle structural injustices that drive environmental damage while respecting indigenous knowledge and enabling marginalized group participation. Stakeholders need to implement governance methods that involve everyone, including local communities together with civil society organizations and traditional leaders.

To guarantee transparency and fairness, we must hold all corporations responsible for their environmental and social effects, regardless of their domestic or foreign status. Alternative livelihood investments, alongside green technology advancements and conservation efforts, reduce harmful extraction reliance while creating environmentally aligned economic opportunities. The findings of this chapter demonstrate that Ghana's environmental issues within the extractive industry are intrinsically linked to justice, power dynamics, and development processes. The political ecology perspective enables effective comprehension and responses to the multifaceted interactions among resource utilization practices and their impacts on social fairness and environmental health.

References

Acheampong, J., Dorasamy, N., & Kumasey, A. (2024). Livelihood access and challenges in mining resettlement communities: Insights from Ghana. *Evolutionary Studies in Imaginative Culture, 8*(4), 643–657.

Adjuik, Y., & Robert, J. (2018). The expansion of Chinese businesses in Ghana: Implications for Ghana's economic development. *International Journal of Scientific and Research Publications, 8*(4), 1–28.

Africa Defence Forum (ADF). (2023, December 19). Illegal Chinese gold mining leaves an open wound in Ghana. *Africa Defence Forum.*

AfricaNews. (2024, October 6). Thousands demonstrate in Accra against illegal mining in Ghana. *AfricaNews.*

Aikins, E. R. (2024). Ghana must stop galamsey before it sinks the country. *ISS Africa.*

Akyeampong, E., & Xu, L. (2023). Chinese Technology and the transformation of the rural economy in Ghana: Evidence from Galamsey in the Ashanti and Savannah regions. *African Affairs, 122*(488), 329–351.

Alden, C. (2007). *China in Africa.* Zed Books.

Amoah, L. G. A. (2012). Africa in China: Affirming African agency in Africa-China relations at the people to people level. In *China-Africa partnership the Quest for a Win-Win Relationship* (pp. 104–115). Inter Region Economic Network.

Ampaw, E. M., Chai, J., Jiang, Y., Dumor, K., & Edem, A. K. (2023). Why is Ghana losing the war against illegal gold mining (Galamsey)? An artificial neural network-based investigation. *Environmental Science and Pollution Research, 30*(29), 73730–73752.

Anim-Gyampo, M., Berdie, B. S., Bessah, E., & Agodzo, S. K. (2021). Effects of illegal artisanal gold mining operations on groundwater quality in Ghana: the case of Ahafo-Ano South District. In *Water Quality-Factors and Impacts. IntechOpen.*

Antwi-Boateng, O., & Akudugu, M. A. (2020). Golden migrants: The rise and impact of illegal Chinese small-scale mining in Ghana. *Politics & Policy, 48*(1), 135–167.

Aryee, B. N., Ntibery, B. K., & Atorkui, E. (2003). Trends in the Small-scale Mining of Precious Minerals in Ghana: A Perspective on its Environmental Impact. *Journal of Cleaner production, 11*(2), 131–140.

Aryee, B. N. A. (2001). Ghana's mining sector: Its contribution to the national economy. *Resources Policy, 27*(2), 61–75.

Asante, R. (2018). China and Africa: Model of South-South cooperation? *China Quarterly of International Strategic Studies, 4*(2), 259–279.

Attuquayefio, D. K., Owusu, E. H., & Ofori, B. Y. (2017). Impact of mining and forest regeneration on small mammal biodiversity in the Western Region of Ghana. *Environmental Monitoring and Assessment, 189*, 1–9.

Auty, R. M. (1993). *Sustaining development in mineral economies: The resource curse thesis*. Routledge.

Auty, R. M. (2001). *Resource abundance and economic development*. Oxford University Press.

Awewomom, J., Benyade, B. K., Osei, F. E., Azanu, D., Opoku, F., Sackey, L. N., & Akoto, O. (2024). A review of health hazards associated with exposure to galamsey-related pollutants. *Health Sciences Investigations Journal, 5*(2), 726–734.

Ayelazuno, J. A. (2011). Continuous Primitive Accumulation in Ghana: The Real-life Stories of Dispossessed Peasants in Three Mining Communities. *Review of African Political Economy, 38*(130), 537–550.

Ayelazuno, J. A. (2014). The 'New Extractivism' in Ghana: A Critical Review of Its Development Prospects. *The Extractive Industries and Society* 1: 292–302.

Aziabah, M. A., & Ayelazuno, J. A. (2024). The failure of the militarised fight against 'Galamsey'in Ghana A critical overview of the class and political dynamics. *Journal of Planning and Land Management, 3*(2), 38–51

Bebbington, A., Humphreys Bebbington, D., Bury, J., Lingan, J., Muñoz, J. P., & Scurrah, M. (2008). Mining and social movements: Struggles over livelihood and rural territorial development in the Andes. *World Development, 36*(12), 2888–2905.

Bryant, R. L. (1997). Beyond the impasse: The power of political ecology in Third World environmental research. *Area, 29*(1), 5–19.

Bryant, R. L., & Bailey, S. (1997). *Third world political ecology*. Routledge.

Burgess, S., & Beilstein, J. (2013). This means war? China's scramble for minerals and resource nationalism in Southern Africa. *Contemporary Security Policy, 34*(1), 120–143.

Chen, C. K. (2016). China in Africa: A threat to African countries? *Strategic Review for Southern Africa, 38*(2), 23.

Cheru, F., & Obi, C. (2011, September/October). De-coding China-Africa relations: Partnership for development or '(neo) colonialism by invitation'? *The World Financial Review*, 72–75. https://www.diva-portal.org/smash/geta2:445203/FULLTEXT01.pdf

Chin, G. T., & Gallagher, K. P. (2019). Coordinated credit spaces: The globalization of Chinese development finance. *Development and Change, 50*(1), 245–274.

Citinewsroom.com. (2022, September 16). We'll shut down operations if galamsey makes water untreatable - GWCL. *Citinewsroom*.

Crooks, J. A. (2002). Characterizing ecosystem-level consequences of biological invasions: The role of ecosystem engineers. *Oikos, 97*(2), 153–166.

Debrah, E., & Asante, R. (2019). Sino-Ghana bilateral relations and Chinese migrants' illegal gold mining in Ghana. *Asian Journal of Political Science, 27*(3), 286–307.

Diop, C. A. (1987). *Black Africa: The economic and cultural basis for a federated state*. Expanded, Subsequent edition. Lawrence Hill Books.

Dzakpasu, P. E., Adom, D., & Panin, K. B. O. (2024). Conserving Ghana's biodiversity: A spotlight on the potentials in green informatics. *African Social Science and Humanities Journal, 5*(4), 397–404.

Elmqvist, T., Maltby, E., Barker, T., Mortimer, M., Perrings, C., Aronson, J., et al. (2012). Biodiversity, ecosystems, and ecosystem services. In *The Economics of Ecosystems and Biodiversity: Ecological and Economic Foundations* (pp. 41–111). Routledge.

Essah, M., & Andrews, N. (2016). Linking or de-linking sustainable mining practices and corporate social responsibility? Insights from Ghana. *Resources Policy, 50*, 75–85.

Gilbert, D., & Albert, O. B. (2016). Illegal small-scale gold mining in Ghana: A threat to food security. *Journal of Food Security, 4*(5), 112–119.

Global Initiative Against Transnational Organized Crime. (2021, July 6). Gold, guns and China: Ghana's fight to end Galamsey. *Global Initiative*.

Green, M. A. (2024). There's mining, then there's galamsey. *Wilson Center*.

Gyampo, R. E. V. (2014). Making Ghana's oil money count: Lessons from gold mining. *International Journal of Development and Economic Sustainability, 2*(1), 25–38.

Harvey, D. (2003). *The new imperialism*. Oxford University Press.

Haslam, P. A., Schafer, J., & Beaudet, P. (2009). *Introduction to international development: Approaches, actors, and issues*. Oxford University Press.

Haslam, T. J., Wang, H. and Deng, T. (2015) China-Africa trade and investment: Moving beyond the neocolonial debate, *Journal of Economics, Business and Management, 3*(9).pp. 875–882. https://www.joebm.com/index.php?m=content&c=index&a=show&catid=50&id=609

Hennessy, L. (2014). Where there is no company: Indigenous peoples, sustainability, and the challenges of mid-stream mining reforms in Guyana's small-scale gold sector. *New Political Economy, 20*(1), 126–153. https://doi.org/10.1080/13563467.2014.914158

Hilson, G. (2002). The environmental impact of small-scale gold mining in Ghana: Identifying problems and possible solutions. *Geographical Journal, 168*(1), 57–72.

Hilson, G., Hilson, A., & Adu-Darko, E. (2014). Chinese participation in Ghana's informal gold mining economy: Drivers, implications, and clarifications. *Journal of Rural Studies, 34*, 292–303.

Hinwood, A., Heyworth, J., Tanner, H., McCullough, C., & Lund, M. (2011). Water quality of mine void pit lakes used for recreation. *Epidemiology, 22*(1), S296.

Karl, T. L. (1997). *The paradox of plenty: Oil booms and petro-states.* University of California Press.

Kuffour, R. A., Tiimub, B. M., & Agyapong, D. (2018). Impacts of illegal mining (galamsey) on the environment (water and soil) at Bontefufuo area in the Amansie West district. *Journal of Environmental Earth Sciences, 8*(7), 98–107.

Kumah, R. (2023). Chinese participation in Ghana's illegal small-scale gold mining: Linking local pull factors to distributional inequities. *The Extractive Industries and Society, 16*, 101356.

Kwofie S, Awuah A and Yankey IK (2015) Support to Civil Society Organisations to Increase Natural Resources Management and Environmental Governance in Ghana. *Journal of Economics and Sustainable Development 6*(10): 148–159.

Lal, R. (2015). Restoring soil quality to mitigate soil degradation. *Sustainability, 7*(5), 5875–5895.

Lartey, V. C, (2024). Safeguarding Ghana's Future The galamsey crisis and the call for accountability through collective action. *Ghana Web.* Retrieved December 10, 2024, from https://www.ghanaweb.com/GhanaHomePage/features/Safeguarding-Ghana-s-Future-The-galamsey-crisis-and-the-call-for-accountability-through-collective-action-1954757#google_vignette.

MacNeil, K. S. (2018). Let's Name It: Identifying Cultural, Structural and Extractive Violence in Indigenous and Extractive Industry Relations. *Journal of Northern Studies, 12*(2), 81–103.

Maldonado, J. K. (2008). *Putting a price-tag on humanity: Development-forced displaced communities' fight for more than just compensation* (Doctoral dissertation, ProQuest).

Mlambo, C., Kushamba, A., & Simawu, M. B. (2016). China-Africa relations: What lies beneath? *The Chinese Economy, 49*(4), 257–276.

Mohammed, A. S., Graham, E., & Dary, S. K. (2022). Rising expectations and dying hopes: Local perceptions of oil and gas extraction in Ghana. *Energy Research & Social Science, 88*, 102529. https://www.sciencedirect.com/science/article/abs/pii/S2214629622000366

Mohammed, A. S., Tuokuu, F. X. D., & Adda, E. B. (2023). Livelihood access and challenges of coastal communities: Insights from Ghana. *Journal of Global Responsibility.* https://doi.org/10.1108/JGR-02-2022-0017

Moody, S. (2011). China in Sub-Saharan Africa: Demand extracting supply. *International Affairs Review, 20*(1), 1–22.

Munishi, L. K., Ndakidemi, P. A., Blake, W., Comber, S., & Hutchinson, T. H. (2021). Toxic metals in East African agro-ecosystems: Key risks for sustainable food production. *Journal of Environmental Management*, 294, 112973.

Ofori SA, Dwomoh J, Yeboah EO, et al. (2024) A ecological study of galamsey activities in Ghana and their physiological toxicity. *Asian Journal of Toxicology, Environmental, and Occupational Health 2*(1): 40–57

Oberman, E. (2023). Illegal mining in Ghana: The negative impact on WASH, typhoid, and other infectious diseases. Retrieved April 24, 2025, from https://www.coalitionagainsttyphoid.org/illegal-mining-in-ghana-the-negative-impact-on-wash-typhoid-and-other-infectious-diseases/.

Osei, M. K., Aboagye, L. M., Ofori, P., & Annor, B. (2018). Biodiversity in Ghana. *In Global Biodiversity* (pp. 81–111). Apple Academic Press.

Panford, K. (2017). *Africa's natural resources and underdevelopment* (pp. 978–971). Palgrave Macmillan US.

Robbins, P. (2011). *Political ecology: A critical introduction* (2nd ed.). Wiley-Blackwell.

Sachs, J. D., & Warner, A. M. (2001). The curse of natural resources. *European Economic Review, 45*(4), 827–838.

Sarpong, S. A. (2010). *Multinationals and the social perspectives an assessment of the mining communities in Western Ghana*. Cardiff University (United Kingdom).

Scanes, C. G. (2018). Human activity and habitat loss: destruction, fragmentation, and degradation. In *Animals and human society* (pp. 451–482). Academic Press.

Sibiri, H. (2021). Present and emerging issues detrimental to Ghana-China relations. In *Sixty years of Ghana-China relations: Friendship, friction and the future* (pp. 145–164). University of Ghana Press.

Sindzingre, A. N., (2011). The conditions for long-term growth in Sub-Saharan Africa: China as a model, a constraint and an opportunity. Cahiers du Centre Emile Durkheim Working Papers, p.48.

Sivakumar, M. V. K. (2007). Interactions between climate and desertification. *Agricultural and Forest Meteorology, 142*(2–4), 143–155.

Taylor, I. (2014). *Africa rising? BRICS-Diversifying dependency*. Boydell & Brewer Ltd.

Tengapoe, K., Baddianaah, I., & Agyemang, I. (2023). Anthropogenic induced land use land cover dynamics of the Black Volta River Corridor in north-western Ghana, 2011–2021. *Trees, Forests and People*, 14, 100449.

Teschner, B. A. (2012). Small-scale mining in Ghana: The government and the galamsey. *Resources Policy, 37*(3), 308–314.

Tuokuu, F. X. D., Gruber, J. S., Idemudia, U., & Kayira, J. (2018). Challenges and opportunities of environmental policy implementation: Empirical evidence from Ghana's gold mining sector. *Resources Policy, 59*, 435–445.

Zhao, S. (2014). A neo-colonialist predator or development partner? China's engagement and rebalance in Africa. *Journal of Contemporary China, 23*(90), 1033–1052.

China's Belt and Road Initiative and the "Green Turn" in Africa

Abdou Rahim Lema, Amabilly Bonacina, and Adam Laroussi

Introduction

Africa–China relations have deepened and widened over the past decades, with the engagement characterised by increased economic cooperation, investment, infrastructure development, and people-to-people interactions. Since it overtook the United States in 2009, China has been Africa's largest trading partner. Beijing is also the leading contributor to Africa's lagging infrastructure development. Thus, China is playing an outsized role in Africa. The rapid growth of China's engagement with Africa in the last two decades is equally matched by a considerable increase in academic outputs on China's role in and impact on the continent, especially with

A. R. Lema (✉) • A. Bonacina
Department of Political Science, Université de Montréal, Montreal, QC, Canada
e-mail: abdou.rahim.lema.mohamed@umontreal.ca;
amabilly.bonacina@umontreal.ca

A. Laroussi
École Nationale d'Administration Publique, Montréal, QC, Canada
e-mail: adam.ben.abdallah@umontreal.ca

L. G. Adu Amoah (ed.), *Africa-China Relations*,
https://doi.org/10.1007/978-981-95-4370-0_13

regard to how China's pre-eminence in Africa promotes or inhibits the continent's development. For quite some time, the dominant assumption in much of the Sino-African relations literature was that China sets the terms and conditions of the engagement and unilaterally determines the outcomes (Lee, 2013; Lampert & Mohan, 2015). Such Sino-centrism effectively underplays African agency, both state and non-state African agency. In that regard, Africa is presented as lacking agency, and Africans are assumed to be childlike, inferior, and the helpless victims (Lampert & Mohan, 2015). This is assumed to allow China to exert power over and exploit the continent at will (Chen, 2015).

However, there have been strong pushbacks on these premises in recent studies. Known as the African agency literature, this research corpus calls for the recognition of the agency of African actors in their relationship with China. Led by some of the most prominent critical Africanist voices in the field, the corpus brings a much-needed novel perspective, different from tired narratives that depict African countries as passive recipients of the whims of outside powers (Crabtree, 2018; Soulé-Kohndou, 2018, 2019). Instead, these studies argue that African actors are very active in shaping their engagement with China.

This chapter contributes to this growing body of research by providing a contextual analysis of China's engagement with African countries in the green energy transition. We analyse this "green turn" in Africa–China relations and focus on two specific solar power plants in Kenya and the Central African Republic (CAR) as illustrative cases of the growing dynamics. Based on an analysis of secondary data and official reports about the projects, these cases help us get a better picture of how the "green turn" has been co-constructed by the two parties and with it the political economy dynamics.

These cases are relevant because they show—in very different contexts—how African countries are currently experiencing growing dynamics of energy transition in collaboration with Chinese partners. Kenya inaugurated a major solar power plant in Garissa, and CAR a solar power plant near Bangui—all built in collaboration with Beijing.

While both countries faced challenges in accessing electricity (14% of the population in CAR in 2024 and 36% in Kenya in 2015), Kenya has made significant progress, reaching 76% access in 2022, thanks, in part, to its cooperation with China. A comparison between these two States allows us to explore whether green development follows similar trajectories, thus offering avenues for reflection based on recent and little-studied cases in this context. The choice of cases also represents two opposing political-institutional, economic, and social situations, that is, a stable and democratic country (Kenya), which has a greater capacity to exercise agency, and a more fragile, chronically unstable, and authoritarian country (CAR), which is assumed to have less capacity but finds ways to exercise what Lonsdale (2000) refers to as "agency in tight corners", as we suggest below.

The chapter is structured as follows. Following the introduction, we review the relevant literature on African agency in Africa–China relations. The review is divided into two subsections, with the first part discussing the legacy of Africa's marginalisation in Africa–China relations, and the second, the (African) "agency turn" in Africa–China relations research. Following the literature review, we elaborate on the "green turn" in Africa–China relations. Before concluding the chapter, we briefly discuss the two illustrative cases of our green turn argument in Africa–China relations. The illustrative cases include the Garissa and Sakaï solar power plants in Kenya and CAR, respectively.

The Legacy of Africa's Marginalisation and Africa–China Relations

Africa has long been relegated to the margins of international politics, with the continent mostly associated with gloomy concepts such as marginalisation, underdevelopment, dependence, and exploitation (Bayart, 1993; Bayart & Ellis, 2000; Amin, 1978). The marginalisation of the African continent is pervasive in the literature of international politics because Africa is considered a subject of great power politics rather than a central actor in its own right (see Duggan & Hodzi, 2021). Consequently, Africa is considered an insignificant actor faced with the brutal reality of international power politics. According to Odoom and Andrews (2017, p. 43), however, rather than being insignificant and inconsequential, the continent suffers from "representational deficiency", because the major analytical constructs provided by established (Western) international relations (IR) theory have long failed to accurately capture and explain Africa's dynamic role in international affairs. Otherwise, despite the obvious power asymmetries, Africa has always been far from being a peripheral actor. Instead, it has constantly been a strong agent of world politics in its very own ways (see Bayart, 1993; Bayart & Ellis, 2000).

China's recent global rise and its growing engagement with Africa did little to change the "representational deficiency" the continent faces. Instead, China's rise and its renewed interest in the continent only revived the same old questions of Africa's place in the world. This is not surprising because, according to Ding et al. (2022), China's relations with Africa are construed in relation to Africa's relations with the West, as "[m]ost academic writings tend to view China in Africa from a Western perspective: Africa, China, and their relations are conceptualised and evaluated according to Western norms and standards" (Ding et al., 2022, p. 410). As such, the literature tends to impose the dominant (Western) perspectives on China's engagement with Africa by recycling the old gloomy concepts.

Substituting China for Western powers, Africa is presented as helpless, clueless, and dependent on the new power in town (Crabtree, 2018; Soulé-Kohndou, 2016, 2018). Illustrative of this logic is Naim's (2009) assertion that China is a "rogue" actor in Africa that has been "underwriting a world that is more corrupt, chaotic and authoritarian". Africa is "China's second continent", Howard French (2015) sums it up, whereby the "neo-coloniser" seeks to reproduce and deepen existing pathologies in the continent by further entrenching African dependency and underdevelopment. Undoubtedly, Africans continue to be "spoken of or spoken for" (Mohan, 2013, p. 1257). As a result, Carmody and Kragelund (2016, p. 1) argue that, for a long time, studies on the subject of Sino-African relations have "presented an unbalanced picture in which an all-powerful China subjugated weak African states, thereby replicating previous Orientalist tropes about Africa".

In response to these persisting "Orientalist tropes about Africa", there have been many calls for course correction in recent years. For instance, Giles Mohan and Ben Lambert (2013) argue that African actors, whether state or non-state actors, had agency in their relationships with China, through which they constantly shape the engagement. Nevertheless, Pádraig Carmody and Peter Kragelund (2016) warn that, in the context of Africa–China relations, recent efforts to emphasise African agency may unintentionally support "internalist" explanations of African underdevelopment because positing Africans to be in the driving seat or as being co-pilots in their engagement with China may imply that the elites have the power to fundamentally reshape the nature of that engagement. Obviously, recognising African agency does not necessarily mean denying or ignoring the constraints restricting African actors given the perennial asymmetrical power dynamics between the two parties. The constraints, whether in the form of great power rivalries, structural economic disparities, or institutional weaknesses, are real and persistent (Brown & Harman, 2013). However, as Lonsdale (2000) suggests, African agency does still operate even in those "tight corners". Taking that fact very seriously will allow us to go beyond the tired tropes of an Africa that is victimised, chaotic, violent, and poor. The next section discusses the African agency literature in Africa–China relations.

The African "Agency Turn" in Africa–China Relations Research

Scholarly discussions on Sino-African relations in the past decade have witnessed a considerable shift towards African agency[1]. This includes attempts by Corkin (2016), Mohan and Lampert (2013), and Lampert and Mohan (2015) to shed light on the importance of African agency in understanding China's engagement with the African continent. Likewise, Wang (2022a, 2022b) recently takes on individual agency within structural and institutional constraints to propose both a political championship analysis of infrastructure delivery and presidential extraversion. Clearly, the question is no longer whether African countries have agency vis-à-vis their power asymmetry with China because, in line with Lonsdale's "agency in tight corners", African (state and non-state) actors constantly shape the engagement (Lonsdale, 2000). The reality of asymmetric power between Africa and China may reduce the range of actions available to African actors when they interact with their Chinese counterparts, but that does not necessarily eliminate their options entirely (Tull & Blasiak, 2011).

The recent focus on African agency in the literature has shifted the research focus onto the myriad ways in which African actors shape the continent's engagement with China and allowed researchers to better analyse how African agents exercise their capacity to do and act in their engagement with Beijing (Soulé, 2020). For instance, Giles Mohan and Ben Lambert (2013, p. 92) assert that "African actors have negotiated, shaped, and even driven Chinese engagements in Africa in important ways". As Chiyemura (2019) observes, the African agency research corpus examines African agency from two different but interrelated perspectives: African state officials' agency[2] and African non-state actors' agency.

The first perspective is mostly interested in examining how African government officials exercise agency when engaging the Chinese. This is what led Soulé-Kohndou (2016, 2019) to examine the bureaucratic agency in Benin and the asymmetrical power play between the small West African country and China. She argues that, when it comes to negotiating infrastructure development deals, civil servants and the executive arm of the state influence the engagement patterns before, during, and after contract negotiations. Likewise, Phillips (2018) shows that, since its oil discovery in 2007, the Ghanaian government has been able to exercise agency on aspects of brokering relations with the Chinese, Americans, and traditional development banks in Ghana's bilateral and multilateral relations. But that exercise was limited in terms of transforming the structural basis of the engagements. This finding is similar to Carmody and Kragelund's (2016) work on China's engagement with both Zambia and Angola, where the Zambian government exercised limited agency, and the Angolans exercised constrained agency.

Similarly, a study by Procopio (2018) also argues that Kenyans exercise agency when interacting with the Chinese in the sectors of health, trade, and education. Moreover, in an edited volume by Gadzala (2015), multiple authors explore African agency by both strong and weak states when dealing with China, demonstrating how African political elites in Nigeria, Angola, Ethiopia, Ghana, and South Africa, amongst others, are skilful at obtaining concessions from the Chinese state. A case in point, de Carvalho et al. (2022) pinpoint the ability of Angolan elites to restrict or even outrightly deny Chinese firms access to oil fields in their study.

The second perspective underscores agency exercised by African non-state actors in their in/direct interactions with the Chinese. This aspect of African agency in relation to China did not initially stimulate much research interest compared to state officials' agency. But a growing number of studies show how African non-state actors influence engagement patterns in relation to China and Chinese actors. In that regard, Lampert and Mohan's (2015) ethnographic research in Nigeria and Ghana is instructive. It shows that Nigerian and Ghanaian traders exercise agency in ways that ensure they retain value and control of the interactions with the Chinese across various scales and times. In another study on China's engagement in these two African countries, Mohan and Lampert (2013) show that Nigerian and Ghanaian entrepreneurs were able to exercise agency using their social, political, and patronage networks to shape their interactions with the Chinese in businesses. In these case studies, the Chinese were forced to adapt to African non-state actors' demands, showing Chinese flexibility and adaptability in the process. These research outputs have helped demonstrate that to fully understand the dynamics of Africa–China relations, one has to take into account how African state and non-state actors shape or influence China's growing engagement with the continent. These are all very important research as they help cement African agency in understanding Africa–China relations.

The "Green Turn" in Africa–China Relations

China has emerged as a formidable global force in green transition efforts worldwide. China's dominance has become so critical in green technology industries that any country wishing to develop its domestic green economy must engage with it in some way (IEA, 2016). In 2023, China accounted for over half of the world's newly installed renewable energy capacity. Similarly, the country's total investment in the new energy sector reached US$676 billion last year, constituting 38% of the global total (Catsaros, 2024). In addition, China manufactures about 60% of global wind farm equipment (Hayley, 2024) and over 80% of solar panels (Mackenzie, 2023), along with other essential green components.

Interestingly, examining Africa–China relations from a green development perspective reveals complementary advantages and the prospect of a "win-win" partnership, with implications that extend beyond the two regions (Chen et al., 2024). Indeed, as Chen et al. (2024) argue, green development is a key area of mutual interest for both China and African countries. More specifically, as a leader in green technology and renewable energy, China has become an essential partner for countries looking to transition to green development. China is the world's largest producer and supplier of solar cells and modules, which aligns perfectly with Africa's needs. Africa has enormous renewable energy potential, as well as 30% of the known reserves of the critical minerals central to the energy transition. Indeed, the International Energy Agency (IEA) forecasts that photovoltaic solar energy will comprise 47% of the technology's mix for mini-grids and off-the-grid systems power generation in sub-Saharan Africa by 2040. Africa also possesses abundant renewable energy resources, with solar, wind, and hydropower reserves accounting for 40%, 32%, and 12% of global reserves, respectively. This offers enormous potential for renewable energy development. Data released by the International Renewable Energy Agency (IRENA) showed that between 2011 and 2020, Africa's solar installed capacity achieved an annual growth rate of 54%, which is two and a half times that of wind energy, nearly four times that of geothermal, and almost 17 times that of hydropower (IRENA and AfDB, 2022).

Thus, Africa offers China significant opportunities for investment in green growth thanks to its richness in natural resources and the need for sustainable energy solutions. China has already played a pivotal role in projects such as the Great Green Wall in the Sahel and various renewable energy installations across the continent, including solar, wind, geothermal, and hydropower plants. In the past, China's energy investments in Africa have primarily focused on large hydropower and coal-fired power projects. However, in recent years there has been a shift towards solar power projects, with Chinese investments in Africa's renewable energy sector growing at an average annual rate of 26% from 2010 to 2020, with solar, hydropower, and wind being the leading technologies (Zheng, 2024).

In general, Chinese manufacturers are looking to Africa to offload stocks of solar panels, batteries, EVs, and other green technologies amid mounting export restrictions on entering Europe and the United States. And, as Beijing cuts down on lending for big infrastructure projects, its narrowed focus gives more prominence to green energy sectors in which it has invested heavily in recent years (Lema, 2023; Siele, 2024). As a result, electricity generation from renewable energy sources like wind and solar is becoming economically viable and technologically mature in many African countries. More specifically, compared to conventional energy generation infrastructure, renewable energy systems are relatively quick to install with much more flexible applications in remote rural areas and can offer better prospects for local job creation and industrial development (Puig et al., 2021; Chiyemura et al., 2023).

Chinese photovoltaic companies have advantages through excellent technology and can provide high-quality and competitively priced PV products to African countries. In addition, these Chinese solar companies have established marketing systems over the years, excellent local teams, and efficient after-sales services. These efforts have enabled them to meet the growing energy demands and diverse application scenarios in the African market (Zheng, 2024). For example, Longi Green Energy Technology is reported to have directly supplied over 1 gigawatt of PV modules to more than 30 African countries. The modules are used across various sectors including national power grids, industry, commerce, agriculture, hospitals, schools, and public utilities. And in addition to exporting PV modules, the company is said to have also stepped up collaboration with educational institutions to provide training in new energy (Zheng, 2024).

In short, Africa–China cooperation in the renewable energy sector has a promising outlook because China has accumulated massive generation and technological capacity for the wind and solar energy sectors. According to China's National Energy Administration (2022), the total installed renewable generation capacity reached 1063 GW in 2021, with wind and solar energy reaching 328 GW and 306 GW, respectively. Likewise, as mentioned above, electricity demand in Africa is expected to double by 2040, with renewables accounting for three-quarters of new generation (Lema et al., 2021; Chiyemura et al., 2023).

This mutual interest in green development was officially cemented at the 2021 Forum on China–Africa Cooperation (FOCAC) in Dakar, Senegal. The 2021 FOCAC meeting and declaration of the Chinese and African leaders confirmed the aspiration from both sides to promote cooperation in renewable energy (Ministry of Foreign Affairs, 2021). Specifically, the Forum adopted the "Declaration on China–Africa Cooperation on Combating Climate Change" (FOCAC, 2021a). Since then, policymakers from both sides have increasingly prioritised the green development agenda in their engagements, with Beijing particularly focusing on "greening" China's Belt and Road Initiative (BRI) and the country's Go Global strategy in general (Bertuzzi et al., 2019; Gourdon et al., 2022; Chiyemura et al., 2023). This is illustrated by the calls from African countries for China to step up its support for the development of renewable energies. China also reaffirmed its commitment to halting the construction of new coal-fired projects on the continent (Gourdon et al., 2022). At the same time, according to the Boston University Global Development Policy Center (GDP), China committed $4.6 billion in new loans to African countries in 2023—an increase from 2022 and the first annual increase since a 2016 peak, but it was still less than half of what was committed annually between 2013 and 2018—of which about $500 million went to hydropower and solar projects (Engel et al., 2024).

The recently concluded 2024 FOCAC in Beijing underscores the breadth and depth of this green partnership. China committed to new initiatives aimed at supporting Africa's energy transition, including solar energy systems and broader clean energy projects, which is well in line with Africa's goal of ensuring that the global energy transition benefits its development and industrialisation, especially through local value addition in critical mineral processing (Chen et al., 2024). This year's FOCAC outcome documents—the Beijing Declaration (FOCAC, 2024a) and the Beijing Action Plan (2025–2027) (FOCAC, 2024b)—provided more specific details to the 2021 Declaration. Climate and energy topics were addressed in a much more detailed and specific manner than previously.

In more specific terms, while the Dakar Declaration addressed energy and climate commitments in a single paragraph, merely advocating for "a green, low-carbon, circular and sustainable way of development" (FOCAC, 2021b; also see Chen et al., 2024), the Beijing Declaration and Action Plan separated the two agendas, detailing the specific agreements and projects needed to achieve common objectives. This includes the China–Africa Environmental Cooperation Centre, the China–Africa Marine Science and Blue Economy Cooperation Centre, the China–Africa Geosciences Cooperation Centre, the China–Africa Green Envoys Program, the China–Africa Green Innovation Program, and the Africa Solar Belt Program. Moreover, the provided details both recognised and embraced the targets and principles of the UN Framework Convention on Climate Change and its Kyoto Protocol, and the Paris Agreement, the Nairobi Declaration, and the Declaration on China–Africa Cooperation on Combating Climate Change (FOCAC, 2024a, 2024b).

Furthermore, according to the latest Beijing Action Plan (2025–2027) signed in September 2024 during the FOCAC Beijing Summit, "The African side appreciates China for assisting Africa in carrying out green development and environmental protection projects and building low-carbon demonstration zones in Africa and is willing to explore with China a green and sustainable way of energy cooperation" (FOCAC, 2024b). For its part, China pledged to "encourage investments in a range of renewable energy projects across Africa, including solar, wind, green hydrogen, hydroelectric, geothermal power initiatives". In order to meet these commitments, China and African countries agreed to "promote the exchanges of expertise, best practices, and innovative solutions in renewable energy, implement comprehensive capacity-building programs to empower African professionals, entrepreneurs, and communities in the renewable energy sector". These efforts clearly show that energy cooperation is today one of the key sectors for the sustainable development of the African continent, and it is constantly being pushed into the Africa–China agenda.

Below, we detail two specific illustrative cases of solar power plants from Kenya and the Central African Republic (CAR). The choice of these countries underscores the fact that many African countries, whether they are democratic and stable (Kenya) or undemocratic and fragile (CAR), are pushing for a green energy transition as a way of dealing with the growing and disproportionately catastrophic effects of climate change on the continent.

The Garissa Solar Power Plant: A Strategic Partnership for Renewable Energy in Kenya–China Relations

Located in Garissa County, north-east Kenya, the Garissa solar power plant is very important for understanding African agentivity in green development and in the political phenomenon of cooperation with China. Although it represents a major milestone in Kenya's energy development, the plant is also an opportunity to continue and support the country's electrification campaign, which began in 2018.[3] With a capacity of 55 megawatts, it is one of the largest in East and Central Africa. Spread over 85 hectares, this impressive infrastructure includes over 200,000 solar panels, transforming sunlight into clean, renewable energy. This is the first time that Kenya has developed a large-scale solar power plant to harness its abundant solar energy resources to diversify the electricity generation mix and reduce energy costs.[4] In addition to creating jobs and stimulating economic activities, as well as helping to combat global warming, the project contributes around 2% to the national energy mix and has significantly reduced energy costs in the country, promoting the development of clean, reliable, sustainable, and affordable electricity.[5]

The Garissa solar power plant is the fruit of a wider cooperation between Kenya and China in green transition. Indeed, it was a Chinese company that won the contract to build the plant. Jiangxi Corporation for International Economic and Technical Cooperation was awarded the construction contract at a budgeted cost of KSh13.7 billion (US$135.7 million), with construction activities to be partly financed by the Chinese Exim Bank of China. This partnership testifies to China's commitment to supporting the development of renewable energies in Africa, and to Kenya's desire to diversify its economic partners.[6] But the solar power plant project also marks an important milestone in Kenya's energy transition. It paves the way for similar projects across Africa and positions the country as a leader in renewable energies on the continent. The project is a concrete example of how to leverage international partnerships to advance efforts to transition to renewable energies.[7]

It was undertaken to facilitate access to electricity in the country, as the energy generated by the Garissa solar power plant supplies around 625,000 homes, helping to improve living conditions for the population. The plant also enables Kenya to reduce its dependence on fossil fuels and enhance its (green) energy security. The plant is reported to have helped Kenya save around 24,470 tons of standard coal and reduce carbon dioxide emissions by around 64,000 tons a year (Zheng, 2024). Furthermore, since it began operations following the official launch by President Uhuru Kenyatta on December 13, 2019, the solar power plant has generated over 76 million kilowatt-hours annually, meeting the electricity needs of 70,000 households and more than 380,000 people (Zheng, 2024).

Covering 85 hectares, the solar project was funded by a $136 million loan from the Export-Import Bank of China and built by a Chinese company, the Jiangxi Corporation for International Economic and Technical Cooperation. And as Kenya's first and still only major solar power plant, Garissa represents a noteworthy step towards the country's goal of 100% renewable energy by 2030[8] (Mbugua & Langat, 2023). Kenya is already well on its way to this goal, in part thanks to supportive policies such as VAT exemptions on renewable energy products, and in part thanks to abundant supplies (Rapid Transition Alliance, 2022). As of 2021, roughly 81% of the country's installed power capacity came from renewable sources,[9] predominantly geothermal, hydropower, and wind. It should be noted that there are more than six projects similar to Garissa currently underway.

While projects such as Garissa are attracting a great deal of attention from the media and political elites, partly due to the Sino-African cooperation agreements they are part of, the off-grid pay-as-you-go solar technology companies that are developing alongside this project are not receiving sufficient attention, despite their significant impact on the economic, social, and political context of African states, and Kenya in particular. According to Park (2021), these off-grid solar companies have radically altered the dynamics of the sustainable energy transition market in Kenya and other sub-Saharan African countries. For example, these solar companies operating in Kenya and other sub-Saharan African countries received $223 million in investment in the form of debt, equity, and grants in 2016, up from just $3 million in 2012. What's more, these companies are increasingly involved in Sino-African agreements, reinforcing their impact on African economies.

The Sakaï Solar Power Plant: A Strategic Partnership for Renewable Energy in Central African Republic–China Relations

The lack of energy is a reality and a persistent problem in the Central African Republic (CAR). Power outages, for example, can last up to 16 hours a day. However, this issue must be understood in relation to the difficult political context in which the country finds itself. Since 2013, CAR has faced a series of internal crises, such as coups d'état, civil war, and armed rebellions (International Crisis Group, 2024; Hakeenah, 2023). As the country struggles with these persisting challenges and state fragility, investing in energy production capacity is an essential public policy for the reconstruction efforts and the resumption of social and economic development in the post-crisis context. The World Bank notes that a measly 14.3% of CAR's over five million people have electricity access, with the capital Bangui having the highest access rate at an estimated 35%, while only 0.4% of rural Central Africans have access (World Bank, 2022). The discrepancy in access to electricity illustrates a national problem that has persisted for decades—the difficulty of accessing goods and services in rural areas—and portrays the challenge of CAR in extending state authority beyond the capital (Bonacina, 2018).

Energy production is limited by factors including an inadequate legal and institutional framework, insufficient internal capacity, and a lack of financing, among other challenges. To address the electricity access problems, CAR came up with the 2015–2030 Investment Project under which several dams will be constructed to help with electricity generation. The dams include the Dimoli hydroelectric scheme (180 MW), Lobaye hydroelectric scheme (75 MW), Kotto hydroelectric scheme (40 MW), and Lancrenon hydroelectric scheme (20 MW), which is on the border with Cameroon. The plan will also see the rehabilitation of the Boali II hydroelectric plant (10 MW to 15 MW). In total, these projects are estimated to cost an estimated US$3.7 billion. The deal for the rehabilitation of the Boali II hydroelectric plant was signed between CAR authorities and the China Gezhouaba Group Company (CGGC) in Beijing during the China–Africa Forum Summit in September 2018. Indeed, Chinese companies have successfully managed to secure multi-billion dollar projects across Africa and are the front-runners in CAR's energy development projects (Hakeenah, 2023; Africa Energy Portal, 2023).

Despite the current difficulties and the low level of socioeconomic development, CAR has enormous potential for the production of sustainable energy, especially solar energy (Renew Africa, 2023). Although heavily dependent on fossil fuels, the country has made efforts to increase the diversification of its energy matrix, taking part in the Sustainable Energy for All initiative that aims to guarantee universal access to modern, efficient, and renewable energy production.[10] Indeed, CAR aims to have at least 10% of its energy produced by renewable sources and increase the number of people with access to electricity to 50% by 2030 (Komode, 2014).

It is in that context that the Sakaï solar power plant is undertaken. The Sakaï solar power plant is a significant investment in the limited context of energy production in CAR. Inaugurated in 2023, CAR's first large-scale photovoltaic solar power plant has a production capacity of 15 MW of energy and is currently responsible for 30% of the capital's electricity (Wansi, 2023). Located 10 km from Bangui, the Sakaï solar field started operation after three years of work. The plant comprises 33,432 solar panels spread over 16 hectares. It currently supplies 15 kilowatts of electricity and aims to reduce the electricity supply deficit (RFI, 2023). The deal for undertaking the project was signed in 2018 during a meeting between Chinese President Xi Jinping and his Central African counterpart Faustin Archange Touadera on the sidelines of the China–Africa summit in Beijing.

Built in partnership with China Energy Engineering Group subsidiary Tianjin Electric Power Construction Company, the project is one of several projects to improve the country's energy infrastructure, as set out in the 2015–2030 Investment Project (Hakeenah, 2023). It is worth noting that Chinese participation in infrastructure investments in CAR has increased in recent years. In addition to the Sakaï plant, for example, China is involved in the construction of the Danzi solar power plant, a project financed by the World Bank and implemented by the Chinese company Shanxi Construction Investment Group (Takouleu, 2023). Moreover, the Chinese are also set to help rehabilitate the Boali II hydroelectric power plant (Hakeenah, 2023). Both projects are part of President Touadera's Government Emergency Project for Access to Electricity (Puracell), which also includes grid integration projects (Takouleu, 2024).

In the case of CAR, we can observe that the African nation actively led the initiative, exemplifying the agency of African state officials. The engagement with China in this case was shaped by CAR, as demonstrated, reiterating Lonsdale's "agency in tight corners" and illustrating how African actors have engaged in negotiations with their Chinese counterparts. Additionally, l'Energie Centrafricaine (ENERCA) is in charge of managing the facility, which was built with local workers (Xinhua, 2022).

Conclusion

Africa–China relations have deepened and widened over the past decades, with the engagement characterised by increased economic cooperation, investment, infrastructure development, and people-to-people interactions. The rapid growth of China's engagement with Africa in the last two decades is equally matched by a considerable increase in academic outputs on China's role and impact on the continent, especially with regard to how China's pre-eminence in Africa promotes or inhibits the continent's development. For quite some time, the dominant assumption in much of the Sino-African relations literature was that China sets the terms and conditions of the engagement and unilaterally determines the outcomes. Such Sino-centrism effectively underplays African agency, both state and non-state African agency.

However, there have been strong pushbacks on these premises in recent studies. Known as the African agency literature, this research corpus calls for the recognition of the agency of African actors in their relationship with China. Led by some of the most prominent critical Africanist voices in the field, the corpus brings a much-needed novel perspective, different from tired narratives that depict African countries as passive recipients of the whims of outside powers. Instead, these studies argue that African actors are very active in shaping their engagement with China.

By offering a contextual review of China's involvement with African nations in the green energy transition, this chapter adds to this expanding body of research while illuminating a rather different picture, away from Sino-centrism. The co-construction of these initiatives is made evident by examining how these projects are planned and executed. Documentation of other cases will be necessary for the argument of co-construction of the "green turn" to be generalisable, but several initiatives across the continent indicate that this turn is a reality and that it is shaping Sino-African relations. African nations are actively looking for investments that align with their realities and necessities. Solar power plant projects like Garissa and Sakaï give us a better idea of how the two parties have co-constructed the "green turn" and show that African agency is feasible and manifests in collaboration with Chinese partners, despite the diverse circumstances of African nations.

Therefore, fitting neatly into the overall theme of the book, this chapter highlights the active role of African actors in shaping their engagement with China. For example, contrary to the reductionist narratives that portray Africa as passively subservient to external powers, including China, we argue that African countries are not mere recipients of foreign influence. Instead, they are proactively seeking partnerships aligned with their specific contexts and development priorities. Concrete examples such as the Chinese-backed Garissa and Sakai solar power plant projects the chapter analysed underscore this process of co-construction—particularly around the emerging "green turn"—and affirm Africa's agency in its collaborations with Chinese partners.

Despite the diversity of national contexts across the continent, these initiatives reflect a broader pattern of engagement: an active, voluntary, albeit asymmetrical, partnership. Sino-African relations, therefore, cannot be reduced to narratives of dependency, coercion, pawnship, or peonage. While structural imbalances persist, African actors exert real influence over the terms and outcomes of their cooperation with China. Kenyan President William Ruto captured[11] this sentiment during his recent public address at Peking University in Beijing, China, stating:

> Kenya and China are not merely trade partners; we are co-architects of a new world order—one that is fair, inclusive, and sustainable [...] I wish to commend China for its leadership in renewable energy technologies, particularly in solar power and electric vehicles. Without China, many of these technologies would remain unaffordable for much of the developing world. Today, solar panels, e-bikes, and electric buses are commonplace in African towns. This is what meaningful South–South co-operation looks like.

While China has often faced allegations of "debt-trap diplomacy" and "neo-colonialism" in Africa, academic scholarship has largely debunked these claims (Challeny, 2017; Rithmire & Li, 2019; Brautigam, 2020). Nevertheless, such narratives still persist in political discourse and media representations (Li & Wang, 2025). Our analysis shows that Chinese engagement in Africa is not unilateral; rather, it is actively shaped by host countries, whose political elites, bureaucracies, and civil society actors play a critical role in influencing both Chinese behaviour and the outcomes of Chinese-financed projects. In short, despite the evident power asymmetry,

African actors are not passive bystanders but co-creators in shaping the evolving dynamics of their partnership with China.

Abbreviations

BRI	Belt and Road Initiative
CAR	Central African Republic
ENERCA	Energie Centrafricaine
FOCAC	Forum on China–Africa Cooperation
GDP	Boston University Global Development Policy Center
IEA	International Energy Agency
IR	International Relations
IRENA	International Renewable Energy Agency

Notes

1. We use the "African agency" in a unified way in this text. As Gadzala (2015) points out, it is possible to speak in a unified way in the context of Sino-African relations, since Chinese action, vis-à-vis the continent, follows the same pattern of approach (similar rhetoric and objectives). This does not exclude that, ultimately, each relationship between China and an African country is unique.
2. We understand African state officials' agency as the agency of government officials of the African states.
3. Kenya National Electrification Strategy: Key Highlights (2018). The World Bank.
4. REREC: https://www.rerec.co.ke/garissa-solar-power-plant.php
5. REREC: https://www.rerec.co.ke/garissa-solar-power-plant.php
6. REREC: https://www.rerec.co.ke/garissa-solar-power-plant.php
7. REREC: https://www.rerec.co.ke/garissa-solar-power-plant.php
8. https://shorturl.at/tvSb8
9. https://www.trade.gov/country-commercial-guides/kenya-energy-electrical-power-systems
10. https://www.nepad.org/countries/central-african-republic
11. https://www.kbc.co.ke/ruto-says-kenya-committed-to-partnering-china-to-champion-interests-of-global-south/

References

Africa Energy Portal. (2023). CAR: near Bangui, the Sakaï solar power plant (15 MW) comes into service. https://africa-energy-portal.org/news/car-near-bangui-sakai-solar-power-plant-15-mw-comes-service.

Amin, S. (1978). Unequal development: An essay on the social formations of peripheral capitalism. *Science and Society, 42*(2), 219–222.

Bayart, J. F. (1993). *The State in Africa. The politics of the belly.* Longman.

Bayart, J. F., & Ellis, S. (2000). Africa in the world: A history of extraversion. *African Affairs, 99*(395), 217–267.

Bertuzzi, M., Melonio, T., Pornet, A., & Tremel, L. (2019). Vers de «Nouvelles routes de la soie» durables ? *Policy Paper*, 1–48.

Bonacina, A. (2018). A República Centro-Africana: tensionamentos históricos e desdobramentos políticos do governo Seleka. Trabalho de Conclusão de Curso, Porto Alegre: Universidade Federal do Rio Grande do Sul. https://lume.ufrgs.br/handle/10183/196071.

Brautigam, D. (2020). A critical look at Chinese "debt-trap diplomacy": The rise of a meme. *Area development and policy, 5*(1), 1–14.

Brown, W., & Harman, S. (2013). *African agency in international politics.* In *African agency in international politics* (pp. 1–16). Routledge.

Carmody, P., & Kragelund, P. (2016). Who is in charge-state power and agency in Sino-African relations. *Cornell International Law Journal, 49*, 1.

Catsaros, O. (2024). Global clean energy investment jumps 17%, hits $1.8 trillion in 2023, according to BloombergNEF report. *BloombergNEF.* https://about.bnef.com/blog/global-clean-energy-investment-jumps-17-hits-1-8-trillion-in-2023-according-to-bloombergnef-report/.

Challeny, B. (2017). China's debt-trap diplomacy. *Project Syndicate.* https://www.project-syndicate.org/commentary/china-one-belt-one-road-loans-debt-by-brahma-chellaney-2017-01.

Chen, X., Benkenstein, A., & Gruzd, S. (2024). Win-Win green partnership: China is capable, Is Africa ready? *SAIIA Policy Insights 157.*

Chen, Y. (2015). China's investment and trade in Africa: Neo-colonialism or mutual benefit. *Cardozo International & Comparative Law Review, 24*, 511.

Chiyemura, F. (2019). *The winds of change in Africa-China relations?: Contextualising African Agency in Ethiopia-China Engagement in Wind Energy Infrastructure Financing and Development.* Open University (United Kingdom).

Chiyemura, F., Shen, W., Burgess, M., Mulugetta, Y., & Wang, Y. (2023). A dynamic institutional analysis of China's engagement with Africa's renewable energy market. *Environmental Politics, 32*(7), 1140–1162.

Crabtree, J. (2018, April 25). Africa needs to know what it wants from China, expert says. Here are two key issues. *CNBC.* https://www.cnbc.com/2018/04/25/africa-needs-to-know-what-it-wants-from-china-expert-says.html.

Corkin, L. (2016). Uncovering African agency: Angola's management of China's credit lines. Routledge.

de Carvalho, P., Kopiński, D., & Taylor, I. (2022). A marriage of convenience on the rocks? Revisiting the Sino–Angolan relationship. *Africa Spectrum, 57*(1), 5–29.

Ding, J., Ratz, C., & Bergman, M. M. (2022). What do we see when looking at China's engagements in Africa? An analysis of mainstream academic perspectives. *Journal of Contemporary China, 31*(135), 398–411.

Duggan, N., & Hodzi, O. (2021). The challenges of China-European Union security cooperation in Africa. *Asia Europe Journal, 19*(1), 43–57.

Engel, L., Hwang, J., Morro, D., & Bien-Aime, V. Y.. (2024). Relative risk and the rate of return: Chinese loans to Africa database, 2000–2023. *Global Development Policy Center/Global China Initiative (GCI) Policy Brief. Boston University.*

FOCAC. (2021a). Declaration on China-Africa cooperation on combatting climate change. http://www.focac.org/eng/zywx_1/zywj/202201/t20220124_10632445.htm.

FOCAC. (2021b). Dakar Declaration of the Eighth Ministerial Conference of the Forum on China-Africa Cooperation. http://www.focac.org/eng/zywx_1/zywj/202201/t20220124_10632443.htm.

FOCAC. (2024a). Beijing declaration on jointly building an all-weather China-Africa Community with a shared future for the new era. https://www.mfa.gov.cn/eng/xw/zyxw/202409/t20240905_11485993.html.

FOCAC. (2024b). Forum on China-Africa Cooperation Beijing Action Plan (2025–2027). http://dm.china-embassy.gov.cn/eng/zgxw/202409/t20240905_11485719.htm.

French, H. W. (2015). *China's second continent: How a million migrants are building a new empire in Africa*. Vintage.

Gadzala, A. W. (Ed.). (2015). *Africa and China: How Africans and their governments are shaping relations with China*. Rowman & Littlefield.

Gourdon, J., Lambert, M., & Macé, A. (2022). La nouvelle stratégie énergétique de la Chine en Afrique: Enjeux et défis. *FERDI Notes brèves/Policy briefs, 232.*

Hakeenah, N. (2023). La Chine met en ligne une centrale solaire en République centrafricaine. Porjet Afrique-Chine. https://projetafriquechine.com/2023/05/03/chine-centrale-solaire-republique-centrafricaine/.

Hayley, A. (2024). Explainer: China's dominance in wind turbine manufacturing. *Reuters*.https://www.reuters.com/business/energy/chinas-dominance-wind-turbine-manufacturing-2024-04-10.

IEA. (2016). *Boosting the power sector in Sub-Saharan Africa: China's involvement*. International Energy Agency.

International Crisis Group. (2024). Bringing lasting peace to the Central African Republic | Crisis Group. https://www.crisisgroup.org/africa/central-africa/central-african-republic/bringing-lasting-peace-central-african-republic.

IRENA and AfDB. (2022). Renewable energy market analysis: Africa and its regions – A summary for policy makers. *International Renewable Energy Agency and African Development Bank*. www.irena.org/publications.

Komode, E. N. (2014). Acces universel aux services energetiques integrant le developpement des energies renouvelables et de l'efficacite energetique: cas de la Republique centrafricaine. Rapport provisoire. CEMAC et CEEAC. https://www.se4all-africa.org/fileadmin/uploads/se4all/Documents/Country_RAGAs/Central_African_Republic_RAGA_FR_Released.pdf.

Lampert, B., & Mohan, G. (2015). Making space for African agency in China-Africa engagements. In A. W. Gadzala (Ed.), *Africa and China: How Africans and their governments are shaping relations with China* (pp. 109–126). Rowman & Littlefield.

Lee, C. K. (2013). *From rhetorical to theoretical agendas in China-Africa studies*. SSRC.

Lema, A. R. (2023). *From a 'project of the century' to 'small is beautiful': The changing face of the BRI in Africa*. The Munk School Munk School of Global Affairs & Public Policy. University of Toronto.

Lema, R., Bhamidipati, P. L., Gregersen, C., Hansen, U. E., & Kirchherr, J. (2021). China's investments in renewable energy in Africa: Creating co-benefits or just cashing-in? *World Development, 141*, 105365.

Li, H., & Wang, Y. (2025). Adaptive governance at work: How Chinese state actors respond to overseas pushback on the Belt and Road Initiative. *The China Quarterly, 262*, 1–17.

Lonsdale, J. (2000). Agency in tight corners: Narrative and initiative in African history. *Journal of African Cultural Studies, 13*(1), 5–16.

Mackenzie, W. (2023). China to hold over 80% of global solar manufacturing capacity from 2023–2026. *Press Release*. https://www.woodmac.com/press-releases/china-dominance-on-global-solar-supply-chain/.

Mbugua, S., & Langat, W. (2023, January 31). Solar power to the people. *Dialogue Earth*. https://dialogue.earth/en/energy/solar-power-to-the-people/.

Ministry of Foreign Affairs. (2021). *Declaration on China-Africa cooperation on combating climate change*. https://www.mfa.gov.cn/eng/zy/gb/202405/t20240531_11367450.html.

Mohan, G. (2013). Beyond the enclave: Towards a critical political economy of China and Africa. *Development and Change, 44*(6), 1255–1272.

Mohan, G., & Lampert, B. (2013). Negotiating China: Reinserting African agency into China–Africa relations. *African Affairs, 112*(446), 92–110.

Naim, M. (2009). Rogue aid. *Foreign policy*, (159), 96.

National Energy Administration. (2022). Statistics on power sector in 2021, http://www.nea.gov.cn/2022-01/26/c_1310441589.htm.

Odoom, I., & Andrews, N. (2017). What/who is still missing in International Relations scholarship? Situating Africa as an agent in IR theorising. *Third World Quarterly, 38*(1), 42–60.

Park, J. (2021). Theorizing and learning from Kenya's evolving solar energy enterprise Development. *Energy Research & Social Science, 81*. https://doi.org/10.1016/j.erss.2021.102254

Phillips, J. (2018). Who's in charge of Sino-African resource politics? Situating African state agency in Ghana. *African Affairs, 118*(470), 101–124.

Procopio, M. (2018). Kenyan agency in Kenya–China relations: contestation, cooperation and passivity. In New Directions in Africa–China Studies (pp. 173–188). Routledge.

Puig, D., Magda, M. G., Daniel, K., Yacob, M., Atef, M., Maximilian, J., Yohannes, H., & Nebojša, N. (2021). An action agenda for Africa's electricity sector. *Science, 373*(6555), 616–619. https://doi.org/10.1126/science.abh1975

Rapid Transition Alliance. (2022). Doing development differently: How Kenya is rapidly emerging as Africa's renewable energy superpower. https://rapidtransition.org/stories/doing-development-differently-how-kenya-is-rapidly-emerging-as-africas-renewable-energy-superpower/.

Renew Africa. (2023). First large scale solar plant in Central Africa Republic (CAR) switches on. *Renew Africa* (blog). https://renewafrica.biz/news/solar/first-large-scale-solar-plant-in-central-africa-republic-car-switches-on/.

RFI. (2023). Centrafrique: création d'une nouvelle centrale solaire, un plus pour les artisans de Bangui. https://www.rfi.fr/fr/podcasts/afrique-%C3%A9conomie/20230420-centrafrique-cr%C3%A9ation-d-une-nouvelle-centrale-solaire-un-plus-pour-les-artisans-de-bangui.

Rithmire, M., & Li, Y. (2019). Chinese infrastructure investments in Sri Lanka: A pearl or a teardrop on the Belt and Road? *Harvard Business School*. Case 719-046. https://www.hbs.edu/faculty/Pages/item.aspx?num=55410.

Siele, M. K.N. (2024). China targets 'green infrastructure' deals in $50B pledge to Africa. *Samafor*. https://www.semafor.com/article/09/05/2024/focac-china-50-billion-africa-promise-with-green-infrastructure-deals.

Soulé-Kohndou, F. (2016). Passive agents? Bureaucratic agency in Africa-China negotiations: A case study of Benin. *London School of Economics (LSE) Global South Unit Working Paper, 3*.

Soulé-Kohndou, F. (2018). Bureaucratic agency and power asymmetry in Benin–China relations. In *New directions in Africa–China studies* (pp. 189–204). Routledge.

Soulé-Kohndou, F. (2019). How to negotiate infrastructure deals with China: four things African governments need to get right. The Conversation.

Soulé-Kohndou, F. (2020). 'Africa+ 1'summit diplomacy and the 'new scramble'narrative: Recentering African agency. *African Affairs, 119*(477), 633–646.

Takouleu, J. M. (2023). CAR: The Country's Second Photovoltaic Solar Power Plant(25 MWp) Inaugurated at Danzi. *Afrik 21*. https://www.afrik21.africa/en/car-the-countrys-second-photovoltaic-solar-power-plant25-mwp-inaugurated-at-danzi/.

Takouleu, J. M. (2024). Electrification: Central Africa Remains the continent's soft spot. *Africa Energy Portal*. https://africa-energy-portal.org/blogs/electrification-central-africa-remains-continents-soft-spot.

Tull, D. & Blasiak, R. (2011). Weak states and successful elites: Extraversion strategies in Africa (No. RP 9/2011). SWP Research paper.

Wang, Y. (2022a). Presidential extraversion: Understanding the politics of Sino-African mega-infrastructure projects. World Development, 158, 105976.

Wang, Y. (2022b). Executive agency and state capacity in development: Comparing Sino-African railways in Kenya and Ethiopia. *Comparative Politics, 54*(2), 349–377.

Wansi, B.-I. (2023). CAR: Near Bangui, the Sakaï Solar Power Plant (15 MW) Comes into Service. *Afrik, 21*, avril 27. https://www.afrik21.africa/en/car-near-bangui-the-sakai-solar-power-plant-15-mw-comes-into-service/

World Bank. (2022). Central African republic: Increasing electricity supply and access and supporting the health system. *World Bank Group*. https://www.worldbank.org/en/news/press-release/2022/06/03/afw-central-african-republic-increasing-electricity-supply-and-access-and-supporting-the-health-system.

Xinhua. (2022). Centrafrique: la centrale photovoltaïque construite par la Chine soulage les pénuries d'électricité (REPORTAGE). *FOCAC*. Retrieved mars 02, 2025, from http://www.focac.org/fra/zfzs_2/202207/t20220712_10719000.htm

Zheng, X. (2024). China's prowess in solar aids Africa's green transition. *China Daily*. https://www.chinadaily.com.cn/a/202409/06/WS66da6c27a3103711928a6782.html.

Conclusion: W(h)ither Africa–China Relations?

Lloyd G. Adu Amoah

The "end of empire" has been accompanied by the flourishing of other means of subjugation.
—Kwame Nkrumah (*2004*, p. 52)

Political decolonization and formal independence in Africa have not meant the end of imperialism. They have only meant a change in the guise *of imperialism.*
—Chinweizu (*1992*, p. 769)

It is indeed not enough to reduce alien power on our economies—vital as that stage is. It is urgent that we seek ways of increasing African power on the world economy at the same time. Africans must move from being pawns in the games of others to becoming true players on the chessboard of global destiny.
—Adebayo Adedeji (*1992*, p. 431)

L. G. Adu Amoah (✉)
Department of Political Science, University of Ghana, Accra, Ghana

Centre for Asian Studies(CAS), University of Ghana, Accra, Ghana
e-mail: alloydgeorgeadu@ug.edu.gh

L. G. Adu Amoah (ed.), *Africa-China Relations*,
https://doi.org/10.1007/978-981-95-4370-0_14

Introduction

As the colonial era faded in Africa in the 1950s and 1960s under the twin pressures of liberation struggles and the ravages of the Second World War (which weakened Britain and France among other imperial powers), the continent's future became the staple of global discussions for academics, the media and informed opinion. The new African states of the emergent postcolonial era saw their new future in modernization. O'Connell (1968), writing in that period, gave a Parsons-Durkheim account of modernization, thus:

> Modernisation is a process that includes the development of mental attitudes that look inventively for causal relations between happenings, and attitudes that seek to structure and control the flow of events through the historical understanding of time past and the planned uses of time ahead; it involves multiplying tools and machines in a society and imparting the skills or techniques needed to manipulate those technological instruments; and it requires social structures that become increasingly complex and differentiated, that demand advanced administrative capacity and that contain a built-in willingness to accept and initiate change.(26)

In the quote above, O'Connell points to the machine-technology-techniques aspects of modernization and thus gestures to the industrialization drive—more broadly, industrial capitalism—which was the dominant choice that came to define the nation-building endeavours of the new African countries. Chinweizu (1992) saw this industrialization drive as essentially an example of African mimicry:

> Modernization was understood, by Africa and the West alike, as a process which would turn African societies into black replicas of twentieth century societies. *The capitalist industrial societies* were the generally preferred model; the socialist industrial societies, though the preferred model for a minority of the African élite, were repugnant to the majority of the African leadership as well as to the West. (770; italics added)

Modernization, and with it industrialization, as driving notions of social organization for postcolonial Africa, came to be embedded in the idea and practice of development, which itself recalled the response to the ravages of an emergent industrial capitalism (Cowen & Shenton, 2005) in its Western European heartlands in the eighteenth and nineteenth centuries.

Under the aegis of the American-led post-World War II international political and financial architecture and through the active involvement (including funding) of foundations such as Carnegie, Rockefeller, as well as the Social Science Research Council, an industrial capitalist consensus (Berman, 1983) on development was forged. This consensus permeated the international civil service, global policy circles, academia, policy and the administrative infrastructure of postcolonial states. This consensus stipulated that "......Third-World development should be carried out mainly in terms of stable, nonradical, constitutional, and, if possible, peaceful and pro-American policies.......The scholars and policymakers supplemented economic determinism with sociological and psychological determinism. Both groups also largely assumed the converse, namely, the beneficence for socio-economic transformation of stable, constitutional political systems" (Berman, 1983, p. 118). Berman (1983) puts this consensus in a more barefaced way, showing how a bureaucratic, political and intellectual elite was forged for the realization of this consensus and its ends in postcolonial Africa:

> The interests of the United States in the Third World, as popularly understood at the time by mainstream social scientists and policy makers, were defined in terms of gradual movement toward a form of *Western democracy*, *continued alignment to the world capitalist system*, *continued access to strategic raw materials*, *order*, and *stability*, and at best a policy not antagonistic to the United States—all of which were to be encouraged by the *nurturing of an indigenous elite that understood the benefits that could accrue from such policies.* (119; italics added)

I turn in the next sections to the last two decades of the twentieth century as well as the first two decades of this century and how the international political economy evolved in the maw of a globalizing capitalism and its new instantiations and the place of Africa–China relations within it.

Critiques of Global Capitalism

The Halcyon Era of Critiques of Global Capitalism

By the early 1970s, dependency theory had emerged as the most sustained intellectual response to the "continued alignment to the world capitalist system" (Berman, 1983, p. 119) of the Global South in the work of a slew of theorists and activists such as Prebisch (1950), Nkrumah (2004), Baran and Sweezy (1966), Baran (1957), Frank (1971), Dos Santos (1970) and Amin (1974). Frank (2004) captures the nub of their argument well when he avers that "we cannot hope to formulate adequate development theory and policy for the majority of the world's population who suffer from underdevelopment without first learning how their past economic and social history gave rise to their present underdevelopment" (86). "Their past economic and social history" refers to the ways in which industrial capitalism, through racism, imperialism and colonialism (Chinweizu, 1992), having journeyed beyond its Western European and North American heartlands, has essentially underdeveloped (Frank, 2004) countries of the Global South through uneven and combined development and, with it, unequal exchange (Hickel et al., 2022)—including ecological unequal exchange(Frey et al., 2019)—leading to relations of dependency. Indeed, the reality of unequal exchange and emerging dependency was well expressed in the declining terms of trade for non-industrial countries, mainly in the Global South, in the 1950s, which was statistically highlighted by the study commissioned by the General Agreement on Tariffs and Trade (GATT) in 1957 and led by the Austrian-American economist Gottfried Harberler. In the report of this study (GATT, 1958) in question, the summary of findings (64 points in all) is revealing in a selection provided below:

> 7. Since the end of 1955, and leaving aside the effects of the Suez crisis, the slowing-down in economic activity in North America and Western Europe has given rise to an average decline in the prices of primary products which in early 1958 reached 5 per cent. Its impact upon the position of non-industrial countries taken as a whole is aggravated by the simultaneous rise-by about 6 per cent-in the price of manufactured goods.
>
> 14. Since before the war, the volume of imports into the non-industrial countries taken as a whole has risen more sharply than the volume of their exports.
>
> 16. The non-industrial countries have also been in deficit on account of their international transactions in services, both in 1928 and in the 1950's.
>
> 17. While the flow of private long term capital has failed to develop in line with the value of world trade, official grants and loans to the non-industrial world have provided in total a substitute for private lending surpassing its previous level.
>
> 23. Imports of non-industrial countries have developed faster than world trade and increasingly consist of capital goods.

> 26. It would be unwise to count upon any improvement in the terms of trade of non-industrial countries to raise their ability to purchase imports.
> 62. We think that there is some substance in the feeling of disquiet among primary producing countries that the present rules and conventions about commercial policies are relatively unfavourable to them. (3, 4-6, 11)

This capitalist structure of the global economy and its debilitating impact on the Global South (Amin, 1972, 1982, 1985, 1987) led to strident protests by the Group of 77 (formed in 1964; hereafter G77), which utilized the international forum provided by the United Nations(UN) to push for the setting up of the United Nations Conference on Trade and Development(UNCTAD) as well as the United Nations Industrial Development Organization (UNIDO). A decade later, in 1974, the G77 ensured the adoption of UN General Assembly Resolutions 3201 and 3202, which declared a New International Economic Order (NIEO) with its programme of action, respectively. These were the means by which the G77 sought to challenge and change the "structure of rules, laws, customs and organizations which together determined the workings of the capitalist world…." (Chinweizu, 1992, p. 772). It is useful to recall here the views of Adebayo Adedeji on the NIEO and Africa. As Executive Secretary of the United Nations Economic Commission for Africa (UNECA), Adedeji argued that, while Africa had played a major role in the G77 and the NIEO, it would not be able "to participate on an equal and equitable basis in any NIEO should it ever emerge, unless it first put its own economies in order at the national and regional levels and adopted a truly economic decolonization strategy" (Adedeji, 1992, p. 421). This economic decolonization strategy was to be directed at the global capitalist system and was anchored in ideas like pragmatic state interventionism, an aversion to a liberalized export and import regime that was against tariff and non-tariff barriers, and the rejection of some conceptual orthodoxies in development economics, such as making a "sacred cow of foreign exchange earnings" and therefore not attaching "excessive importance to foreign trade as the basis for initiating development, particularly the type of foreign trade with which Africa has been engaged both before and since independence" (Adedeji, 1992, p. 423), among others. These ideas were captured in UNECA's *Revised Framework of Principles for the Implementation of the New International Economic Order in Africa, 1976–1981–1985*, which informed the overall tone and tenor of the *Lagos Plan of Action for the Economic Development of Africa, 1980–2000* (hereafter *Lagos Plan of Action* [published in 1981]), Africa's last authentic long-term anti-global capitalism, collective effort at autonomous, self-reflexive socio-economic transformation. To be sure, it can be argued that 1981 symbolized the last year of the halcyon era of opposition to the capitalist underpinnings of international economic relations; I provide reasons in the next section.

The Fall and (Re)emergence of Critiques of Global Capitalism

In many ways, it can be argued that the World Bank's strategy for Africa's development (this was captured in a report also known as the Berg Report, written by economist Elliot Berg with just one African co-author, the Ghanaian K.Y. Amoako), *Accelerated Development in Sub-Saharan Africa: Agenda for Action*, which was published in the same year as the *Lagos Plan of Action* in 1981, effectively undercut the anti-global capitalism push back of the Global South's development project. Fundamentally, the Berg Report laid the intellectual basis for introducing the era of Structural Adjustment policies (see Loxley, 1983) and neoliberal capitalism across the Global South in a manner that ignored the historical underpinnings of underdevelopment and foisted the blame (of underdevelopment) on inept Global South policymakers:

> Largely ignoring external factors blighting African development, such as declining terms of trade for primary products and the impact of failed past aid policies, including the bank's own, the report identified policy errors by African governments as the source of malaise, and called for a stiff dose of reform: the adjustment of overvalued exchange rates, greater emphasis on agricultural exports and increased prices for agricultural producers, reduction of subsidies for urban consumers, downsizing of state bureaucracies, privatization of inefficient parastatals, and improved public sector management.(Gerhart, 1997; foreign affairs.com)

It should not be forgotten that essentially, what was directed at Africa were neoliberal policies that had been applied in Latin America, starting in Chile in the 1970s, which Gunder (1976) referred to as "Economic Genocide in Chile". These raft of unhindered market policies, which Gunder (1976) aptly describes below, came to be known under the catch-all rubric of the Washington Consensus (Marangos, 2009):

> The Junta's economic programme consists of freeing almost all prices to raise them several-fold to 'world levels' and increasing the money supply concomitantly. A 'free' capital market is fostered as well, which beyond concentrating capital into conglomerates also creates its own financial instruments above and beyond the control and even the accounting of the state, and which at the same time increases the amount of monetary means of payment and their velocity of circulation. Fortifying the same process to the same effect still further, 'freedom' must be promoted by destroying or yellow-dog-co-opting the organisation of labour and eliminating its bargaining power, and through all means preventing money wages from keeping pace with inflation in both private and public employment. In short, real wages are drastically reduced by bringing prices but not wages to 'world' levels. Both of these 'freedoms' generate a runaway inflation whose consequences, and intended effects, are to shift income and wealth from labour to capital and from smaller to bigger capital. (880)

By the second decade of the twenty-first century, neoliberal capitalism had undergone further complexity in what is now described as the Wall Street Consensus (WSC) (Gabor, 2021), marked by "the restructuring of development policy into investment opportunities" (Glatzer et al., 2024, p. 464). In other words, in the era of mature neoliberalism in the Global South, developing countries are being made the new frontier for international finance through deliberate policy measures led by their central banks and finance ministries at the behest of key public and private actors and players in advanced capitalist countries. In a recent work, Endrejat et al. (2025) draw attention, using the European context, to how financialized insurance is catalyzing capitalist accumulation on a global scale, thereby questioning its vaunted countercyclical stabilizer role in a neoliberal capitalist world. These analyses by scholars of the continuous revivification of neoliberalism and with it the fresh instantiations of global capitalism reflects as well the recognition of the enduring capitalist structure of global economic relations.

This structuralist analysis seems to have made a comeback as a research programme (Kvangraven, 2020) over the last two decades. The *Cambridge Review of International Affairs*, for example, published one special issue (Special Issue on Uneven and Combined Development [UCD]) and a forum (UCD and International Political Economy [IPE]) in 2020 and 2021, respectively, on the capitalist structure of global economic relations. In one of these articles, Oatley (2021) insisted, for example, that "Mainstream American international political economy (IPE) has gradually lost relevance as a framework for understanding developments in the global political economy. It offers little help for understanding the impact of the China Shock, the development and consequences of the Global Financial Crisis, or the anti-system politics that began to emerge in 2016" and suggests as a panacea "the development of theoretical frameworks that are *intrinsically systemic and dynamic*", such as "the Uneven and Combined Development, and the Political Economy of Complex Interdependence, perspectives, supplemented by greater attention to system parameters, provide a strong foundation upon which to build such frameworks" (p. 318; italics added). Through a Special Issue in the journal, *Development in Practice*, commemorating the Golden Jubilee of the declaration of the NIEO, scholars (Mabefam & Yajalin, 2025; Engel & Mabefam, 2025) point to the enduring capitalist structure framing of the international political economy, which de Oliveira and Kvangraven (2023) insist, and rightly so, is the product of Global South intellectual insight.

The problem of structure in international relations, in particular, and social theory more generally implicates or better still entangles its opposite number, agency. In this sense, the agency-structure problem has been examined by a slew of scholars such as Waltz (1979), Bull (1977), Wendt (1987) and Buzan et al. (1993) in the discipline of international relations (IR). But as Wight (2006) correctly notes, such engagements have been more implicit than explicit regarding the agency-structure matter. Anchored in work that draws on reflections from sociology, such as those of Durkheim (1976) and Parsons (1949), Wight[1] argues that IR needs to be better attuned and engaged with what he describes as "two traditions and five models" (Wight, 2006, p. 123) in the agent-structure literature. The two traditions refer to the interpretation of social reality, such as those constituted by demographic and ecological facts (such as birth and death rates, economic indices, population figures and the like) on one hand and those constructed by the accretion of norms, rules, beliefs and conventions. The former are essentially either constraining or enabling, while the latter deals with subject formation or better still subjectivity. For Wight (2006), this split "mirrors that between a materialist account of structure and a more idealist account" (125). Drawing on these two traditions, Porpora (1989) argues that generally any discourse on the agency-structure problem is wound around four models (which, though inexhaustive, serve as a useful typology), viz: (i) patterns of aggregate behaviour that are stable over time; (ii) law-like regularities among social facts; (iii) collective rules and resources that structure behaviour; (iv) systems of human relationships among social positions (added by Wight, 2006,[2] p. 127); and (v) relations of difference that constitute and define the properties of elements. I do not intend to be detained by the substantive and still pending questions of the agent-structure problem but have been at pains to sketch out its continuing relevance (both in its material and idealist understandings), as opposed to its demise, to understanding our contemporary international political economy. Indeed, Wight (2006) pointed to this putative demise by insisting that "Despite the frequency with which the concept of structure appears in… IR literature the concept remains ambiguous and imprecise…. More often than not structure is defined implicitly rather than explicitly" (123), arguing as well that

> …. not all theoretical positions are as *preoccupied with making explicit what they mean by structure*. In general, poststructuralists and positivists (neoliberal political economists for example) are happy to use the term structure but only instrumentally: it is 'as if' structure existed; even if both mean different things by structure. Since the status of claims regarding structure in these accounts is not ontological, there is little need for them to make clear how they use the term. As long as the postulated term helps explain/predict the phenomena there is no need to examine it further. This has the effect of letting them off the ontological hook. (122; parenthesis and italics added)

African Agency in Africa–China Relations

The nub of my labours thus far in the section above has been to carefully lay out the ontological basis for the claim that one cannot truly make sense of contemporary Africa–China relations without recognizing that "agents always bring their structures with them" (Wight, 1999, p. 110). For Africa–China relations, the pertinent question to ask is just who are the agents and what is this structure? The structure, to my mind, is that spawned by global neoliberal capitalism with its age-old imperial tendencies (Amoah, 2016, 2024; Uysal, 2021; Luce, 2015; Marini, 1972). In a still predominantly state-centric international system, I privilege state actors (and that is not to say non-state actors do not matter) in Africa–China relations and therefore focus on African states and the Chinese state (party-state for that matter) as my key agents in this chapter. Wight (1999) provides his compelling contribution to the theory of agency underpinned by the Spivakan (1996) degree of manoeuverability of subjectivity of the agent, without which one cannot meaningfully talk about the intentionality and accountability of agency and, therefore, the philosophical self. This freedom of subjectivity is ultimately about the power to act or better still bring about "change in something" (including the selfsame agent) (Bhaskar cited in Wight, 1999, p. 132) within the constraints of the social world and, therefore, structure, which essentially precedes this freedom. Within this sketched-out framework of agency, there have been analyses of African agency (agency of African states, to be more precise) and its enduring limitations in the international arena (Brown, 2012; Andreasson, 2013; Brown & Harman, 2013). But these reflections, while recognizing that the structure of the international political economy matters, insist on the need for a shift in focus to Africa's agency in order to understand the continent's "persistently peripheral role in international relations" (Andreasson, 2013, p. 143). Given Africa's continuing and even worsening peripheralization, the intervention of this chapter, in particular, and this volume, generally, in the Africa agency debate is to draw attention once again to the pertinence of structure with respect to the polarizing and exploitative tendencies of global capitalism. Agency is hobbled by structure and indeed influences the power to make change that defines it; it is akin to the shell and the tortoise (one cannot speak of a tortoise without its shell and vice versa; the two are mutually constituted). At this point, I wish to turn to my concerns regarding Africa–China relations in the coming decades. I want to argue that if the capitalist structure of the international political economy matters, then whether or not Africa is able to address its perennially peripheral status in the world must be understood, in critical respects, as a function of China's role in dismantling or maintaining this structure. This should be the key litmus test of Africa–China relations in recent times and going forward.

Africa, China and Global Capitalism

The chapters in this volume grapple with the agential and structural, with varying emphasis, and explicitly or implicitly in their engagement with Africa–China relations. At stake in the analyses in this volume is African states as hosts of largely Chinese state capital (within what Lee, 2017, p. xiii frames as a "varieties of capital"; chapters in this volume have shown how FDI from Chinese private and/or state-owned or backed companies has proved puny in Africa–China interactions), under globalized neoliberal capitalism, leading to and marked, if not defined, by uneven, contradictory and tensional realities and outcomes. To be sure, the very idea and reality of offshore Chinese state capital is telling, given that this would have been considered a misnomer even a generation after the founding of the People's Republic of China. But the normalization of Chinese state capital must be tied to China's emergence as a capitalist state under the tutelage of the United States in what Hung (2009) refers to as its embedding into the development of global capitalism.

A concatenation of both domestic and international factors - key among them the rise of East Asia as a hub and anchor of global capitalism (and with it the making of the semi-periphery), the election of Nixon to the American presidency, America's loss of the Vietnam War, the Sino-Soviet split, the death of Mao and the rise to power again of Deng Xiaoping and an ailing American economy in the 1970s - aided and abetted China's plugging into global capitalism and its eventual transformation into that system's semi-periphery dynamo. Nixon, a known Cold War warrior, insistent on the containment of the Soviet Union and communism (as Vice-President, he urged the use of tactical nuclear weapons during the Indo-China Crises of 1954 and a full-scale assault on Cuba over the Bay of Pigs fiasco), made a round-about turn. Once he became president after the 1968 elections, Nixon pursued fresh American foreign policy moves in which China in particular featured prominently. These American foreign policy departures were encapsulated in the "enunciation of the Nixon Doctrine as a formula for politico-military retrenchment and the opening to China" (Litwak, 1984, p. 52). It can be argued that all this succeeded, in part, in curbing China's revolutionary tendencies or maybe completely defanging them. China was effectively transformed from a potential revisionist to a status quo power. As Ingleson (2024) ably shows, Nixon must be seen as one of the critical movers of China's joining the global capitalist order through the dismantling of the gold standard and fixed exchange regime under his New Economic Policy announced on 15th August 1971 (this was preceded by the lifting of trade restrictions imposed on China during the Korean War in the same month). These measures allowed the free transnational movement of capital like never before and transformed China into an important destination for US investment, taking advantage of its market as well as its unorganized and therefore cheap labour. Thus, "…by the1980s these changes in global capitalism would enable China's own manufacturing capacity to grow exponentially, as it took advantage of corporate America's pursuit of cheap labor" (Ingleson, 2024, p. 33), underpinning thereby its debt-financed investments, FDI inflows, and export-growth model of development.

Heavily thus invested in global capitalism and benefitting from it in terms of its global power status as well as accumulation processes, it is no wonder then that "China shows no interest, intention, or capacity to challenge or replace the existing institutional infrastructure of twenty- first-century capitalism" (Lee, 2017, p. xiv). It is being suggested here that this reality of China's commitment to global capitalism should frame discourses and analyses of Africa's putative partnership with China beyond its otherwise win-win claims, to incorporate and entertain more fully the realities and dangers (both historical and contemporary) of Africa's peonage and pawnage, which are papered over or entirely ignored. The claims of partnership with Africa, without a clear view of China's investment in maintaining global capitalism, are at best a linguistic and an ideational trap, which mask or worse erase the realities and dangers of peonage and pawnage, as the preceding 13 chapters have shown. By and through a semi-peripheral capitalist China, the agency of African states is called forth in a global neoliberal capitalist world marked by inter-core, inter-semi-periphery and core and inter-semi-periphery competition. Drawing on the framework of the Second Cold War (Schindler et al., 2024), Zajontz (2025) views African agency through the concept of "polyalignment", which purports to move this agency beyond just a reactive tendency (in response to global structural shifts), but also acknowledges Wai's (2018) insistence that it must also be able to "inscribe or originate .... world-historical processes" (12).

Polyalignment, while optimistic about African agency, may not really cut it, for after all, the Second Cold War is about network-centric nodes of power and accumulation, in which African states are simply aligned. The real agential issue then is still a reactive one that confronts the problematic of what I term polyexploitation, for which African agency now confronts semi-periphery and core capitalist states trying to exploit (politically, economically, technologically and culturally) the continent—a particular polydominance (understood as domination by multiple powers in the core and now semi-periphery). For clarity, by polyexploitation it is meant the contemporary juncture of Africa's ongoing subjection to global extraction processes not just by core states but concurrently separately by or in concert with semi-peripheral states as well; essentially a new and complex exploitation regimen since Africa was drawn into the Western imperial orbit in the last five hundred years. So in polyalignment, the reactive African agency does not vanish at all. To be sure, though, this reactive or responsorial agency may yet be at best an idealized one, given that in the specific case of Africa–China relations, these relations may be justifiably read as a fundamentally elite project of Africa's (as well as China's too; see Amoah this volume) comprador state and non-state elites (Amoah, 2011; Mgbeoji, 2014; Zajontz, 2020; Carmody & Hampwaye, 2025; Esiyiyas, 2025) for whom China provides financial, political and other benefits.

In effect, contemporary Africa–China relations provide a critical moment for authentic African agency that is both reactive (and therefore survivalist) to the structuralist accumulation regime of global capitalism (with all its deathly effects) and seeks to challenge and dismantle it on a global scale. It is within this context that the future of Africa–China relations must be properly inscribed and with it the issues of partnership, peonage and pawnage unpacked. In this sense, I propose the construction of a New International Living Order (NILO; an extension of the NIEO as an anti-systemic vision) in pursuit of an equitable, anti-extractionist, climate and environmentally sound, decent basic standard of living for all order of living as the primary goal of this authentic African agency both in response to—and as well as a means to inscribe and originate a world historical process in the Waian sense—China in particular and the global capitalist system in general. For in the final analysis for Africa, the global spanning China it confronts must be tied to "the unique paths followed by the Chinese state and corporate actors to join the forces shaping global capitalism…." (Gonzalez-Vicente, 2024, p. 1042).

Abbreviations

GATT	General Agreement on Tariffs and Trade
NIEO	New International Economic Order
NILO	New International Living Order
UNCTAD	United Nations Conference on Trade and Development
UNECA	United Nations Economic Commission for Africa
UNIDO	United Nations Industrial Development Organization

Notes

1. Wight's work provides one of the most elaborate and focused philosophical treatment of the agency-structure problem in the international political economy literature.

2. See Wight (2006) and Porpora (1987, 1989) for a fuller and denser discursive engagement of these two traditions and five models which is beyond the scope of this work.

References

Adedeji, A. (1992). Comparative strategies of economic decolonization in Africa. In A. A. Mazrui & C. Wondji (Eds.), *Africa since 1935. General history of Africa* (Vol. 8, pp. 393–431). UNESCO and Heinamann.

Amin, S. (1972). Underdevelopment and Dependence in Black Africa—Origins and Contemporary Forms. *The Journal of Modern African Studies, 10*(4), 503–524.

Amin, S. (1974). *Accumulation on a world scale: A critique of the theory of underdevelopment.* Monthly Review Press.

Amin, S. (1982). After the new international economic order: The future of international economic relations. *Journal of Contemporary Asia, 12*(4), 432–450.

Amin, S. (1985). Modes of production, history and unequal development. *Science & Society, 48*(2), 2194–2207.

Amin, S. (1987). A note on the concept of delinking. *Review (Fernand Braudel Center), 10*(3), 435–444.

Amoah, L. G. A. (2011). Public policy formation in Africa in the wake of the global financial meltdown: Building blocks for a new mind in a multipolar world. In T. Dietz, K. Havnevik, M. Kaag, & T. Oestigaard (Eds.), *African engagements: Africa negotiating an emerging multipolar world* (pp. 327–345). Brill.

Amoah, L. G. A. (2016). China, Architecture and Ghana's spaces: Concrete signs of a soft Chinese Imperium? *Journal of Asian and African Studies, 51*(2), 238–255.

Amoah, L. G. A. (2024). Diplomacy of architecture and the Ghana National Mosque Complex: Concrete sign of a soft Turkish imperium? *Third World Quarterly*, 0(-0), 1–24.

Andreasson, S. (2013). Elusive Agency. Africa's persistently peripheral role in international relations. In W. Brown & S. Harman (Eds.), *African Agency in international politics* (pp. 143–157). Routledge.

Baran, P. (1957). *The political economy of growth.* Monthly Review Press.

Baran, P., & Sweezy, P. (1966). *Monopoly capital.* Monthly Review Press.

Berman, E. H. (1983). *The influence of the Carnegie, Ford, and Rockefeller Foundations on American Foreign Policy: The ideology of philanthropy.* State University of New York Press.

Brown, W. (2012). A question of agency: Africa in international politics. *Third World Quarterly, 33*(10), 1889–1908.

Brown, W., & Harman, S. (2013). *African Agency in international politics.* Routledge.

Bull, H. (1977). *The Anarchical Society: Study of order in world politics.* Macmillan.

Buzan, B., Little, R., & Jones, C. (1993). *The logic of anarchy: Neorealism to structural realism.* Columbia University Press.

Carmody, P., & Hampwaye, G. (2025). Post-Peak China in Africa? *Insights from Zambia. Critical African Studies, 0*(0), 1–21.

Chinweizu (1992). Africa and the capitalist countries. In *Africa since 1935. General History of Africa*, eds., Ali A. Mazrui and C. Wondji, vol. 8, 769–795. UNESCO and Heinamann.

Cowen, M. P., & Shenton, R. W. (2005). *Doctrines of development.* Routledge.

Dos Santos, T. (1970). The structure of dependence. *American Economic Review, 60*(2), 231–236.

Durkheim, E. (1976). *The elementary forms of the religious life* (2nd ed.). Allen & Unwin.

Endrejat, V., Bulfone, F., & van der Heide, A. (2025). The slumbering giant: Towards a political economy of financialised insurance. *Review of International Political Economy, 0*(0), 1–33.

Engel, S., & Mabefam, M. (2025). The Bretton Woods twins and reform agendas: From the NIEO to the Bridgetown Agenda. *Development in Practice, 0*(0), 2–12.

Esiyiyas, A. D. (2025). Sovereignty or surrender: Confronting Africa's comprador class. *Tricontinental: The Seventh Pan-Afric Newsletter*, 1–9.

Frank, A. G. (1971). *Capitalism and underdevelopment in Latin America: Historical studies of Chile and Brazil.* Penguin.

Frank, A. G. (1976). Genocide in Chile: Open Letter to Milton Friedman and Arnold Harberger. *Economic and Political Weekly, 11*(24), 880–888.

Frank, A. G. (2004). The development of underdevelopment. In K. A. Mingst & J. L. Snyder (Eds.), *Essential readings in world politics* (2nd ed., pp. 86–93). W. W. Norton & Company, Inc.

Frey, S. R., Gellert, P. K., & Dahms, H. F. (2019). *Ecologically unequal exchange: Environmental injustice in comparative and historical perspective.* Palgrave Macmillan.

Gabor, D. (2021). The Wall Street Consensus. *Development and Change, 52*, 429–459.

General Agreement on Tariffs and Trade (GATT). (1958). *Trends in international trade: A report by a panel of Experts.* GATT.

Gerhart, G. (1997). *Review: Accelerated development in Sub-Saharan Africa: An agenda for action.* Retrieved August, 3, 2025, from https://www.foreignaffairs.com/reviews/capsule-review/1997-09-01/accelerated-development-sub-saharan-africa-agenda-action

Glatzer, N., Neumann, M., & Müller, F. (2024). New constitutionalism across the North-South divide—neoliberalization through development cooperation agreements. *Review of International Political Economy, 31*(2), 463–486.
Gonzalez-Vicente, R. (2024). In the name of the nation: Authoritarian practices, capitalaccumulation, and the radical simplification of development in China's global vision. *Globalizations, 21*(6), 1041–1056.
Hickel, J., Dorninger, C., Wieland, H., & Suwandi, I. (2022). Imperialist appropriation in the world economy: Drain from the global South through unequal exchange, 1990–2015. *Global Environmental Change, 73*, 1–13.
Hung, H.-G. (Ed.). (2009). *China and the transformation of global capitalism.* The Johns Hopkins University Press.
Ingleson, O. I. (2024). *Made in China: When US-China interests converged to transform global trade.* Harvard University Press.
Kvangraven, I. H. (2020). Beyond the stereotype: Restating the relevance of the Dependency Research Programme. *Development and Change, 52*(1), 76–112. https://doi.org/10.1111/dech.12593
Lee, C. K. (2017). *The specter of global China: Politics, labour and foreign investment in Africa.* The University of Chicago Press.
Litwak, R. S. (1984). *Detenté and the Nixon Doctrine: American Foreign Policy and the pursuit of stability, 1969–1976.* Cambridge University Press.
Loxley, J.(1983). The Berg Report and the model of accumulation in Sub-Saharan Africa. *Review of African Political Economy*, No. 27/28, 197–204.
Mabefam, M., & Yajalin, J. E. (2025). New international economic order at 50: A reflection on the vision through Samir Amin's lens. *Development in Practice, 0*(0), 1–15.
Marangos, J. (2009). What happened to the Washington Consensus? The evolution of international development policy. *The Journal of Socio-Economics, 38*, 197–208.
Marini, R. M. (1972). Brazilian subimperialism. *Monthly Review, 23*(9), 14–24.
Mgbeoji, I. (2014). The comprador complex: Africa's IPRs Elites, neo-colonialism and the enduring control of African IPR agenda by external interests. *Intellectual Property Journal, 26*, 315–332.
Nkrumah, K. (2004). *Neo-colonialism: The last stage of imperialism.* Panaf.
Oatley, T. (2021). Regaining relevance: IPE and a changing global political economy. *Cambridge Review of International Affairs, 34*(2), 318–327. https://doi.org/10.1080/09557571.2021.1888880
O'Connell, J. (1968). The politics of modernisation and its effect on administration. In A. Adedeji (Ed.), *Nigerian administration and its political setting* (pp. 26–33). Hutchinson Educational.
de Oliveira, F. A., & Kvangraven, I. H. (2023). Back to Dakar: Decolonizing international political economy through dependency theory. *Review of International Political Economy, 30*(5), 1676–1700.

Parsons, T. (1949). *The structure of social action: A study in social theory with special reference to a group of recent European writers* (2nd ed.). Free Press.

Porpora, D. (1987). *The concept of social structure*. Greenwood Press.

Porpora, D. (1989). Four concepts of social structure. *Journal for the Theory of Social Behaviour, 19*(2), 195–212.

Prebisch, R. (1950). *The economic development of Latin America and its principal problems*. United Nations.

Schindler, S., Alami, I., DiCarlo, J., Jepson, N., Rolf, S., Bayırbağ, M. K., Cyuzuzo, L., De Boom, M., Farahani, A. F., Liu, I. T., McNicol, H., Miao, J. T., Nock, P., Teri, G., Seoane, M. F. V., Ward, K., Zajontz, T., & Zhao, Y. (2024). The second cold war: US-China competition for centrality in infrastructure, digital, production, and finance networks. *Geopolitics, 29*(4), 1083–1120.

Spivakan, G. C. (1996). Subaltern talk: Interview with editors. In D. Landry & G. Maclean (Eds.), *The Spivak Reader* (pp. 297–308). Routledge.

United Nations Economic Commission for Africa (UNECA). (1976). *Revised framework of principles for the implementation of the new international economic order in Africa, 1976–1981–1985*. UNECA.

United Nations Economic Commission for Africa (UNECA). (1981). *Lagos Plan of action for the economic development of Africa, 1980–2000*. UNECA.

Uysal, G. (2021). Turkey's Sub-Imperialism in Sub-Saharan Africa. *Review of Radical Political Economics, 53*(3), 442–461.

Wai, Z. (2018). Africa in/and international relations: An introduction. In M. I. de Heredia & Z. Wai (Eds.), *Recentering Africa in international relations: Beyond Lack, peripherality, and failure* (pp. 1–30). Palgrave Macmillan.

Waltz, K. (1979). *Theory of international politics*. Addison-Wesley.

Wendt, A. (1987). The agent–structure problem in international relations theory. *International Organization, 41*(3), 335–370.

Wight, C. (1999). They shoot dead horses don't they? Locating agency in the Agent-Structure Problematique. *European Journal of International Relations, 5*(1), 109–142.

Wight, C. (2006). *Agents, structures and international relations: Politics as ontology*. Oxford University Press.

Zajontz, T. (2020). The Chinese infrastructural fix in Africa: Lessons from the Sino-Zambian 'road bonanza'. *Oxford Development Studies, 50*(1), 14–29.

Zajontz, T. (2025). Locating Africa in the Second Cold War: The geopolitical economy of Kenyan polyalignment. *Third World Quarterly, 0*(0), 1–21.

Index[1]

A

[1] Note: Page numbers followed by 'n' refer to notes.

L. G. Adu Amoah (ed.), *Africa-China Relations*,
https://doi.org/10.1007/978-981-95-4370-0

FSC
www.fsc.org
MIX
Papier | Fördert gute Waldnutzung
FSC® C083411

Kolibri 360 GmbH
Ferdinand-Jühlke-Straße 7
99095 Erfurt, Deutschland
produktsicherheit@kolibri360.de